"Building thoughtfully on the work of the late insightful and richly rewarding labour of love. As....., researched, the book draws on the author's deep knowledge of geopolitical reality and how it manifests itself in post-Imperial cricket, enabling an ambitious brief to be admirably met. At times, indeed, you wonder how the game has survived the context in which it is played. If you want to know why cricket is the world's most racialized, politicized and fascinating ballgame, look no further." – *Rob Steen, Senior Lecturer and award-winning sports journalist, University of Brighton, UK*

"Cricket is one of a few sports where nation vs nation remained a primary contest well into the new millennium. Inexorably tied to a colonial past, cricket also reflected the aspiration of its new nations and nationhoods over the last five decades. In a masterful work of scholarship, Wagg gives us an engaging, comprehensive new history of modern cricket. From the relentless churn of events, achievements and controversies around the cricketing globe, he teases out the sport's engagements with the zeitgeist: the tussle between the old world and the new, the tumult of race and gender, the advent of 'professionalism', globalisation and the corporatisation of cricket. As much as the book is about modern cricket around the world, Wagg has also skilfully identified the world's footprints on modern cricket." – *Sharda Ugra, Senior Editor, ESPNcricinfo and ESPN India*

Cricket: A Political History of the Global Game, 1945–2017

Cricket is an enduring paradox. On the one hand, it symbolises much that is outmoded: imperialism; a leisured elite; a rural, aristocratic Englishness. On the other, it endures as a global game and does so by skilful adaptation, trading partly on its mythic past and partly on its capacity to repackage itself. This ambitious new history recounts the politics of cricket around the world since the Second World War, examining key cultural and political themes, including decolonisation, racism, gender, globalisation, corruption and commercialisation.

Part One looks at the transformation of cricket cultures in the ten territories of the former British Empire in the years immediately after 1945, a time when decolonisation and the search for national identity touched every cricket playing region in the world. Part Two focuses on globalisation and the game's evolution as an international sport, analysing: social change and the Ashes; the campaigns for new cricket formats; the development of the women's game; the new breed of coach; the limits to the game's global expansion; and the rise of India as the world's leading cricket power.

Cricket: A Political History of the Global Game, 1945–2017 is fascinating reading for anybody interested in the contemporary history of sport.

Stephen Wagg is a professor in the Carnegie School of Sport at Leeds Beckett University, UK.

Routledge Research in Sports History

The *Routledge Research in Sports History* series presents leading research in the development and historical significance of modern sport through a collection of historiographical, regional and thematic studies which span a variety of periods, sports and geographical areas. Showcasing groundbreaking, cross-disciplinary work from established and emerging sport historians, the series provides a crucial contribution to the wider study of sport and society.
Available in this series:

4 **Making Sport History**
   Disciplines, Identities and the Historiography of Sport
   Edited by Pascal Delheye

5 **A Social History of Tennis in Britain**
   Robert Lake

6 **Association Football**
   A Study in Figurational Sociology
   Graham Curry and Eric Dunning

7 **Taekwondo**
   From a Martial Art to a Martial Sport
   Udo Moenig

8 **The Black Press and Black Baseball, 1915–1955**
   A Devil's Bargain
   Brian Carroll

9 **Football and Literature in South America**
   David Wood

10 **Cricket: A Political History of the Global Game, 1945–2017**
   Stephen Wagg

www.routledge.com/sport/series/RRSH

Cricket: A Political History of the Global Game, 1945–2017

Stephen Wagg

LONDON AND NEW YORK

First published 2018
by Routledge

2 Park Square, Milton Park, Abingdon, Oxfordshire OX14 4RN
52 Vanderbilt Avenue, New York, NY 10017

Routledge is an imprint of the Taylor & Francis Group, an informa business

First issued in paperback 2018

Copyright © 2018 Stephen Wagg

The right of Stephen Wagg to be identified as author of this work has been asserted by him in accordance with sections 77 and 78 of the Copyright, Designs and Patents Act 1988.

All rights reserved. No part of this book may be reprinted or reproduced or utilised in any form or by any electronic, mechanical, or other means, now known or hereafter invented, including photocopying and recording, or in any information storage or retrieval system, without permission in writing from the publishers.

Notice:
Product or corporate names may be trademarks or registered trademarks, nd are used only for identification and explanation without intent to infringe.

British Library Cataloguing-in-Publication Data
A catalogue record for this book is available from the British Library

Library of Congress Cataloging-in-Publication Data
Names: Wagg, Stephen, author.
Title: Cricket : a political history of the global game, 1945-2017 / Stephen Wagg.
Description: Milton Park, Abingdon, Oxon ; New York, NY : Routledge, 2018. | Includes bibliographical references and index.
Identifiers: LCCN 2017024353| ISBN 9781138839854 (hardback) | ISBN 9781315733210 (ebook)
Subjects: LCSH: Cricket—History. | Cricket—Political aspects.
Classification: LCC GV913 .W33 2018 | DDC 796.35809—dc23
LC record available at https://lccn.loc.gov/2017024353

ISBN: 978-1-138-83985-4 (hbk)
ISBN: 978-0-367-18611-1 (pbk)

Typeset in Sabon
by Swales & Willis, Exeter, Devon, UK

In Memoriam

Stephen and Elizabeth Wagg, Ted and Florrie Hardy, my grandparents
Tom and Anne Wagg, my father and mother
Mike Marqusee, who spoke truth to cricket power

Contents

Acknowledgements · xi

PART I
Cricket and the end of empire · 1

1 Fossilised reactionaries? English cricket since 1945 · 3

2 A nation of blow-ins? Cricket in Australia since 1945 · 18

3 'The partnership of the horse and its rider': cricket in Southern Africa since 1945 · 36

4 A relative lack of interest: cricket in New Zealand since 1945 · 60

5 Father, king, statesman, general, prince, don: West Indian cricket culture since 1945 · 73

6 The soul of a nation, long suppressed? Cricket in India since 1945 · 90

7 Cricket in a hard country: Pakistani cricket since 1947 · 108

8 'We rule here, you rule there': cricket in East Pakistan and Bangladesh since 1947 · 126

9 After brewing tea for the empire: cricket in Sri Lanka since 1945 · 139

PART II
Cricket in the age of globalisation   157

10 Straight-shooting blokes: social distinction,
    masculinity and myth in the Ashes, 1945 to 2015   159

11 'Everyone seemed to be "with it"': cricket politics
    and the coming of the one-day game, 1940–1970   180

12 'Paint a picture, and keep it the right way up':
    cricket and the mass media 1945–2015   199

13 Women's cricket: the feminism that dared
    not speak its name – a brief history   223

14 Remove the gunk in the middle . . .: the coming of
    Twenty20 and the Indian Premier League   250

15 Have you made this team great, or have they made you?
    Cricket, coaching and globalisation   263

16 Beyond the boundaries: the drive to globalise
    cricket, and its limits   284

Afterword   312
Index   314

Acknowledgements

My thanks to:

Simon Whitmore for the chance to write this book.

Tony Collins, Ron Greenall, Jon Gemmell, Willem Van Schendel, Sharda Ugra, Raf Nicholson, Dil Porter and Rob Steen for reading and commenting on drafts of what I'd written.

Robert Curphey in Lord's library for his friendly assistance.

Kausik Bandyopadhyay for sending me his article on Bangladeshi cricket.

Ivor Dembina for longstanding friendship and a place to stay.

My friends at Grace Road and Dunton Bassett for always-enjoyable cricket conversation.

Helen Cooper for kindly allowing her artwork to be shown on the cover.

Catherine Hanley for editorial help.

Part I

Cricket and the end of empire

To an extent apparently unparalleled in the world of sport, international cricket bears the contours of the old British Empire. Aside from the 'Mother Country' herself, all the nine countries entitled to play Test cricket are either former British dominions or colonies. This section will consist of nine chapters which will detail the development after the Second World War of cricket cultures in these ten countries. This development took place largely against a backdrop of decolonisation, a process by which no cricket culture in the world was unaffected.

Chapter 1

Fossilised reactionaries?
English cricket since 1945

This chapter will look at the social and political progress of English first-class cricket since the Second World War. It will draw on the manifold histories of the English game, in particular those by the American-born Marxist writer Mike Marqusee[1] (1953–2015) and the English educationalist Sir Derek Birley[2] (1926–2002), as well as on journalistic accounts and cricket biographies. Cricket, and especially English cricket, has a vast literature. Much of this literature may be seen as an often unacknowledged and even unconscious meditation on the decline and dismantlement of the British Empire and on consequent changes both in the British class structure and in British national identity. It also expresses an enduring paradox. English cricket governance has often been disparaged for its purportedly high-handed, stick-in-the-mud conservatism and as presiding over a timeless activity still wedded to its eighteenth-century origins. For cannier observers, though, this is anything but the case. Indeed Marqusee characterised the period from the late 1960s to the late 1990s in English cricket history as one of 'permanent revolution' and 'modernization without end'.[3] And Francis Wheen, in his foreword to Marqusee's book *Anyone But England*, argued that the Marylebone Cricket Club (MCC), for much of its history the stewards of English cricket, 'who are usually denounced as fossilised reactionaries' were:

> Not reactionary enough. Given their hostility to almost everybody outside their magic circle – black people, women, undeferential foreigners – one would expect them also to shun such modern barbarians as PR consultants, marketing whizkids and corporate hospitality-merchants. Go to any county ground and you will see this isn't the case.[4]

... on which the sun never sets? The 1940s and 50s

Brylcreem Summer is the title of a book by the historian Eric Midwinter. It's an affectionate reference to the Middlesex and England cricketer Denis Compton, whose batting exploits with teammate Bill Edrich (both scored over 3,000 runs in the summer of 1947) typified the re-embrace of peacetime pleasures in post-war Britain and who gained a contract to advertise Brylcreem, the popular men's hair preparation, in 1949. This time of apparent optimism and plenty has been seen by several of the game's historians as a false dawn.

Cricket had played an important part in maintaining wartime morale in England. A British Empire XI, assembled by the patrician administrator Sir Pelham Warner in 1944, had played regular games against a London Counties team. These fixtures had been inscribed not only by empire but by social class, the former side being composed of amateurs and the latter of professionals,[5] a distinction still considered indispensable to the successful navigation of cricket as a flagship of English national identity. Moreover, more than 90,000 people came to Lord's to watch the last of five 'Victory Tests' between England an Australian Services XI in 1945.[6]

The prevailing, class-based myth[7] of English cricket was that it was always played with an attacking mentality, under the reliable leadership of independent-minded amateur gentlemen. The Jackson Committee in 1944 had called for attacking play to be maintained in the coming post-war era but ruled strongly against shortened forms of the game: two-day matches, which might have proved popular but were often deemed to be less cerebral, were rejected.[8] The same year the Bishop of Leicester, Guy Smith (Winchester and Oxford) had told *Wisden*, the cricketers' almanac, that 'cricket will always have a stable place in the nation'.[9] In this regard the season of 1947 represented a high tide of patriotic cricket euphoria. County and international cricket drew large crowds and England beat the (all white) South African visitors 3–0 in the Test series. 'On a sunny day of good cricket', cricket writer John Arlott wrote twenty years later, 'people will say "It's like 1947"'.[10] 'Are they still in?' he recalls people saying of Compton and Edrich. 'Everyone knew who "they" were'.[11]

Before very long, however, this elation was beginning to be read as imperial hubris amid indications that English cricket should look to its laurels. In November 1947, W.D. Isaacs wrote from Barbados to *The Times* to warn of the importance of the MCC sending a strong team to the West Indies that winter, on account of the growing strength of Caribbean cricket and of 'the awakening to political consciousness of the labouring classes and the clamour for responsible government in each colony as a prelude to federation and Dominion status'.[12] (England lost the series.) Moreover, the Australian touring side that came to England in 1948 won the Ashes Test series 4–0, although the MCC were to a degree mollified by healthy attendances and gate receipts: 132,000 people came to the Lord's Test and the Leeds Test attracted 158,000.[13] Birley, for one, saw England's failure as down to lack of leadership: England captain Norman Yardley 'was a fine cricketer and a nice chap, but scarcely a man of steel or a master-tactician'.[14] Sentiments of this kind effectively launched a debate that was to dominate English cricket for the next two decades and was probably not finally put to bed until the early 1990s. In this debate, two myths – one of the amateur, possessed of a gentlemanly blithe spirit, and the other of a dogged professional, fearful for his livelihood – were relentlessly played off against each other. This popular dichotomy helped to contour half a century of soul-searching and tinkering on the part of the English cricket authorities.

County cricket ceased to thrive during the 1950s. Attendances fell[15] and the county clubs were soon in financial difficulties. Rowland Bowen wrote that the immediate post-war years had been 'a period of delusion' and that the decline in the attendance at county matches had coincided with the abolition of petrol rationing (in 1950).[16] Aside from a diversification of leisure-time options for the English public, Eric Midwinter blamed inflation, rising wages (meaning that cricket faced stiffer completion from other occupations) and the growing reluctance of the elite universities of Oxford and Cambridge to admit students on their sport ability alone – traditionally a key source of county captains.[17] According to Birley, by 1953 Test match revenue was already keeping counties financially afloat.[18]

English cricket now seemed to call for more professionalism, in the sense of tactical and technical preparation. In 1949, in the wake of the Test series defeat of 1948, Harry Altham, another historian of the game and a master at Winchester, one of the country's elite public schools, was made Chairman of the MCC Youth Cricket Association and President of the English Schools Cricket Association. He was also appointed Chairman of a Special Committee to inquire into the future welfare of English cricket. Three years later he published the first edition of the *MCC Coaching Manual*.

The entry of the word 'coaching' into the ongoing discourse about English cricket entailed a necessary challenge to the central myth that the country's cricket rested on the dashing and spontaneous batsmanship and shrewd captaincy of the gentleman amateur. Such traits, by definition, could not be taught – they were inherent in the privately educated, upper middle-class male. But, sometimes with conspicuous reluctance, team leadership, both at national and at county level, was being passed to lower-born tacticians. In 1953, the MCC appointed their first professional captain of the twentieth century, Yorkshireman Len Hutton, and no doubt influenced his receiving of a knighthood from Sir Anthony Eden's Conservative government in 1956. County cricket also saw the decline of the amateur captain.[19] In a post-war cricket world of declining deference and growing meritocracy, the insistence of some county clubs on appointing amateur captains of modest playing ability became increasingly anomalous. A slew of middle-class amateurs who lacked the ability to play cricket at first-class level were appointed to captain county clubs in the 1940s and 50s. Their poor performances with bat and ball and their often peremptory manner in dealing with their teams made for much ill feeling in county dressing rooms.[20]

Influential spokespeople such as Rowland Bowen railed against the spectre of professionalism now haunting English cricket politics. A major and veteran of the Indian Army and the War Office, Bowen decried the apparent decline of the 'Oxbridge' amateur and argued that, although the English game had contrived to retain it 'religious aura', coaching it had brought 'a dreadful uniformity'.[21] Conservative cricket commentators (a description that described most of them) grumbled about the 'defensiveness' of Hutton's captaincy. In the *Daily Telegraph* leading Establishment scribe E.W. Swanton wrote: 'If our new captain ever errs from an excess of adventure, there is at least one critic who will observe with the most sympathetic eye'.[22] The MCC would appoint a commission on the amateur–professional distinction in 1958, chaired by the Duke of Norfolk. It concluded that 'the distinctiveness of the amateur cricketer' was not obsolete, but 'of great value to the game and should be preserved'.[23] Those (many) who harboured this sentiment became dewy-eyed when in 1961 the county championship was won by Hampshire, traditionally seen as the birthplace of English cricket and captained by Old Etonian *bon viveur* Colin Ingleby-Mackenzie.[24] Nevertheless the distinction was abolished in 1963, bringing lasting regret to the English game's many patrician commentators, including Swanton, who wrote several years later:

> I deplored the loss of the independent player and reminded my readers 'the evolution of the game has been stimulated from its beginnings by the fusion of the two strains, each of which had drawn strength and inspiration from the other. English cricket has been at its best when there has been a reasonably even balance'.[25]

But this notion of 'two strains' was merely cricket's version of the Conservative 'One Nation' myth world in which swashbuckling amateurs worked together with honest-to-goodness working-class professionals in patriotic harmony. Particular cricket philosophies were never the exclusive properties of one social class. Indeed different approaches could be manifested in the same person: Cambridge-educated Bob Barber, who played county cricket in the late 1950s and early 60s is described on one authoritative cricket website as a player who, having been 'a cautious amateur with Lancashire, changed counties and became a carefree cricketer with Warwickshire'.[26] And, as the writer Tim Quelch remarks perceptively, despite the enduring obsession with amateurism, English Test success in the 1950s was procured through a 'contradictory, tough combative, professional style of play that was practised as dutifully by its leading unpaid players as it was by its paid ones'.[27]

Revenge of the undeferential foreigners; enter the marketing whiz kids

The One Nation ideology that governed cricket discourse was therefore increasingly at odds with actual MCC policy. And the rise of professionalism was not its only challenge. Swanton's 'two strains' applied equally to the British Empire and its subjects and English cricket governance had, historically, been rooted in the upper and upper middle classes, spanning land ownership, colonial administration, the military, and high finance; this elite had, in Marqusee's words, 'learned to pose as the guardians of national values, transcending particular class interests'.[28] This entailed placing cricket, like the Royal Family, above the market and the vulgarities of trade and commerce. In the 1960s, however, the MCC had to come to terms with decolonisation and with the less esteemed elites of advertising and sponsorship.

As we have seen, English cricket authorities were made aware of the increased cricketing prowess and rising political ferment in the West Indies in the late 1940s. Moreover, they lost a Test series in the Caribbean in the winter of 1947–8 and were convincingly beaten for the first time on home soil by West Indies in 1950. This latter result was received with equanimity by the English cricket press. In *The Cricketer* magazine Swanton, a devoted imperialist, recognised an authentic amateur spirit in the West Indian batting 'which, like that of the Australians, is always, for our good, mocking the utilitarian and the humdrum'.[29] Moreover, West Indian migrants in the crowd brought a public gaiety to the event previously not witnessed at the cricket grounds of what was still a comparatively staid, Anglo Saxon culture. Calypso player Lord Kitchener recalled:

> After we won the match, I took my guitar and I call a few West Indians, and I went around the cricket field singing. And I had an answering chorus behind me and we went around the field singing and dancing. So, while we're dancing, up come a policeman and arrested me. And while he was taking me out of the field, the English people boo him. They said, 'Leave him alone! Let him enjoy himself. They won the match, let him enjoy himself.' And he had to let me loose, because he was embarrassed. So I took the crowd with me, singing and dancing, from Lord's into Piccadilly in the heart of London. And while we're singing and dancing going into Piccadilly, the people opened their windows wondering what's happening. I think it was the first time they'd ever seen such a thing in England. And we're dancing Trinidad style, like mas,[30] and dance right down Piccadilly and dance round Eros.[31]

At the time the British government had made no obvious moves to grant independence to British colonies. Indeed, as historian John Newsinger has argued, the Attlee Labour administration (1945–51) 'was wholeheartedly committed to the preservation of as much of the British Empire as was possible, although it did use different rhetoric from Churchill and the Conservatives'.[32] The stewards of English cricket were entitled to feel that all was well with the empire and that its children were merely coming of age within the imperial family.

There followed, however, a sequence of blows to this national self-assurance in cricket and a fraying of the bonds that had previously bound the MCC to the cricket-playing subject territories. On their tour of the West Indies in the winter of 1953–4, amid a growing movement for independence, the England team were received with considerable hostility and riot squads attended several of the Test matches.[33] The England players were, among other things, accused of taking umpiring decisions badly[34] and, during the period of decolonisation and after, a string of expressions of abuse, dissent and accusations of cheating were levelled by English cricket personnel at what were now Commonwealth opponents. On the winter tour of 1958–9 England players accused the Australian bowlers Gordon Rorke and Ian Meckiff of throwing the ball.[35] Similar accusations were made against the South African fast bowler Geoff Griffin, who toured England in 1960, against the Pakistani spinner Haseeb Ahsan in 1962[36] and against the West Indian fast bowler Charlie Griffith in 1963. Prior to the Test series in England in 1976 England captain South African-born Tony Greig caused enduring controversy when he said 'These West Indians, if they get on top they are magnificent cricketers. But if they're down, they grovel, and I intend [. . .] to make them grovel'.[37] On tour in India in 1981–2 another England captain, Keith Fletcher, angrily knocked the bails off his wicket, having been given out,[38] and umpiring controversies followed on England's tours of Pakistan in 1982 and 1987. In the latter instance the tour itself was placed in doubt following an angry exchange between England captain Mike Gatting and umpire Shakoor Rana.[39] Through the 1980s there was much indignation in English cricket circles at what was alleged to be intimidatory fast bowling by West Indies.[40] A letter to *Wisden Cricket Monthly* in June 1990 read 'Until we can breed 7ft monsters willing to break bones and shatter faces, we cannot compete against these threatening West Indians'.[41] During the Test series in England in 1988, the home side's batsmen could not cope with the West Indian pace attack and lost a five-match rubber 4–0, with one draw; in desperation, England appointed four different captains during this one summer – a high point in post-imperial comeuppance.

The lost empire reverberated on English first-class cricket culture in other important ways.

First, in 1967 following the Clark Report of the previous year, which had recommended freer movement of players between counties and in an attempt to boost flagging attendances at county cricket, clubs were allowed to sign an overseas player. For some this represented a recognition of a global labour market for cricket and of the counties as the only full-time professional cricket circuit. Inevitably, though, it raised questions about a (further) weakening of the England team. The influential cricket correspondent Christopher Martin-Jenkins reflected years later that in 1962 the top seven batsmen in the county averages had all been English and of Test class; in 1983 only three of the top ten had qualified for England and one of them (Geoffrey Boycott) was 42.[42] English cricket thus presented a comparatively early version of what is now a popular complaint – that imported players inhibit the development of indigenous sports talent.

Second, the MCC's corresponding anxiety to maintain a credible Test team made for considerable flexibility with regard to nationality. The most notable and controversial case here concerned Basil D'Oliveira, born in Cape Town in 1931 and of Indian-Portuguese ancestry, who migrated to Britain in 1960 and, qualifying by residence, made his debut for England in 1966. South Africa had ceased to be a British dominion in 1961, principally to protect its racist social and political system of apartheid. Under this system, D'Oliveira had been classified as 'Coloured', a grouping with reduced civil rights who were not permitted to play sport with whites. When D'Oliveira was selected to tour South Africa in 1968 the South African government refused to accept him and a political rift, virtually without precedent, opened up in English cricket culture.

D'Oliveira had initially been omitted from the MCC touring party and was included only as a replacement. It is now known that the MCC had had advanced warning that D'Oliveira would not be accepted by the South African government: a message to this effect had been sent via Lord Cobham. Cobham was an archetypal MCC grandee – he had played county cricket (he'd captained Worcestershire); he was the son and grandson of MCC presidents; he was a former Governor General; and he had extensive business interests in South Africa. He relayed the message informally and it was withheld from the MCC membership. There was an outcry at the MCC's handling of the affair, but the British sport press was largely unsympathetic to the protestors; one cricket correspondent called them 'furious, emotional and self-righteous' and another accused them of not knowing 'a South African cricket pitch from a Norwegian fjord'. John Arlott stood virtually alone in decrying the initial omission of D'Oliveira: nobody with an open mind, he wrote, would believe that it had been made for valid cricket reasons. Moreover, what encouragement did it give to the British-born children of West Indian, Indian, Pakistani and African immigrants who would soon qualify to play for England?[43]

A Special General Meeting of the MCC was called at which David Sheppard, a former England batsman and now a Church of England bishop, proposed two resolutions, one condemning the mishandling of the affair and another that England cease cricket tours of South Africa while that country operated the apartheid system. He was seconded by former Cambridge University (and future England) captain Mike Brearley. Both motions were voted down.[44]

In time, post-war migration from British colonies, along with the Gleneagles Agreement of 1977 under which Commonwealth countries undertook to discourage contact and competition between their sportsmen and sporting organisations, teams or individuals from South Africa, led to a number of other cricketers born outside the UK becoming eligible to play for England. This in turn triggered often ugly ruminations as to who was, or was not, a proper Englishman and whether or not British birth guaranteed loyalty to the cause. Roland Butcher, a Barbadian by birth who had come to England aged 13 in 1966, made his England debut in 1980. He was followed in 1986 by Phillip DeFreitas (b. Dominica, 1966) Devon Malcolm (b. Jamaica, 1963; England debut 1989) and Chris Lewis, a Guyanese by birth, in 1990. Along with these a number of white Africans with British parentage were allowed, their home country now excluded from international cricket, to qualify for England – notably, South Africans Allan Lamb (who played for England between 1982 and 1992), brothers Chris and Robin Smith (1983–6 and 1988–96, respectively) and Graeme Hick, who had played initially for Zimbabwe (1991–2001). The key precedent for these selections, however, was the qualification in 1972 of Tony Greig, another white South African, to represent England on account of his Scottish parents. While his father's wartime record in Bomber Command was cited to appease the doubters,[45] Greig, like a number of others, became the target of some reactionary English nationalism – for example, John Woodcock, cricket writer for *The Times*, stressed that Greig was 'an Englishman, not by birth or upbringing, but only by adoption. It is not the same as being English through and through'[46] – a judgement coloured by Grieg's assistance in the defection of a number of Test cricketers to World Series Cricket in 1977 (see Chapter 2). This (essentially racist) sentiment received its most rancorous expression in 'Is it in the blood', an article in *Wisden Cricket Monthly* in 1995 which questioned the commitment to the national cause of cricketers born outside the UK.

It is, of course, part of the enduring paradox of English cricket that, amid this post-imperial anguish over 'race', national identity and rumoured 'enemies within', it would not only maintain its 'mediaeval cathedral' aura, so decried by Rowland Bowen[47] and others, but consider allowing it to be used for marketing purposes. Indeed, sponsorship began in cricket comparatively early – in 1963, with a trophy (the Gillette Cup) which bore the sponsor's name. The Gillette Cup was, in effect, the inauguration of one-day cricket in England and ran counter to the conventional wisdom that had been expressed at the MCC in the immediate post-war period. It was followed in 1969 and 1972 by further one-day competitions sponsored by tobacco companies (the John Player League and the Benson and Hedges Cup, respectively).

There were some important acknowledgements tacit in these moves. With attendances at county matches continuing to plummet, the MCC now accepted that the shorter format and guaranteed result entailed in one-day cricket might revive county cricket as a spectator sport. Equally, there was an acceptance that most of these spectators would be watching via television, the BBC having undertaken to broadcast all three competitions.

Television coverage, along with access to the ambience of a timelessly sanctified national game, was what attracted the sponsors. As Midwinter pointed out, looking back from the early 1990s, the new competitions had brought a more even distribution of trophies among the counties,[48] but, during what was effectively the same period (1966–91) county attendances had dwindled from 500,000 to 170,000. Gate money was now therefore a minor factor in county income, 70% of which now came from sponsors and the Test and County Cricket Board (TCCB), constituted in 1968.[49] Moreover, following boundary changes brought about by the Local Government Act of 1972 several county cricket headquarters and main grounds were no longer in the original counties; the Act had effectively signalled the rise of municipalities and made counties begin to look like an administrative anachronism.[50] Some county cricket clubs – Essex[51] and Leicestershire,[52] for example – were facing extinction.

The nexus of sponsorship and broadcasting – particularly television – now became central to English cricket governance and survival. In 1989 one of England's historic Test match venues – the Oval in South London – became the 'Fosters Oval', in honour of the Australian lager brand. In 1992 the TCCB permitted the painting of sponsors' logos on the pitch in Test matches,[53] Cornhill Insurance being the beneficiary in this instance. In 1999 the contract for the televising of England's Test matches, hitherto the preserve of the BBC as the nation's public service broadcaster, was awarded to Channel 4, a channel charged since its inception in 1982 with catering to minorities. Michael Jackson, Chief Executive of Channel 4, said their coverage would seek to reflect 'the younger multi-cultural audience of the game' and that the channel would also try to win new fans to cricket. The deal, he said, had been struck because 'our and the ECB's interests coincide. Not because of the size of our cheque book'. Significantly Channel 4 would cede one Test match to the satellite TV channel, Sky Sports,[54] founded in 1991 and owned by Australian-born, American magnate Rupert Murdoch's media conglomerate News International. In 1998, the recently elected Labour government, having cast aside the last vestiges of socialism and re-branded as 'New Labour', was persuaded to omit home Test matches from the list of sporting events deemed of national importance and therefore to be broadcast free of charge on terrestrial television. Predictably, in 2004 pending the expiry of the second Channel 4 contract, the rights to show England's home Tests passed to Sky, who, as was pointed out, could easily outbid terrestrial broadcasters but who would deliver a much smaller audience.[55]

By then commercial sponsorship had long since gained acceptance at the commanding heights of English cricket, Cornhill having first sponsored a Test match in 1978 and the Prudential insurance company having sponsored cricket's World Cup between 1975 and 1983. Mike Marqusee wrote perceptively about the nature of the sponsors and of their motivation, pointing out that half of the 40-odd companies sponsoring English cricket in 1992 were from the finance and insurance sector and a further third from food and drink retail. Not all of these companies would be seeking a high public profile so much as influence in the City of London financial markets.[56] (Brit Insurance sponsored the England cricket team from 2010 to 2014 before giving way to Waitrose, the upmarket grocery store chain.) The satellite TV deal thus consecrated Test cricket as a prestigious niche market, in which a range of status-seeking companies could 'lease an English national identity from the TCCB' and borrow a sense of 'prudence and permanence' from a game through 'its long association with the English ruling class'.[57]

All professionals now: English cricket and technocracy

Following the tenures of Ted Dexter and M.J.K. Smith between 1961 and 1966, the England captaincy saw little of the blue-blooded amateur credentials on which a series of Establishment commentators had insisted. Dexter, whose lofty bearing had earned him the nickname of 'Lord Ted', had been a figure from a pre-meritocratic age: during his time at Cambridge University (1955–8) he had not attended a single lecture, spending most of his three undergraduate years playing golf and cricket.[58] Smith had played rugby for England while still at Oxford University; he had captained Warwickshire at cricket while, like many amateurs, enjoying a sinecure as club assistant secretary. England captains thereafter were of humbler social origin and/or exhibited none of the independent spirit of MCC legend. After Smith and Establishment favourite Colin Cowdrey came Brian Close, the son of a Yorkshire weaver with no airs or graces and an approach to cricket that was grudging and unequivocally professional. If the virtues formerly ascribed to the amateur captain ever returned to the England captaincy, they did so most notably in the person of Mike Brearley, who led England intermittently between 1977 and 1981. Brearley certainly had much of the traditional profile. He was educated at an 'independent' school at which his father taught and had degrees in Classics and Moral Sciences from Cambridge University. Primarily a batsman, he captained both Cambridge and Middlesex, but, as with many amateur captains of yore, his Test match average (22.88) did not qualify him for selection as a player. Instead he was feted for his handling of men. Swanton claimed him for tradition, calling him a 'natural leader' and eagerly bracketing him with Yardley, Dexter and Smith[59] while others adapted him to modernity – John Arlott, for example, praised Brearley, not for any qualities inherent in his class background, but for the fact that he had studied psychoanalysis.[60] Brearley thus became seen as an exponent of 'man management skills', a view of him sealed in 1981 when he succeeded the volatile working-class all-rounder Ian Botham as captain following the Second Test in the home series against Australia and seemingly transformed Botham's performance. In 2003 Conservative politician Tim Yeo nominated

Brearley as 'The Greatest Briton' on Personnel Today, a website dedicated to 'HR [Human Resources] news'. Yeo wrote:

> Brearley later said that Botham was 'very headstrong, a very strong personality. He needed someone who would put his arm around him and tell him about the immense talent he possessed. He needed someone who would remind him of the role he had to play because of his unlimited ability'.

Brearley's skill was in motivating his team and commanding respect, despite his own limited abilities'.[61] Brearley published a book, *The Art of Captaincy*, in 1985; it was re-published in 2001.[62] What had once been regarded as an inherent ruling class trait was now re-packaged as an area of expertise that could be acquired through study and careful analysis and rendered in its own vocabulary – often decried as 'management-speak'. Brearley now works as a psychotherapist, occasional journalist and motivational speaker.

For English cricket, the last glimpse of the amateur myth was probably in 1992 when 35-year-old David Gower, one of England's best batsmen of the post-war era, whose nonchalance often recalled pre-war times, was left out of the England party to tour India and Sri Lanka. By then the science and professionalism implied in Brearley's man management had begun to extend to physical fitness and mental preparation. M.J.K Smith said in 2012: 'In our time, the players hardly did any physical exercises, gym, etc. We kept ourselves fit only through playing cricket'.[63] By the 1980s a body of opinion ran counter to this off-the-cuff approach and, in 1986, England had appointed ex-Test player Micky Stewart as team manager with 'a brief to oversee discipline, fitness and technical supervision'.[64] His regime was based on embryonic sport science and was fully embraced by Keith Fletcher, who succeeded Stewart in 1992. Gower, a gifted and relaxed *bon viveur*, was immediately seen as a casualty of this utilitarianism. Ex-England captain and fast bowler Bob Willis stated that 'No number of dossiers on the opposition, fielding charts, training routines and fitness assessments can be a replacement for talent' and the playwright Harold Pinter complained that 'All this training is a pain in the arse. It doesn't make you a better player'. A motion of No Confidence in England's selectors was tabled by angry MCC members and carried at a meeting in Westminster in January 1993. This vote, however, was outweighed by subsequent postal votes.[65] For English first-class cricket, this could be seen as amateurism's last hurrah. (This theme is taken up again Chapter 15.)

Thereafter, English cricket proceeded to an ostensibly greater marketisation. In 1996 the TCCB (shortly to become the England and Wales Cricket Board: ECB) approached Tory peer Lord MacLaurin, at the time chairman of Tesco supermarkets, to be its chairman. MacLaurin was convinced that, compared to Australians and South Africans, too many English cricketers lacked 'the toughness, the mental resilience, the sheer bloody-mindedness that it takes to win'.[66] He also perceived that the financial crisis afflicting county cricket remained and that none of the eighteen clubs was solvent. Moreover, three major ECB sponsors, including Britannic Insurance who had sponsored the county championship, were withdrawing. He proposed a business plan, called *Raising the Standard*, which called for a streamlining of local cricket and, most importantly, the splitting of the county championship into two divisions – an idea with a long heritage in English cricket.[67] The latter met with much initial opposition from the counties, but the plan was accepted in full the following year. The championship has been constituted in two divisions since 2000 and matches have been contested over four days – the latter to provide a better nursery for Test cricket, on which county clubs now relied financially. This reliance was further reflected in the introduction of central contracts for a squad of England players, a move designed to remove them largely from the county circuit and, thus, lessen their workloads. An important new revenue stream for counties was opened up in 2003 with the inauguration of Twenty20 cricket (see Chapter 14).

Between 1994 and 2004 there was a 40% decline in the number of recreational cricketers in England and Wales[68] and, largely because it is so expensive to run, the twenty-first century has seen a big decline in cricket in state schools. Ex-Test cricketer Phil DeFreitas said in 2015: 'I have been saying it for years: it won't be long before everyone in the England side is privately educated'; in 2015, only three England players had been to state schools.[69] Moreover these privately educated young men had likely passed through a cricket academy or 'centre of excellence' on their way to county and international cricket. These centres are part of a post-MacLaurin technocracy designed to promote higher standards than those promoted by club and village cricket. The historic cricket clubs at Cambridge and Oxford Universities have both operated as parts of centres of cricketing excellence since 2010. These centres include the other universities in the respective towns (Anglia Ruskin University and Oxford Brookes University). That same year the university clubs re-branded as Cambridge and Oxford Marylebone Cricket Club Universities and the only first-class match they play is the annual one against each other. Similar MCC centres were founded and given first-class status at the universities of Durham and Loughborough and the combined universities of Leeds, Leeds Metropolitan (now Leeds Beckett) and Bradford in 2001 and Cardiff in 2012; all enjoy first-class status.

Beyond the academies, there was the cricket charity *Chance to Shine*, launched in 2005. *Shine* was, in effect, a cricket missionary body, funded by the ECB, private donors, corporate sponsors (who currently include Lycamobile mobile phone services, Yorkshire Tea and Waitrose supermarkets) and the British government (via Sport England). Part of its mission was to close the gap opened out in cricket provision during the previous thirty years between state and private schools and it attempts to do so by taking a version of cricket into state primary and secondary schools. There were ironies here, as the sports writer David Conn pointed out in 2009:

> Graham Able, the master of Dulwich College in South London, is a trustee of the Cricket Foundation and a passionate supporter of *Chance to Shine*, but his own school embodies the almost ludicrous inequality that remains between the private and state sectors. Able says Dulwich College – where it costs £27,330 a year to board – has, for 1,450 boys aged between seven and 18, eight full grass cricket fields. That, according to Southwark Council, is two more than exist for the whole borough, where just one state school, Bacon's City Technology College, has a single grass cricket field.[70]

English cricket has perpetually found ways of mitigating the decline in public interest, and consequent financial crisis, that set in in the 1950s. One way and another it has defied the predictions of commentators such as Rowland Bowen, who wrote in 1970: 'I personally think the game will last but [. . .] not even on a minor key, but as something rough and ready, something for which there will be no money'.[71]

Notes

1 Mike Marqusee's influential *Anyone But England* was published in three editions – first by Verso in 1994 with the subtitle *Cricket and the National Malaise*. A second expanded edition was published by Two Heads in 1998 as *Anyone But England: Cricket, Race and Class*. In 2005, a third edition, with a new afterword, and this time called *Anyone But England: An Outsider Looks at English Cricket* was published by Aurum Press.
2 *A Social History of English Cricket*, first published by Aurum Press in 1999 and reissued a number of times since, most recently in 2013.
3 Mike Marqusee *Anyone But England: An Outsider Looks at English Cricket* London: Aurum Press 2005 p.114.
4 Ibid. p.12.
5 Eric Midwinter *The Lost Seasons: Cricket in Wartime 1939–45* London: Methuen 1987 p.53.
6 Eric Midwinter *Brylcreem Summer: The 1947 Cricket Season* London: The Kingswood Press 1991 p.7.
7 I use the word 'myth' here to imply not a misconception but to an idea invariably not subject to challenge –'depoliticised speech' as the French writer Roland Barthes has it: see Roland Barthes *Mythologies* St Albans: Paladin 1976 pp.142–5.
8 Derek Birley *A Social History of English Cricket* London: Aurum Press 2003 p.269.
9 Midwinter *The Lost Seasons* p.151.
10 John Arlott *Vintage Summer: 1947* London: Eyre and Spottiswoode 1967 p.17.
11 Ibid. p.18.
12 Marcus Williams (ed.) *The Way to Lord's: Cricketing Letters to The Times* London: Fontana 1984 pp.89–90.

13 Birley *A Social History* p.276.
14 Ibid.
15 Birley *A Social History* p.281.
16 Rowland Bowen *Cricket: A History of Its Growth and Development Throughout the World* London: Eyre and Spottiswoode 1970 p.205.
17 Eric Midwinter *The Illustrated History of County Cricket* London: The Kingswood Press 1992 pp.70–1.
18 Birley *A Social History* p.288.
19 See Stephen Wagg '"Time, gentlemen, please": the decline of amateur captaincy in English county cricket' in *Contemporary British History* Vol.14 No.2 Summer 2000 pp.31–59 (Also published as Adrian Smith and Dilwyn Porter eds. *Amateurs and Professionals in Post-War British Sport* London: Frank Cass 2000).
20 Wagg '"Time, gentlemen, please" pp.31–59.
21 Bowen *Cricket: A History* pp.207–8.
22 Birley *A Social History* pp.283–4.
23 Quoted in Marqusee *Anyone* p.118.
24 Ingleby-Mackenzie's carefree upper-class life and his reflections on the 'champagne cricket' that Hampshire had played that year were narrated in his memoir of the following year: *Many a Slip* London: Oldbourne 1962.
25 E.W. Swanton *Sort of a Cricket Person* London: Collins 1972 p.201.
26 http://www.espncricinfo.com/england/content/player/8982.html Access 16 March 2016.
27 Tim Quelch *Bent Arms and Sticky Wicket: England's Troubled Reign as Test Match Kings During the Fifties* Durrington, West Sussex: Pitch Publishing 2012 p.11.
28 Marqusee *Anyone* p.74.
29 Swanton was writing of the first day of the Lord's Test, 24 June 1950. Reproduced in E.W. Swanton *As I Said at the Time* (ed. George Plumptre) London: Unwin Hyman 1986 p.165.
30 'Masquerade', a Caribbean carnival.
31 Garry Steckles 'The triumph of Calypso cricket' http://caribbean-beat.com/issue-100/triumph-calypso-cricket Access 17 March 2016.
32 John Newsinger *The Blood Never Dried: A People's History of the British Empire* London: Bookmarks 2013 p.176.
33 See Alex Bannister *Cricket Cauldron: With Hutton in the Caribbean* London: Pavilion Books 1990 (first published 1954).
34 Bannister *Cricket Cauldron* p.178.
35 Arunabha Sengupta 'Ian Meckiff – the bowler who was "thrown out"' http://www.cricketcountry.com/articles/ian-meckiff-the-bowler-who-was-thrown-out-83372 Posted 7 January 2014, Access 17 March 2016.
36 See Osman Samiuddin *The Unquiet Ones: A History of Pakistan Cricket* Noida: Uttar Pradesh Harper Sport 2014 pp.120–2; see also http://www.espncricinfo.com/pakistan/content/player/40380.html Access 12 January 2017.
37 Brian Viner 'Tony Greig: An innings as captain, rebel and a good man [Obituary]' http://www.telegraph.co.uk/sport/cricket/news/9770989/Tony-Greig-An-innings-as-captain-rebel-and-a-good-man.html Posted 29 December 2012, Access 17 March 2016.
38 Birley *A Social History* p.330.
39 The incident occurred on 7 December 1987. See '1987: Gatting Row Halts Play in Pakistan' http://news.bbc.co.uk/onthisday/hi/dates/stories/december/9/newsid_2536000/2536829.stm Access 17 March 2016.
40 Fully discussed in Michele Savidge and Alastair McLellan *Real Quick: A Celebration of the West Indies Pace Quartets* London: Blandford 1995.
41 Simon Lister *Fire in Babylon: How the West Indies Cricket Team Brought a People to its Feet* London: Yellow Jersey Press 2015 p.316.

42 Christopher Martin-Jenkins *Twenty Years On: Cricket's Years of Change 1963–1983* London: Willow Books 1984 p.13. For a full discussion, see Alastair McLennan *The Enemy Within: The Impact of Overseas Players on English Cricket* London: Blandford 1994.
43 Quoted in Peter Oborne *Basil D'Oliveira: Cricket and Conspiracy: The Untold Story* London: Time Warner Books 2005 pp.216–18.
44 For a full account, see Oborne *Basil D'Oliveira* pp.142–60.
45 See David Lemmon *Changing Seasons: A History of Cricket in England 1945–1996* London: Andre Deutsch 1997 pp.278–9.
46 Quoted in Birley *A Social History* p.316.
47 See Bowen *Cricket: A History* p.253.
48 Midwinter *The Illustrated History* p.82.
49 Ibid. p.74.
50 Ibid. p.86.
51 See Lemmon *Changing Seasons* pp.221–2.
52 When Mike Turner was made secretary-manager of Leicestershire in 1960 he was told that 'the foreseeable life of the club was no more than five years'. See 'Mike Turner: A Profile [Obituary, 2015]' http://www.leicscricketmembers.co.uk/mike-turner.html Access 19 March 2016.
53 Discussed by Marqusee *Anyone* p.136.
54 'Channel 4 wins rights to home Tests' http://news.bbc.co.uk/1/hi/sport/cricket/194168.stm Posted 16 October 1998, Access 19 March 2016.
55 Marqusee *Anyone* p.324.
56 Ibid. pp.139–40.
57 Ibid. pp.140–1.
58 See Alan Lee *Lord Ted: The Dexter Enigma* London: Vista 1996 p.32.
59 In *Barclays World of Cricket* September 1980. Reproduced in Swanton *As I Said at the Time* pp.17–19.
60 In *Wisden Cricket Monthly* October 1981. Reproduced in John Arlott 'Brearley: Has there ever been a better captain?' in David Rayvern Allen (ed.) *Arlott on Cricket: His Writings on the Game* London: Fontana 1985 pp.287–90. See p.288.
61 Tim Yeo 'The greatest Briton: Mike Brearley' http://www.personneltoday.com/hr/the-greatest-briton-mike-brearley/ Posted 28 January 2003, Access 20 March 2016.
62 Mike Brearley *The Art of Captaincy* London: Channel Four Books 2001.
63 Mike Smith (Interview with Ijaz Chaudhry) 'Why bother to change your style as long as you're scoring?' http://www.espncricinfo.com/magazine/content/story/582194.html Posted 21 September 2012, Access 20 March 2016.
64 See 'Micky Stewart' http://www.espncricinfo.com/england/content/player/20376.html Access 20 March 2016.
65 See Rob Steen *David Gower: A Man Out of Time* London: Vista 1996 pp.288–393.
66 Ian MacLaurin *Tiger by the Tail: A Life in Business from Tesco to Test Cricket* London: Macmillan 1999 p.189.
67 Rowland Bowen, for one, suggested it in a memorandum around 1950: Bowen *Cricket: A History* p.254.
68 Marqusee *Anyone* pp.338–9.
69 Simon Briggs 'English cricket's public school revolution' http://www.telegraph.co.uk/sport/cricket/international/england/11546893/English-crickets-public-school-revolution.html Posted 17 April 2015, Access 20 March 2016.
70 David Conn 'Chance to Shine sheds light on English cricket's eager underclass' *The Guardian* 8 July 2009 https://www.theguardian.com/sport/blog/2009/jul/08/england-cricket-schools-david-conn Access 7 March 2017.
71 Bowen *Cricket: A History* p.253.

Chapter 2

A nation of blow-ins?
Cricket in Australia since 1945

In March 1999, John Howard, Australia's Prime Minister and Leader of the right-wing Liberal Party, issued what was called a 'Preamble', which was his contribution to a national debate over whether or not the country should become a republic. In this preamble, he declared that the 'Australian nation is woven together of people from many ancestries and arrivals.'[1] Predictably, commentators were quick to produce their own versions of this preamble, one of them being Bill Leak, cartoonist for the equally right-wing newspaper *The Australian*, owned by Rupert Murdoch's News Corp Australia. In Leak's version Australia was 'a nation of blow-ins and we've got the lot here – bog Irish, reffos, dagos, wogs, slopes, you name it.'[2] This catalogue of derogatory terms for, in order, migrants, Irish people, refugees, Italians and Spaniards, black people and South East Asians could, of course, be read either as a reactionary rant or as a comment on the hypocrisy of politicians. Either way it provides a useful introduction to this chapter, which entails a discussion of cricket as a flagship for a changing Australian national identity in the period since 1945. Sport is widely seen as having a central place in Australian national life and cricket, especially in the immediate post-Second World War period, has been preeminent in that regard. For example, two cricketers – Don Bradman, who played for Australia between 1928 and 1948, and Keith Miller, whose Test career ran for ten years from 1946 – received state funerals, Bradman in 2001 and Miller in 2004. The family of Richie Benaud, who represented Australia between 1952 and 1964 and subsequently commentated on cricket on Australian TV and radio, politely declined a state funeral on his death in 2015.[3] The chapter explores the fluctuations and contradictions in Australia's post-war cricket culture and can be read as a companion to Chapter 10 on social class and the historic Ashes series.

A conservative gerontocracy: the Menzies years

Australia had been constituted as a dominion under the British crown in 1901 and the British parliament's power to legislate for Australia (and any other Commonwealth country) was ceded under the Statute of Westminster of 1931. After 1945, it is widely accepted, Australia maintained for two decades or so a largely Anglophile cricket culture, whose unofficial patron was the equally Anglophile Robert Menzies. Menzies was Australia's Prime Minister from 1939 to 1941 and again from 1949 to 1966[4] – the latter period a time of reconstruction, economic boom and large-scale immigration.[5] Post-war Prime Minister Ben Chifley and his Immigration Minister Arthur Calwell had inaugurated a 'populate or perish' policy in 1945. 'Calwell calculated that Australia would need 70,000 immigrants per year and set his sights on Britain to provide most of these: "It is my hope that for every foreign migrant there will be 10 people from the United Kingdom"'.[6]

The Sheffield Shield, the country's first-class cricket competition which Australian states had contested since 1892, was donated by the British Conservative politician Henry Holroyd, Lord Sheffield, and along with Britain and South Africa, Australia had been a founder member of the Imperial Cricket Conference in 1909. As noted in Chapter 1, the two countries staged a series of Victory Tests at the end of the Second World War and these took place in an atmosphere of shared patriotic euphoria: the biographer of Lindsay Hassett, who captained Australia in the series, referred to these games as 'The Happy Series'.[7] In deference to their gentlemanly visitors, when England were due to tour Australia in 1946–7, Australian players were required by the Australian Cricket Board (ACB) to wear dinner jackets for formal occasions.[8] Moreover, when the Australian Test team arrived in Britain in 1948, as a gesture symbolising the continuing bond between Australia and the Mother Country, they brought with them 17,000 food parcels, a gift from the people of Victoria.[9] The Ashes series in Australia in 1950–1 is remembered by the country's leading cricket writer as 'congenial'[10] and the following one, in England in the Coronation year of 1953, was noted for its gentlemanly accord. Australian journalist and ex-cricketer Jack Fingleton thanked the two captains, Hassett and Len Hutton (England's first professional captain), for contesting the series 'in such a friendly manner'.[11]

The administration of Australian cricket in this period appeared also to be based on the British model of masters-and-men; their style of governance during the Menzies years is universally rendered as autocratic and penny-pinching.[12] Leading Australian cricket writer Gideon Haigh has characterised them as a 'conservative gerontocracy'.[13] This had a number of important implications for cricket, both in Australia and beyond.

Australian players' remuneration from Test cricket was negligible, largely because the Board sailed under a flag of imported British amateurism. Richie Benaud, who first played for Australia in 1952, remembered being told by Board member Frank Cash: 'Never let money interfere with your cricket . . . only play for the love of the game'.[14] Players held outside jobs but often depended on the forbearance of their employers because of their long absences – in the case of the 1953 tour, for instance, Benaud estimated that he would be away from home for a little under eight months.[15] The players worked as salesmen or in banks and often retired from the game early to secure their long-term employment outside of cricket. They were usually short of money – it's said, for example, that Don Tallon, who kept wicket for Australia between 1946 and 1953, played in tattered gloves because he couldn't afford a new pair.[16] As in other countries, some cricketers earned money from journalism but could expect censure if they were critical of the Board. In 1951 the New South Wales player Sid Barnes was selected to play for Australia in the Third Test against West Indies. The Board rescinded his selection but refused to say why. Rumours circulated as to Barnes' possible misdemeanours and he appealed, unsuccessfully, to the Board to dispel them. Barnes won a libel action against one of the Board's supporters in 1952, but never played for Australia again. The Board's action is widely assumed to have been because Barnes had been publicly critical of them.[17] Incidents such as this helped to make player resentment a paradigm for Australian cricketers' relationship with the Board.

The Board was also parochial in its outlook and in the early 1950s rebuffed invitations from India, South Africa and New Zealand to tour.[18] The Board's reluctance here could have been borne of several factors – among them, concern over tour expenses and the length of time players would have to spend away from their jobs and, thus, require allowances – further overtures from the Indian cricket board in 1956 and 1957 contained guarantees of tax exemption.[19] The Board's Anglo-centric perspective also suggests that they seldom made a move without being certain that the authorities at Lord's would approve it. Indeed, the Board only agreed to revisit the question when MCC Secretary Ronnie Aird came to Australia to insist that the Board join the English in becoming 'cricket missionaries to the less popular Test countries'. New Zealand, widely disparaged in Australian cricket circles at the time, were a case in point.[20] The MCC further urged the Board to visit India and Pakistan in 1957.[21]

Test-playing relations had, however, been long established with West Indies who had first toured Australia in 1930–1. When they returned for a further series in 1951–2 it was, as Haigh points out, to a backdrop of considerable political irony. Although still captained by members of the white Caribbean planter class, the West Indies team was predominantly black and the host country still operated a 'White Australia' immigration policy, operant since the Immigration Restriction Act of 1901.[22] Aimed principally to exclude migrants from the Asia Pacific region, this policy was steadily modified in the 1950s and early 60s and abandoned in 1973 but still lent a legitimacy to popular racism and the warm reception accorded to the West Indian side 'probably had more to do with an instinctive respect for sportsmen than any enlightened indifference to pigmentation'.[23] When his team arrived in the Caribbean to tour in 1955, Australian captain Ian

Johnson launched a 'charm offensive', making sure to tell local reporters to 'forget the White Australia policy'.[24] (Fifteen years later Prime Minister Menzies would feel obliged to consult the South African ambassador to Australia about the acceptability of batsman Grahame Thomas joining the forthcoming tour of his country, which then operated the apartheid system of state racism. Thomas was dark-skinned and was rumoured to have had a Cherokee Indian grandfather. Remarkably, perhaps, the ambassador foresaw no problem.[25] Menzies, indeed, subscribed to what was probably the dominant view of white administrators in the British Empire after the Second World War: that racial policies were an internal affair for the country concerned. At the time of the Sharpeville massacre of black protesters by South African police in 1960 he stated that the incident, like the system of apartheid that had provoked the protest, was a 'domestic matter' and rebuked 'busy-bodies' at the United Nations for suggesting otherwise.[26] He openly deplored the 'premature grant of self-government' to nations of 'uneducated' non-white peoples.[27])

West Indies returned in late 1960 for what may have been regarded as both the zenith and a watershed for gentlemanly Test cricket in Australia. Two principal factors defined the series. One was sportsmanship and the general acceptance of umpiring decisions – West Indies captain Frank Worrall, for example, decreed that his team show no dissent.[28] The other was the adventurous nature of the cricket played, beginning with an exciting tied Test (the first in Test history) at Brisbane in December. These factors and others together seem to crystallise a number of convergent trends in Australian cricket culture and governance.

The city of Melbourne rewarded the West Indian team with a ticker tape send-off in February 1961: 'Commerce in this Australian city stood almost still as the smiling cricketers from the West Indies, the vanquished not the victors, were given a send-off the like of which is normally reserved for Royalty and national heroes. Open cars paraded the happy players from the Caribbean among hundreds of thousands of Australians who had been sentimentalised through the media of cricket as it should be played'.[29]

Nevertheless, 'brighter cricket' remained a matter of contention in the Australian game. For one thing, there were mutterings in the Australian camp that the West Indians had been accorded all the credit when Australia had played the more adventurous game.[30] More importantly, the series had been against a widely recognised trend in Australian popular and consumer culture. Attendances at Sheffield Shield matches had boomed immediately after the Second World War but dwindled in the 1950s – a response, according to historians, to slow batting and defensive play.[31] Other sports, notably Australian Rules and association football, were attracting a growing public[32] and, kept at arm's length by the conservative cricket board, who thought it would diminish attendances still further, Australian radio turned instead to golf and tennis.[33] Beyond this, post-war Australia was experiencing full employment and a consumer boom. Leisure options now extended beyond sport and embraced holidays, hotels, shopping and eating out.[34] As early as 1952 ex-Australian captain Vic Richardson had called for limited-overs cricket[35] and the board had appointed a committee to explore this option in 1956.[36] During the late 1950s and early 60s home crowds for Test matches declined to their lowest number since the 1920s.[37] Moreover, the number of cricketers in Australia was going down and the board had no junior development programme in the 1950s.[38] Thus, having kept the broadcasting media at arm's length, the Australian board began to relent in the late 1950s. The first Test to be shown on Australian television was the game against England at Brisbane in December 1958 and was broadcast by the Australian Broadcasting Corporation (ABC). The Board thus began to do business with ABC, the public service broadcaster, but, doubtless observing what it took to be MCC proprieties, it remained hostile to commercial TV and to advertising. It remained so, despite the MCC themselves signing a sponsorship deal for a one-day cricket tournament with the Gillette razor company in 1962. This stance would prove crucial for the direction of Australian cricket, and cricket generally, in the 1970s.

Sportsmanship had been central to Australia's Anglophile cricket identity for much of its existence hitherto and had been most notably expressed in the fabled 'Bodyline' series of 1932–3, during which Australians had believed that they and not England were upholding the game's purportedly chivalrous traditions. Australian selector Bill Johnson had described England's tactics in that series as 'the most unsportsmanlike act ever witnessed on an Australian cricket field'.[39] But, as in all other cricket-playing countries, on-field etiquette in Australian cricket was, in effect, a theatre for contending over what it was to be Australian. The series of 1960–1 notwithstanding, the Australian game was witnessing a growing competitiveness. In 1950 English cricket commentator John Arlott observed in Australian cricket 'a single-minded determination to win the game – to win within the laws, but if necessary, to the last limit within them'. Haigh suggests that this caused 'a minor storm' in Australia when cricket discourse still largely embraced the English myth of fair play.[40] Indeed, in his book on the Australia–England Test matches of 1946–7, the leading Australian journalist Clif Cary had rebuked Australian captain and national icon Don Bradman for his 'grim outlook' which was 'more in keeping with his civilian occupation of a stockbroker'.[41] Moreover there would continue to be strong expression in Australian cricket of the gentlemanly amateur ethic. Recalling the Ashes series of 1950–1, Australia's captain Ian Johnson spoke of quite happily 'walking' for a catch that neither the umpires, nor the English close fielders had noticed.[42] And the website dedicated to the Nottinghamshire ground, Trent Bridge, records an incident in the First Ashes Test of 1964, in 'a display of sportsmanship that might raise an eyebrow in modern encounters, [Australian wicketkeeper] Wally Grout declined to remove the bails for what would have been a routine run out after England batsman Fred Titmus collided with the bowler in attempting a quick single'.[43]

In the 1970s Australian cricket would acquire a more outrightly aggressive demeanour and this would have to do with the greater involvement of the commercial media, with trends in wider Australian society, with an evolving sense of national identity and with what some perceived as an Americanisation of the country's popular culture. Certainly the seeds of this were visible soon after the Second World War. Covering the Ashes series of 1950–1 for the *Manchester Evening News*, reporter John Kay observed a nascent celebrity market for cricketers waiting to be tapped:

> At Melbourne the young boys and girls go almost hysterical... I know several English cricketers who used to breathe a sigh of relief whenever they reached the security of their quarters without the loss of a tie, a button, or even a cap... no film stars ever had more adulation that did the cricketers of England and Australia – especially the young ones – for the few brief days around Christmas at Melbourne in the year 1950.[44]

C'mon Aussie, c'mon: Australian cricket culture after the 'Packer Revolution'

The history of Australian cricket since the late 1970s – and, indeed, the history of cricket generally in that period – has been informed most signally by what's been called the 'Packer Revolution' – a series of crucial innovations that consecrated a marriage between sport and television.[45]

Attendances at Test matches in Australia after the Second World War appear to have peaked with the series of 1946–7; thereafter, as Australian cricket historians agree, there were fluctuations (notably in 1960–1) within an overall steady decline.[46] Some kind of low was reached in the Ashes Test at Old Trafford, Manchester in 1964, when each side scored over 600 runs in their first innings, leaving scarcely any time for a second. There was a growing lobby against 'safety first' cricket led by such figures as the country's dashing 1950s cricket icon Keith Miller, who called for the Ashes to be 'dumped' in 1971.[47] Among a rising generation of Test cricketers there appeared to be similar dissatisfaction: for example in 1968, Ian Chappell, who had first played for Australia in 1964 and would take over the captaincy in 1971, responded to the bleak pragmatism of his captain, Bill Lawry, with a terse 'If that's Test cricket, you can stick it up your fucking arse'.[48] This malaise, coupled with the continued refusal of the Australian Cricket Board (ACB) to do business with commercial television, provided the conditions for the inauguration of World Series Cricket in 1977.

Kerry Packer was the grandson of Tasmanian Robert Packer, who had founded the family's media empire. His father Frank, the conservative founder of the Australian Consolidated Press and backer of Menzies' Liberal

Party, had been an early sponsor of Australian cricket, offering financial incentives for fast scoring in the 1958–9 season.[49] Packer Senior had developed the commercial TV station Channel Nine and when, in 1976, the ACB refused to grant the channel television rights for the forthcoming Test series against England, his son and business heir Kerry retaliated by staging his own cricket series, for which he hired many of the world's best players. The transaction of the Packer matches, styled as 'World Series Cricket' (WSC), is widely chronicled – indeed, along with the fabled 'Bodyline' series of 1932–3, it is probably the most revisited chapter in cricket history.[50] The chief legacy of WSC was the recasting of cricket events and the men who enacted them as creatures chiefly of television and of the commercialised popular culture that encompassed television. This in turn had a number of important implications for Australian national identity-in-cricket.

Advised by Richie Benaud, who himself was fully cognisant of public impatience with the slowness of the contemporary game,[51] WSC inaugurated a limited-overs format for a newly flamboyant cricket, played in coloured clothing, often at night and with a white ball and supported by intensive advertising campaigns. In part these latter entailed a number of what Andrews and Grainger call 'vernacular initiatives' in which, amid a process of 'cloying yet infectious *C'Mon Aussie C'Mon* promotions', various WSC players were effectively 'Disneyized', giving them cartoon versions of their own public personalities.[52] This process was in train, under the tutelage of entrepreneurs such as John Cornell, a Channel Nine producer, who had launched the career of Paul Hogan (famed later for playing ironised bush ranger 'Crocodile Dundee') and was already marketing several Australian cricketers.[53] To expedite the devising of these for-public-consumption identities, forty of the world's leading cricketers, including twenty-eight Australians, were contracted not only to WSC, but to PBL Marketing, an arm of the Packer empire. In the construction of these cartoon identities the marketers took account of popular trends and mythologies. In the early 1970s observers had registered a growing restiveness, both on and off the field, in Australian cricket. In 1972 a leading umpire spoke of an 'increase in foul language and bad sportsmanship'[54] and, during the same period, as Richard Cashman has suggested, the 'reputation of the Australian crowd as a good-natured, fair-minded and knowledgeable assembly began to nosedive'.[55] To the marketers the time seemed right for a revisitation of the 'larrikin' and 'ocker' stereotypes – images of aggressive, proudly unsophisticated, tinny-wielding masculinity established in Australian popular culture since the early 1900s, but comparatively dormant during the Menzies years. Australian Test players, who had been arguing with their board over money for decades, welcomed the extra income that all this yielded and the commercialisation of Australian elite cricket was sealed in a rapprochement between Packer and the ACB in 1979, when the ACB signed a ten-year promotion deal with PBL Marketing. In the subsequent alchemy of growing professionalism, accumulated grievance and promotional artifice, the Australian cricket team during this period became, for many, a traveling troupe of glowering, disputatious, drooping-moustachioed lager-drinking white males. Many of the current team appeared in a TV advert for Toohey's draught lager the following year in 1980,[56] and the lager motif reached its apogee when Australia's tour of England in 1989 was sponsored by the Australian beer brand Castlemaine XXXX.

This lager-soaked, faux-uncouth narrative placed the country's leading cricketers at the heart of what the Australian film director Mark Hartley has called the theme of 'Ozploitation' in late twentieth-century popular culture.[57] Harte and Whimpress, understandably, describe three leading Australian cricketers of this period – Dennis Lillee (Australia 1971–84), Rodney Marsh and Greg Chappell (both 1970–84) – as 'made-for-television heroes'.[58] Lillee's 'fiery temperament' and periodic ill-discipline was seen as a commercial asset by PBL Marketing, who intervened to stop him being suspended in 1981 following an angry altercation with the Pakistani player Javed Miandad.[59] Probably the greatest beneficiary of the market in cricket identities was the Victorian player Merv Hughes (Australia 1985–94) who grew a huge moustache and reinvented himself as a cartoon larrikin of cottage industry proportions.[60] Hughes even published a book composed entirely of the letters and messages he had received in his capacity as national larrikin.[61]

These presentations of self resonated well with an increasingly egalitarian public which was moving perceptibly away from Anglophile deference. For instance, Test player Ashley Mallett (Australia 1968–80) has written tellingly about the popular appeal of his team-mate Doug Walters, who represented Australia between 1965 and 1981:

> Cricket fans embraced him as one of their own, for here was a national batting hero who did the sort of stuff they did: he drank and he smoked, he had a bet and a laugh. They loved it when, in 1977, news broke that before his 250 for Australia against New Zealand at Christchurch, he spent the previous night in the hotel bar with a team-mate.[62]

The most important caveat to be made about these celebrations of the common man is that they were, ultimately, steeped in whiteness.[63] Moreover, it seems clear that they have been superseded in the twenty-first century by celebrations of men, and of masculinities, that were not nearly so common. The chapter concludes by expanding upon these two observations.

Australia fair? Cricket and national identity in the twenty-first century

As the 'White Australia' policy (finally abandoned in 1973) demonstrates, 'race' has loomed large as an issue in Australian society since 1945; in the country's cricket culture it has, arguably, been the elephant in the room. By the 1980s a political and intellectual battle was joined over the country's national identity. In this battle, the political and cultural right, perceiving Australia to be predominantly of white, British-descended ethnicity, squared off against the forces of 'multiculturalism', the latter seeking recognition for essentially two constituencies: migrants from Asia and the long-resident Aboriginal community. For the right the debate was dominated by the conservative historian Geoffrey Blainey, who in a series of speeches and writing in the mid-1980s, warned of the 'Asianisation' of Australia.[64] Blainey's intervention set the tone for much subsequent anti-immigrant politicking in Australia, and concomitant argument over national identity, notably by Liberal Party politician John Howard who, as Leader of the Opposition from 1985, immediately embraced opposition to multiculturalism as a political platform.[65] Howard was Australia's Prime Minister from 1996 to 2007 and was known both for his steadfast refusal to acknowledge any wrongs done to Aboriginals by 'White Australia' and for his 'Pacific Solution' (2001–7) of transporting asylum seekers to remote islands in the Pacific Ocean.

In 2010 Howard unsuccessfully sought the presidency of the International Cricket Council. Like Menzies, he always associated himself closely with the Australian cricket team, regarding it as a flagship for national identity. Critics have argued that the team continued largely to represent the myth of white Australia that Howard sought always to defend. The Australian team of the mid-1970s, for example, was known for 'sledging' – a term originating in the 1960s for the old-established practice of fielders making provocative remarks to break the batsman's concentration. This was wholly in keeping with the 'larrikin' ethos, but could take the form of racial abuse – as when in 1974 Australian fielders on tour in New Zealand taunted home batsman Glenn Turner for having an Indian wife. (Turner's wife, Sukhinder Gill, was Punjabi. She served as mayor of the New Zealand city of Dunedin from 1995 to 2004.)

Nor have ethnic minorities been well represented in Australian teams. For example, only two players to play for the country since 1945 – Jason Gillespie and Dan Christian – have an indigenous Australian heritage. Gillespie (Australia 1996–2006) descends on his father's side from the Kamilaroi people of New South Wales (he also has a Greek mother), and Christian (who played one-day internationals between 2012 and 2014) has Wiradjuri (also New South Wales) ancestry. In 1988 a squad of Aboriginal cricketers toured the UK to mark the 120th anniversary of a similar tour by Aboriginal players in 1868; one history dismisses this celebration as 'another blot on Australia's use of their indigenous peoples for self-gratifying motives'.[66] Moreover, as David Utting has shown, the ACB in its promotional literature ceased to style itself as 'a powerful part of the Australian mainstream, "coming out" between 1998 and 2009 to clearly promote a view of Australian culture which aligned with John Howard's view of Australian identity, and after 2009 dropped any allusion to its place in Australian cultural development'.[67]

Perhaps inevitably, however, political challenges to the enduringly white conception of the nation's cricket family endorsed by Menzies and Howard have begun to be felt. Most of the early and most notable graduates of the Australian Cricket Academy – founded in 1987 as a joint initiative of the Australian Institute of Sport (AIS) and the ACB – were white. In 2013 Melbourne cricket reporter Adam Cooper reflected that the national team had:

> Remained firmly Anglo-Celtic in origin, save for exceptions such as Len Pascoe (of Yugoslavian descent),[68] Dav Whatmore (born in Sri Lanka), Kepler Wessels (born in South Africa) and Andrew Symonds, who has a Caribbean heritage. This week 20 years ago, for example, Australia fielded a Test team whose first names could be those of *Home and Away*[69] regulars: Mark, David, Justin, Mark, Steve, Allan, Ian, Paul, Shane, Merv and Craig.[70]

However, Australian cricket officials now recognised that 'four in ten Australian households have got a parent who was born overseas' and some clubs were recognising these new demographics:

> Sunshine Heights Cricket Club, in Melbourne's western suburbs, is a remarkably progressive club, having welcomed people from South Sudan, Uganda, Vietnam, India, the Philippines and Afghanistan – many of them refugees – into the fold. Since adopting an open policy of encouraging diversity, dating back to the 1960s, the club has been recognised for the measures it has taken in making the club more inclusive.[71]

Among the cricketers from migrant and/or ethnic minority communities, it was Asians, according to Indian cricket writer Sharda Ugra, who had faced the most difficulties. One told Ugra that much of their travail originated in:

> The '80s and '90s [known] as 'the Billy Birmingham era' in Australian cricket. Birmingham was a comedian known for successful audio parodies of the Channel Nine commentary team, packaged as *The 12th Man*. Much of the popularity of the sketches stemmed from jokes around Indian, Pakistani and Sri Lankan surnames and accents. The enormously successful Billy Birmingham phenomenon in those decades led, Jeh [Ugra's informant] believes, to 'the marginalisation of Asian cricketers' and gave rise to the 'curry muncher' epithet. 'Many young Asian boys coming into the system were turned off from playing men's cricket for the abuse they copped – why would I turn up every Saturday and listen to the abuse?'.

28 Cricket and the end of empire

In 1992 Richard Chee Quee (born Sydney, 1971) became the first player of Chinese origin to play first-class cricket in Australia. Chee Quee said that he experienced racism, and that it bothered him, particularly once he started playing for New South Wales.[72] However, '[t]here are hundreds of registered cricket clubs across Australia' Ugra wrote optimistically, 'and each account of an exclusionary or "blokey, boozy" environment can be countered with examples of inclusion or attempts to change'.[73]

In the still-largely-white elite of Australian cricket there has, nevertheless, been perceptible change. One clear feature here has been the onset of critical reassessments of the nation's most celebrated cricketing son, Don Bradman. In truth, there had always been some reservation among public chroniclers about the national lionising of Bradman. While Bradman was still playing Test cricket (he retired in 1948), Australian cricket writer Ray Robinson, observing that Bradman had been given seventeen more lines in *Who's Who* than Josef Stalin, contended that what had been written about Bradman 'mostly leaves an impression wholly preposterous'.[74] Talk of Bradman's estrangement from his team-mates was rife during his playing days and, on his death in 2001, one obituary remarked that Bradman had achieved almost everything in life 'save for one thing: the affection of his peers'.[75] Indeed, such has been the re-evaluation of Bradman in Australia, that one blogger was recently moved to ask 'Is the war on Don Bradman's reputation a fair thing?'[76]

The testimony both of Bradman's admirers and of his critics can combine to explain this 'war'. One of Bradman's biographers points to a paradox in Bradman's unmistakable aspiration to join the country's Anglophile elite:

> He was born only a few years after this country was federated [in 1901] and developed an affection and an affinity with the royals from 1930. Bradman is knighted and was a freemason. He admires the stable institutions of parliament, democracy and the law, which have been inherited from Britain. The contradiction in all this is the fact that Bradman did a great deal, arguably more than any other individual Australian in the twentieth century, to define a character that was distinctly, culturally Australian. He did not mimic the accents or demeanours of those from the Mother Country. Bradman used his skills to destroy and humiliate the representatives of England at every opportunity.[77]

Bradman, thus described, represented what the historian Richard Holt has called a 'cultural nationalism' founded on a 'Jack's as good as his master' attitude.[78] But for many Australians in the twenty-first century the concept of 'master' no longer applies: indeed, although a proposal to abandon the British monarchy was defeated in a referendum of 1999, republicanism is strong in Australia and is currently the official policy of the Labor Party, the Green Party and the Liberal Prime Minister Malcolm Turnbull. Moreover, since so many families do not trace their origins to the UK, Britain is not their 'Mother Country'. And the country has seen arguments for multiculturalism and feminism enter the political mainstream. As Brett Hutchins, who led the revisionist critique of Bradman, wrote of Bradman's funeral: 'At the risk of sounding disrespectful, it was predominantly white males mourning a dead white male'.[79] Criticism, however, has not been confined to the things Bradman represented. Since his death he has been periodically redefined as a cold fish, mean with money and anti-Catholic (a religion embraced by a number of his team-mates). Crucially, he seldom joined colleagues for a drink ('I did not think it my duty to breast the bar and engage in a beer-drinking contest') and his parsimony, as Chair of the ACB in the mid-1970s in dealing with the Australian players, was said to be a major factor in their defection to Packer. It was also claimed that he had been estranged from his own family, absent from the funerals of close relatives and suspected of involvement in a financial scandal in the mid-1940s for which another man went to prison.[80] This offended against the historic and egalitarian Australian ideal of 'mateship', deeply engrained in the national mythology and heavily stressed in the larrikin-inspired commercial popular culture of the late twentieth century.[81] Nor was it marriageable with the family-centred view of Australia popularised in the television soap operas *Neighbours* (set in a fictitious Melbourne suburb and begun 1985) or *Home and Away* (which takes place in a fictitious resort on the coast of New South Wales and started in 1988).

It would be wrong, however, to assume that Bradman's successors in the baggy green caps have disposed entirely of his legacy. Certainly, what was perceived in Bradman as undue ruthlessness has, with the receding of the gentlemanly ethos, simply been less disparaged in his successors. For example, of Steve Waugh, who captained Australia from 1999 to 2004, it was written that he had 'the gift of reducing complex matters to simple ones: he sees without prejudice how best to exploit the opposition's weakness, how best to deploy his own strengths. The approach, cold-blooded, scientific, is that of a general'.[82] Waugh is one of a number of Australian Test cricketers of the twenty-first century who have, like Bradman, ascended into a comfortable upper middle-class life and a status as proud professionals and national figures. Unlike him, however, they have in many cases produced extensive and prideful narrations of the self, strongly redolent of the 'reflexive self-identity' explored by the sociologist Anthony Giddens in the early 1990s.[83] Waugh (168 Tests 1985–2004), Adam Gilchrist (96 Tests 1999–2008) and Ricky Ponting (168 Tests 1995–2012) have all produced huge autobiographies: Waugh's runs to 816 pages, Ponting's to 699 and Gilchrist's lasts for over 600. In these books they offer numerous team-bonded colour pictures of Australian sides, along with detailed tour reminiscences, family snaps, tributes to Mum, Dad, wives and children and the recurrent rhetoric of 'living the dream' and of 'the journey' that their lives thus far have constituted.[84] These men show none of Bradman's emotional reticence. Justin Langer (Australia 1993–2007) narrates his self in the form of a two-page personal treatise.[85] Addressing readers of his autobiography *True Colours: My Life*, Adam Gilchrist explains the title thus: 'Life is an array of colours, the vibrant red of love though to the blackness of pain, and every shade in between'.[86] Waugh was no less restrained, reviewing his career to date with a mixture of family and national pride:

> Cricket had given me many cherished memories, but to be carried around the SCG [Sydney Cricket Ground] on the shoulders of my team-mates, with an Aussie flag draped around my neck and the crowd going berserk, was as good as it could possibly be. To then be greeted by Lynette [his wife], Rosalie, Austin and Lilian [their children] on the ground was to know I was blessed and lucky to have a supportive and loving family who'd sacrificed so much to allow me to fulfil my dream.[87]

And Bradman's parsimony has been replaced by philanthropy: in 2005, for example, Steve and Lynette Waugh set up the Steve Waugh Foundation, supporting people with rare diseases.[88] This doing of good works is a prominent facet of contemporary celebrity: as Jo Littler argues, 'public displays of support for "the afflicted" can be a way for celebrities to appear to raise their profile above the zone of the crudely commercial into the sanctified, quasi-religious realm of altruism and charity, whilst revealing or constructing an added dimension of personality: of compassion and caring'.[89]

These personal journeys, team-bondings and narrations have been wedded to an emergent 'Aussie' identity: 'I know that self-belief is the essence of personal progress', stated Langer, alongside 'I feel like I could run through a brick wall when I am wearing the baggy green cap'.[90] As Waugh has made clear this new Aussie identity reaches both backward, to the imperial era, and forward to a multicultural Australia. On the way to the Ashes series in 2001 the Australian squad visited Gallipoli, in Turkey, scene of a battle in the First World War in which Australian troops died alongside British and New Zealanders fighting the army of the Ottoman Empire. The event is marked by Anzac Day in Australia, but the remembrance is widely shunned by the Australian left because of its colonial, 'Mother Country' associations. The visit, recalls Waugh:

> Had a profound effect on most of the squad. We waited for a couple of days and then each member of the squad stood up and tried to explain what the experience had meant to them. Like many I was moved by the words of [physiotherapist] Patrick Farhart, who is of Lebanese descent. He said that, for the first time in his life, even though he'd been born in Australia, he felt 100% Australian as he stood among the trenches.[91]

John Hirst, an Australian historian and a republican, recognised a new post-imperial perception of Gallipoli: whereas once republican critics had asked 'What sort of cringing colonial outfit was it that thought it did not properly exist until it took part in an imperial war?', now they preferred to remember that:

> In May 1915 an experienced English war correspondent, Ellis Ashmead-Bartlett, declared that the Australian troops at the Gallipoli landing were superb, as good or better than the British. The self-doubt of the Australians lifted at that moment. They felt themselves to be a proper nation. They had passed the test; no one could look down on them now.[92]

Notes

1 http://www.home.aone.net.au/~byzantium/preambles/pm.html Access 13 July 2016.
2 http://www.home.aone.net.au/~byzantium/preambles/bl.html Access 13 July 2016.
3 'Richie Benaud family declines Australia state funeral' http://www.bbc.co.uk/news/world-australia-32274167 Access 14 July 2016.
4 Gideon Haigh *The Summer Game: Australian Test Cricket 1945–71* Melbourne: Test Publishing 1997 p.67.
5 See, for example, Stephen Bell *Australian Manufacturing and the State: The Politics of Industry in the Post-War Era* Cambridge: Cambridge University Press 1993; Stuart Macintyre *Australia's Boldest Experiment: War and Reconstruction in the 1940s* Sydney: NewSouth Publishing 2015.
6 http://www.poheritage.com/the-collection/exhibitions/ten-pound-poms-pos-part-in-postwar-emigration-to-australia/populate-or-perish Access 15th July 2016.
7 R.S. Whitington *The Quiet Australian: The Lindsay Hassett Story* Melbourne: Wren Publishing 1973 p.80.
8 Chis Harte, with Bernard Whimpress *A History of Australian Cricket* London: Andre Deutsch 2003 p.394.
9 Harte, with Whimpress *A History of Australian Cricket* p.405.
10 Haigh *The Summer Game* p.41.
11 J.H. Fingleton *The Ashes Crown the Year* London: Collins 1954 p.307.
12 See in particular Harte, with Whimpress *A History of Australian Cricket*. Their narrative is consistently critical of what they see as the short-sightedness of the Australian Board.
13 Haigh *The Summer Game* p.61.
14 Richie Benaud *Over But Not Out* London: Hodder and Stoughton 2011 p.75.
15 Benaud *Over But* p.74.
16 Haigh *The Summer Game* pp.22–3.
17 See Sidney Barnes *It Isn't Cricket* London: William Kimber 1953 pp.144–68. See also Haigh *The Summer Game* pp.54–8 and Harte, with Whimpress *A History of Australian Cricket* pp.422–3.
18 Harte, with Whimpress *A History of Australian Cricket* pp.421 and 432.
19 Harte, with Whimpress *A History of Australian Cricket* p.454.

20 See, for example, Harte, with Whimpress *A History of Australian Cricket* p.468.
21 Harte, with Whimpress *A History of Australian Cricket* pp.438 and 454.
22 For an overview see James Jupp *From White Australia to Woomera: The Story of Australian Immigration* Melbourne: Cambridge University Press 2002.
23 Haigh *The Summer Game* p.44.
24 See Ian Johnson obituary http://www.espncricinfo.com/wisdenalmanack/content/story/155319.html Access 16 July 2016; see also Harte, with Whimpress p.439.
25 See Haigh *The Summer Game* pp.223–4.
26 Sir Robert Menzies *Afternoon Light: Some Memories of Men and Events* London: Cassell 1967 p.193.
27 Menzies *Afternoon Light* p.191.
28 Haigh *The Summer Game* p.140.
29 'West Indies in Australia, 1960–1' http://www.espncricinfo.com/wisdenalmanack/content/story/155246.html Access 20 July 2016.
30 Haigh *The Summer Game* p.156.
31 See, for example, Richard Cashman *'Ave a Go Yer Mug! Australian Cricket Crowds From Larrikin to Ocker* Sydney: William Collins 1984 pp. 104 and 123 and Haigh *The Summer Game* pp.138–9.
32 Harte, with Whimpress *A History of Australian Cricket* p.417.
33 Harte, with Whimpress *A History of Australian Cricket* p.446.
34 See, for example, Paul Hogben and Judith O'Callaghan, 'Leisure Capital: Sydney and the Post-War Leisure Boom' in *Proceedings of the Society of Architectural Historians, Australia and New Zealand: 30, Open*, edited by Alexandra Brown and Andrew Leach (Gold Coast, Qld: SAHANZ, 2013), Vol. 1, pp. 125–37. https://www.griffith.edu.au/__.../R01_01_Hogben-OCallaghan_Leisure-Capital.pdf Access 21 July 2016.
35 Harte, with Whimpress *A History of Australian Cricket* p.423.
36 Harte, with Whimpress *A History of Australian Cricket* p.446.
37 Haigh *The Summer Game* p.265.
38 Harte, with Whimpress *A History of Australian Cricket* pp.423 and 446.
39 Quoted in Rob Steen *Floodlights and Touchlines: A History of Spectator Sport* London: Bloomsbury 2014 p.314.
40 See John Arlott *Concerning Cricket: Studies of the Play and the Players* London: Longmans, Green & Co. 1949. The quotation appears in Haigh *The Summer Game* p.41.
41 Clif Cary *Cricket Controversy: Test Matches in Australia 1946–7* London: T. Werner Laurie Ltd 1948 p.4.
42 Haigh *The Summer Game* p.41.
43 http://www.trentbridge.co.uk/news/2012/june/an-illustrious-history-ashes-tests-at-trent-bridge.html Access 22 July 2016.
44 John Kay *Ashes to Hassett: A Review of the M.C.C. Tour of Australia, 1950–51* Manchester: John Sherratt & Son 1951 pp. 54 and 150.
45 See David L. Andrews and Andrew D. Grainger 'The "Packer Affair" and the early marriage of television and sport' in Stephen Wagg (ed.) *Myths and Milestones in the History of Sport* Basingstoke: Palgrave Macmillan 2011 pp.239–61.
46 See Cashman *'Ave a Go* p.104; Harte, with Whimpress p.425, 472–6; Haigh *The Summer Game* pp.138–9.
47 Haigh *The Summer Game* p.317.

48 Haigh *The Summer Game* p.287.
49 Haigh *The Summer Game* p.270.
50 See, for example, Henry Blofeld *The Packer Affair* Newton Abbot: Readers' Union 1978, an account of how Packer's plan was hatched and carried out, and Gideon Haigh's *The Cricket War* (Melbourne: Text Publishing, 1993), a detailed, behind-the-scenes account of WSC games. See also Harte, with Whimpress pp.579–605. A drama series called *Howzat! Kerry Packer's War*, scripted by the Australian writer Christopher Lee, premiered on Channel Nine in August 2012.
51 Robert Craddock 'Richie Benaud and Kerry Packer had different styles but they combined to launch World Series Cricket' http://www.dailytelegraph.com.au/sport/cricket/richie-benaud-and-kerry-packer-had-different-styles-but-they-combined-to-launch-world-series-cricket/news-story/49406d1ff6e8bb67e79bab26f2bb0eec?nk=89cf0428b15da4243230306dbab08ab8-1469701387 Posted 10 April 2015, Access 28 July 2016.
52 Andrews and Grainger 'The "Packer Affair"' p.249.
53 Paul Barry *The Rise and Rise of Kerry Packer* Ultimo, New South Wales: Bantam 1993.
54 Harte, with Whimpress *A History of Australian Cricket* p.542.
55 Cashman *'Ave a Go* p.135.
56 See Russell Jackson 'The Joy of Six: Great Australian sport adverts' *The Guardian* 9 July 2013 https://www.theguardian.com/sport/blog/2013/jul/09/joy-of-six-australian-sport-adverts Access 28 July 2016.
57 See interview with Hartley at https://www.youtube.com/watch?v=rTnZFGPfCGg Posted 25April 2014, Access 28 July 2016.
58 Harte, with Whimpress *A History of Australian Cricket* p.643.
59 Harte, with Whimpress *A History of Australian Cricket* p.630.
60 An odyssey described in Rod Nicholson *Merv: Merv Hughes* Scoresby, Victoria: Magenta Press 1990.
61 See Merv Hughes *Dear Merv* Crows Nest, New South Wales: Allen and Unwin 2001.
62 Ashley Mallett *One of a Kind: The Doug Walters Story* Crows Nest, New South Wales: Allen and Unwin 2008 p.xvi.
63 For a useful discussion see Jan Larbalestier 'White Over Black: Discourses of Whiteness in Australian Culture' *Borderlands* (e-journal) Vol.3 No.2 2004 http://www.borderlands.net.au/vol3no2_2004/larbalestier_white.htm Access 29 July 2016.
64 Notably in a speech on 17 March 1984 in the Victorian city of Warrnambool and later in his book Geoffrey Blainey *All for Australia* Sydney: Methuen Haynes 1984.
65 For excellent summaries, see 'When talk of racism is just not cricket' (Unattributed) http://www.smh.com.au/articles/2005/12/15/1134500961607.html Posted 16 December 2005, Access 29 July 2016 and Tim Soutphommasane, Race Discrimination Commissioner, Keynote Speech to Asian Studies Association of Australia Annual Conference, 'AsiaScapes: Contesting Borders' University of Western Australia, 10 July 2014 https://www.humanrights.gov.au/news/speeches/asianisation-australia Access 29 July 2016.
66 Harte, with Whimpress *A History of Australian Cricket* p.668.
67 David Utting 'Multicultural cricket? National identity and the Australian Cricket Board's annual report' *Journal of Australian Studies* Vol. 39 No. 3 2015 pp.362–80, p.362 http://dx.doi.org/10.1080/14443058.2015.1051085 Access 29 July 2016.

68 Pascoe was born in Bridgetown, Western Australia in 1950 to Macedonian immigrants. His original surname was 'Durtanovich'. In his autobiography team-mate Geoff Lawson says that Pascoe took a lot of baiting about his origins, especially from Ian and Greg Chappell. See Chris Ryan 'When will we see c Nguyen b Yunupingu?' *Wisden Cricketers' Almanack Australia 2003–04* South Yarra, Victoria: Hardie Grant 2003 pp.23–8, p.24.
69 Popular Australian TV soap opera.
70 Adam Cooper 'Australian cricket's simmering melting pot' http://www.espncricinfo.com/magazine/content/story/622727.html Posted 27 February 2013, Access 29 July 2016.
71 Copper 'Australian cricket's simmering'.
72 Ryan 'When will we see' p.26. Chee Quee retired in 2006.
73 Sharda Ugra 'Fawad Ahmed and the vanishing of Billy Birmingham: How ethnic diversity and the south Asian diaspora became front and centre in Australian cricket policy' *The Fearless Nadia Occasional Papers on India-Australia Relations* Summer 2015 Vol.1 http://www.aii.unimelb.edu.au/publications/fawad-ahmed-and-vanishing-billy-birmingham-how-ethnic-diversity-and-south-asian Access 29 July 2016.
74 Ray Robinson *Between Wickets* London: Fontana 1958 (first published 1945).
75 Scyld Berry 'The other side of Don Bradman' http://www.telegraph.co.uk/sport/cricket/3000015/The-other-side-of-Don-Bradman.html Posted 3 March 2001, Access 30 July 2016.
76 Spiro Zavos 'Is the war on Don Bradman's reputation a fair thing?' http://www.theroar.com.au/2012/12/23/spiro-is-the-war-on-bradmans-reputation-a-fair-thing/ Posted 23 December 2012, Access 30 July 2016.
77 Roland Perry *The Don: A Biography* Sydney: Pan Macmillan 1995 p.585.
78 Richard Holt *Sport and the British: A Modern History* Oxford: Oxford University Press 1989 pp.230–2.
79 Brett Hutchins 'Unity, difference and the "national game": Cricket and Australian national identity' in Stephen Wagg (ed.) *Cricket and National Identity in the Postcolonial Age* Abingdon: Routledge 2005 pp.9–27 p.18.
80 See Brett Hutchins *Don Bradman: Challenging the Myth* Melbourne: Cambridge University Press 2005 pp.154–7.
81 Arunabha Sengupta '10 cricketers whom Sir Don Bradman rubbed the wrong way' http://www.cricketcountry.com/articles/10-cricketers-whom-sir-don-bradman-rubbed-the-wrong-way-17275 Posted 25 August 2012, Access 30 July 2016.
82 Simon Barnes 'The man who changed the game' *Wisden Cricketer's Almanack* 2003 http://www.espncricinfo.com/magazine/content/story/132151.html Access 30 July 2016.
83 See Anthony Giddens *Modernity and Self-Identity: Self and Society in the Late Modern Age* Cambridge: Polity Press 1991.
84 See, in particular, Ricky Ponting *Ponting: At the Close of Play* London: HarperCollins 2013.
85 Justin Langer *Seeing the Sunrise* Crows Nest, New South Wales: Allen & Unwin 2008 pp.2–3.
86 Adam Gilchrist *True Colours: My Life* Sydney: Pan Macmillan 2008 p.xi.
87 Steve Waugh *Out of my Comfort Zone: The Autobiography* Melbourne: Michael Joseph 2006 p.719.

88 http://www.stevewaughfoundation.com.au/
89 Jo Littler '"I feel your pain": cosmopolitan charity and the public fashioning of the celebrity soul' *Social Semiotics* Vol. 18 No. 2 June 2008 pp.237–51, p.237.
90 Langer *Seeing* p.2.
91 Waugh *Out of* pp.597–8.
92 John Hirst 'Anzac Day: the curious notion of Australia's "birth" at Gallipoli' *Sydney Morning Herald* 24 April 2014 http://www.smh.com.au/comment/anzac-day-the-curious-notion-of-australias-birth-at-gallipoli-20140424-zqyll.html Access 31 July 2016.

Chapter 3

'The partnership of the horse and its rider'

Cricket in Southern Africa since 1945

There can be few societies in the world whose history is more starkly contoured by institutionalised racism than the societies of the Republic of South Africa and Zimbabwe (known as Southern Rhodesia between 1898 and 1979). In each of these countries the indigenous black population was suppressed with considerable brutality by encroaching whites and a system of racial domination established, the legacy of which is today still clearly inscribed in the cricket cultures of the two countries. The central figure in the history of this domination is the British imperialist, politician and businessman Cecil Rhodes, who was Prime Minister of Cape Colony from 1890 to 1896 and who gave his name to the territory since renamed Zimbabwe. Rhodes was an unabashed white supremacist, whose Glen Grey Act, passed by the Cape parliament in 1894, can be seen as part of the foundation for the apartheid system that characterised South African society during the four decades that followed the Second World War. Proposing the Act, Rhodes said of indigenous Africans 'I think the natives should be a source of great assistance to most of us. At any rate, if the whites maintain their position as the supreme race, the day may come when we shall all be thankful that we have the natives with us in their proper position'.[1] Another Englishman, Godfrey Huggins, Prime Minister of Rhodesia between 1933 and 1956, expressed a similar sentiment in the 1950s, suggesting that the whites and blacks of Rhodesia lived in 'partnership', adding the ugly qualification that this was akin to the partnership 'between the horse and its rider'.[2] As this chapter will show, these racist convictions, and the draconian enactments that accompanied them, still reverberate in the South African and Zimbabwean cricket cultures.

Abnormal sport in an abnormal society: cricket under apartheid

Cricket had been brought to southern Africa via British troops who came and colonised the Cape after the Napoleonic Wars (1803–15). In the process they had driven out a large contingent of Dutch farmers, known as Boers, whose forebears, many employed by the Dutch East India Company, had settled the area in the mid-seventeenth century. The Dutch departure, in the late 1830s and early 40s, was known in Boer history as 'The Great Trek'. This trek and the subsequent discovery of diamonds in the Kimberley area of the Northern Cape (in the 1860s) and of gold in the Boer region of the Transvaal (in the 1880s) had had huge implications for the future of the country and, in particular, for its black inhabitants. Seeking land, the Boers had fought brutal campaigns (which they called 'Kaffir wars') against the resident African tribes, killing many and enslaving others.[3] Meanwhile, the powerful nexus of white politicians and the mining companies which had formed to exploit the country's diamond and gold deposits had set about converting black Africans from a rural peasantry into a politically powerless proletariat. Rhodes' Glen Grey Act had been designed to establish a system of individual (as opposed to communal) land tenure, and it created a labour tax to force African men into paid employment, principally in the mines. A further Act (the Native Land Act of 1913) had however preserved the fiction of Africans as peasants, assuming them for administrative purposes to be living in barren areas, designated as 'homelands'. This measure precluded the possibility of African workers needing higher wages.[4] Mineworkers were confined within compounds, with no trade union rights and few freedoms.[5]

Whatever sporting activity had flourished among African workers during this period had likely done so at the instigation of white authorities. Africans and 'Coloureds' (people of 'mixed race') had played cricket and formed clubs in the late nineteenth century[6] and, in the 1920s, liberal elements had promoted sport among Africans as a means, among other things, to combat the spread of communism.[7] During the 1930s the Native Affairs Department organised black cricket teams[8] and in 1933 the Chamber of Mines had donated a cup to Bantu (black) cricket, The Native Recruiting Corporation (NRC) trophy.[9]

A colour bar had been officially established in South African cricket in 1894 after consultation with Rhodes.[10] Between the two world wars a colour bar had also been established in the mines, largely at the behest of landless white workers who now competed with blacks for jobs. The Rand Revolt of 1922, led by militant white workers in favour of this colour bar, had also effectively sealed a political alliance between the white working class and the Afrikaner (i.e. Dutch descended) Nationalist Party, founded seven years earlier, that would dominate South African politics for the next seventy years. The leaders of the Nationalist Party had traded strongly on Boer mythology and espoused an explicitly fascist doctrine which they had rendered as 'Christian Nationalism'.[11] The Nationalists won the General Election of 1948 and during the 1950s the pre-existing policies of racial separation and constriction of black African liberty were hardened into an all-embracing framework of racist legislation known as 'apartheid' (literally 'apart-hood').[12] This legislation and, in particular, the 'pass laws' which in

1952 established an internal passport system that governed the movement of Africans from one place to another, triggered angry protests. Moreover, black African independence movements were beginning to thrive across the continent – Ghana, for example, gained independence in 1957 – and in February 1960 British Conservative Prime Minister Harold Macmillan warned in the South African parliament of this 'wind of change' blowing across Africa. 'Whether we like it or not,' he said, 'this growth of national consciousness is a political fact'.[13] Macmillan received a cold reception and the following month in the Transvaal (now Gauteng) township of Sharpeville sixty-nine African anti-apartheid demonstrators were shot dead by police. After this the leaders of the main African political parties – the African National Congress (ANC) and the Pan African Congress (PAC) – were either jailed, exiled or obliged to go underground. Nelson Mandela, leader of the ANC, was imprisoned for life in 1964.

South Africa meanwhile thrived economically – perhaps expectably, given its guaranteed supply of cheap and unfree labour – and foreign capital poured into the country: the economy grew by 76% between 1960 and 1970.[14] To a significant degree cricket reflected the country's political and social arrangements. While no specific law enforced the segregation of sport, cricket was nevertheless racially divided.[15] As Archer and Bouillon observe, South African first-class cricket was founded historically on a 'combination of elitism and racism'.[16] First-class cricket was exclusively white and predominantly English. Provincial teams had competed since 1889 for the Currie Cup, donated by the Scottish shipping tycoon Sir Donald Currie, and the British cricket connection had been further nurtured in the early 1900s by the mining magnate Sir Abe Bailey, a close associate of Rhodes and regular commuter to the UK. Bailey had promoted a tour of England by a South African team in 1907, the success of which 'was an expression of the British in extending their control over that country in the years leading up to the First World War'.[17] Two years later, again at Bailey's instigation, the Imperial Cricket Conference, comprising England, South Africa and Australia, had formed. Dutch South Africans in general shunned cricket, understandably identifying the game with the imperial oppressors who had provoked the Great Trek: before the early 1960s few Afrikaner schools played cricket and the first cricket book to be published in Afrikaans did not appear until 1955.[18] Thus, in the period that followed the Second World War, elite white South African players saw themselves as members of a similarly white, white-flannelled imperial family – a sentiment strongly reflected, for example, in the memoirs of the South African Test player Dudley Nourse. Nourse, like many South African players, had an English heritage: his father, also a South African Test player, had been born in England. He had been named 'Dudley' after the Earl of Dudley, Governor General of Australia where his father had been playing cricket at the time of his birth in 1910.[19] This imperial cricket intimacy was sustained during the twenty years that followed the Second World War: the South African team toured Britain in 1947, 1951, 1955, 1960 and 1965 and Australia in the winters of 1952–3 and 1963–4. England (MCC) toured South Africa in the winters of 1948–9, 1956–7 and 1964–5 and Australia visited in 1957–8. It survived – indeed was, perhaps, strengthened – by South Africa's secession from the Commonwealth in 1961, the country having the previous year been re-constituted as a republic.[20] Moreover, white cricket in South Africa thrived during this period: the number of white South African cricketers doubled between 1955 and 1970 and the Nationalist government had begun to see the prowess of the South African cricket team as 'a political asset'.[21] Black cricket, meanwhile, although strong in Eastern Cape, Kimberley, Cape Town and Johannesburg, suffered, like all other aspects of life in black South Africa, for lack of finance and facilities, a situation exacerbated by the Group Areas Act of 1950 confining black Africans to particular places: for instance, as Jon Gemmell points out, under the Act black cricketers lost access to cricket grounds in three suburbs in the Western Cape.[22] Nevertheless, inter-college games between black cricketers were very popular in the 1960s and 70s and attracted crowds measured in their thousands.[23] Cricket was segregated at an administrative level with different Boards of Control for the Africans, Malays, Coloureds and Whites. This was an example of apartheid strategists' 'multi-national' vision of a future South Africa which would seek to define each of these different racialised groups as separate states within a state.

Historically, the game was most popular among the black middle class, who tended to identify with 'British values'.[24] All the same, as Nauright suggests, 'Coloured, Indian and African cricket culture developed its own forms in the twentieth century, sometimes different from the dominant white culture surrounding the game. Defensive batting was not supported and quality of stroke play and shot making was paramount'.[25] Black cricket, however, remained largely invisible to the cricket public outside of and, to a significant degree, within South Africa itself.[26] A remarkable illustration of this invisibility would come in 1973 when John Passmore, an eminent white cricket administrator and benefactor of Western Province, confessed that until four years earlier he had been 'completely unaware that Africans either played, or wanted to play, cricket'.[27]

During this period, however, opposition to apartheid, both in South Africa and in the wider cricket world, had been growing. In 1948 broadcaster John Arlott, a member of the British Liberal Party, arrived in South Africa to cover the forthcoming Test series between South Africa and the MCC. Travelling around the country he was taken aback by the scale of black poverty amid white plenty;[28] in March 1950, speaking on the BBC's radio programme *Any Questions* he told his audience that 'the existing government in South Africa is predominantly a Nazi one'. He continued:

> Anything can happen to a native in South Africa – any form of violence carrying through as far as murder, and you may rest assured that the person who kills him or ill-treats him won't suffer in any real way at all. The present government that is there at the moment is now issuing forms to ascertain everybody's race, and they give you the blanks to fill in – you can fill yourself in as European, African, Asiatic or other Coloured... The greatest claim for our party is that when asked to fill in our race on leaving the Union [of South Africa] we filled in on the relevant line the word 'human'.[29]

Arlott's intervention will have served as an early notification, especially to progressive sections of the British sporting public, of the brutalities of apartheid. But it cut little ice with the MCC, many of whose members still saw South Africa, as Rhodes had, as the cradle of white Western civilisation and/or had financial interests in the country's mining industry. However, world opinion was moving against apartheid South Africa, driven by emergent political forces both at home and abroad. In South Africa black African sportspeople and white sympathisers began to form non-racial governing bodies in opposition to the existing whites-only organisations and a significant blow against apartheid was struck in 1956 when the non-racial South African Table Tennis Board was recognised ahead of its white counterpart by the International Table Tennis Federation. Moreover campaigners, such as SANROC (the South African Non-Racial Olympic Committee, founded in 1962) sought to prevent South Africa sending a whites-only team to the Olympics: South Africa had done this in 1960, but their participation in the Olympics could not be agreed in 1964 or in 1968[30] and the country was expelled from the Olympic movement in 1970, the first nation to suffer this fate.[31]

The chief factor behind apartheid South Africa's growing pariah status was the decolonisation that took place after the Second World War. By the 1960s international sports governance had to contend with the growing lobby of emergent sovereign states that had gained independence from the European imperial powers. The Olympic movement, historically anxious to expand its membership and at the same time to maintain that 'politics' had no place in sport, was increasingly confronted by the prospect of boycotts by new nations who stood against South Africa's state racism. Around fifty of these nations organised an alternative to the Olympics – the Games of the New Emerging Forces (GANEFO) in Jakarta in 1963 – and fear of mass withdrawals obliged the international Olympic Committee (IOC) to act. World cricket governance faced a similar dilemma. As Jon Gemmell states, the black cricket-playing countries led the way in calling for South Africa's isolation, invoking the United Nations Declaration of Human Rights of 1948 and, in 1969, calling for any cricketer who had played or coached in South Africa to be banned.[32] The previous year, as we saw in Chapter 1, the

Nationalist government had refused to accept Basil D'Oliveira, born a 'Cape Coloured' but qualified for England by residence, as a member of the MCC party due to tour South Africa. The tour was called off.[33] The same year in a suggestion of an ever-widening racial divide in the country, ex-South African cricket captain Jackie McGlew had announced that in 1970 he would stand as a candidate for the Nationalist Party in the provincial elections in Natal; he described anti-apartheid demonstrators as 'hooligans'.[34]

In 1970 the proposed tour of the UK by the South African cricket team was cancelled at the insistence of British Home Secretary James Callaghan on the ostensible ground that he could not guarantee public order if it went ahead. Callaghan also informed the MCC that the Commonwealth Games, scheduled to begin in Edinburgh in July, would be in jeopardy if the tour were not cancelled.[35] The South African Council of Sport (SACOS), formed three years later, campaigned successfully on the slogan 'No Normal Sport in an Abnormal Society'.

South Africa's isolation from world cricket (and all other international sport) was further affirmed by the Gleneagles Agreement of 1977, under which Commonwealth leaders undertook to discourage contact and competition between their sportspeople and sports organisations, teams or individuals from South Africa. By now it was not only South African sport organisations and personnel who might provoke a boycott, but anyone who had associated with them: for example, a boycott of the Montreal Olympic Games of 1976 was threatened if New Zealand were admitted, New Zealand having recently hosted the South African rugby team.

The South African government responded to these developments with a mixture of undisguised intransigence and *faux* reform. In 1956 sport had become a state matter when it had come under the jurisdiction of the Ministry of the Interior. The minister concerned, T.E. Donges, along with Prime Minister Hendrik Verwoerd, had been among the chief architects of apartheid and, in general, the South African government's stance during Donges' time as minister (1956–61) and beyond was that inter-racial sport would not be countenanced in South Africa. The government of Johannes 'John' Vorster (1966–78) took, on the face of it, a more nuanced position, arguing in 1971 that sport in South Africa would now be conducted on a 'multinational' basis. This new approach was drafted by the far right, all-male secret Afrikaner society, the Broederbond, and represented a switch from biologically based to cultural racism. Drawing on the historical 'homelands' policy, the Nationalist government now suggested that the country's black people constituted a series of distinct nations with their own ways of life. The previous year the Black Homelands Citizenship Act had effectively cancelled the (partial) citizenship of black South Africans and instead designated them as citizens of the 'homelands' or 'Bantustans', several of which were now claimed to be independent nations.[36] Multiracial cricket would not be permitted; nor would non-whites be allowed to join the

South African Cricket Association. Black teams could, however, play touring teams effectively as representing separate nations.[37] The policy seemed designed to reassure white conservatives that apartheid was intact, yet to suggest to anxious cricket administrators around the world that the regime was softening.

The politics of South African cricket during the 1970s were characterised by a series of initiatives and quasi-initiatives designed to promote multiracial cricket. This resulted in some marginal change. Black players began to appear at club and provincial level – the 'Coloured' batsman Abdullatief 'Tiffie' Barnes first appeared for Transvaal in 1971, for example, and black spin bowler Omar Henry made his debut for Western Province in 1973. The British millionaire businessman Derrick Robbins brought several cricket teams on private tours to South Africa in the mid-1970s and their opposition occasionally featured non-white players such as Barnes. These initiatives were driven by a number of factors, chief of which, for the white authorities, was to be thought to be bringing about sufficient change for South Africa to be re-admitted to Test cricket. Indeed, in 1979, a delegation from the International Cricket Conference recommended that a team selected from all the Test-playing countries tour South Africa. The recommendation was not acted upon.[38]

Other, broader, considerations were in play however. The Nationalist government, while concerned to appease a right wing wedded to apartheid, was increasingly mindful of two things. First, the extractive sector of the South African economy (chiefly, gold and diamond mining) which apartheid had furnished with a permanent supply of cheap labour, was being overtaken by manufacturing industry. Unlike mining, manufacture required a workforce that was both highly skilled and remunerated sufficiently to buy goods on the domestic market. This imperative was heightened by growing international hostility, which harmed inward investment.[39] Second, as Callinicos and Rogers argued, the Carnation Revolution – a coup by middle-ranking army officers against the dictatorship of Marcello Caetano in Portugal in 1974, which became a mass movement – hastened the progress of decolonisation in Southern Africa. The Portuguese colony of Angola achieved independence the following year and in 1976 the black township of Soweto, on the edge of Johannesburg, erupted in protest against the compulsory teaching of Afrikaans in local schools.[40]

Thus, changes in South African cricket governance were accompanied by broader adjustments in racial legislation. Under the Industrial Conciliation Amendment Act of 1979 trade union rights were extended to black workers and the Federation of South African Trade Unions was formed, followed by the National Union of Mineworkers in 1982. The Riekert Commission of the same year recommended that black workers already resident in urban areas should receive preferential treatment in seeking work. Anti-apartheid activist Sheena Duncan suggested: 'The Riekert report is a very clever and highly sophisticated piece of work which will probably result in a longer period in which the status quo will be maintained through the creation of a relatively small African privileged group which may serve as a buffer against unrest.'[41] The Prohibition of Mixed Marriages Act of 1949, designed to preserve white 'racial purity' was repealed in 1985. Petty apartheid – the segregation of daily life on public transport, in restaurants, on beaches and so on – was allowed to wither; grand apartheid – the apparatus of white rule – remained intact. In cricket two principal developments ran in parallel to these changes: at the instigation of white former Test cricketer Ali Bacher a scheme to 'bring cricket to the townships' was instigated and a series of 'rebel tours' by overseas cricketers was staged.

Bacher was South African cricket's leading diplomat. As captain of the South African team ultimately prevented from touring England in 1970 he had stated pointedly that he would welcome multiracial cricket in his country 'as soon as the government finds it practical'.[42] (This would have paralleled the dismantlement of petty apartheid. But the notion of 'multiracial cricket' within an otherwise racist framework was unacceptable to most opponents of apartheid: hence their favoured slogan 'No Normal Sport in an Abnormal Society'.) The tours and the township programmes were thus primarily designed once again to present an acceptable political face to the international cricket world. The programmes – called Bakers Mini Cricket, having been sponsored by Bakers biscuit brand – were inaugurated in 1983 and enabled black boys and girls to play cricket with a soft ball. Politically, it was vital to South Africa's efforts at international rehabilitation: it traded on the notion that black cricket was currently a negligible presence in the nation's cricket culture, but that a remedy, in the form of a missionary 'development' initiative, was now being applied. The 'rebel tours', although state-funded, achieved little; indeed, they were counter-productive. For example, far from 'forging links', the several West Indian cricketers who participated in the rebel tour of 1983 received life bans and became ' the unforgiven' – social outcasts on their respective islands.[43] Moreover, the games contributed to escalating political turmoil in the republic. South Africa was experiencing an unprecedented level of strikes and violence was once again rife in the townships. Now black protesters came to the rebel tour games and cheered heartily for South Africa's opponents.[44] The final rebel tour, in 1990 by an England XI under the captaincy of Mike Gatting, was conducted amid angry protests. Shunned by black Africans and showing little understanding of the situation they had walked into, they returned home to little reproof and expressed no regret.[45]

In the end South Africa was re-admitted to international cricket for the only reason that many observers had argued that it could be: the abandonment of apartheid. By the late 1980s, as Worger and Byrnes argued, the contradictions in South African society had moved beyond the capacity of apartheid to reform itself: 'Foreign investors withdrew; international banks called in their loans; the value of South African currency collapsed; the price of gold fell to less than one-half of the high of the 1970s; economic output declined; and inflation became chronic'.[46] In 1990 F.W. de Klerk, a former supporter of apartheid who had succeeded P.W. Botha as prime minister the previous year, lifted the ban on membership of the African National Congress and released its leader, Nelson Mandela (with whom the government had been negotiating for some time) from prison. On the day of the release, with angry demonstrations escalating, Bacher negotiated a curtailment of the Gatting cricket tour, claiming this gesture to be in support of de Klerk. White South African cricketer Mike Proctor commented that 'the release of Mandela and the unbanning of the ANC were more important to South Africa at that time than a cricket tour'.[47]

Cricket and the Rainbow Nation: the South African game after apartheid

One thing is broadly agreed by observers of post-apartheid South Africa: the passing of white rule has not brought a materially better life – nor, indeed, much substantial change of any kind – to the majority of the black population. Ten years after the end of apartheid a report by the United Nations Development Program (UNDP) revealed huge and growing in equalities in the country:

> The UNDP report notes that although absolute poverty and the poverty gap declined between 1995 and 2002 from 51.1 percent of the population to 48.5 percent of the population, using the national poverty line of R354 per adult per month, the population has grown in the same period – thus increasing the number of poor from 20.2 million in 1995 to 21.9 million in 2002. Blacks constitute the poorest layer of the population, making up over 90 percent of the 21.9 million poor. In seven of the nine provinces more than 50 percent of the population lives in poverty. The report defines extreme poverty as those living on less than one US dollar per day. In South Africa the number of people in this situation has increased from 9.5 percent in 1995 (3.7 million) to 10.5 percent in 2002 (4.7 million). The rate has increased for all ethnic groups and all provinces. The poverty gap, indicating the depth of poverty, has also increased between 1995 and 2002. South Africa also has one of the most unequal distribution of incomes in the world, with approximately 60 percent of the population earning less than R42,000 per annum (about US$7,000), whereas 2.2 percent of the population have an income exceeding R360,000 per annum (about US$50,000).[48]

There has been no sign of a reversal of this pattern and writers such as William Gumede have accused the African National Congress, which has governed South Africa since the ending of apartheid, of 'leadership paralysis' and of frittering away the political legitimacy they had accumulated through their role in the struggle against white minority rule.[49] The widespread disappointment with the ANC has been heightened by the fact that it was for most of its history a socialist party, its mission to promote social equality and human rights having been enshrined in its Freedom Charter of 1955. Few observers analysed the ANC's failure to fulfil this mission more acutely than the Canadian journalist Naomi Klein, who argued that the ANC had taken office with minimal room for political manoeuvre:

> Want to redistribute land? Impossible – at the last minute, the negotiators agreed to add a clause to the new constitution that protects all private property, making land reform virtually impossible. Want to create jobs for millions of unemployed workers? Can't – hundreds of factories were actually about to close because the ANC had signed on to the GATT, the precursor to the World Trade Organization, which made it illegal to subsidize the auto plants and textile factories. Want to get free AIDS drugs to the townships, where the disease is spreading with terrifying speed? That violates an intellectual property rights commitment under the WTO, which the ANC joined with no public debate as a continuation of the GATT. Need money to build more and larger houses for the poor and to bring free electricity to the townships? Sorry – the budget is being eaten up servicing the massive debt, passed on quietly by the apartheid government. Print more money? Tell that to the apartheid-era head of the central bank. Free water for all? Not likely. The World Bank, with its large in-country contingent of economists, researchers and trainers (a self-proclaimed 'Knowledge Bank'), is making private-sector partnerships the service norm. Want to impose currency controls to guard against wild speculation? That would violate the $850 million IMF deal, signed, conveniently enough, right before the elections. Raise the minimum wage to close the apartheid income gap? Nope. The IMF deal promises 'wage restraint.' And don't even think about ignoring these commitments – any change will be regarded as evidence of dangerous national untrustworthiness, a lack of commitment to 'reform,' an absence of a 'rules-based system.' All of which will lead to currency crashes, aid cuts and capital flight. The bottom line was that South Africa was free but simultaneously captured; each one of these arcane acronyms represented a different thread in the web that pinned down the limbs of the new government.[50]

All this has had stark implications for cricket culture in a society officially liberated from state racism. In particular it has described a vicious circle wherein black politicians, helpless to deal with economic inequalities, have pushed all the harder for the more symbolic change represented by a multiracial national cricket team; at the same time, enduring black poverty has made this change largely impossible to realise.

In 1992, white South African cricket captain Kepler Wessels was pictured being embraced by Steve Tshwete at the World Cup in Australia.[51] Wessels was an Afrikaner from Orange Free State and Tshwete a black activist and ex-prisoner of the apartheid regime who would become the ANC's first sports minister. Their embrace – used initially to publicise the government's whites-only referendum on ending apartheid[52] – would become cricket's symbol of the 'Rainbow Nation' heralded two years later by the black Anglican Archbishop of Cape Town, Desmond Tutu. However, progress toward a 'rainbow' South African team has been minimal. As in so many other walks of South African life, despite the lip service paid to multiracialism, a white power structure has remained largely undisturbed.

The contradiction at the heart of South African cricket politics was typified by, and played out in, the person of Johannes 'Hansie' Cronje, national team captain between 1994 and 2000. Cronje was an Afrikaner blue blood: his family had been farmers (central to Boer mythology) and members of the Dutch Reform Church (a – perhaps the – major bulwark of apartheid) and he had attended the Grey College, a prestigious private school in Bloemfontein.[53] A team-mate recalled that Cronje believed in 'transformation' – the word adopted in post-apartheid politics to refer to the promotion of a multiracial society and the subject of a charter published by the post-apartheid United Cricket Board of South Africa UCBSA[54] in 1999[55] – and would drive long distances to give cricket coaching to underprivileged black children.[56] 'Hansie was never against developing previously disadvantaged people', said his friend the white pastor Ray McCauley, 'but he felt that the way the UCB went about it was not fair towards the team and not fair to the [black] players who were forced into the side – many times to their own detriment. Hansie himself had worked hard to get to the top. He believed that young black players (like the white players) had to prove themselves'.[57] Indeed Cronje briefly resigned the captaincy in 1998 in protest against 'affirmative action' in team selection.[58]

This aptly summed up the racial politics of elite South African cricket at the turn of the century. In 1999 there had been only five black South African-born Test cricketers and this five included Basil D'Oliveira, who had played for England and not for the country of his birth. Four of the five (D'Oliveira, Paul Adams, Omar Henry and Herschelle Gibbs) were classified as 'Coloured' and came from the Western Cape. Henry had been 40 years old when he had made his debut for South Africa in 1992.[59] Steve Tshwete, now ANC sport minister, declared that he could no longer support the South African team because it did not properly represent the nation.[60] White players and officials meanwhile grumbled about 'political interference', a 'culture of entitlement', 'quotas' and the loss of 'merit' as the criterion for team selection. Kevin Pietersen was not untypical in this regard: born to a white South African father and an English mother in Natal in 1980, he claimed to have been dropped from the Natal team in 1999 because of affirmative action:

To me, every single person in this world needs to be treated exactly the same and that should have included me, as a promising 20-year-old cricketer, in the summer of 1999/2000. As far as I was concerned I should not have been discriminated against because of something that happened years before my time. I must emphasise at this point that I am not racist. Apartheid was none of my doing.[61]

(Pietersen came to play in England the following year and, qualifying through his English mother, was selected for England in 2005.)

These popular and enduring white defences of the status quo in South African cricket ignore crucial factors. First, as Desai and Vahed point out, the ANC approved the re-admission of South Africa to the ICC in 1991, before reaching a political settlement with the outgoing Nationalist government. This, they argue, meant a loss of leverage and therefore a continuation of white hegemony in post-apartheid cricket.[62] Second, despite the United Cricket Board of South Africa's 'Statement of Intent' that it would use cricket to redress past injustices,[63] the lack of material assistance available from the ANC government has made cricket development dependent either on the revenue that the South African team can generate or on corporate investment. The former consideration strengthens the hand of white administrators who warn against weakening the side with positive discrimination.[64] The latter one had brought initiatives such as Bakers Mini Cricket and it has also brought funding from the mining companies (Anglo American and de Beers) to send promising young black cricketers to white, cricket-playing schools.[65] The best example here is Makhaya Ntini, who played 101 Tests for South Africa between 1998 and 2009. Ntini (b.1977) was from the Xhosa village of Mdingi in the Border region of Cape Province. In the 1990s the village was inhabited mostly by migrant farm and mine workers and their families and had 80% unemployment. Ntini was given a bursary to attend Dale College in King William's Town, known for its sporting achievements. He went on to receive cricket coaching at the Bradman Academy in Adelaide and the MRF Pace Foundation in Chennai, India.[66] Several black Test players have been developed in this way, but this has done nothing for community cricket structures and has heightened the tension, present in so many contemporary societies, between financing elite sport on the one hand and promoting mass participation on the other. This is a key consideration because in South Africa black players have poor diet, must travel long distances to play or be coached and have little money for equipment.[67] The country's cricket authorities have settled for raising a handful of talented black players out of the poverty that afflicts the huge majority of black South Africans.

Meanwhile, commercial developments have conspired to place ever greater emphasis upon the standards which, it is so often asserted, black cricketers have not been able to meet. In the season of 2004–5 inter-province cricket, previously contested by eleven teams, was re-constituted and based now on six franchises: The Dolphins (KwaZulu-Natal), the Cobras (Western Cape), the Warriors (Eastern Cape), the Lions (Gauteng), the Titans (Northern Gauteng), and the Knights (Free State). These franchises depended on commercial sponsorship, further strengthening the already popular argument that teams could not afford to 'carry' players for reasons of 'political correctness'.

At the same time the global labour market in cricket had generated new threats to South African national team-building. One is the so-called Kolpak ruling in the European Court of Justice in 2003. This ruling, which established the right of Slovak handball player Maros Kolpak to play in Germany, simultaneously affirmed the free movement of labour within the European Union. Moreover, the Cotonou agreement, struck between the European Union (EU) and the African, Caribbean and Pacific Group of States ('ACP countries') in 2000, made the ruling applicable to a number of cricket-playing countries, including South Africa, Zimbabwe and several Caribbean nations. In 2008 the EU stated that the Cotonou treaty should govern the movement of goods and services, not labour. However, by 2009 fifty South Africans had gone to English clubs as 'Kolpak' players. The same year, as the cricket writer Rob Steen pointed out, England could, in theory, have been 'about to embark on a tour of South Africa with a first-choice XI culled solely from players born or schooled in South Africa'.[68] Thus Cricket South Africa (CSA), which had taken over the running of the professional game in 2006, now became further preoccupied with maintaining playing standards, in 2008 reversing their initial decision to ban Kolpak players from South African cricket.[69]

To the 'Kolpak' difficulties could be added the rewards offered by the Indian Premier League, begun in 2008 and designed for a satellite TV audience. With prospect of a burgeoning industry of televised 'big bash' cricket tournaments came the likelihood that the game's most flamboyant performers would become freelance 'portfolio' players, with no loyalty to their clubs or national cricket cultures.[70]

The intractability of the transformation issue has had at least two, mutually reinforcing, implications. One is that the country's cricket memories will remain overwhelmingly white. For example, since South Africa's re-admission to international competition, cricket writers have been wont to write wistfully of the country's 'lost generation' of players.[71] These accounts are always about the white players (Peter and Graeme Pollock, Barry Richards, Mike Proctor and others) unable to play Test cricket because of apartheid South Africa's exclusion from international sport. There is no lament for the legions of unnamed black cricketers held back by apartheid, although occasionally a black cricketer denied by state racism is remembered – as with the 'Coloured' Durban spin bowler Baboo Ebrahim.[72]

The second is that, given the factors in play – the ANC government's inability to confront black poverty and the growing imperative to maintain a winning international team – transformation as an issue will endure for a long time to come, often abetted by media outlets working to the now-familiar 24-hour news cycle. Reportage has often been framed around the tacit notion that politics could (and should) be kept out of sport. The purportedly liberal British *Guardian* noted when the Transformation Charter for cricket was announced in 1999 that white selectors would now 'be answerable to politically inclined administrators'.[73] In 2008 Cricket South Africa chief executive Gerald Majola called a hasty press conference to overrule CSA president Norman Arendse; Arendse had refused to ratify the South African touring party for Bangladesh because it didn't meet the current target of seven black players. (It had only four.)[74] Three months later Arendse was obliged to insist that he had not 'interfered' with team selection for the recent tour of India.[75] Some cricket media continued to revisit (and attempt to re-ignite) the transformation issue. For instance, in March 2015 Cricinfo writer Firdose Moonda reported that the South African Cricketers Association (SACA) was considering legal action against the CSA over a proposal to raise the quota from five to six in franchise cricket.[76] And in August 2016, another Cricinfo journalist Gaurav Kalra broached the matter of quotas to white South African Test cricketer Daryll Cullinan with the following lengthy and apparently leading question: 'People on the outside find it difficult to understand, but here you are in a very competitive sporting environment and you look over your shoulder and see England, Australia, these teams that don't have to deal with all of this. You've got to play the match on the cricket field and then deal with all of this baggage that comes from outside of it. Did that create a certain resentment within the squad?' Cullinan gave a comparatively nuanced reply but, elsewhere in the conversation, suggested that black South Africans preferred football and his remark in this context that 'My issue is that cricket is inherently not a black man's game in South Africa' was selected as the headline for the article.[77] Predictably this brought a rejoinder a few days later from former Cricket South Africa president, Dr Mtutuzeli Nyoka, that cricket was indeed a black man's sport and that black cricketers had not been given opportunities.[78] Some months earlier, in the *Rand Daily Mail* (formerly an anti-apartheid newspaper, now a website), academic and leading critic Ashwin Desai had gone to the heart of the transformation issue. For failing to meet their transformation targets, Sport Minister Fikile Mbalul had forbidden CSA, among other sport bodies, to bid for international tournaments – something Desai dismissed as symptomatic of the gestural politics that had characterised this controversy:

> It is now some 25 years since South African sport made undertakings that it would become more representative of the population, and Mbalula now seeks to stop international competition in the country because transformation is slow. In an election year, he will no doubt try to portray this action as something radical, a show of black nationalist

muscle flexed in enclaves where whites, Indians, and coloureds cohere disproportionately. It's an interesting reversal of the bread-and-circuses method of rule. Instead of distracting a restive population with circuses, he makes a show of cancelling them – with the hope, of course, that this obscures the absence of bread.[79]

These (apparently valid) criticisms notwithstanding, clear progress has been made at elite level. Indeed, in September 2016 the Proteas,[80] the national team, committed to new targets requiring them to play an 'average minimum of 54% black players and average minimum of 18% black African players over the season' and, in doing so, CSA president Chris Nenzani pointed out that 'The Test starting XI that played in the recent Test series against New Zealand contained six players of colour and two Black Africans and the ODI starting XI had as many as eight players of colour (73%) in their most recent series against the West Indies and Australia'.[81]

A nation of gentlemen? Cricket in Zimbabwe since 1945

The modern history of Zimbabwe parallels that of South Africa in a number of ways. What is now Zimbabwe was colonised in the 1890s. It was seized by the Pioneer Column, the brutal military arm of Cecil Rhodes' British South Africa Company, which crushed subsequent uprisings of the indigenous tribes, the Ndebele and the Shona. Rhodes was attracted by local mineral deposits – consisting chiefly of gold and diamonds – and instituted a compound system similar to the one established in the South African mines: African workers called it 'chibaro', or forced labour.[82] In 1895 the territory was named 'Rhodesia', after its chief plunderer. In 1923 the British Crown declared that this territory did not, after all, belong to the British South Africa Company and it was reconstituted as a self-governing British colony under white rule. In 1930, under the Land Apportionment Act, Africans were banned from owning land outside of demarcated 'reserves' – the equivalent of South African 'homelands' – and white farmers became prosperous growing sugarcane, coffee, cotton, tobacco, and several varieties of high-yield hybrid maize. The Native Land Husbandry Act of 1951 forced many African peasants off the land and obliged them to seek work from white employers; the Act stimulated much nationalist protest.[83] By 1970 all land unsuitable for any agricultural purpose was in African hands; 98% of land useable for afforestation or fruit or cattle farming was owned by whites.[84]

By now cricket was long-established as a key element in white Rhodesian settler culture. Indeed Surrey's Montague Parker Bowden, who had captained England against South Africa in 1889, had been a member of Rhodes' Pioneer Column; white Rhodesia had strong cricket links with the UK and white South Africa and cricket matches had been arranged as soon as the white invaders had established Fort Salisbury in 1890.[85] Rhodesia occasionally played in the Currie Cup and the MCC had brought a team to Rhodesia in 1938. In 1944 two Rhodesians had played for the Rest of the Empire XI against a British team in Cairo. Rhodesia was also a regular destination for private tour parties of English county cricketers. For example, Alec and Eric Bedser of Surrey were members of an MCC party that, as was the custom, took a working holiday there in 1949, on the way home from their Test series in South Africa. They played games against local white opposition and took in Victoria Falls, a trip up the Zambesi River and a visit to Rhodes' grave in the Matopos Hills.[86] Mixed-race Commonwealth teams also visited in the early 1960s and the racism visited on black members of these teams was seen by the organisers as a minor hiccup. Organiser Ron Roberts wrote to E.W. Swanton in 1962: 'We have had a few incidents of Europeans refusing to serve our non-Europeans [. . .] but these little setbacks have been accepted philosophically'.[87] Rhodesia also occasionally supplied players to the South African Test side, beginning with Denis Tomlinson and Bob Crisp in 1935 and most notably including Bulawayo-born Colin Bland, who appeared in 21 Tests for South Africa between 1961 and 1967.

In the early 1960s the two main African resistance movements – the Zimbabwe African People's Union (ZAPU) founded in 1961 and the Zimbabwe African National Union (ZANU) formed in 1963 – and fear of nationalism prompted the rise of the Rhodesian Front (RF), which drew most of its support from white farmers. In 1965 the RF government declared Unilateral Independence from Britain. In the diplomatic wrangle between UK and Rhodesia that followed, racism was not deemed an important issue and the British Labour government under Harold Wilson offered the RF independence without black majority rule. Rhodesia during this time managed to block the outflow of capital from the country and the nationalist movement launched a guerrilla offensive in 1967.

As in South Africa, growing isolation from the outside world and mounting revulsion at racist governance seems only to have hardened the white Rhodesians' affection for cricket. In 1972 white South African cricketer Mike Proctor beat RF Prime Minister Ian Smith in a poll for 'Rhodesian of the Year'.[88] Moreover racist exclusion was not always extended to visiting cricketers. In 1970 black Barbadian and West Indies captain Garfield Sobers came to Rhodesia to play in a single wicket competition and was photographed with Smith. An international furore ensued, during which Guyana Prime Minister Forbes Burnham banned Sobers from entering the island and Indian Prime Minister Indira Gandhi similarly refused to admit him as a member of the West Indies team due to tour India.[89] (Dr Eric Williams, Prime Minister of Trinidad and Tobago, interceded and persuaded Sobers to apologise.) Australia toured Rhodesia in 1966 but the following year the British government intervened to prevent Yorkshire County Cricket Club from doing so.[90]

In 1980, with the guerrilla war effectively won, the British government under Margaret Thatcher entrusted political power to ZANU PF, under Robert Mugabe, and the country was renamed 'Zimbabwe', a Shona word meaning a hallowed place. The acceptance of Mugabe was on the basis that ZANU plainly carried the most popular support but it was grudging because of the belief in the British Establishment that he was Marxist intending to nationalise the country's economy. Independence and majority rule were followed by factional hostility between ZANU and ZAPU which was not resolved until 1988 when the two parties merged.

Although the exact time and place of the remark do not seem to have been established, Mugabe stated in 1983 that: 'Cricket civilises people and creates good gentlemen. I want everyone to play cricket in Zimbabwe; I want ours to be a nation of gentlemen'.[91] In view of the now widely acknowledged brutality of his regime, this remark has been treated with scepticism, but there has been strong, if uneven, support for cricket in independent Zimbabwe. As in majority-rule South Africa, a transformation programme was instituted. There seems to have been no strong tradition of black people playing cricket in Rhodesia, although there were black cricketers: for example, in 1972 Peter Chingoka, born in Bulawayo in 1954 and later President of the Zimbabwe Cricket Union, became the first black Rhodesian to play in the country's Logan Cup.[92] A talent-awareness programme was launched in line with the government's 'Africanisation' policy'.[93] This was primarily aimed at the discovery and development of black cricketers, white cricket being long-established and the Indian-Rhodesian game also on a sound footing – indeed, in 1958 a team of Indian Rhodesians had played a visiting side of South African 'coloureds' captained by Basil D'Oliveira.[94] A scholarship scheme for young black cricketers was set up and steps taken to found clubs for black cricketers – an example being Takashinga, founded in 1990 and initially linked to Churchill High School in Harare and later transplanted to the suburb of Highfields.[95] Understandably, the term 'Africanisation' became problematic since a great many whites and Asians had been born in the country and were therefore entitled to see themselves as Africans.[96]

In 1992, on the strength of the performances of a largely white team, Zimbabwe had been awarded Test status by the ICC. By then, however, 'structural adjustment' programmes, wherein the Mugabe government, like most governments around the world, was obliged by the International Monetary Fund and the World Bank to reduce state spending, had been instigated. The effects of this, coupled with international sanctions and the reduction in aid and investment, sent the Zimbabwean economy crashing: between 2000 and 2005 it contracted by over 40% and by the beginning of 2007 80% of the population were said to be living below the poverty line.[97] Mugabe reacted with a mixture of violence and cronyism. An opposition political party – the Movement for Democratic Change – had been formed in 1999 and its supporters now faced widespread intimidation. In 2001 and

2002 men described as veterans of the guerrilla war were allowed to invade white-owned farms; much land ended up in the hands of 'fat cat' supporters of Mugabe, the only people who could afford to cultivate it.[98] Between 2000 and 2007 3.4 million Zimbabweans left the country.[99]

Notwithstanding some successes in the transformation programme – for example, in 2001 Harare batsman Hamilton Masakadza became the first black player to score a century for Zimbabwe – unsurprisingly, off-the-field turmoil affected the progress of Zimbabwean cricket. In 2003, during the World Cup co-hosted by South Africa and Zimbabwe, Henry Olonga, a black member of the Zimbabwean side and Andy Flower, a white, took the field against Namibia wearing black armbands which they said were to be 'mourning the death of democracy in our beloved Zimbabwe'.[100] The following year team captain Heath Streak, whose family farm near Bulawayo had been invaded in 2001,[101] resigned along with a number of other white players. As in South Africa after Kolpak, Zimbabwean cricket began to haemorrhage players to other cricket-playing countries, notably England.

Zimbabwean cricket now became further scarred by accusations of racism and counter-accusations of corruption, while international disquiet over ZANU governance began to parallel concern raised by the earlier Smith regime. In 2008 the British (Labour) government announced that the Zimbabwe cricket team would be refused entry to the UK for the following year's Test series. Secretary of State for Culture, Media and Sport Andy Burnham stated that this was because 'The Zimbabwean government has ceased to observe the principle of the rule of law. It has terrorised its own citizens, including the ruthless and violent suppression of legitimate political opposition'.[102] With Mugabe accusing his opponents of racism and imperialism it seemed that cricket, an enduring symbol of white dominance, might not have much of a future in Zimbabwe. As Jon Gemmell commented perceptively: 'Cricket is not a major sport in Zimbabwe; it was a minority white pastime that has been Africanised under the present regime. It is more multiracial than in the past, but could be sacrificed by ZANU PF as a further example of colonial influence'.[103] This prospect had been strengthened two years earlier when the government had dissolved the board of Zimbabwe Cricket (ZC), whereupon Brigadier Gibson Mashingaidze, chair of ZANU's Sport and Recreation Commission, had declared: 'we are starting afresh. We are not bothered about [losing] Test status. Those who want to go to India, Canada or wherever, can go. The government will not be held at ransom by individuals'.[104] Since then a number of white players, including Streak and Flower, have made their peace with the authorities and returned to Zimbabwean cricket as coaches. In 2014 Streak wanted to move on from the now-familiar grumblings about quotas and political interference which had been his rationale for walking out ten years earlier. With talented black players now available to the Zimbabwe team, Streak now suggested that financial mismanagement had been the problem:

It was really more people taking advantage of the political situation at that time. The Zimbabwe Cricket Union was making a lot of money and people who had no background or history in cricket suddenly were very interested in becoming a part of the hierarchy in Zimbabwe cricket. That is where the problem started.[105]

The same year two monitors of the Zimbabwean cricket scene claimed that Zimbabwe Cricket's current financial crisis was partly attributable to the mismanagement of a $6 million loan given to ZC by the ICC: it was placed in an interest free account at Metabank, on whose board sat several members of the ZC hierarchy.[106] Six months earlier the Zimbabwe players had refused to report for training over unpaid match fees and announced that they were forming a union.[107] At the time of writing it appeared that Zimbabwe was indeed prepared to risk losing Test cricket: by 2016 Zimbabwe had played only thirteen Tests in five years and none in 2015 – a situation attributed to the more lucrative possibilities of limited-overs cricket.[108]

Notes

1. On moving the second reading of the Glen Grey Act, Cape House, 20 July 1894. See Vindex [F. Verschoyle] *Cecil Rhodes: His Political Life and Speeches 1881–1900* London: Chapman and Hall 1900 p.372.
2. See, for example, Larry W. Bowman *Politics in Rhodesia: White Power in an African State* Cambridge, Massachusetts: Harvard University Press 1973 p.26 https://archive.org/stream/politicsinrhodes00bowm/politicsinrhodes00bowm_djvu.txt Access 5 September 2016.
3. Alex Callinicos and John Rogers *South Africa After Soweto* London: Pluto Press 1977 pp.18–19.
4. Callinicos and Rogers *South Africa After Soweto* pp.22–5.
5. Callinicos and Rogers *South Africa After Soweto* p.94.
6. Robert Archer and Antoine Bouillon *The South African Game: Sport and Racism* London: Zed Press 1982.
7. See Jon Gemmell *The Politics of South African Cricket* London: Routledge 2004 pp.53–4.
8. Gemmell *The Politics* p.54.
9. This ran under the auspices of the (black) South African African Cricket Board (SAACB) until 1959, when the SAACB affiliated to the non-racial South African Cricket Board of Control (SACBOC) and ran non-racial tournaments between 1961 and 1964. SAACB was reconstituted in 1964–5 and ran the NRC Cup until 1975. See André Odendaal, Krish Reddy, Andrew Samson *The Blue Book: A History of Western Province Cricket, 1890–2011* Auckland Park, SA: Fanele 2012 p.140.
10. See André Odendaal 'Cricket and representations of beauty: Newlands Cricket Ground and the roots of apartheid in South African cricket' in Anthony Bateman and Jeffrey Hill (eds.) *The Cambridge Companion to Cricket* Cambridge: Cambridge University Press 2011 pp.218–37, p.228. This initiative was taken by cricket officials in Western Province, home to Cape Town's Newlands, South Africa's premier cricket ground, which had opened six years earlier. The move was made in order to exclude fast bowler Krom Hendricks from the South

African team. Krom was a Cape Malay. The Cape Malays were descended from enslaved Javanese, first brought to South Africa in the seventeenth century by the Dutch East India Company.
11 Callinicos and Rogers *South Africa After Soweto* p.7. It has been argued that the Dutch Reformed Church was the co-author of apartheid – 'some would say its initiator'. See Allister Sparks *The Mind of South Africa* London: Arrow Books 1997 p.153.
12 Jon Gemmell provides a detailed summary of the various apartheid laws: see Gemmell *The Politics* pp.57–61.
13 http://news.bbc.co.uk/onthisday/hi/dates/stories/february/3/newsid_2714000/2714525.stm Access 7 September 2016.
14 See Callinicos and Rogers *South Africa After Soweto* p.4.
15 Grant Jarvie *Class, Race and Sport in South Africa's Political Economy* London: Routledge and Kegan Paul 1985 p.50.
16 Archer and Bouillon *The South African Game* p.85.
17 Geoffrey Levett 'Constructing imperial identity: the 1907 cricket tour of England' in Bruce Murray and Goolam Vahed (eds.) *Empire and Cricket: The South African Experience 1884–1914* Pretoria: Unisa Press 2009 pp.241–57, p.257.
18 Archer and Bouillon *The South African Game* p.87.
19 See Dudley Nourse *Cricket in the Blood* London: Hodder and Stoughton 1951 p.11.
20 This meant, of course, that South Africa was now outside of the Imperial Cricket Conference, yet 'white' sides continued to play against them.
21 Archer and Bouillon *The South African Game* pp.87–8.
22 Gemmell 'South African cricket: "The Rainbow Nation must have a Rainbow Team"' in Jon Gemmell and Boria Majumdar (eds.) *Cricket, Race and the 2007 World Cup* Abingdon: Routledge 2008 pp.39–60 pp.40 and 43. The areas were Vasco, Green Point and Mowbray.
23 Gemmell 'South African Cricket' p.41.
24 Archer and Bouillon *The South African Game* p.88.
25 John Nauright *Sport, Cultures and Identities in South Africa* London: Leicester University Press 1997 p.36.
26 Ibid. p.38.
27 Gemmell 'South African Cricket' p.46.
28 See John Arlott *Basingstoke Boy: The Biography* London: Willow Books 1990 pp.175–6.
29 David Rayvern Allen *Arlott: The Authorised Biography* London: HarperCollins 1996 pp.145–6. For a full account of the furore that followed Arlott's comments see pp.137–53.
30 See Stephen Wagg 'In this shrinking world: "race", the Olympics and the wind of change' in Jonathan Long and Karl Spracklen (eds.) *Sport and Challenges to Racism* Basingstoke: Palgrave Macmillan 2011 pp.37–52.
31 Jarvie *Class, Race* p.54.
32 Gemmell *The Politics* p.137.
33 This became one of the most discussed incidents in cricket's history and, to a degree, D'Oliveira became depicted as a depoliticised hero, placed outside of the history of struggle, succeeding with quiet dignity against formidable odds. See in particular Peter Oborne *Basil D'Oliveira: Cricket and Conspiracy – The Untold Story* London: Little, Brown 2005.
34 Douglas Alexander 'Former Test captain comes under fire' *The Age* 12 November 1968 p.4 https://news.google.com/newspapers?nid=1300&dat=19681112&id=39IQAAAAIBAJ&sjid=eZMDAAAAIBAJ&pg=3358,2293573&hl=en Access 9 September 2016.

35 http://news.bbc.co.uk/onthisday/hi/dates/stories/may/22/newsid_2504000/2504573.stm Access 8 September 2016.
36 No other country accepted them as such. See, for example, Colin Bundy 'The Transkei: or how to keep black labour cheap' *New Society* 21 October 1976 pp.121–3.
37 For a good summary, see Gemmell *The Politics* pp.66–8.
38 See Gemmell *The Politics* pp.163–4.
39 See Gemmell *The Politics* p.65.
40 Callinicos and Rogers *South Africa After Soweto* p.5.
41 See http://www.sahistory.org.za/dated-event/recommendations-riekert-commission-investigate-employment-conditions-black-workers-are-t Access 11 September 2016.
42 See Gemmell *The Politics* p.93.
43 See Siddhartha Vaidyanathan 'The Unforgiven' http://www.espncricinfo.com/magazine/content/story/286356.html Posted 2 August 2007, Access 11 September 2016.
44 Gemmell *The Politics* p.165.
45 Paul Weaver 'English rebels who ignored apartheid cause still show a lack of shame' *The Guardian* 11 January 2010 https://www.theguardian.com/sport/2010/jan/11/rebel-tour-1990-england-players-south-africa Access 11 September 2016.
46 William H. Worger and Rita M. Byrnes 'History of South Africa (Part 2: The Republic of South Africa: 1961–present)' http://www.nationsonline.org/oneworld/History/South-Africa-history2.htm Access 11 September 2016.
47 Quoted in Gemmell *The Politics* p.177.
48 World Socialist Web Site 'United Nations report highlights growing inequality in South Africa' http://www.wsws.org/en/articles/2004/05/safr-m21.html Posted 21 May 2004, Access 15 September 2016.
49 William Gumede *Restless Nation: Making Sense of Troubled Times* Cape Town: Tafelberg 2012.
50 See Naomi Klein *The Shock Doctrine: The Rise of Disaster Capitalism* London: Allen Lane 2007 p.203. Klein's chapter 'Democracy born in chains: South Africa's constricted freedom' can be read in full at the *Common Dreams* website: http://www.commondreams.org/views/2011/02/14/democracy-born-chains-south-africas-constricted-freedom Posted 14 February 2011, Access 15 September 2016.
51 The picture can be seen at: https://www.google.com/culturalinstitute/beta/asset/steve-tshwete-kepler-wessels-and-draft-sport-constitution/cQE5WVCObxF_gg Access 15 September 2016.
52 The referendum took place five days before South Africa were due to play England in Sydney in the semi-final of the World Cup. The ICC had only agreed to admit South Africa to the tournament on the condition that there was a 'Yes' vote and, if there was not, the team would have to come home – see Firdose Moonda 'We left knowing that we put South Africa on the map' http://www.espncricinfo.com/wctimeline/content/current/story/812993.html Posted 30 December 2014, Access 13 January 2017.
53 See Garth King *The Hansie Cronje Story: An Authorised Biography* Oxford: Monarch Books 2007 pp. 19, 24 and 90.
54 See 'A brief history of the process that led to the formation of the UCBSA' http://static.espncricinfo.com/db/NATIONAL/RSA/ABOUT_THE_UCB/HISTORY.html Access12 May 2017.

55 https://www.theguardian.com/sport/1999/jan/02/cricket8 Access 16 September 2016. Lowry wrote that South Africa's white cricket selectors would now be 'answerable to politically inclined administrators'.
56 King *The Hansie* p.137.
57 King *The Hansie* p.139.
58 King *The Hansie* p.140; see also Gemmell 'South African cricket: the Rainbow Nation' p.51.
59 See Ian Hawkey 'Mandela and beyond' in Rob Steen (ed.) *The New Ball, Volume Two: Universal Stories* Edinburgh: Mainstream 1999 pp.39–55, p.43.
60 Ibid. p.40.
61 Kevin Pietersen *Crossing the Boundary* London: Ebury Press 2006 p.62.
62 Ashwin Desai and Goolam Vahed 'Beyond the Nation? Colour and class in South African cricket' in Ashwin Desai (ed.) *The Race to Transform: Sport in Post-Apartheid South Africa* Cape Town: HSRC Press 2010 pp.176–221 p. 178.
63 Gemmell *The Politics* p.104.
64 Desai and Vahed 'Beyond' p.180.
65 Desai and Vahed 'Beyond' p.183.
66 Hawkey 'Mandela and beyond' pp.44–5.
67 Desai and Vahed 'Beyond' pp.183–5.
68 Rob Steen 'Anyone for England?' http://www.espncricinfo.com/magazine/content/story/427344.html Posted 30 September 2009, Access 16 September 2016.
69 Desai and Vahed 'Beyond' pp.199–201.
70 Desai and Vehad 'Beyond' p.202. See also Chris Rumford 'Twenty20, global disembedding, and the rise of the 'portfolio player' *Sport in Society* Vol.14 No.10 2011 pp.1358–68.
71 See, for instance, Martin Chandler 'The lost generation' http://www.cricketweb.net/the-lost-generation/ Posted 25 May 2012, Access 16 September 2016.
72 Sidharth Monga 'Baboo's story' http://www.espncricinfo.com/magazine/content/story/496754.html Posted 18th January 2011, Access 16 September 2016.
73 Johan Lowry 'Non white charter can bowl out selectors' *The Guardian* 2 January 1999 https://www.theguardian.com/sport/1999/jan/02/cricket8 Access 16 September 2016.
74 Telford Vice 'Majola ends quota row' *The Guardian* 12 February 2008 https://www.theguardian.com/sport/2008/feb/12/cricket.sport Access 16 September 2016.
75 Cricinfo staff 'I did not interfere in team selection for India – Arendse' http://www.espncricinfo.com/southafrica/content/story/353082.html Posted 31 May 2008, Access 16 September 2016.
76 Firdose Moonda 'Legal threat over abrupt SA quota change' http://www.espncricinfo.com/southafrica/content/story/855925.html Posted 26 March 2015, Access 16th September 2016.
77 Gaurav Kalra 'My issue is that cricket is inherently not a black man's game in South Africa'. Cricinfo http://www.espncricinfo.com/magazine/content/story/1050081.html Posted 27 August 2016, Access 16 September 2016
78 '"Cricket is inherently a black man's sport" – Dr Mtutuzeli Nyoka' http://www.enca.com/media/video/cricket-is-inherently-a-black-mans-sport-dr-mtutuzeli-nyoka Posted 30 August 2016, Access 16 September 2016.
79 Ashwin Desai 'Fikile Mbalula: Hypocrite who hides government's failings' http://www.rdm.co.za/sport/2016/05/03/fikile-mbalula-hypocrite-who-hides-government-s-failings Posted 3 May 2016, Access 16 September 2016.
80 'Proteas' – South African flowers representing hope and change – replaced 'Springboks' as the national team's nickname in 1992.

81 'Proteas commit to transformation targets' http://www.sport24.co.za/Cricket/Proteas/proteas-commit-to-transformation-targets-20160903 Posted 5 September 2016, Access 16 September 2016.
82 Callinicos and Rogers *South Africa After Soweto* pp.93–4.
83 See David Martin and Phyllis Johnson *The Struggle for Zimbabwe: The Chimurenga War* London: Faber & Faber 1982 p.xiv. See also William R. Duggan 'The Native Land Husbandry Act of 1951 and the rural African middle class of Southern Rhodesia' *African Affairs* Vol. 79 No.315 1980 pp.227–40.
84 Callinicos and Rogers *South Africa After Soweto* p.95.
85 Jonty Winch *Cricket's Rich Heritage: A History of Rhodesian and Zimbabwean Cricket 1890–1982* Bulawayo: Books of Zimbabwe 1983 p.1.
86 Alec and Eric Bedser *Our Cricket Story* London: Evans Brothers 1951 pp.194–7.
87 E.W. Swanton *As I Said At the Time: A Lifetime of Cricket* (edited by George Plumptre) London: Unwin 1987 p.492.
88 Andrew Novak 'Sport and racial discrimination in colonial Zimbabwe: a reanalysis' *International Journal of the History of Sport* Vol. 29 No. 6, 1 April 2012 pp. 850–67, p.853.
89 See Aviston D. Downes 'Sport and international diplomacy: the case of the Commonwealth Caribbean and the anti-apartheid campaign, 1959–1992' *The Sports Historian* Vol.22 No.2 November 2002 pp.23–45.
90 See Charles Little 'Rebellion, race and Rhodesia: international cricket relations with Rhodesia during UDI' in Dominic Malcolm, Jon Gemmell and Nalin Mehta (eds.) *The Changing Face of Cricket: From Imperial to Global Game* Abingdon: Routledge 2010 pp.93–106, pp.95–6.
91 See, for example, Lucy Fleming 'Mugabe turns 90: Nine things you may not know' BBC News http://www.bbc.co.uk/news/world-africa-26257237 Posted 21 February 2014, Access 23 September 2016.
92 Novak p.854; the Logan Cup was donated by Scottish-born diamond magnate James Douglas Logan in 1903 – see Dean Allen *Empire, War and Cricket in South Africa: Logan of Matjiesfontein* Cape Town: Zebra Press 2015.
93 Trevor Chesterfield 'Zimbabwe: what of the future?' in Jon Gemmell and Boria Majumdar (eds.) *Cricket, Race and the 2007 World Cup* Abingdon: Routledge 2008 pp.133–51, p.138.
94 See Jonty Winch 'Jayanti – a cricketing anachronism as Zimbabwe's "forgotten" players make a fresh start' *Sport in Society* Vol.16 No.1 2013 pp.56–70.
95 See Liam Brickhill 'The Takashinga way' http://www.espncricinfo.com/magazine/content/story/570904.html Posted 22 July 2012, Access 23 September 2016. See also Telford Vice 'Local side with a nationalist agenda' *The Guardian* 20 April 2004 https://www.theguardian.com/sport/2004/apr/20/cricket Access 23 September 2016.
96 Chesterfield 'Zimbabwe' p.138.
97 Leo Zeilig 'Zimbabwe: Imperialism, hypocrisy and fake nationalism' *International Socialism* No.119 Summer 2008 pp.93–110, p.100.
98 Zeilig 'Zimbabwe' p.97.
99 Zeilig 'Zimbabwe' p.102.
100 Liam Brickhill 'Olonga and Flower make a stand' http://www.espncricinfo.com/wctimeline/content/current/story/825253.html Posted 2 February 2015, Access 24 September 2016.
101 'Streak family tells of gun-wielding raid on Zimbabwe farm' http://www.espncricinfo.com/ci/content/story/104770.html Posted 8 March 2001, Access 24 September 2016.

102 Jon Gemmell 'Cricket: who benefits from the Zimbabwe ban?' http://bleacher report.com/articles/33750-cricket-who-benefits-from-zimbabwe-ban Posted 30 June 2008, Access 24 September 2016. As Gemmell pointed out elsewhere, many of the people supporting a ban on cricket ties with Mugabe's Zimbabwe had argued for 'building bridges' to apartheid South Africa. He also suggested that a more apt comparison was between Zimbabwe and Pakistan: if people were sufficiently concerned about Mugabe's authoritarian rule to want to ban the Zimbabwe cricket team, why hadn't they been similarly concerned about successive military dictatorships in Pakistan? See Jon Gemmell 'So far beyond the pale: international morality and cricket boycotts' in Chris Rumford and Stephen Wagg (eds.) *Cricket and Globalization* Newcastle: Cambridge Scholars Publishing 2010 pp.60–82.
103 Gemmell 'Cricket: Who benefits. . . .?'
104 Chesterfield 'Zimbabwe' p.148.
105 Subash Jayaraman 'If things were managed properly, Zimbabwe could be a mid-ranked side' http://www.espncricinfo.com/magazine/content/story/779047.html Posted 10 September 2014, Access 24 September 2016.
106 Tristan Holme and Liam Brickhill 'Zimbabwe Cricket mismanaged $6m ICC loan' http://www.espncricinfo.com/zimbabwe/content/story/724593.html Posted 3 March 2014, Access 24 September 2016.
107 Tristan Holme 'Disunity threatens Zimbabwe players' prospects of a better future' http://www.espncricinfo.com/magazine/content/story/942029.html Posted 19 November 2015, Access 24 September 2016.
108 Sakshi Gupta 'Why are Zimbabwe ignoring Test cricket?' http://www.cricketcountry.com/articles/why-are-zimbabwe-ignoring-test-cricket-402106 Posted 17 February 2016, Access 24 September 2016.

Chapter 4

A relative lack of interest
Cricket in New Zealand since 1945

British journalist Christopher Martin-Jenkins covered cricket for the BBC and the broadsheet newspapers. In his memoirs, first published in 2012, he reflected on his visits to seven of the nine Test-playing countries other than his own. Of New Zealand he wrote:

> From the selfish viewpoint the wonderful thing about tours to this country was the relative lack of interest in cricket. There were more days off than usual, less demand for interviews on my tour as BBC correspondent, or for feature articles when I returned in later years for the *Telegraph* and *Times*.[1]

This chapter analyses New Zealand's recent history as the (widely designated) poor relation among the cricket-playing 'white' dominions of the dismantled British Empire. The 'relative lack of interest' in cricket in New Zealand is paralleled in the nation's academy since only one notable scholar – Prof. Greg Ryan, a historian at Lincoln University in Christchurch – has devoted much attention to the country's cricket culture and the chapter necessarily draws quite heavily on his (excellent) work.

New Zealand was colonised by Britain in the mid-nineteenth century and given a measure of self-government which was formalised with the conferring of dominion status in 1907. As with other areas of white British settlement wars were fought with the indigenous population. In New Zealand's case, there were wars over land ownership between white militias and local Maori tribespeople between the mid-1840s and the early 1870s. Originally called 'Maori Wars', since the Second World War, through the writing of historians such as Sir Keith Sinclair,[2] Maori history has been more sympathetically interpreted: Sinclair, in particular, argued strongly against the then-prevailing idea (widely known now as 'The South Island Myth') that New Zealand was culture-less before the arrival there of whites.[3] These conflicts are nowadays generally known as The New Zealand Wars, after the book of the same name published by historian James Belich,[4] and the country's whites generally referred to by the Maori word 'Pakeha'. In August 2016 the New Zealand government announced that there would be a national day commemorating these wars.[5] The wars were preceded by the Treaty of Waitangi, signed in 1840. Interpreted by the settlers as conceding sovereignty to Britain, and thus as the foundation document of New Zealand as a nation, the treaty has been the subject of dispute ever since and the Waitangi Tribunal was established as a permanent commission of inquiry in 1975. In 1960, the second New Zealand Labour government re-designated an existing national holiday as Waitangi Day. This was re-named New Zealand Day in 1973, but the National Party government of Robert Muldoon reverted to Waitangi Day in 1976, partly in deference to Maori wishes.

All this suggests that New Zealand, in comparison to other Test cricket-playing nations governed by white, settler-descended elites, has a pattern of historic ethnic relations more nuanced and less virulently or institutionally racist than those of Southern Africa or even of neighbouring Australia. This has been reflected in the country's cricket culture wherein debates about national identity and access to the game, while not without controversy or racial stereotyping, have on the whole lacked either the crudeness or the divisiveness evidenced elsewhere in the cricket world.

'Britain's Farm': cricket in New Zealand, 1945-1980

The 'Dominion of New Zealand' became simply 'New Zealand' in 1947 when the Labour Prime Minister Peter Fraser decided finally to adopt the Statute of Westminster of 1931, facilitating complete self-rule. Ties to Britain remained close, however. In the 1940s non-Maori New Zealanders constituted 95% of the people and 96% of them identified as British, so that, when New Zealand citizenship and passports became available in 1948, few British migrants applied.[6] The government continued to prefer British migrants or those from northern Europe. 1947 saw the arrival of the 'Ten Pound Poms' – British who found it cheaper to come to live in New Zealand than to take a holiday at home. Between 1945 and 1971 New Zealand took in 77,000 migrants from the UK.[7] This was paralleled by a trade relationship with Britain, which flourished in the 1950s and 60s and declined only after the entry of the UK into the European Economic Community (EEC). Of the fifty-five years since 1945 an appraisal of New Zealand exports states:

> The starkest change over this time is the declining contribution of the United Kingdom, which in 1955 took 65.3 percent of New Zealand's exports. By the year ended June 1973, during which Britain formally entered the European Economic Community, this had fallen to 26.8 percent. By the year ended June 1990 its share had fallen to 7.2 percent and in the year ended June 2000 its share was 6.2 percent.[8]

During that time Britain's status as a world power had fallen and in any case British culinary tastes had moved away from 'butter, cheese and frozen lamb'. New Zealand had started to export more to the Pacific Rim and was no longer 'Britain's Farm'.[9]

It is authoritatively asserted that New Zealand cricket was slow to assimilate these important changes. As Greg Ryan wrote in 2005, for much of the period that followed the Second World War, the country's cricket remained shackled by Anglophilia and, more specifically, the 'amateur virtues' of the English game.[10] Certainly Martin-Jenkins of the BBC always relished teaming up with his opposite number former RAF pilot Iain Gallaway, the 'most charming and accomplished of the New Zealand cricket commentators . . . A traditionalist if ever there was, who always referred to Britain as "home" although he had been a Kiwi all his life'.[11] The great hero of Gallaway's generation was likely to have been the explorer Edmund Hillary, whose ascent of Everest with Tensing Norgay, announced on the eve of the British queen's coronation in 1953, was immediately rewarded with a knighthood. Hillary 'encapsulated the masculine qualities celebrated in Kiwi culture, becoming the nation's favourite icon and represented on the $5 note. An imperial hero and a pioneer, the first and the best, laconic and humanitarian, a gentleman with a larrikin streak'.[12]

In practice this abiding affection for the Mother Country meant a notably relaxed attitude to losing among the administrators of New Zealand cricket and, despite the attainment of Test status in 1930, an apparent contentment with playing to a poor national standard. For example, despite a relatively successful tour of England in 1949, during which they drew all four Test matches and lost only one first-class match, New Zealand did not win a Test match until 1956, when they beat West Indies at Eden Park in Auckland. This does not seem to have caused as much of a stir as it might have. For example, New Zealand's wicketkeeper that day, Simpson 'Sam' Guillen, significantly a black Trinidadian who had toured New Zealand with West Indies in 1952 and then migrated to the country, had no idea that it was his team's first Test win: 'I didn't know. I was surprised. I thought New Zealand had won Test matches before. I heard the talk going around and I wondered what was going on. Then, of course, the papers had it printed and then I knew'.[13] And, despite 'thousands of Aucklanders mobbing the players and a nation soon to celebrate the news via radio', Jack Alabaster, another member of the side, recalled little of them when reminiscing in 2016:

> If there were ticker tape parades or telegrams from the Prime Minister, Alabaster doesn't recall them. Certainly there were no receptions at city hall in Invercargill. He had work to do. 'As far as I was concerned I had to get back smartly and go back to school [he was a teacher at Southland Boys' High School]. I recall some time on the Wednesday [the day after the victory] I was back at school'.[14]

One New Zealand editor even offered the dampening comment that 'the edge' of West Indies endeavour had perhaps been 'a little dulled'.[15]

As Ryan suggests, the New Zealand cricket authorities during this period spent too much time approaching Lord's with requests for the MCC to tour and too little time developing cricket links to other nations. Neighbouring Australia were the most frequent visitors between the late 1940s and the late 1960s and their visits, while popular, failed to lift the standard of the home team's play. For example, Australia sent a strong team in 1946 and that year, in what was later ratified as the first Test match between the two countries, New Zealand were beaten in less than nine hours. There was a big crowd, however, and record takings of £3,000 for the New Zealand Cricket Council (NZCC) board.[16] Then, between 1949 and 1969, Australia despatched a series of B teams often accompanied by murmurs of encouragement: in 1957, for instance, the Australian captain, 21-year-old Ian Craig, said in his farewell speech that New Zealand cricket was 'handicapped by an inferiority complex'.[17] In 1960, after another Australian side captained by Craig had won one and drawn three non-Test matches, Phil Tressider wrote in the *Sydney Morning Herald* that 'The New Zealand team has surprised the touring Australians by its high standard'. However, a member of the Australian party, 24-year-old Bobby Simpson, insisted that the standard of the game in New Zealand 'is not improving'.[18] New Zealand didn't win another Test match until January 1962, when they beat South Africa in Cape Town: each side won two of a five-Test series and one game was drawn. They didn't win a Test match at home until the Third Test against India at Christchurch in 1968 (India won the series 3–1) and they didn't win a series until 1969–70, when they beat Pakistan in Lahore in the second of a three-Test series, the other two matches being drawn.

Ryan notes a continuing invocation of the amateur spirit during these years of setback. For example, in 1954 a writer in the *New Zealand Listener* expressed the hope that success would not be achieved at the expense of 'that easy friendliness and sportsmanship, on and off the field, which help us to remember that cricket is still a game even when it is played by international sides'.[19] Other factors have been adduced, particularly in Ryan's analysis, to explain New Zealand's modest performances during the 1950s and 60s: the country's comparatively small population, (1.72 million in 1945); the high cost of travel, both internally to New Zealand and abroad; and the often inclement New Zealand weather, unconducive to good cricket.[20] Moreover New Zealand only had a small number of first-class sides and, therefore, of matches: when in 1956 Northern Districts entered the Plunket Shield (donated by William Plunket, Governor General of New Zealand in 1906) this brought the number of competing teams to seven, the others being Auckland, Wellington, Canterbury, Otago, Hawke's Bay and Central Districts. The latter had only competed for the shield since 1950.

On top of this, as we have seen, New Zealand's leading cricketers were all part-timers and, in this sense, amateurism in New Zealand cricket was born of necessity. Moreover, as some historians have observed, the sense of social superiority inherent in British amateurism was often bulwarked in New Zealand by a belief on the part of New Zealanders that their society was founded on free, rather than convict or bonded labour.[21] This was thought to set them above Australians, areas of whose territory, notably Queensland, New South Wales, Tasmania and Norfolk Island, had begun as penal settlements.

When New Zealand cricket finally did accept professionalism (both as a set of attitudes and as an embrace of the cash nexus) it was not done without recriminations on the part of the game's administrators similar to those heard from the Australian Cricket Board during the same period. The impetus for change seemed to come to New Zealand via English county cricket. The New Zealand press had always given extensive coverage to the county championship[22] and, from time to time, New Zealanders had played county cricket: for example, wicketkeeper Ken James, one of New Zealand's first Test players, had qualified for Northamptonshire in 1935, as had Bill Merritt in 1938 and John Guy twenty years later. And the patronage of furniture magnate Sir Julien Cahn (who gave him a sinecure as nominal manager of a furniture store) had enabled Wellington batsman C.S. 'Stewie' Dempster to participate in what many regard as the hypocrisy of amateur captaincy with Leicestershire between 1936 and 1938.[23] However, the first Kiwi batsman to make a sustained career in county cricket was Glenn Turner, who made his debut for Worcestershire in 1968, the first year that counties were able to sign one overseas player who would not be subject to the normal residential qualification.

Turner is regarded as New Zealand cricket's 'first real professional'.[24] His dedication to practice ('I used to practise in front of the mirror the forward-defensive, the backward defensive, the drive, the various shots. I did that as soon as I could hold the bat')[25] and single-minded approach to batting, compared by some to that of England's Geoffrey Boycott,[26] set him against the country's cricket traditions. While batsmen who became preoccupied with their own scores and income might antagonise team-mates, the criticism of Turner by the New Zealand cricket hierarchy was largely self-serving. 'I was supposed to be playing for the dirty dollar – not many, I might add', he said later. 'I had to cross over from amateurism to professionalism, and there was a strong feeling among the administration and our country as a whole that you ought not to play for money'.[27] This strong feeling was expressed by leading spokespeople such as Arthur Carman, a Quaker pacifist and editor of the *New Zealand Cricket Almanack*, who wrote in 1977 that it would be 'a sad day when players perform for financial gain rather than for the sake of sport itself and for the honour of representing one's country or province'.[28] Likewise NZCC chair Walter Hadlee, an accountant known for his parsimony and 'a stickler for an amateur ethos',[29] resented Turner's demands for more investment in players and infrastructure and even suspended him in June 1977. In the late 1950s and early 60s Hadlee also argued strongly against the appointment of a coach to accompany the New Zealand squad.[30] Hadlee's stand seems to have been designed to protect an amateur hypocrisy similar to that which had, until the early 1960s, prevailed in England. As Martin Chandler wrote in 2013:

> In 1976, when he led New Zealand to Pakistan and India, he [Turner] was paid less than any other member of the side. Each member of the squad, all of whom were amateurs except Turner, received a tour allowance, and all the amateurs were also paid at least something by their employers. As a professional cricketer there was no commercial organisation there to make up the shortfall for Turner.[31]

Turner played 41 Tests for New Zealand, scoring over 2,800 runs at an impressive average of nearly 45. He was part of, and has come to typify, a modernisation and maturation of New Zealand cricket at international level:

> In the pre-Turner era, New Zealand had played 83 Tests, of which they had won four, drawn 38, and lost 41. Turner's performances changed things around significantly – as New Zealand won 11 Tests in 14 years, losing 26 and drawing 30. The win-loss ratio, which was 9 per cent previously, had gone up to 42 per cent in Turner's era.[32]

It is not without irony that the man to help complete this maturation was Walter Hadlee's son Richard, who played 86 Tests for New Zealand between 1973 and 1990 and was the first bowler to take 400 Test wickets. Like a number of New Zealand cricketers by that time he plied his trade abroad, representing Nottinghamshire in the English county championship between 1978 and 1987 and playing a season for Tasmania 1979–80.

Aside from access to cricket labour markets overseas, the staging of one-day internationals (the first being against Pakistan at Christchurch in 1973) offered the opportunity to boost both the status and the income of New Zealand cricket, although, as Ryan points out, these were often played at low-capacity venues.[33]

In 1981, New Zealand having been relatively prosperous in one-day cricket, an incident occurred which revealed the growing complexity of the interface between emergent professionalism and the widely invoked 'spirit of the game'. In a Benson and Hedges World Cup best-of-five final at Melbourne Cricket Ground Australian captain Greg Chappell instructed his brother Trevor to bowl the final ball of the game underarm, minimising the chances of New Zealand scoring the six they needed to tie the game. New Zealand Prime Minister Robert Muldoon was outraged, calling it 'the most disgusting incident I can recall in the history of cricket' and identifying the Australians' yellow outfits as 'a sign of cowardice'.[34] The strong impression at the time was one of wounded Kiwi innocence versus ruthless Aussie pragmatism. Paul Ford wrote recently that 'Nobody came close to the Chappells in terms of their impact on our country's sporting psyche – together they demonstrated a mercilessness and ruthlessness that undermined the much admired New Zealand trait of giving someone a fair go'.[35] Some re-visitations of this incident, however, suggest that the key differences were within cricket cultures, rather than between them. Muldoon was joined by Australian Prime Minister Malcolm Fraser and Australian administrator and national icon Sir Donald Bradman in his condemnation and 'Greg Chappell said he always got more abuse in Australia than New Zealand'.[36] Richie Benaud, historically a spokesperson for Australian cricketers, was particularly swingeing in his criticism.[37] 'New Zealand, meanwhile, were "pissed off" according to McKechnie [the batsman facing the underarm delivery] but no more than that. "An hour or two after the game, when we'd all had a shower and were back at the hotel, we were joking about it, trying to work out how you could hit a six off an underarm"'.[38]

Cricket in New Zealand: a national sport?

Recently New Zealand cricket has been dominated by the politics of social inclusion and, more specifically, by attempts to account for (and, if possible, to remedy) the marginalisation to cricket culture of the country's chief ethnic minorities – the Maori and the Pacific Islanders.

Although a number of players of Maori heritage have played cricket for New Zealand, they have been seen widely as peripheral to the game. For example, in 2001 a team of New Zealand Maoris contested (and won) the short-lived Pacifica Cup, participating alongside Fiji, Papua New Guinea, the Cook Islands, Samoa, Vanuatu and New Caledonia.[39] A dozen years later, in 2013, Maori cricket coach Graeme Stewart announced a tour of the Cook Islands by a Northern District Maori squad. He stressed the historical significance of this – 'We will be playing just kilometres from the spot said to be the departure point for the fleet of waka [canoes] that set off for Aotearoa', he told the press.[40] The following year Stewart organised some senior games between Maori sides. He hoped, he said, to revive the Pacifica Cup: 'If we can set that up again . . . it may give the young, aspiring Maori cricketers the inspiration to represent New Zealand'.[41] On 2 August 2015, to help celebrate Maori Language Week, New Zealand played a one-day international (ODI) against Zimbabwe in Harare under the name Aotearoa, Aotearoa being the Maori name for New Zealand. Four months later 18-year-old Zak Gibson, a fast bowler from Te Awamutu, on New Zealand's North Island, became the first recipient of New Zealand Cricket (NZC)'s new Maori Cricket Scholarship.[42]

Similar hopes were reposed in the New Zealand's Pacifika community following the debut of Ross Taylor (full name: Luteru Ross Poutoa Lote Taylor) in 2007. Taylor had been born to a Samoan mother and Pakeha father in Wellington in 1984 and was now the poster boy for a campaign to bring more Pacific Island New Zealanders to international level. 'Not trying to be biased', said Ben Mailata, Auckland cricket's Pacific Island development officer in 2012, 'but Pacific Islanders are natural athletes, with good hand-eye co-ordination and are big hitters of the cricket ball. If we can tap into the talent and provide coaching and refine skills, then I can see us dominating the sport in 10 to 20-years'.[43]

Two principal factors seem to have driven these campaigns.

The first has to do with intrinsic value given to social inclusion in New Zealand society. The country has a strong leftish tradition. For example, it developed a nuclear-free policy in the 1960s, which effectively destroyed the ANZUS defence treaty signed with Australia and the United States in 1951.[44] It has a strong environmental movement, which spawned the Green Party of Aotearoa New Zealand in 1990, and an equally strong feminist presence.[45] These strands of the New Zealand left came together most decisively in 1981 in an anti-racist campaign to protest a tour of the country by a rugby team representing apartheid South Africa. The disorder that attended the tour is frequently styled in New Zealand as 'the closest this country has come to civil war'.[46] Besides this, as we have seen, the protection and advancement of Maori rights are a recurrent theme in New Zealand politics. So, when in 2003 ex-New Zealand captain Martin Crowe commented of Kiwi bowler Daryl Tuffey 'Tuffey is a Maori and, traditionally, not many Maori make good cricketers because they don't have the patience or the temperament to play through a whole day, leave alone over a Test match',[47] this remark caused less of an outcry than might have been expected in countries where it was less of an affront to popular opinion. Crowe immediately apologised, but *NZ Herald* columnist Richard Boock did not spare him. Until Crowe's intervention, wrote Boock:

> The reasons for low Maori participation levels in cricket had seemed pretty straightforward, or so some of us thought. Apathetic and sometimes-bigoted local associations, costs, the strangeness of the game and an understandable dislike of English colonialism had combined to repel almost anyone with brown skin. There was no suggestion they couldn't play cricket, it was just that they had some very good reasons for not wanting to.[48]

New Zealand Cricket operations manager John Reid was quick to make clear that Crowe did not speak for NZC but readily identified Maori and Pacific Islander communities as areas of low recruitment. This, he ventured, was an issue of class, as much as race: 'Cricket is still perceived by many as a white middle-class game. And if you look at many other sports in New Zealand, Maori and Pacific Islanders make a strong contribution in comparison'.[49]

Thus, the second factor – the importance of NZC widening both their recruitment and their domestic market – was flagged up. In this regard New Zealand cricket faced a cluster of problems in the twenty-first century.

First, as Paul Ford wrote recently, 'unlike in the subcontinent, where cricket rules hearts and minds, in New Zealand everything starts and ends with rugby'[50] and, in particular, the All Blacks national team. The primary significance of the All Blacks is that they are winners on the world stage. It's arguable that the All Blacks, who have won the last two World Cups (in 2011 and 2015) and have few serious rivals in international rugby, have profited from the rise of neoliberal popular culture in New Zealand, as elsewhere, in the 1980s. In the wake of 'Rogernomics' – the free market policies adopted by Labour finance minister Roger Douglas between 1984 and 1988 – New Zealand became more open to globalisation and, in its public culture, more unsympathetic to failure. This has meant, among other things, that New Zealanders have been exposed to a greater range of sport and leisure options and that the country's media have become more impatient with the shortcomings of the national cricket side – the latter probably linked to the rise in sponsorship, sponsors not wishing to be associated with losers. 'New Zealand Cricket takes for granted the extraordinary amount of coverage it enjoys', said veteran sports broadcaster Murray 'Deaks' Deaker in 2012. 'That coverage bears no resemblance to the lack of success it has on the international scene'.[51] Competition from other sports went well beyond rugby: as Deaker pointed out 'as many fans turned up to speedway events in one night as there would be for an entire season of domestic cricket, yet the discrepancy of media coverage between the two sports was stark'.[52]

Second, and related to this, the national cricket team is losing media coverage. As Andrew Alderson pointed out, when New Zealand beat Sri Lanka in Colombo in November 2012, they did so 'in front of zero media – either print, digital or broadcast – from their own country. This is a far cry from the days when the *Herald* used to send a reporter around the country to cover Auckland and another to follow Northern Districts during the summer months'.[53] NZC had long since lost free-to-air television coverage, New Zealand Tests having been available only on pay TV since 1998.[54]

Third, as with other Test-playing countries, there was increasing competition from other cricket leagues. After 2003 the country's cricketers could avail themselves of the Kolpak ruling. There were other enticements, notably, since 2008, the lucrative Indian Premier League. The short-lived Indian Cricket League, also started in 2008, attracted six Kiwi Test players; because it was not sanctioned by the International Cricket Council the six were banned from playing for New Zealand again. Of these, at least three were deemed still good enough to play Test cricket.[55]

So NZC had every reason to be increasing its outreach work. However, its prospects of success in this work were limited: if the problems of racial exclusion were dealt with, the difficulties deriving from social class remained. In this regard NZC faced similar problems to those encountered in most Test-playing countries: cricket is expensive to play and will not necessarily appeal to groups defined as excluded from it. In the early twenty-first century there was a general decline in the number of people playing cricket in New Zealand[56] and secondary school-aged children playing cricket in the country dropped from 17,794 in 2000 to 9,937 in 2014.[57] Adam Parore, who in 1990 became the first Maori to play cricket for New Zealand, went to an elite private school[58] and, as in England, South Africa and elsewhere, such schools, along with a growing contingent of development officers, are likely to increase in importance as a source of first-class cricketers. Indeed, as Ryan points out, most Maoris and Pacific Islanders in New Zealand are in low-paid, low-status occupations and, in neoliberal times, are more likely have long working hours and to be subject to casualisation. This makes them more likely to choose shorter and cheaper leisure-sport options than cricket, which would explain the growing popularity since the late 1980s of the sport of kilikiti among Maori and Pacifika.[59]

Yet, despite dwindling media interest at home, first-class cricket survives in New Zealand, largely through the fruits of globalisation and the growth of new media. As Alderson observed in 2012:

> New Zealand Cricket does not necessarily have to worry about revenue from media coverage overseas because in April it secured an eight-year deal outsourcing broadcast rights from all tours to Pitch International, a deal understood to be worth in excess of US$100 million ($122 million). PI specialises in selling the rights to television, radio, internet and mobile phone content globally.[60]

Moreover the players have held their own at international level. Following a drawn two-match Test series in England in 2015, ex-England captain Michael Vaughan commented: 'The way New Zealand play, they put you under pressure in every single session. The bowling matches the batting in aggression. If you look at the 10 days of cricket, New Zealand won seven and a half. If we played a third Test, New Zealand would go on to win'.[61] And, importantly, public enthusiasm kindled by the World Cup of 1992, which New Zealand had helped to stage and in which they had reached the semi-final, seemed to return in 2015 when they were beaten in the final by Australia. On the tournament website, beneath the headline 'WORLD CUP HAS SEEN NEW ZEALAND FALL IN LOVE WITH CRICKET AGAIN' former Kiwi captain Stephen Fleming pressed an argument recurrent in the nation's cricket circles: that more should be made of the 'Trans-Tasman rivalry'[62] with Australia: 'there is no doubt our relationship with our nearest neighbour Australia has got out of kilter. We simply have not been playing them often enough'.[63]

Notes

1. Christopher Martin-Jenkins *CMJ: A Cricketing Life* London: Simon and Schuster 2013 p.272.
2. See, for example, Stephen Chan 'Obituary: Sir Keith Sinclair' *The Independent* 3 August 1993 http://www.independent.co.uk/news/people/obituary-sir-keith-sinclair-1459112.html Access 1 October 2016.
3. See, for example, Richard Reeve 'The South Island myth: observations on the poetics of mystery in three local poets' http://www.nzepc.auckland.ac.nz/features/bluff06/reeve.asp Access 1 October 2016.
4. James Belich *The New Zealand Wars and the Victorian Interpretation of Racial Conflict* Oxford: Oxford University Press 1986.
5. Elton Rikihana Smallman 'Government announces Land Wars Day at Turangawaewae' http://www.stuff.co.nz/national/83329239/Government-announces-Land-Wars-Day-at-Turangawaewae Posted 19 August 2016, Access 1 October 2016.
6. Philippa Mein Smith *A Concise History of New Zealand* Cambridge: Cambridge University Press 2005 p.172.
7. Mein Smith *A Concise History* p.183.
8. From Statistics New Zealand http://www2.stats.govt.nz/domino/external/PASFull/pasfull.nsf/b45013b35df34b774c2567ed00092825/4c2567ef00247c6acc256965007ea4a8?OpenDocument Access 1 October 2016.
9. Mein Smith *A Concise History* pp.196 and 202.
10. Greg Ryan 'Kiwi or English? Cricket on the margins of New Zealand national identity' in Stephen Wagg (ed.) *Cricket and National Identity in the Postcolonial Age* Abingdon: Routledge 2005 pp.28–47, p.29.
11. Martin-Jenkins *CMJ* p.274.
12. Mein Smith *A Concise History* p.190.
13. Matt Richens 'NZ's oldest test cricketer Sam Guillen dies' http://www.stuff.co.nz/sport/cricket/8380115/NZs-oldest-test-cricketer-Sam-Guillen-dies Posted 5 March 2013, Access 1 October 2016.
14. Mark Geenty 'Like finding a gold nugget' – memories fresh of first test win, 60 years on' http://www.stuff.co.nz/sport/cricket/77780694/like-finding-a-gold-nugget—memories-fresh-of-first-test-win-60-years-on Access 1 October 2016.
15. Quoted in Ryan 'Kiwi or English?' p.28.
16. Chris Harte, with Bernard Whimpress *A History of Australian Cricket* London: Andre Deutsch 2003 p.393.
17. Harte, with Whimpress *A History of Australian Cricket* p.454.
18. Harte, with Whimpress *A History of Australian Cricket* p.469.
19. Quoted in Ryan 'Kiwi or English?' p.33.
20. Ryan 'Kiwi or English?' pp.30–1.
21. See, for example, Charlotte Macdonald 'Ways of belonging: sporting spaces in New Zealand history' in Giselle Byrnes (ed.) *The New Oxford History of New Zealand* Melbourne, Victoria: Oxford University Press 2009 pp.269–96, p.274.
22. Greg Ryan 'New Zealand cricket and the colonial relationship' in Anthony Bateman and Jeffrey Hill (eds.) *The Cambridge Companion to Cricket* Cambridge: Cambridge University Press 2011 pp.116–30, p.126.
23. http://www.espncricinfo.com/newzealand/content/player/36827.html Access 2 October 2016.
24. Abhishek Mukherjee 'Glenn Turner: New Zealand and Worcestershire giant' http://www.cricketcountry.com/articles/glenn-turner-new-zealand-and-worcestershire-giant-26991 Posted 26 May 2016, Access 3 October 2016.
25. Mukherjee 'Glenn Turner'.

26 Worcestershire colleague Basil D'Oliveira was among those to compare Turner's 'hunger for runs' to Boycott's well-known appetite for the same commodity. See Martin Chandler 'New Zealand's first professional cricketer' http://www.cricket web.net/new-zealands-first-professional-cricketer/ Posted 23 January 2016, Access 3 October 2016.
27 Mukherjee 'Glenn Turner'.
28 See Ryan 'Kiwi or British?' p.35.
29 See Andrew Alderson 'Cricket: Modern game dotted with personality clashes' http://www.nzherald.co.nz/sport/news/article.cfm?c_id=4&objectid=10854330 Posted 16 December 2012, Access 3 October 2016.
30 See Don Cameron 'Obituary: Walter Hadlee' http://www.nzherald.co.nz/sport/news/article.cfm?c_id=4&objectid=10403606 Posted 29 September 2006, Access 3 October 2016.
31 Chandler 'New Zealand's first professional'.
32 Mekherjee 'Glenn Turner'.
33 Ryan 'Kiwi or English?' p.35.
34 Tom Hunt 'The delivery that lingered … with a bad odour' http://www.stuff.co.nz/dominion-post/capital-life/8252526/The-delivery-that-lingered-with-a-bad-odour Posted 2 February 2013, Access 4 October 2016.
35 Paul Ford 'The villain who wasn't' http://www.thecricketmonthly.com/story/1010179/the-villain-who-wasn-t Posted June 2016, Access 4 October 2016.
36 Martin Williamson 'Underhand, underarm' http://www.espncricinfo.com/magazine/content/story/498574.html Posted 29 January 2011, Access 4 October 2016.
37 https://www.youtube.com/watch?v=mIL6KZox6Ao Access 4 October 2016.
38 Williamson 'Underhand'.
39 Unattributed 'Pacifica Cup: Tournament huge success, but likely to be last of its kind' http://www.espncricinfo.com/magazine/content/story/99606.html Posted 22 February 2001, Access 4 October 2016.
40 Greg Taipari 'Cricket: squad set for pioneering tour' http://www.nzherald.co.nz/rotorua-daily-post/news/article.cfm?c_id=1503438&objectid=11118675 Posted 3 September 2013, Access 4 October 2016.
41 Greg Stutchbury 'First Maori matches considered catalyst for New Zealand game' http://articles.chicagotribune.com/2014-03-20/sports/sns-rt-uk-cricket-zealand-maori-20140320_1_cricket-new-zealand-rugby-super-rugby Posted 20 March 2014, Access 5 October 2016.
42 'Fast bowler Zak Gibson awarded inaugural NZC Maori Cricket Scholarship' http://www.blackcaps.co.nz/news-items/fast-bowler-zak-gibson-awarded-inaugural-nzc-maori-cricket-scholarship Posted 28 November 2015, Access 5 October 2016.
43 Heath Moore 'Rise of Pacific Island cricket heralds big future impact' http://pacific.scoop.co.nz/2012/03/rise-of-pacific-island-cricket-heralds-big-future-impact/ Posted 14 March 2012, Access 5 October 2016.
44 Mein Smith *A Concise History* pp.179–82.
45 See, for example, Christine Dann *Up From Under – Women and Liberation in New Zealand 1970–1985* Port Nicholson, New Zealand: Allen & Unwin 1988.
46 See, for example, Nikki Macdonald 'Waging war on and off the pitch: A look back at the 1981 Springbok Tour' http://www.stuff.co.nz/dominion-post/news/5331035/Waging-war-on-and-off-the-pitch Posted 23 July 2011, Access 5 October 2016.
47 Katherine Hoby 'Crowe: cricket not the game for Maori' http://www.nzherald.co.nz/nz/news/article.cfm?c_id=1&objectid=3052026 Posted 17 January 2003, Access 5 October 2016.

48 Richard Boock 'Off the ball: Crowe's view on Maori unacceptable' http://www.nzherald.co.nz/sport/news/article.cfm?c_id=4&objectid=3051941 Posted 17 January 2003, Access 5 October 2016.
49 Hoby 'Crowe: Cricket'.
50 Paul Ford 'Cricket in rugby country' http://www.espncricinfo.com/travel/content/current/story/816435.html Posted January 2015, Access 5 October 2016.
51 Andrew Alderson 'The Shame Game: Cricket and the media – a romance that went sour' http://www.nzherald.co.nz/sport/news/article.cfm?c_id=4&objectid=10851721 Posted 3 December 2012, Access 5 October 2016.
52 Alderson 'The Shame Game'.
53 Alderson 'The Shame Game'.
54 Ryan 'Kiwi or British?' p.40.
55 Unattributed 'NZ Cricket bans six rebels' http://www.stuff.co.nz/sport/cricket/196745 Posted 1 January 2009, Access 5 October 2016.
56 Ryan 'Few and far' p.72.
57 Sarah Harvey 'Decline in NZ school kids playing cricket calls for different approach' http://www.stuff.co.nz/sport/cricket/67468457/decline-in-nz-school-kids-playing-cricket-calls-for-different-approach Posted 22 March 2015, Access 6 October 2016.
58 Ryan 'Few and far' p.68.
59 Ryan 'Few and far' pp.72–3. See also Heather Jarvis 'Samoa's version of cricket, kilikiti, on display in Melbourne tournament' http://www.abc.net.au/news/2014-04-10/an-samoa27s-version-of-cricket2c-kilikiti2c-on-display-in-me/5380372?section=vic Posted 10 April 2014, Access 6 October 2016.
60 Alderson 'The Shame Game'.
61 Stephan Shemilt 'England v New Zealand: Hosts slip to 199-run defeat and series draw' Posted 2 June 2015, Access 7 October 2016.
62 Ryan 'Kiwi or British?' p.36.
63 http://www.icc-cricket.com/cricket-world-cup/news/2015/columns/87655/stephen-fleming-world-cup-has-seen-new-zealand-fall-in-love-with-cricket-again Access 7 October 2016.

Chapter 5

Father, king, statesman, general, prince, don

West Indian cricket culture since 1945

Nowhere in the world have politics, cricket and the public chronicling of the game's history been more closely interwoven than in the Caribbean. The Trinidadian Marxist writer and political activist C.L.R. James, who in 1963 published what many regard as the first book to deal seriously with the relationship between politics and sport,[1] was also a leading figure in the island's main political party, the People's National Movement (PNM) and an advisor to its first leader, Dr Eric Williams. Michael Manley, the leader of the People's National Party (PNP) of Jamaica from 1969 to 1992, wrote a copious history of West Indies cricket that came out in 1988.[2] The Antiguan writer Leonard 'Tim' Hector wrote extensively about Caribbean politics and published many articles about West Indies cricket as reflected in those politics.[3] And Hilary Beckles, Professor of History at the University of West Indies and author of a number of works on Caribbean cricket, was until 2013 a member of the West Indies Cricket Board (WICB) and contributes regularly to debates on the region's cricket politics. Beckles' influential two-volume account of the development of West Indies cricket appeared in 1998.[4] As these authors variously acknowledge, and as this chapter seeks to show, the politics of West Indian cricket have been contoured successively by 'race', colonisation, nationalism and globalisation. Beckles suggests that Caribbean cricket has passed through three stages or paradigms: the *colonial* (when the cricket-playing territories were British colonies), the *nationalist* (the time of the independence movement and the early decades of independence) and the coming of *globalisation* (time of opening up of Caribbean economies to global economic forces). The chapter follows broadly this pattern.[5]

'Alexander must go': cricket and West Indian nationalism

Unlike the other nine countries entitled to play Test cricket, the West Indies are not a nation as such. They are a series of islands[6] in the Caribbean basin, once occupied and colonised by Britain, reconstituted briefly as a federation under British tutelage between 1958 and 1961, and now established as individual sovereign states. The region's cricket culture has closely reflected these changes. The principal elements in the local populations are (a) white, European settler-descended West Indians – the numerical minority (by far) but dominant in commerce and land ownership (b) black, African slave-descended West Indians – the great majority and (c) Indo-West Indians, descended from labourers brought to the Caribbean as indentured workers. The majority of these workers went to Trinidad and British Guiana – what is now Guyana. Around a dozen of the islands play cricket.

The often tumultuous events that occurred in the thirty years that followed the Second World War, in West Indian cricket and in the wider Caribbean society, had their roots in the political difficulties and upheavals of the 1930s. Working and living conditions on the islands, always severe, had deteriorated. Between 1900 and 1930 the sugar industry in Jamaica had been centralised so that the number of sugar factories fell from 111 to 39, while the annual output of sugar had multiplied eightfold over the same period. In 1927 the US government had ceased to admit West Indian migrants. The population of Kingston, the Jamaican capital, swelled by 73% between 1921 and 1943. Social tensions grew.[7] In Trinidad there had been a hunger march by workers in the island's oil fields in 1933 and strikes and riots in its sugar belt; oil workers' leader Tubal 'Buzz' Butler called for a general strike in 1937. The same year, when Barbadian police tried to deport Clement Payne, a workers' organiser, there was a riot and mass looting in the capital, Bridgetown, and forty-six people died in riots in Kingston in 1938.[8] *Warning from the West Indies*, an important study by the Scottish historian William Miller Macmillan, published 1936, told of great poverty on the islands.[9]

Out of this turbulence emerged several strong labour movements which in time spawned socialist political parties: for instance, the PNP in Jamaica, the Democratic Labour Party in Barbados (both in 1938) the PNM in Trinidad and Tobago (in 1956).

Before 1945 West Indian cricket had reflected little of this militancy. The paternalist, colonial racism that had pervaded Caribbean society had had two important manifestations in the early West Indies teams: first, black players, who had first been admitted to the side in 1890, played always under the captaincy of whites (or 'near whites') and, second, West Indian batsmen tended, for the most part, to be white and bowlers to be black. (This ran parallel to the general division of labour in English county cricket between high-born amateur batsmen and working-class bowlers.)

West Indian captains had invariably been drawn from white, well-connected families – planters, merchants or colonial administrators. For example, Aucher Warner, who had captained the first West Indian team to tour England in 1900, was the Oxford-educated son of the Attorney General of Trinidad and Tobago who himself later became Solicitor General of the island. Kingston-born R.K. Nunes, who had captained West Indies on the award of Test status in 1928, was also a lawyer and had played for Surrey Second XI in 1919; Manley describes him as 'of a family that came as near to aristocracy as the colonies can produce'.[10] Trinidadians George 'Jackie' Grant and his brother Rolph, who had captained the team in the 1930s, were from a wealthy Port of Spain commercial family and were both educated at Cambridge University. The family of John Goddard (captain 1947–57) were wealthy Barbadian rum merchants. An important departure from both the aforementioned norms was George Headley.

Headley was the first in what would become a succession of great West Indian batsmen – James placed him a close second to Donald Bradman as the greatest batsman he had ever seen.[11] He was also Caribbean sport's first working-class hero. He captained West Indies in one Test, against England at Kingston in 1947. By then the captaincy had become a political issue, a focus for those campaigning for independence from Britain and for a more equal, racially unsegregated society. For example, Trinidadian Learie Constantine who, through his mother, was the grandson of slaves[12] and who played eighteen Tests for West Indies between 1928 and 1939, had once said:

> Cricket in the West Indies is the most glaring example of the black man being kept in his place ... The heart of our cricket is rotted by racist politics. I only hope that before I die, I see a West Indian cricket team chosen on merit alone, and captained by a black man, win a rubber against England.[13]

(Constantine himself hoped to be a lawyer, but, given Trinidad's racialised labour market, had to settle for a clerical job with an oil company.)[14] An early initiative was taken by near-white Jamaican politician Noel 'Crab' Nettersole, deputy leader of the PNP, who lobbied strongly for Headley to be given the West Indies captaincy. The notion of a black captaincy had had some longstanding support within the British Establishment, since Sir Pelham Warner (brother of Aucher, devout imperialist and a major figure at the MCC) had for some time argued that such an appointment would convey a greater sense of social justice and discourage radical ideas on the islands.[15] However, as Manley suggests, the West Indies selectors occupied 'the more remote parts of the social structure'[16] and, in the end, conceded Headley only a single Test.

This left the issue open to the left and to the nationalists, whose hand was strengthened by the emergence, after the Second World War, of three more illustrious black-skinned batting talents. Frank Worrell (51 Tests 1948–63), Everton Weekes (48 Tests 1948–58) and Clyde Walcott (44 Tests 1948–60) had all been born in the mid-1920s on the island of Barbados. Like Headley they were all outstanding batsmen and thus, like him, they were living challenges to the notion that batting was the province of the purportedly more cerebral white man. Headley had had a Test average of 61; Weekes followed with 59, Walcott's was 57 and Worrell's 49. Moreover, as Manley observed later, all three were 'clever men'.[17] In the Caribbean, in the more egalitarian and politically turbulent climate that characterised the islands after the Second World, the performances of 'The Three Ws' contrasted sharply with the record of, say, the white Barbadian John Goddard who was made West Indies captain in 1947, aged 29, after only 4 Tests and with a batting average of 24. Politically, as C.L.R. James realised, Worrell would become the most important W of the three.

Feeling against the white colonists and their settler allies often ran high during this period and, as observed in Chapter 1, was made particularly manifest when West Indies played England. Len Hutton's team that visited in the winter of 1953–4 got an especially rough ride in British Guiana, where the British government had declared a state of emergency in October 1953, imprisoning the People's Progressive Party (PPP) leader and democratically elected Chief Minister Cheddi Jagan.[18] (British troops would stay in British Guiana, defending a government appointed from London and ignoring continued PPP success at the polls, until 1964.) There was also an angry reception in Jamaica, where Hutton had to deal with the (improbable) accusation that he had insulted the island's Chief Minister, Alexander Bustamente.[19] Trevor Bailey, who played for England on that tour, recalled later his irritation with white West Indians and expatriate Englishmen who insisted 'England simply had to win. Their reason was that their life would not be worth living if the West Indies were victorious'; it would 'make the native uppity'.[20] James, similarly, recognised that cricket was popular culture in the Caribbean: 'The islands are small – during big cricket people talk fanatically about nothing else. Every street corner is a seething cauldron of cricket experiences, cricket memories, fears, suspicions, hopes, aspirations'.[21] James therefore renewed the drive for a black captain, using Worrell, a charismatic and educated figure, as both his candidate and, by extension, as a symbol of the possibility of black self-government. James was, moreover, in no hurry to achieve this objective since a good deal of political capital needed to be accumulated in the pursuit of it. Worrell was actually offered the captaincy in 1957 but had to decline it because he was studying in England at Manchester University. James was unconcerned. Identifying England and Australia as key target audiences, the important thing, he wrote later, was

> To continue to send to populations of white people, black or brown men under a white captain. The more brilliantly the black men played, the more it would emphasise to millions of English people 'Yes, they are fine players but, funny, isn't it, they cannot be responsible for themselves – they have to have a white man to lead them'.[22]

In 1960, though, James seized the moment. With social unrest growing and the West Indies side being captained by Jamaican Cambridge blue Franz Copeland Murray 'Gerry' Alexander, James wrote an article in *The Nation*, a mouthpiece both for the PNM and the independence movement, insisting that 'Alexander Must Go'. The edition sold out overnight and Worrell was made captain.[23]

Similarly, for much of West Indian cricket history, the issue of fast bowling had provided memorable vignettes of class and/or racial conflict, pitting black, working-class bowlers against white patrician batsmen. The West Indies had always had fast bowlers in their team and they had always been black: as James wrote: 'This was the traditional order, a line of white batsmen and a line of black bowlers'.[24] Some of these bowlers were very accomplished. George John (b. St Vincent 1883), who had played before West Indies gained Test status, featured heavily in *Beyond a Boundary* – James said of him: 'John was not hostile, he was hostility itself'.[25] Barbadian Manny Martindale (10 Tests between 1933 and 1939, with 37 wickets at 22 runs per wicket) was rated the sixth best West Indian fast bowler ever – some accolade – by Michael Manley.[26] And Hophnie Hobah Hines Johnson, making his debut at the age of 37, had taken 10 wickets against England at his native Kingston in 1948. On occasion, with the implication that he was behaving above his station, a West Indian fast bowler had been asked to curb his hostility. In February 1930, during the Test against England, Learie Constantine is said to have been asked by the England manager Harry Mallett to cut down his short-pitched deliveries; he did so, but noticed that England's Bill Voce was subject to no comparable restriction.[27] In 1959, when West Indies toured India, another 'real quick', Jamaican fast bowler Roy Gilchrist, was sent home by team captain Gerry Alexander for bowling beamers (head-high full tosses) at Swaranjit Singh, who had been a contemporary of Alexander at Cambridge University. The incident was still being discussed in the Caribbean in 2016. Jackie Hendricks, a West Indies wicketkeeper on the tour, recalled:

> Singh had been travelling around India during the tour, criticising the home team for what was perceived as their fear of Gilchrist. He [Singh] came out to bat wearing a beautiful, sky blue turban. Gillie bowled and he [Singh] played a lovely cover drive and held the pose. 'Great shot, eh?' [Singh said] Gilchrist had responded with a beamer. 'The ball hit me plumb in my chest – from Gilchrist's hand to my chest – and it passed somewhere close to the turban, almost unrolling it' remembered Hendricks. The next ball was another beamer and Singh, clearly unnerved, appealed to Alexander: 'Gerry, you going to make this happen? This man is out to kill me'.[28]

In the volatile political climate prevailing in the Caribbean in 1959, the banished Gilchrist became a *cause celebre*. To the WICB he was trouble. As it happened, Gilchrist's short and sometimes violent temper was widely acknowledged – indeed, eight years later he would hold his wife's face to a hot iron during a row.[29] However, for nationalist politicians and for many West Indians talking on street corners, Gilchrist was a political metaphor – a black man born into plantation poverty, demeaned and cast aside by high-handed white administrators. As James saw it, by simply dismissing Gilchrist the WICB were both evading their responsibilities and making a political mistake: 'He was a West Indian Test cricketer. Unless the Board discovered a way of scrubbing him white he would be considered one of us'. James recommended that Frank Worrell, whom Gilchrist was known to respect, be asked to intercede in the matter.[30] Thirty years later Michael Manley went further, describing Gilchrist as no more than a victim of the islands' oppressive social conditions – 'a difficult young man, full of aggression, difficult to handle, burdened with those tensions which so often run like scars across the landscape of the personalities of people who come from poverty'.[31]

In 1958 ten Caribbean territories were brought together to form the West Indian Federation. The federation had been resisted by island assemblies, which were dominated by white planters, but in general had the support of the trade unions, who thought it would hasten the award of independence. The federation foundered after three years, chiefly because the project engendered comparatively little enthusiasm in either Jamaica or Trinidad, two of the major islands, which were going through a period of prosperity – the former through bauxite mining and manufacture and the latter through oil exports. Jamaica withdrew in 1961 and the federation was dissolved.[32] Both islands became fully independent the following year, followed by Barbados in 1966, the same year as Guyana became a self-governing commonwealth under the British crown. Some historians now see this as a heavy defeat for the Caribbean left and the region's working class. A federated West Indies would have wielded considerable political and economic power, but it was defeated by a combination of British intransigence and the increased involvement of the United States in the region in the 1940s and 50s.[33] African American historian Gerald Horne argues that US intervention brought two key political developments. First, the situating of American military bases in the region during the 1940s brought (a more virulent) Jim Crow racism to societies already structured by colonial racism and, second, Cold War anti-communist initiatives helped to drain the radicalism from the Caribbean labour movement and its affiliated political parties, most of which now embraced social democracy, expelled suspected communists[34] and relaxed their support for labour rights.[35] Jagan, for example, had sought to increase welfare spending, raise the minimum wage and strengthen trade unions.[36] Britain and the United States, fearful of Soviet influence in the region and, more pointedly, concerned to protect the interests of the multinational company Booker Bros McConnell – which had a controlling interest in most of the sugar plantations[37] – had responded with a combination of 'terror bombings, detention of politicians, and black propaganda'.[38]

From 'calypso cricket' to 'Fire in Babylon': West Indian cricket culture, 1960 to 1992

Following the dismantling of the West Indian Federation, the West Indies team became, *de facto*, the flagship for a nationalist project which had no nation. For the preceding decade or more the West Indies team had been styled and regarded as 'calypso cricketers', an appellation probably originating with the celebrations that greeted West Indies' first Test victory over England at Lord's in 1950, which had been led by the calypsonian Lord Kitchener. During the 1960s and early 1970s West Indians teams created a lot of excitement, at home and abroad, and featured some of the greatest players in their history – notably the Barbadians Garfield Sobers (93 Tests 1954–74, and arguably the finest all-round cricketer ever to play the game), fast bowler Wesley Hall (48 Tests 1958–69) and Rohan Kanhai (a dashing Guyanese batsman, descended from migrant Indian indentured labourers, 79 Tests 1957–74).

Three things are notable about the West Indies cricket of the 'calypso' era.

First, West Indies' opening attack featured the same two bowlers throughout the 1960s: Wesley Hall and fellow Barbadian Charlie Griffith (28 Tests 1960–9). As Savidge and McLellan write: 'Hall was treated with affection as well as respect by most of his opponents; Griffith's achievements on the other hand were often viewed with great suspicion'.[39] In Barbados in 1962 a ball from Griffith hit Indian batsman Nari Contractor on the head, inflicting serious injury; Contractor never played for India again.[40] Griffith was often accused of having an illegal action, notably by Australian cricketers-turned-journalists Richie Benaud and Keith Miller.[41] Griffith was actually one of several bowlers across the Test-playing countries who were subject to such accusations, but, doubtless like many West Indians, he felt racialised as a black brute by white critics: 'Charlie . . . was suspicious – partly as a result of the throwing controversy, I imagine – of anyone white', wrote Trevor Bailey in the early 1980s.[42] The treatment of Griffith was, perhaps, a foretaste of the way West Indian fast bowlers would be depicted in the coming years.

Second, there were clear signs in the 1960s that the West Indies team still carried the hopes of many of the poorer sections of the Caribbean public and that the atmosphere was especially tense when West Indies played England, the representatives of the colonial power. There was, for example, a bottle-throwing riot at Port of Spain's Queens Park Oval in January 1960 when a local favourite, Charran Singh, was given out.[43] And Manley noted three riots in rapid succession when England visited in 1968 under the patrician leadership of Colin Cowdrey.[44]

Third, while West Indian virtuosity attracted much admiration, cricket commentary styled them predominantly as lacking durability and a winning mentality. As we saw in Chapter 2 the West Indies team that toured Australia in 1960–1 were feted as 'smiling cricketers' and 'the happy players from the Caribbean', but were nonetheless 'vanquished' (2–1). In 1966 *Wisden* suggested that West Indies' defeat by Sussex at Hove that year 'perhaps reflected the lack of resolution in the batting'.[45] When they toured England in 1969 West Indies were deemed worthy of only a three-Test series (as opposed to the usual five) and were beaten 2–0, with one match drawn. Doubts were also raised about captaincy, which between 1965 and 1973 was in the hands of the cavalier and apolitical Garry Sobers. In particular, Sobers' two declarations in the Test against England at Port of Spain in March 1968, which gifted the game to England, caused enduring consternation in the Caribbean and reinforced the dominant notion of West Indies as talented but erratic. West Indies did not win a Test series between 1968 and 1973. For those prepared to make the connection, these cricket judgements resonated strongly with the popular imperialist notion encapsulated in the statement of Labour MP and former Secretary of State for the Colonies Jim Griffiths, who, following the coup of 1953 in British Guiana, had told the Commons that in this case Britain was dealing with 'people who are growing up. They are adolescents who are politically immature'.[46] This echoed the earlier judgement of Labour Deputy Leader Herbert Morrison who, during the Second World War, had suggested that to give African colonies independence would be 'like giving a child of ten a latch-key, a bank account and a shot-gun'.[47]

West Indies' series in Australia in the winter of 1975–6, which they lost heavily (5–1) and in which the main instruments of their defeat were fast bowlers Dennis Lillee and Jeff Thomson, is regarded as a watershed. Guyanese batsman Clive Lloyd, given the captaincy the previous year, is widely credited with devising a new strategy for the West Indies team, based on the deployment of four fast bowlers. Previous West Indies teams had tended to use only two or, at the most, three fast men and would generally feature at least one spin bowler. Spin bowlers Sonny Ramadin and Alf Valentine had been given much of the credit for West Indies' victory at Lord's in 1950 and Lloyd's cousin, off-spinner Lance Gibbs (79 Tests 1958–76, 309 Test wickets) had been one of the game's greatest ever slow bowlers. West Indies, under the captaincy principally of Lloyd (1974–85) and Antiguan Vivian Richards (1986–91) then embarked on their most successful period which spanned the late 1970s and the early 1990s. This period had a number of important features.

First, the new strategy seemed to be founded on a spirit of federation which rejected the particularisms of individual West Indian states. This appears to have been prompted by the participation of many leading West Indian cricketers in the Packer project of 1978 and their subsequent banning by the WICB. As fast bowler Michael Holding said later: 'When we were banned from international cricket, we bonded together: all the island rubbish went out . . . it was all for the West Indies'.[48] In the process was created what Beckles has described as 'one of the finest expressions of efficient human resources mobilisation since the fulfilment of the national independence agenda'.[49]

Second, a sense of race – and of anti-racism, in particular – was sharpened during this time, both on and off the field. As we saw in Chapter 3, West Indian cricketers who participated in 'rebel tours' of apartheid South Africa in the early 1980s were seen as collaborators with a racist state. They received life bans and became pariahs in their communities.[50] On the field there was a new intolerance of remarks with any racial implication. Richards recalled in his biography a good deal of on-field racial abuse in the Test series against Australia in 1975–6: 'It did not prove easy to concentrate when someone was snarling at you and saying "You f**k off, you black bastard!"'[51] Some months later, prior to a series against West Indies, England captain Tony Greig (who had grown up in Cape Province, South Africa) announced the intention of the England team was to make West Indies 'grovel'. Whatever Greig's intention, the word had connotations of colonial and racial oppression. The word 'grovel', West Indies players were informed, 'was often used to put down the blacks in South Africa. Of course, Greig was a South African so that only served to add fuel to our anger'.[52]

Third, this realisation fed a growing sense on the part of the West Indian players that they were playing for black people, at home as well as abroad. Richards himself wore a wristband of red, green and gold, the Rastafarian colours, and the team were very conscious of their following among the black Caribbean diaspora. Significantly, when West Indies tied up a 3–1 series victory again England the Oval in August 1963, '[t]he pitch was invaded by thousands of West Indians to end a raucously supported series'.[53] When West Indies returned to the Oval in 1984, captain Lloyd, noting the nearness of the ground to the West Indian enclave of Brixton, remarked that the coming Test would be 'a home fixture for us'.[54] In Brixton three years earlier there had been a riot, which had been provoked, according to many locals, by Metropolitan Police Operation Swamp 81 – seen as excessive police surveillance of black people. Disturbances had followed in black communities in Moss Side in Manchester, Liverpool, Bristol, Leicester, Southampton, Handsworth in Birmingham, Derby, Nottingham and Leeds.[55] Most West Indian players had relatives in one or other of these communities. The jubilation engendered by the triumphs of the West Indies team among the people of these communities is recounted in the film *Fire in Babylon*[56] and the book of the same name and inspired by the film.[57]

Fourth, some of West Indies most decisive victories during this were against England. They beat England 3–0 in 1976 (the 'grovel' series), 1–0 in 1980, 2–0 in 1980–1, 5–0 in England in 1984 and 5–0 again in West Indies in 1985–6, followed by a 4–0 victory back in England in 1988. After the final Test in 1984 West Indian supporters in the crowd happily waved banners reading 'BLACKWASH'.[58] In 1988 the English cricket establishment was in apparent disarray, appointing no fewer than four different captains over five Test matches.[59] This was an inescapable token of Britain's loss of empire and comparative decline as a world power. The response of the British cricket establishment and mass media was recriminating. In a view reflected widely in the British sports press David Frith, a right-wing writer from outside the public school–Oxbridge coterie that dominated English cricket politics and lacking some of its gentlemanly diplomacy, wrote in *Wisden Cricket Monthly* in 1991 that the West Indian team was 'the most unpopular in the world. Their game is founded on vengeance and violence and is fringed by arrogance'. He added that '[t]here is more to bowling than the ugly bouncer flying straight at the teeth, and West Indies' bowling success, upon which their 15-year dominance has been based, has been heavily reliant on the short, fast ball. This has seriously depleted cricket as a spectacle'.[60] (In July 1995, as editor of *Wisden Cricket Monthly*, Frith published an article, submitted by an obscure writer with far-right views, called 'Is it in the blood', which questioned the loyalty of England players not born in England. Devon Malcolm, born in Jamaica in 1963, and Phillip DeFreitas, born in Dominica in 1966, sued for defamation and won both damages and an apology in the High Court. Frith was sacked.)

West Indian supporters, welcome on English cricket grounds of the 1950s as happy calypsonians, in 1976 found themselves condemned as louts and told to leave their drums and other musical instruments at home. West Indian captains were instructed to tell their section of the crowd to be quiet.[61] Black people, welcome as migrant colonial subjects, now, as first-generation British citizens, were being redefined as some kind of 'enemy within'. Mike Marqusee said of these supporters: 'Whatever they may have liked to think, they were not West Indians. They were not like their parents. Their loyalty to and pride in the West Indian Test side was a political choice'.[62]

Trouble in paradise: West Indian cricket in the age of globalisation

The West Indian cricket team began to falter in the early 1990s. When they were beaten by Australia at Sabina Park, Kingston, in April 1995 they experienced their first series defeat since 1980. They went on to draw a series away to England 2–2 in the summer of 1995, but, the following February, in the Indian city of Pune, they lost a World Cup match (heavily) to Kenya, a country with a negligible cricket tradition. Ten years earlier such an event had been unthinkable. Since then West Indies cricket has been in decline, and cricket discourse in the Caribbean has been dominated by the vocabulary of crisis. Two important voices in the debate over what had happened to West Indies cricket and what was to be done about it were the Antiguan intellectual Tim Hector, who died in 2002, and Hilary Beckles, who was elevated to the Vice Chancellorship of the University of West Indies in 2015. This chapter concludes with a summary of the crisis – its symptoms, likely causes and proffered solutions.

According to Beckles, the period of crisis coincides broadly with a third paradigm – the age of globalisation.[63] This refers to the increased vulnerability of West Indian nations to neoliberal economics, the vagaries – given the historic dependence of West Indian countries on certain products (sugar, oil, bauxite, bananas . . .) – of international markets and the demands of international financial institutions, such as the World Bank and the International Monetary Fund (IMF). This vulnerability was accentuated by the decline in foreign investment and the reduction in Western aid that followed the end of the Cold War in the early 1990s. West Indian nations now had to accept loans on condition of 'structural adjustment' – often now called 'austerity' measures or, simply, reductions in public spending.[64] It was ironic, as Hector noted in 1999, that:

> The dominance of West Indies cricket began in 1977 [at] precisely the point that Jamaica was structurally adjusted and put under the thumb of IMF surveillance, or if you prefer, external impositions. Trinidad and Tobago went the way of structural adjustment in 1988, Guyana was next. Barbados followed the same course in 1991.[65]

'Structural adjustment', he wrote the following year, 'totally undermined all of our nationalist assumptions, about "we" being as good as "Them" and therefore holding our own, independently, in good times or in bad'.[66]

West Indian cricketers were thus making their way in a new political and economic environment. In another irony, the Packer experience of 1977–8 had reminded them of their worth in the cricket labour market – a worth often not recognised by the WICB. In this regard West Indian batsman Brian Lara was, according to Beckles, a symbol of the new age.[67] Born the tenth of eleven children in Trinidad in 1969, Lara had a seventeen-year Test career during which he accomplished many feats, including the highest ever Test score (400 not out against England in Antigua in 2004), and retired with a Test average of 53. He also gained lucrative cricket employment in England and South Africa and, with the growth of televised cricket, acquired an international celebrity. By the end of the twentieth century he was Caribbean cricket's first multimillionaire. People of such social and financial standing are not so easily bent to the will of national cricket boards, nor are they necessarily drawn to the nationalism of a nation that does not exist. Lara was captain of the West Indies team that refused to travel to South Africa for a Test series in 1998 until it had received a better pay offer. The political symbolism here was clear enough: a sports team which in the previous decade had had a global following among oppressed black people was now, for financial reasons, stalling on a trip to a country where an expectant black populace, recently liberated from the state racism of apartheid, awaited them. Fourteen years later former WICB president Pat Rousseau was still accusing Lara of disrespecting venerated South African president Nelson Mandela.[68] South Africa, who fielded an all-white team for the first four of a five-match series, won the rubber 5–0, four of the Tests by wide margins.

One key difficulty with the emergence of Lara and other West Indian cricketers as celebrities has been with sponsorship. In 2005, for instance, Lara and six other players (including the emergent Chris Gayle) were discarded because they had personal sponsorship deals with a company (Cable and Wireless) that was in direct competition with Digicel, the sponsors of the WICB. The situation called for complex talks involving Grenada Prime Minister Keith Mitchell, WICB president Teddy Griffith, the West Indies Players Association and the two companies.[69] Pay disputes and poor standards of play have remained at the heart of West Indies cricket in the twenty-first century. In 2007 an editorial in the influential *Jamaica Gleaner* suggested that the West Indies withdraw from Test cricket for two to three years in order to develop players of the required standard.[70] Two years later, amid another pay dispute, West Indies players refused to turn out for a Test series against Bangladesh and the WICB was obliged to name a replacement squad.[71]

As in other Test-playing countries, these difficulties have been compounded by the liberalising of the world cricket labour market and the growth of limited-over cricket and, in particular, of Twenty20 – as typified by the career of Chris Gayle. Gayle was born in Rollington Town, a downtown area of Kingston, in 1979 and made his debut for West Indies in 2000. He was immediately marked down as one of several young players 'insufficiently respectful' to senior players.[72] Despite periodically refusing to turn out for West Indies, he nevertheless registered 103 Tests between 2000 and 2014 (an indication, among other things, of the frequency with which Test cricket is now played) and had a respectable batting average of 42. He has made a great deal of money as an attacking batsman on the international limited-over circuit and his CV embraces the Barisal Burners, Dhaka Gladiators, the Jamaica Tallawahs (Jamaica, along with the other cricket-playing West Indian nations, were rebranded in 2013), Kolkata Knight Riders (in the Indian Premier League), Lahore Qalandars, Matabeleland Tuskers, Melbourne Renegades, Royal Challengers Bangalore, Somerset, Sydney Thunder, Western Australia, and Worcestershire. Gayle has in the process cultivated a *faux* 'gangsta' public persona, sporting long dreadlocks, posing with glamorous models in bikinis and (in)famously propositioning a female sports reporter on TV in 2016.[73] In a way that could never have been the case in the previous eras, West Indian cricket needs Gayle more than he needs West Indian cricket. Indeed in 2009, when he was still captain of the West Indies Test side Gayle announced that he 'wouldn't be so sad' if Test cricket died.[74] Gayle is one of a growing number of hitters-for-hire in world cricket. Another in the West Indies is Kieron Pollard, born in Trinidad in 1987 and brought up in poverty by a single mother. Pollard is a specialist one-day cricketer. He attracted four maximum bids in the 2010 IPL auction. He knows there is comparatively little money in Test cricket in the Caribbean and has never played a Test match.

Beckles has flagged up a number of other social factors that have combined to deepen the crisis – in particular, rising unemployment, the decline of village culture and the rise of cable TV, bringing with it imported, often American, cultural influence.[75] Other sports now contend for people's interest in the West Indies: football has global appeal and basketball is growing in popularity, especially in Trinidad. Moreover, three generations have matured in the Caribbean to whom the spirit of West Indian nationalism is unknown. In the late 1990s Beckles was already advocating a West Indian cricket academy in which young cricketers would be tutored both in sport science and in the socialist traditions of Caribbean nationalism.[76] Hector, although he relented later (see Chapter 15) initially took a slightly bleaker view. 'A purposeless society cannot produce purposeful cricket', he wrote in 2000, adding that a scientific approach was 'alien to the West Indian temper'.[77]

At the time of writing there seems little light at the end of the tunnel. Watching West Indies in 2015 English cricket commentator Mark Nicholas remarked: 'Most of the batsmen simply look out of their depth, both technically and mentally'.[78] In the Caribbean the WICB has, predictably, attracted much adverse criticism. A report in 2007 by P.J. Patterson, former Prime Minister of Jamaica, recommended expanding the WICB to include 'additional representatives from the Caribbean Community governments, the private sector, tourism, and the University of the West Indies'.[79] Nine years later this had not been done; in 2016 Beckles called for the report's implementation.[80] In 2016 CARICOM (the twenty-strong free trade association of Caribbean nations) called for the immediate dissolution of the WICB.[81]

Beckles continued to invoke the past to try to stimulate the present and, in doing so, only revealed the political deadlock that now afflicted West Indies cricket. In 2011, in a lecture in St Kitts entitled 'Frank Worrell: The Rise and Fall of West Indies Cricket', Beckles suggested that in the history of West Indies cricket 'Frank Worrell is the Father of the Nation, Sobers is the King of Cricket, Clive Lloyd is the Statesman, Richards is the General of the Army, Brian Lara is the Prince, and Chris Gayle is the Don'. Don was acknowledged as a mafia term and Beckles then drew comparison between a 'don' and 'Dudus' (aka Christopher Coke, a Jamaican drug lord). The intended implication was that the West Indian cricket public should go back to the Caribbean communitarianism signified by Worrell and not be distracted by a bling-laden, itinerant six-hitter. Indeed, Beckles had styled Lara as 'Prince' and Gayle as 'Don' the year before in an article which, among other things, accused Gayle of 'ideological detachment'.[82]

The West Indies Players Association (WIPA) immediately demanded the sacking of Beckles, who at the time was a Director of the WICB.[83] Here, no doubt, was a political irony: a West Indian nationalist historian was being rebuked by a trade union. Beckles insisted he had been misunderstood and a controversy created which was 'designed to distract from the task at hand – that is, diagnosing the crisis in West Indies cricket and developing policies to fix it; also, seeking to assess how we as West Indians will treat with the issue of our cricketers rejecting the West Indies cricket team.'[84]

Notes

1 C.L.R. James *Beyond a Boundary* London: Serpent's Tail 1994 (first published London: Stanley Paul 1963). See also Mike Marqusee 'Thinking beyond boundaries' *Red Pepper* March 2013 http://www.redpepper.org.uk/thinking-beyond-boundaries/ Access 12 October 2016.
2 Michael Manley *A History of West Indies Cricket* London: Andre Deutsch 1988. Hilary McD. Beckles *The Development of West Indies Cricket, Volume 1 The Age of Nationalism, Volume 2 The Age of Globalization* Jamaica: The Press, University of West Indies/ London: Pluto Press 1998.
3 See Tim Hector 'One eye on the ball, one eye on the world: cricket, West Indian nationalism and the spirit of C.L.R. James' Compiled and with editorial commentary by Stephen Wagg in Stephen Wagg (ed.) *Cricket and National Identity in the Postcolonial Age* Abingdon: Routledge 2005 pp.159–77.
4 Hilary McD. Beckles *The Development*.
5 See Beckles *The Development*; Volume 1 looks at the first two paradigms and Volume 2 deals with the third.
6 In this chapter the West Indies will frequently be referred to as a series of islands. This is simply shorthand – most of them are, after all, islands – but British Guiana (now Guyana) is, of course, on the South American mainland.
7 Manley *A History* pp.55–6.
8 See Jan Rogozinski *A Brief History of the Caribbean* Harmondsworth: Plume 2000 pp.313–14.
9 William M. Macmillan *Warning from the West Indies: A Tract for Africa and the Empire* London: Faber & Faber 1936 (re-published Harmondsworth: Penguin 1938).
10 Manley *A History* pp.62–3.
11 James *Beyond* p.139.
12 Arunabha Sengupta 'Baron Learie Constantine: A grandson of slave's amazing journey in life to earn the title of Baron' http://www.cricketcountry.com/articles/baron-learie-constantine-a-grandson-of-slaves-amazing-journey-in-life-to-earn-the-title-of-baron-18122 Posted 21 September 2016, Access 13 October 2016.
13 Quoted in Gideon Haigh 'George Headley: The great black hope' http://www.espncricinfo.com/magazine/content/story/428006.html Posted 3 October 2009, Access 12 October 2016.
14 Gerald Howat *Learie Constantine* London: George Allen & Unwin 1975 p.45.
15 See Beckles *The Development* Volume 1 pp.35–58.
16 Manley *The History* p.60.
17 Manley *The History* p.69.
18 It is widely accepted that the British acted at the insistence of the United States government. See, for example, John Newsinger *The Blood Never Dried: A People's History of the British Empire* London: Bookmarks 2013 pp.235–6.

19 Gerald Howat *Len Hutton: The Biography* London: Mandarin 1990 p.136.
20 Trevor Bailey *Wickets, Catches and the Odd Run* London: Willow Books 1986 p.186.
21 James *Beyond* p.238.
22 James *Beyond* p.233.
23 James *Beyond* pp.239–40. See also Andy Bull 'The forgotten story of ... white West Indian cricketers' *The Guardian* 2 February 2009 https://www.theguardian.com/sport/blog/2009/feb/02/forgotten-story-of-white-west-indian-cricket Access 13 October 2016.
24 James *Beyond* p.94.
25 James *Beyond* p.75.
26 Michele Savidge and Alastair McLellan *Real Quick: A Celebration of the West Indies Pace Quartets* London: Blandford 1995 p.21.
27 Savidge and McLellan *Real Quick* p.23.
28 Garfield Myers 'Alexander had no choice but to send Gilchrist home – Hendriks' http://www.jamaicaobserver.com/news/Alexander-had-no-choice-but-to-send-Gilchrist-home---Hendriks_68900 Posted 31 July 2016, Access 13 October 2016.
29 Abhishek Mukherjee 'Roy Gilchrist: A fast-bowling terror whose career was cut short by his mercurial nature' http://www.cricketcountry.com/articles/roy-gilchrist-a-fast-bowling-terror-whose-career-was-cut-short-by-his-mercurial-nature-28399 Posted 28 June 2016, Access 14 October 2016.
30 James *Beyond* pp.235–6.
31 Manley *A History* p.138.
32 See Rogozinski *A Brief History* pp.321–2.
33 See, for example, Stephen G. Rabe *US Intervention in British Guiana: A Cold War Story* Chapel Hill: University of North Carolina Press 2005.
34 See, for example, Jacqueline Mackenzie and Ken Fuller 'Richard Hart: Caribbean activist and writer' *Morning Star* 3 January 2014 https://www.morningstaronline.co.uk/a-2feb-Richard-Hart-Caribbean-activist-and-writer Access 18 October 2016.
35 See Gerald Horne *Cold War in Hot Zone: The United States Confronts Labor and Independence Struggles in the British West Indies* Philadelphia: Temple University Press 2007.
36 Mark Curtis *Web of Deceit: Britain's Real Role in the World* London: Vintage 2003 pp.349–50.
37 Curtis *Web of Deceit* pp.347–54.
38 See Richard Drayton 'Britain's secret archive of decolonisation' History Workshop Online http://www.historyworkshop.org.uk/britains-secret-archive-of-decolonisation/ Posted 19 April 2012, Access 18 October 2016. See also Richard Drayton 'Anglo-American "liberal" imperialism, British Guiana 1953–64, and the world Since September 11' in William Roger Louis (ed.) *Yet More Adventures With Britannia: Personalities, Politics and Culture in Britain* London: I.B. Tauris 2005 pp.321–42.
39 Savidge and McLellan *Real Quick* p.33.
40 Martin Williamson 'The bouncer that ended a career' http://www.espncricinfo.com/magazine/content/story/807661.html Posted 6 December 2014, Access 18 October 2016.
41 Manley *A History* p.174.
42 Quoted in Savidge and McLellan *Real Quick* p.35.
43 Nasser Khan 'A riot in the Oval' http://www.guardian.co.tt/entertainment/2013-05-01/riot-oval Posted 2 May 2013, Access 18 October 2016.
44 Manley *A History* pp.181–2.

45 Quoted by Patrick Hicks in 'When I watched Sussex tame the mighty West Indians' http://www.espncricinfo.com/magazine/content/story/1023213.html Posted 11 June 2016, Access 18 October 2016.
46 Quoted in Curtis *Web of Deceit* p.352.
47 Quoted in Colin Cross *The Fall of the British Empire 1918–1968* London: Book Club Associates 1968 p.262.
48 Quoted in Savidge and McLellan *Real Quick* p.43.
49 Hilary Beckles 'The Strife of Brian' in Rob Steen (ed.) *The New Ball Volume Two: Universal Stories* London: Mainstream 1999 pp.79–95, p.81.
50 At the time of writing these 'unforgiven' include David Murray, the son of Caribbean cricket hero Everton Weekes, who in 2007 was living in disgrace and destitution in Bridgetown, Barbados. See Siddhartha Vaidyanathan 'The unforgiven' http://www.espncricinfo.com/magazine/content/story/286356.html Posted 2 August 2007, Access 19 October 2016.
51 Viv Richards *Hitting Across the Line: An Autobiography* London: Headline 1992 p.68.
52 Richards *Hitting* p.98.
53 Will Luke 'A brief history: England v West Indies: 1960–1980' http://phone.espncricinfo.com/england-v-west-indies-2012/content/story/292034.html Access 19 October 2016.
54 Quoted in Stephen Wagg 'Calypso kings, dark destroyers: England–West Indies Test cricket and the English press, 1950 to 1984' in Wagg (ed.) *Cricket and National Identity...* pp.181–203, p.181.
55 See http://www.runnymedetrust.org/histories/index.php?mact=OralHistories,cntnt01,default,0&cntnt01qid=35&cntnt01returnid=20 Access 19 October 2016.
56 Stevan Riley (Director) *Fire in Babylon* London: Cowboy Films/Passion Pictures 2010.
57 Simon Lister *Fire in Babylon: How the West Indies Cricket Team Brought a People to its Feet* London: Yellow Jersey Press 2015.
58 'WI in England 1984: One-armed bandits and a Blackwash' http://news.bbc.co.uk/sport1/hi/cricket/8012447.stm Posted 1 May 2009, Access 19 October 2016.
59 See Neil Robinson *Long Shot Summer The Year of Four England Cricket Captains 1988* Stroud: Amberley Publishing 2015.
60 Quoted in Savidge and McLellan *Real Quick* pp.149–50.
61 See Stephen Wagg 'Calypso kings' pp.192–6.
62 Mike Marqusee *Anyone But England: An Outsider Looks at English Cricket* London: Aurum Press 2005 p.252.
63 Beckles *The Development* Volume Two.
64 Rogozinski *A Brief* pp.326–8.
65 Hector 'One eye' p.172.
66 Hector 'One eye' p.173.
67 Beckles *The Development* Volume Two pp.91–4.
68 H.G. Helps 'Did former West Indies cricket star, Brian Lara, disrespect Nelson Mandela?' http://www.mnialive.com/articles/did-former-west-indies-cricket-star-brian-lara-disrespect-nelson-mandela?A=WebApp&CCID=14585&Page=355&Items=3 Posted 19 November 2013, Access 20 October 2016.
69 'Lara dropped over sponsorship row' http://news.bbc.co.uk/sport1/hi/cricket/other_international/west_indies/4321081.stm Posted 6 March 2005, Access 20 October 2016.
70 1 May 2007.
71 'West Indies name replacement squad' http://www.espncricinfo.com/wivbdesh2009/content/story/413237.html Posted 8 July 2009, Access 20 October 2016.

72 http://www.espncricinfo.com/westindies/content/player/51880.html Access 20 October 2016.
73 Donald McRae 'Chris Gayle: "You're with men. You're good-looking. What do you expect?"' *The Guardian* 14 June 2016 https://www.theguardian.com/sport/2016/jun/14/chris-gayle-mel-mclaughlin-sexism-row-west-indies-cricket Access 20 October 2016.
74 See Anna Kessel 'Chris Gayle warns Andrew Strauss to "stay out of his business" over late IPL return' *The Guardian* 12 May 2009 https://www.theguardian.com/sport/2009/may/12/chris-gayle-andrew-strauss-cricket Access 20 October 2016.
75 Beckles *The Development* Volume Two pp.126–7.
76 Beckles *The Development* Volume Two pp.161–7.
77 Hector 'One eye' p.175.
78 Mark Nicholas 'Is it time for the West Indian nations to go it alone?' http://www.espncricinfo.com/magazine/content/story/952847.html Posted 17 December 2015, Access 20 October 2016.
79 Tony Cozier 'Degenerating WICB can't ignore latest call for change' http://www.espncricinfo.com/magazine/content/story/910077.html Posted 16 August 2015, Access 20 October 2016.
80 'Beckles urges WICB to implement Patterson Report reform' http://jamaica-gleaner.com/article/sports/20160407/beckles-urges-wicb-implement-patterson-report-reform Posted 7 April 2016, Access 20 October 2016.
81 Nagraj Gollapudi 'CARICOM resolute in endeavor to dissolve WICB' http://www.espncricinfo.com/westindies/content/story/1033179.html Posted 8 July 2016, Access 20 October 2016.
82 Hilary McD. Beckles '"Prince" Lara and "Don" Gayle: Globalization and the Leadership Crisis in West Indies Cricket' in Rumford and Wagg (eds.) *Cricket and Globalization* pp.172–88, p.175.
83 'WIPA condemns Professor Beckles for comparing Chris Gayle with "Dudus" Coke' http://guyanachronicle.com/2011/05/11/wipa-condemns-professor-beckles-for-comparing-chris-gayle-with-dudus-coke Posted 11 May 2011, Access 20 October 2016.
84 'Sir Hilary says "don" comments misunderstood' http://www.jamaicaobserver.com/sport/Sir-Hilary-says—don—comments-misunderstood_8801924 Posted 14 May 2011, Access 20 October 2016.

Chapter 6

The soul of a nation, long suppressed?
Cricket in India since 1945

When India received her independence from Britain, in August 1947, her incoming Prime Minister, Jawaharlal Nehru, educated at an English public school (Harrow) and Cambridge University and now leader of the Indian Congress Party, addressed the new nation. 'A moment comes', he said, 'which comes but rarely in history, when we step out from the old to the new, when an age ends, and when the soul of a nation, long suppressed, finds utterance'. Later in the speech he observed:

> The service of India means the service of the millions who suffer. It means the ending of poverty and ignorance and disease and inequality of opportunity. The ambition of the greatest man of our generation has been to wipe every tear from every eye. That may be beyond us, but as long as there are tears and suffering, so long our work will not be over.[1]

In the seventy odd years since he gave it, poverty, ignorance and inequality of opportunity have, however, persisted and many an Indian tear has doubtless been shed. Moreover, historians agree that, during that period, Nehru's political legacy has been dismantled and, well before the end of the twentieth century, his Congress Party had foregone its historic grip on the levers of power. Cricket, a game of which Nehru was very fond – he went regularly to watch cricket at Lord's while studying for the bar in London between 1910 and 1912[2] – and with which his legacy was sometimes identified, has in many ways reflected the decline of Nehruism and the corresponding rise of the political and economic forces that Nehru sought to restrain.

An Indian game, accidentally discovered . . . cricket and the birth of a nation

Most cricket writers are familiar with Ashis Nandy's enigmatic declaration in 1989 that cricket 'is an Indian game accidentally discovered by the British'.[3] Since British men undoubtedly brought cricket to India, perhaps the most tenable interpretation of this remark is the one chosen by Indian historian Ramachandra Guha, who, in his widely admired history of the Indian game, points out that the men of the British occupation (or 'raj'), far from urging cricket on the Indian people as part of some colonial project, often opted to play it only among themselves: to 'steal time away from the natives'.[4] The natives, in other words, played their cricket separately. Indeed, as Guha suggests, when ex-Kent captain Lord Harris became Governor of Bombay, capital of the western coastal state of Maharashtra, in 1890 he had, contrary to the claims of his biographer,[5] done little to promote cricket outside of his European social circle. Indeed when in 1891 he was asked to settle a dispute between a dozen European polo players and a thousand native cricketers over the use of Bombay's Esplanade, he had ruled in favour of the polo team.[6]

Indian cricket thrived nevertheless, its progress inevitably circumscribed by the country's caste system and its 'communalism', or religious divisions. Here the initiative had been taken by the Parsi community, whose Zoroastrian religion shared a number of tenets with Christianity and whose mercantile leanings and fairish skin also appealed to British administrators.[7] The Parsis had played their first match against Bombay-based Europeans in 1877 and the rise of Hindu and Muslim cricket had by 1912 given rise to a Quadrangular Tournament. In 1937 a fifth team, comprising cricketers from India's remaining senior religions (Buddhists, Jews and Christians) was added, reconstituting the competition as Pentangular. The matches were played on the now-legendary maidans – vast recreation grounds in south Bombay – and aroused great public interest. Moreover, as James Astill, points out, the communalism that defined the Pentangular competition had meant that, inasmuch as sporting encounters were metaphors for social and political divisions, the fiercest rivalry for many Indians was not with the British.[8]

In the period between the turn of the twentieth century and the Second World War the growth of Indian cricket had been financed by a bejewelled regiment of Indian princes, who hired cricketers, funded teams and underwrote cricket tours. Prominent among these benefactors had been Sir Bhupinder Singh, Maharaja of Patiala in the Punjab region of northern India. The Maharaja had been a pioneer of Indian cricket and had run his own cricket team, donated the Ranji Trophy, the first-class cricket competition currently contested by twenty-eight teams in India, and paid for an Indian team, captained by himself, to tour England in 1911.[9] This was part of a political rapprochement between the Indian aristocracy and the British colonial project, wherein Indian state rulers enjoyed a level of continued autonomy in their respective jurisdictions in return for their sponsorship of cultural activities such as sports. As Mihir Bose points out, under the British Raj, half of India was not ruled by Britain, but by native allies.[10]

This pattern of patronage had helped to raise questions about India's caste system, notably with regard to Palwankar Baloo (1876–1955). Baloo, who is now widely acknowledged as a pioneer of Indian cricket – indeed

Guha's history of Indian cricket began life as a biography of Baloo[11] – was an Untouchable (low status, out-caste), who played for a Hindu team. He was treated as a menial by his teammates when off the field of play and dropped from the team, because of his low social rank, in 1920. This decision was soon reversed, largely because of his prowess as a cricketer (he had been the success of the Indian tour of England in 1911), and made vice-captain – a move that Guha regards as analogous to the appointing of a black player to captain West Indies forty years later.[12]

Patronage had also thrown up arguably India's first cricket hero – Cottari Kanakaiya (C.K.) Nayudu (1895–1967), an attacking batsman whose patron was the Maharaja of Holkar, in central India.[13] Nayudu had played the last of his seven Tests, all of them against England and the only ones played by India before the Second World War, in 1936 (four years after India were given Test status) and finished with a modest batting average of 25. However, his cavalier batting against a visiting MCC team in front of a large and jubilant crowd at the Bombay maidan in 1926 is vividly recreated by British writer James Astill, who judges this occasion to have marked Indian cricket's coming of age.[14]

The forming of the Board of Control for Cricket in India (BCCI) in 1926 and India's Test debut at Lord's in June 1932 took place against a backdrop of religious-political tumult dominated by the Hindu lawyer and pacifist Mohandas Gandhi. Gandhi led successive public protests against British rule and the social exclusion of the Untouchables. He also campaigned for religious pluralism, condemning, when asked, the Pentangular tournament for its apparent divisiveness and the tacit support it might give to the Muslim separatism that would end in the creation of Pakistan: 'I have never understood the reason for having Hindu, Parsi, Muslim and other communal Elevens. I should have thought that such unsportsmanlike divisions would be considered taboo in sporting language and sporting manners'.[15]

The granting of India's independence in 1947 was also the moment of partition of the country, territories in the north east and north west of India becoming the new state of Pakistan. An estimated 15 million people were uprooted from their homes (as Muslims fled what was now effectively designated as Hindu territory, and *vice versa*) and between one and two million people were killed. Since this inter-communal tension to a degree still characterises the Indian political scene (and its cricket culture) there is a sense, as Delhi-based writer William Dalrymple wrote in 2015, that '1947 has yet to come to an end'.[16] The relationship between Indian cricket and religious extremism – manifest chiefly, but not solely, in its relationship with Pakistan – will be discussed later in this chapter.

Partition and independence had a number of immediate consequences for Indian cricket. First, it left India short of fast bowlers. Indeed, one fast bowler, Fazal Mahmood of Lahore, was scheduled to tour Australia with the Indian squad in 1947–8 but, by the time the players were due to depart, the sudden imposing of partition had made him a Pakistani.[17] As several writers point out, fast bowlers tended to come from cities such as Karachi and Lahore in the north of the country and India had had a credible opening pair at the beginning of their Test history: Mohammad Nissar, a Muslim from Lahore and Ladhabhai Nakum Amar Singh, a Hindu from Rakjot in Gujrat. Both had drawn praise from English batsmen following their performances in the 1930s. Neither played Test cricket after 1936 – Singh died of typhoid in 1940 – and India, arguably, could not call on another credible fast bowler until the 1980s: indeed, Nissar and Singh are still thought by some observers to have been among India's best ever.[18]

The absence of fast bowlers helped feed the comparative lack of credibility accorded to the Indian cricket team in the 1950s and 60s. After all fast bowlers have generally been symbols of aggressive masculinity and much post-colonial writing, following Edward Said,[19] has argued that such masculinity defined the rational West, subject peoples of the East being assumed to represent feminine passivity. Prashant Kidambi has suggested Indian cricketers of this period were viewed through a colonial stereotype of the 'effeminacy of educated Indians'.[20] Despite having, the previous February, recorded their first Test win (against England in Madras), India found it difficult to bat against England's fast bowlers Fred Trueman and Alec Bedser when they toured England in the summer of 1952. England won the four-match series 3–0, with one game drawn; in the second innings of the First Test at Headingley, India had lost four wickets without a run on the board. Performances such as this meant that England ordinarily sent a B team to India during this period.[21] India beat visitors Pakistan 2–1 the following winter and the New Zealand tourists 2–0 in 1955–6, but such victories were rare: between Jun 1959 and January 1968 they lost seventeen consecutive away Tests, a record.[22]

India's cricket pitches were in any event not conducive to fast bowling,[23] but she began from the 1960s to produce an array of talented spin bowlers. The most celebrated of these – Bhagwath Chandrasekhar (58 Tests 1964–79), Bishan Singh Bedi (67 Tests 1967–79), Erapalli Prasanna (49 Tests 1962–78) and Srinivas Venkataraghavan (57 Tests 1965–83) – are remembered (and celebrated in the cricket heritage industry)[24] as a quartet, although the four appeared together for India only once, against England at Edgbaston in 1967. They helped establish India in international cricket.

Credit for their development is often accorded to the Nawab of Pataudi who took over the Indian captaincy, aged 21, in 1961: for example, on Pataudi's death in 2011, Prasanna said Pataudi had been 'primarily responsible for developing India's spin quartet in an aggressive role similar to what the West Indians had later in form of the pace quartet'.[25] In this regard, Pataudi was, like Ted Dexter in English cricket during the same period, a politically paradoxical figure – lordly and cavalier in demeanour, but the apostle nevertheless of a modern, more professional approach to the game. He thus embodied the key political changes taking place in post-independence India.

Pataudi was among the last of long line of Anglophile and cricket-loving Indian aristocrats. His father had been to Oxford University, played a handful of games for Worcestershire in the English county championship and, like the illustrious Indian princes Ranjitsinhji (1872–1933) and Duleepsinhji (1905–59) before him, had been selected to play for England – in one Test on the troubled 'Bodyline' tour of Australia in 1932–3. Like many high-born young Indian men before him, Pataudi Jnr, known universally as 'Tiger', had been to an English public school (Winchester) and to his father's Oxford college and had succeeded Dexter as county captain of Sussex in 1966. During the immediate post-independence period, however, princes, for so long the patrons of Indian cricket, lost their privileges. In the sense that it had a partly controlled economy, with for example, a succession of five-year plans stretching through the 1950s and 60s,[26] India under Nehru's Congress Party was a quasi-socialist society during this period. Between 1947 and 1949, at the behest of Congress Home Affairs minister Vallabhbhai Patel, rulers of all the 565 princely states surrendered their power to the new government in return for a payment from the Privy Purse. Patronage of cricket soon passed to big companies such as the multi-faceted Tata and ACC (Associated Cement Companies), both based in Bombay, and the State Bank of India.[27] And, although in 1969 Pataudi provided a foretaste of India's now pervasive celebrity culture by marrying film star Sharmila Tagore – the first Indian actress to pose in a bikini – in 1971 he, along with all other Indian princes, lost both the captaincy of the Indian team and his title (inherited following his father's death, playing polo in 1952) when such things, along with the Privy Purse, were abolished by the government of Nehru's daughter, Indira Gandhi. Parliamentary elections were due and Pataudi was asked by the regional Vishal Haryana Party to stand as candidate for the Gurgaon constituency. Intriguingly Pataudi was immediately opposed by Lala Amarnath, India's first post-independence captain and a cricketer seen as the 'first to kick against the stifling domination of Indian cricket by the local princes and their imperial backers'.[28] Amarnath had famously been sent home from India's tour of England in 1936 by then-captain the Maharajkumar of Vizianagram, allegedly for 'indiscipline'.[29] Amarnath eventually withdrew in favour of the Congress candidate, 'urging the voters not to be "carried away by glamour" but to vote for the "progressive policies of our Prime Minister". Indira Gandhi was then at the height of her popularity . . . and the election itself was being fought by her party under the appealing slogan "Garibi Hatao" [Abolish Poverty]'.[30] Pataudi polled just under 23,000 votes out of nearly 400,000. India's aristocracy was on the wane and her government planners apparently in the ascendancy.

Pataudi's captaincy also coincided with a growth in the popularity of cricket in India, a pattern sustained during the tenure of his successor, Bombay batsman Ajit Wadekar (37 Tests 1966–74). Post-independence India experienced considerable internal tensions, particularly, following the aforementioned abolition of the princely states, between the state and the regions.[31] While some of these conflicts, such as the Telangana rebellion in Hyderabad state in the late 1940s,[32] were essentially peasant revolts against oppressive feudal landlords, much controversy across the country revolved around the status of local languages. The Nehru government feared 'Balkanisation'[33] and argued for uniformity and Hindi – which was spoken by less than half the population – was declared the official language of India in 1950. The result was widespread protests, often in defence of the continued use of English, in the (many) areas in which Hindi was unknown. This, in turn, brought not only riots and disorder but sharpened regional identities, thus, as James Astill suggests, boosting among other things the inter-region cricket competition, the Ranji Trophy.[34]

The expansion of All India Radio (AIR) also increased access to, and interest in, cricket. Ball-by-ball commentary in English of the Indian team's first home series (against West Indies in 1948–9) could now be heard in the country's major cities and by the 1960s commentaries were available in other widely-spoken languages such as Hindi, Bengali and Tamil. By this time, it seems, a fervent cricket nationalism was already in incubation. In the spring of 1965 Pataudi captained India to victory in a home series against New Zealand, clinched by 7 wickets in the final Test in Delhi. During the previous Test he had exercised some of the gentlemanly insouciance to which well-to-do Test captains of the day commonly aspired, declaring India's second innings closed 'largely out of sympathy for our opponents, because we had kept them in the field for the best part of two days'.[35] The Nawab's relaxed attitude may well have chimed with the public ethos encouraged by the Congress Party in which, as Guha observed, 'the nationalist spirit poured into the concrete that built dams and the steel that made factories'[36] – not into sport. But, since in the event New Zealand had barely managed a draw 'Tiger' found himself 'castigated' by the national sports press for 'throwing away certain victory'.[37] Later, on New Year's Day 1967, during a Test match against West Indies at Eden Gardens in Calcutta, there was a riot among spectators. Pataudi later reflected that Indian cricket crowds were ordinarily 'vast, noisy, easily pleased, less partisan than most and well behaved' and he attributed the disturbance to the heat, coming elections and the fact that thousands more tickets had been sold than there were seats available.[38] Hindsight suggests otherwise. Reflecting on what was a period of rising success for the Indian team, Astill notes '[b]etween 1967 and 1975 Indian stadiums saw four serious riots during Test matches, two each in Calcutta and Bombay. They were attributed mainly to overcrowding or general rowdiness'. Yet, for observers such as Astill, the violence was also a sign of:

The nationalist sentiments that India's winning streak had encouraged [...] many Indians, especially those newly attracted to the game, were no longer prepared to settle for individual heroics and an occasional victory. They had started expecting India to win all the time, and when they lost, as Wadekar found out, their anger was terrible.[39]

The closing section of this chapter addresses the effect on Indian cricket culture of the often ugly spiralling of these sentiments and the concomitant growth of India as a largely unfettered capitalist economy.

'I want them with tears in their eyes . . .' Politics, money and cricket in India since 1970

Several developments define India's forty-five-year progress from 1970 to the time of writing: the decline both of the Nehruvian legacy and of Congress Party's domination of Indian politics; the adoption of neoliberal economic policies, most concertedly after 1991; rapid economic growth, particularly in the fields of media and hi-tech services, bringing the southern city of Bangalore to rival India's main industrial centres of Bombay (known as Mumbai since 1995), Madras (Chennai since 1996) and Calcutta (Kolkata since 2001); a widening gap between rich and poor – two groups which, in a population estimated at 1.25 billion in 2013, India has in abundance; the development of a nuclear bomb in 1998; the embrace of Western-style consumerism; and the rise of an often virulent Hindu nationalism. Few doubt the interrelatedness of these developments, all of which have, in way or another, helped to shape the nation's cricket culture. A brief political chronology follows.

Nehru died in 1964. After two brief premierships, the role passed in 1966 to his daughter Indira Gandhi. Gandhi persisted with key Nehruvian policies (five-year plans, friendship with the Soviet Union, campaigns to end rural poverty, support for the Untouchables and other minorities. . .) but, in what is widely perceived as a left–right split with the party faction led by the pro-business politician Morarji Desai, she was expelled from the party in 1969. She formed her own version of the Congress Party and continued to govern, nationalising fourteen banks in the same year and India's mines in 1973. In 1975, an Indian High Court declared Indira Gandhi's election to the Lok Sabha (the Indian parliament) void on grounds of the illegal financing of her party's selection campaign. She now declared a state of emergency which lasted for two years. Losing power to Desai in 1977, Gandhi regained it in 1980, but by now the Nehruvian project was unravelling and the country was entering a period of instability: Mrs Gandhi was murdered in 1984 and Rajiv Gandhi, her son and successor, was assassinated five years later.[40]

Rajiv Gandhi had been more pro-capitalist than his mother, instituting a low-regulation, low-tax regime and relaxing restrictions on the import of consumer durables.[41] His death was followed by a more full-blooded engagement with international trade and finance: in 1991 an Indian coalition government accepted loans from the World Bank and the International Monetary Fund (IMF) and signed joint venture agreements with major international corporations such as Ford and IBM.[42]

These developments took place against a backdrop of rising communal strife and the growth of Hindu nationalism (called Hindutva by its adherents and majoritarianism by more neutral observers).

During the Desai premiership (1977–9) the right wing Hindu nationalist group, the Rashtriya Swayamsevak Sangh (RSS), outlawed since RSS members had murdered Mohandas Gandhi in 1948, was rehabilitated.[43] The 1980s saw an increase in communal violence, mostly against Muslims, and a huge groundswell of Hindu anger began to be generated about a sixteenth-century mosque in the city of Ayodhya, in the northern state of Uttar Pradesh, which, it was now claimed, had been built on the birthplace of Lord Ram, a sacred figure in Hindu mythology. The site became a place of pilgrimage for leaders of the emergent right wing Bharatiya Janata Party (BJP). The mosque was destroyed in 1992 and anti-Muslim violence intensified.[44] The BJP came to power in India in 1998; having professed fear of foreign control, they now encouraged foreign investment and embraced economic liberalisation. As Mike Marqusee, an acute observer of the country's cricket and politics, said of India in 1996: 'The section of the population most integrated into the global marketplace is also the most chauvinist'.[45]

Some see India's descent into communal strife as a break with Nehruvian secularism.[46] Others blame Nehru himself – notably, the Marxist historian Perry Anderson who, among other things, suggests that Nehru pandered to Hindu mysticism and used brutal Hindu communalism to unify post-partition India,[47] and Bose and Jalal, who argue that the Indian National Congress used religiously based majoritarianism 'to parry regional threats'.[48] The Hindutva has been read as one of a range of ways of containing the Indian lower classes[49] and, similarly, as a bid by upper caste Hindus to restore their hegemony.[50]

The influence on the nation's cricket culture of India's embrace of capitalist globalisation and the rise of Hindu nationalism has been marked.

The politics of partition and early independence had alarming implications for India's Muslims, including the elite cricket players and cricket enthusiasts among them. Muhammad Ali Jinnah, leader of the Muslim League and the first leader of Pakistan, had argued explicitly that India's Muslims constituted a separate nation.[51] This had been the rationale for the creation of Pakistan, but it also pre-defined India's remaining Muslims as outsiders – a status further affirmed by Congress's ruling that Hindi become the country's official language – and presented Hindu nationalist politicians with a ready-made resident Other, whom they could, when the situation seemed to demand it, accuse of betrayal. The Bombay Pentangular tournament finished in 1946 – a gesture of secularism but, with persistent Hindu nationalism, one likely only to marginalise religious minorities further.

Cricket authorities in both countries strove, often successfully, to keep communalism at arms' length.

Pakistan played their first series of Test cricket in India in 1952–3, by which time the two new nations had already been at war in the northern territory of Kashmir during 1947–8. As Guha observes, there were pleas for sportsmanship from official spokespeople in both countries but, while decorum was observed on the field of play and the Pakistani players were welcomed in the cricket-mad city of Bombay, there were hostile demonstrations in Nagpur, Calcutta and Delhi.[52] The greatest disturbance seemed to occur in Lucknow, a city with a substantial Muslim population in the northern state of Uttar Pradesh, where Pakistan won the their first Test – the second in a three-match rubber – in October 1952: as Bose writes, the India team bus was stoned by an angry crowd and India captain Amarnath had to beat protesters back with a stick.[53] Indian bowler Fazal Mahmood (later to play for Pakistan) recalled that the Indian players had 'saved their lives by a hair's breadth'.[54]

Indian teams have generally been mixed faith (the side of 1952 had two Muslims, for instance) and, in an enduringly volatile religious-political climate, the reputations of Indian Muslim Test players could be made and destroyed over a short space of time, as with Abbas Ali Baig in 1960. Baig, like Pataudi, was a high-born Muslim who made his name as a dashing batsman at Oxford University. Aged 20 and still a student he had been drafted as a replacement into the Indian side touring England in 1959 and scored a hundred on debut in the Fourth Test in Manchester, dealing comfortably with England's fast bowlers. The following year in Bombay he scored 50 against Australia and, in a foretaste of India's twenty-first-century celebrity culture and a conspicuous breach of its conservative social codes, he was kissed on the cheek by a young woman on his way back to the pavilion.[55] Later in 1960, however, when India toured Pakistan, Baig was widely condemned for a string of low scores, his accusers claiming that he had deliberately undermined his own team for the good of Islam, and his Test career was virtually over: 'A failure in a non-Pakistan series', remarks Bose, 'or by a Hindu in that series, might have been overlooked'.[56]

In 1965, when India and Pakistan fought their second war in Kashmir, the captains of the respective cricket teams, Pataudi and Hanif Mohammad, then both playing for a Rest of the World team in England, sent a telegram to both governments reading 'We wish to express deep regrets at the war between India and Pakistan. We find unity on the cricket field by reaching for a common objective. We fervently hope both countries can meet and find an amicable solution.'[57] But five years later the two countries were at war again, in a conflict that would result in the secession of East Pakistan to become Bangladesh, and they played no more Test matches until 1978. By this time nationalist fervour, to a degree independent of anti-Muslim racism, had begun to engulf the Indian cricket team. As Guha points out, India's first Test win, against England at Madras in 1952, had been the occasion for comparatively little public celebration. When the team returned from a series victory in West Indies in 1971, however, a jubilant crowd of 10,000 greeted them at the airport. Moreover, when they won their next series (in England) 1–0 much of the population of Bombay turned out to applaud them and Prime Minister Indira Gandhi gave them a civic reception.[58]

Mrs Gandhi, it appears, was trying to ride the wave of popular cricket nationalism that was emerging, but this wave has been most successfully negotiated by the rising new Indian middle class and the Hindu nationalists – often, following Marqusee, the same people. This has, perhaps, been most dramatically seen in the city of Bombay, historic centre of Indian cricket culture. In 1973 the city's Brabourne Stadium, founded in 1937, staged its last Test match and, two years later, and was replaced by the Wankhede, a new venue built nearby. Presented as arising from a dispute between the BCCI and the Bombay Cricket Association, Bose interprets this instead as a symbol of the growing influence of Bombay new rich, who lacked the 'colonial cum ritualistic Hindu reticence' of India's longer established plutocrats.[59] Less than twenty years later, Bombay politics had become dominated by Shiv Sena, a fascistic Hindu party founded in the city in the mid-1960s by Bal Thackeray, a political cartoonist, and closely allied to the BJP. In 1991 members of Shiv Sena dug up the pitch at the Wankhede Stadium to prevent Pakistan playing there; the match, and Pakistan's tour, were cancelled. In 1993 a bomb, planted by Muslim members of the city's underworld in retaliation for the destruction of the Ayodhya mosque, killed over 250 people in Bombay,[60] after which Thackeray made the maudlin declaration: 'I want them [Muslims] with tears in their eyes every time India loses to Pakistan'.[61] The threat of Shiv Sena intervention has continued to hang over Indian cricket administration: in 1999 Shiv Sena dug up the pitch at New Delhi's Ferozeshah Kotla Stadium and they continued to protest Indian cricket relations with Pakistan throughout the early twenty first century. In October 2015 they stormed BCCI headquarters at the Wankhede Stadium, chanting anti-Pakistan slogans.[62] Two days later leading Indian cricket writer Sharda Ugra speculated as to whether Mumbai and Chennai should now be struck off the international cricket calendar.[63]

Irrespective of this mayhem, appreciation of cricket in India seemed to undergo change with the rise of the new commercial middle class. And several years later Guha observed: 'With corporate sponsorship and block booking the genuine cricket lover has in any case been displaced by the overworked, overpaid, half-drunk and hyper-nationalist yuppie'.[64] Such spectators demanded victory, rather than cricket: for example, a hail of bottles, emanating from the more expensive seats, greeted India's elimination from the World Cup in Calcutta in 1996 – '"I paid Rs5000 for this rubbish", said one angry spectator'.[65] During a match at the Kotla Stadium in the same tournament an acquaintance of Mike Marqusee asked the mother of some children waving placards that were obscuring his view of the game to rein them and was told: 'If you want to watch the cricket, go home and watch it on television. We are here to make a noise'.[66]

Central to the marriage of cricket, commerce and nationalism has been television. As Satadru Sen writes:

> The dramatic expansion of Indian television after 1982 marked a major movement. First, by taking coverage of cricket matches into new 'viewing publics,' the TV revolution exposed entirely new segments of the population not only to the esoteric rituals of cricket, but also to the culture of athletic nationalism.[67]

These new publics, according to Guha, included housewives and farmers[68] – in the case of the latter, bringing Indian cricket, always largely an urban game,[69] to a rural audience. During this period television coverage of cricket in India was provided by Doordarshan, the government-funded public service broadcaster begun in 1959, and Doordarshan bought the rights to show the World Cup of 1996 from WorldTel, an American sports marketing company founded by expatriate ex-All India Radio commentator and typically new-breed Indian entrepreneur Mark Mascarenhas. Doordarshan, however, defaulted on their payments so the Indian government brokered a deal which allowed satellite channel Star TV, part of News Corporation, Rupert Murdoch's media empire, to share transmission.[70] As Marqusee estimated, around 90% of cricket's public now lived on the sub-continent[71] and to this could be added the substantial South Asian diaspora. The television audience was estimated at 400 million.[72]

Needless to say, entrepreneurs were not slow to take advantage of a market of this size. The American soft drinks corporations Coca Cola and Pepsi used the World Cup as an opportunity to break into the Asian market, Coca Cola paying $3.8 million to be designated as the 'official' soft drink[73] of the tournament and Pepsi being skilfully marketed as the soft drink with 'nothing official about it' – a persuasive selling line with young Indian cricket fans, some of whom were co-opted into the process via Coke's 'Fan of the Match' prize.[74]

This emergence of Indian cricket as such a lucrative popular cultural property also greatly enriched the BCCI. The commodity that BCCI were selling was specifically international cricket. As Bose had commented in 1986 the Indian press by now scarcely bothered to report the inter-zone Ranji Trophy matches. Moreover, the centrality of television and commerce already dictated that one-day-internationals (ODIs), which offered greater spectacle, a shorter format and the certainty of a winner, should take precedence over the traditional five-day Test match. Guha estimates that India played 150 ODIs in the fifteen years between 1974 and 1989 and nearly 300 in the following eleven.[75]

While the World Cup of 1996 was a commercial watershed, other important developments had already taken place, notably when, as Ugra pointed out, for 'the first time, in early 1993, Doordarshan had to pay the BCCI to televise a match and not the other way around. The rights to televised cricket in India were formalised as a commodity owned by the BCCI, which could be sold to the highest bidder'.[76] The TV rights to the 1996 World Cup, staged jointly by India, Pakistan and Sri Lanka, sold for $14 million, a huge sum at the time.[77] Ten years later Mumbai media and entertainment corporation Nimbus paid an equally eye-watering $612 million for the rights to show Indian cricket over the coming four years.[78]

The ongoing conflict between India and Pakistan was also a spur to cricket commerce. For example, it added promotional spice to the frequent ODIs between the two countries staged in Sharjah in the United Arab Emirates, a cricket stadium having opened there in 1982. Beyond the ample television audience the games attracted many South Asian labourers working in Sharjah and the Indian super-rich, for whom Sharjah was a favourite haunt.[79] In 2000 the Star Sports satellite channel, owned jointly by Disney and Murdoch's News Corporation, won the rights to show the three-cornered Carlton & United Series, first held in Australia and featuring the host country, India and Pakistan, in Asia. TV commercials exploited the fact that Indian and Pakistani troops had recently been at war in Kashmir with the slogan 'Qayamat!' – Hindi for 'apocalypse'.[80] When India beat Pakistan in a one-day Group B match of the 2015 ICC Cricket World Cup held in Adelaide they did so in before an estimated television audience of 1 billion, making it the most-watched match in the history of cricket.[81] India captain M.S. Dhoni said, with considerable understatement: 'When we play Pakistan there's definitely more intensity'.[82] India and Pakistan have, however, rarely played each other on home soil in recent times.

Meanwhile, Indian Test cricketers, along with their counterparts from other countries, were signing lucrative advertising contracts which, in the Indian instance especially, turned most of the team into wealthy and socially conspicuous young men. Some, notably the formidable Mumbai batsman Sunil Gavaskar (125 Tests 1971–87, batting average 51), received a degree of hero worship in their home towns[83] and fulfilled an expanded version of the role accorded to many Indian Test cricketers since the 1950s, that of corporate ambassador – in Gavaskar's case for the major textile company Nirlon. But while most Indian Test cricketers since the 1990s have become celebrities to rival the stars of Bollywood and television soap opera, there is acknowledged to be something about the kudos attaching to Sachin Tendulkar, the most feted of all Indian cricketers, which sets him apart. Tendulkar (200 Tests 1989–2013, batting average 54) first played for India at the age of 16. He signed a five-year, 250 million rupee deal with Mascarenhas' WorldTel in 1995, at the age of 22. This made him the world's richest cricketer and the contract was regularly renewed on ever more generous terms. WorldTel was headquartered in Bangalore, hub of India's emergent hi-tech and media industries, and the ostentatious Mascarenhas was a living symbol of India's new wealthy, described in society magazines as 'Mr Big' and referring to Tendulkar as 'My boy'.[84] In India Tendulkar is, as the historian Prashant Kidambi observes, 'the biggest brand of them all'; but the bigger the brand, the wider the appeal, and Tendulkar's attraction stretched well beyond what Kidambi aptly calls the 'raucous embrace' of India's status-hungry nouveau riche[85] To nationalists savouring the virility of a nation now harbouring a nuclear bomb he presented, perhaps, an assured masculinity that dealt calmly with fast bowling in a way that had generally eluded previous generations of Indian batsman. As a devout Hindu and devoted family man,[86] he reassured social conservatives, but he was also an icon to India's poverty-stricken masses. In 1998, the Bombay poet C.P. Surendran wrote memorably:

> Batsmen walk out into the middle alone. Not Tendulkar. Every time Tendulkar walks to the crease, a whole nation, tatters and all, marches with him to the battle arena. A pauper people pleading for relief, remission from the lifelong anxiety of being Indian, by joining in spirit their visored saviour.[87]

At his retirement in 2013 Tendulkar found himself dealing uncomfortably with claims that he was a living god.[88] However, in the often toxic political climate of contemporary India, such designations are not easily shaken off: in May 2016, at the behest of Shiv Sena and other Hindu nationalists, Indian comedian Tanmay Bhat found himself under investigation by Mumbai police for making fun of Sachin Tendulkar.[89]

Conclusion: something won or something lost

Observers of cricket and politics, within India and beyond, have been expectably divided over the merits of the revolution wrought in the country's cricket by capitalist globalisation. James Astill of *The Economist* – a magazine known, according to one commentator, for its 'free market utopianism'[90] – is one of the most recent Western travellers in Indian cricket; in his book of 2013 he broadly welcomes the 'great tamasha' – 'spectacle', 'carnival' or 'commotion' in several Indian languages – that Indian cricket has become and refers dismissively to the 'enterprise-throttling' regime of Nehru and the Congress Party.[91] Another decisive voice of acceptance was that of historian Satadru Sen, who in an essay of 2005 rejected what he saw as 'the ideology of the Nehruvian state, with its rhetoric of secularism, manly asceticism and nationalist internationalism'.[92] He welcomed the marriage of cricket and television and participation of Indian fans in these spectacles and their entry, thus, into the world of global consumption:

> My point is that it is not simply the audience that draws the advertisers; the advertisements also draw and shape the audience, and this dynamic profoundly affects what the audience remembers. People who tune in to watch cricket do not simply come to watch the game. Like Super Bowl audiences in the United States, they come also to watch the advertisements, not least because consuming images of global products like Pepsi and Adidas when those products have been attached to Indian national icons like Tendulkar (and thus domesticated, without being stripped of their cosmopolitan glamour) is an experience of the pleasure of being a modern consumer-citizen. Their memories of cricket, then, include the products that are associated with the cosmopolitan stars of the national game, as well as the stark facts of big money: the statistics of batting averages have been reduced to near-irrelevance by the statistics of players' contracts.
>
> The new crowd in Indian cricket also consumes – and thus remembers – the crowd itself. The panoramic eye of the television camera produces a visual memory of one's fellow-spectators that is significantly different from the observed recollection of the ticket-holder in the stands. The crowd is at once expanded, rendered spectacular, and incited to perform as spectacle. Without television, there would be little incentive for the painted-face carnivals of present-day cricket, which survive as a continuous trace in the memory of the watcher when the specifics of the game itself have faded.[93]

Others have deplored exactly what Sen applauded. In 1988 Indian writer Sujit Mukherjee lamented '[a] large majority of our spectators watch cricket without understanding details of the game . . . and their sole interest is being present at an Indian victory'[94] and, for Mike Marqusee, looking back on the World Cup of 1996, 'the carnival of globalisation [had] turned into an orgy of nationalism'.[95] Twenty years later, as the novelist and campaigner Arundhati Roy reflected that the major companies who, in post-war India, were running the nation's cricket teams, were now also running the nation itself, amassing vast fortunes in the process: in a country, 800 million of whose population had to live on less than 20 Indian rupees (a little under US$3) a day, 100 people by 2014 owned assets equivalent to one quarter of India's gross domestic product.[96] One such, Mukesh Ambani, controller of the huge corporation Reliance Industries Limited and owner of the Mumbai Indians cricket team, in 2014 had a personal fortune of $20.2 billion.[97] He and his family were regular spectators at India's ODIs but, clearly, in the contemporary Indian cricket crowd, some consumer-citizens had almost unimaginably more scope for consumption (and citizenship) than others.

Notes

1. The speech can be read in full at: http://sourcebooks.fordham.edu/halsall/mod/1947nehru1.html Access 4 November 2016.
2. Sankar Ghose *Jawaharlal Nehru, a Biography* Mumbai: Allied Publishers 1993 p.11.
3. Ashis Nandy *The Tao of Cricket: On Games of Destiny and the Destiny of Games* London: Penguin 1989 p.1.
4. Ramachandra Guha *A Corner of a Foreign Field: The Indian History of a British Sport* London: Picador 2003 p.38.
5. See James D. Coldham *Lord Harris* London: George Allen & Unwin 1983 pp.86–7.
6. Guha *A Corner* pp.57–9.
7. James Astill *The Great Tamasha: Cricket, Corruption and the Turbulent Rise of Modern India* London: Wisden Sports Writing 2013 p.11.
8. Astill *The Great* pp.6 and 15.
9. See Richard Cashman *Patrons, Players and the Crowd: The Phenomenon of Indian Cricket* New Delhi: Orient Longman 1980 pp.27–33.
10. Mihir Bose *A Maidan View: The Magic of Indian Cricket* London: George Allen & Unwin 1986 p.3.
11. Gideon Haigh 'A cricket history of India' [Review of *A Corner of a Foreign Field*] http://www.espncricinfo.com/magazine/content/story/343290.html Posted 17 May 2008, Access 15 November 2016.
12. See Guha *A Corner* pp.142–5.
13. Guha *a Corner* p.202.
14. Astill, *The Great* p.7.
15. Ramachandra Guha 'Gandhi and cricket' *The Hindu* 30 September 2001 http://www.thehindu.com/2001/09/30/stories/0730028p.htm Access 15 November 2016.
16. William Dalrymple 'The Great Divide: The violent legacy of Indian Partition' *The New Yorker* 29 June 2015 http://www.newyorker.com/magazine/2015/06/29/the-great-divide-books-dalrymple Access 15 November 2016.
17. See Shaan Agha 'Remembering Fazal Mahmood: Pakistan cricket's first "poster boy"' http://www.dawn.com/news/1185304 Posted 31 May 2015, Access 29 November 2016.
18. Astill *The Great* p.40.
19. Notably in *Orientalism* London: Penguin 2003 [First published 1978].
20. Prashant Kidambi 'Sachin Tendulkar and Indian public culture' in Anthony Bateman and Jeffrey Hill (eds.) *The Cambridge Companion to Cricket* Cambridge: Cambridge University Press 2011 pp.187–202, p.188.
21. Bose *A Maidan View* p.16.
22. Astill *The Great* pp.44–5.
23. Astill *The Great* p.43.
24. See, for example, Suresh Menon 'India's spin quartet remembered' http://www.dreamcricket.com/dreamcricket/news.hspl?nid=16323&ntid=3 Posted 31 October 2011, Access 17th November 2016; and Krishna Shripada 'India's famed spin quartet – the gold standard for hunting in packs' http://www.sportskeeda.com/cricket/indias-famed-spin-quartet-gold-standard-hunting-packs Posted 20 September 2016, Access 17 November 2016.
25. BBC South Asia News 'Tributes paid to Indian cricketer "Tiger" Pataudi' http://www.bbc.co.uk/news/world-south-asia-15030717 Posted 23 September 2011, Access 17 November 2016.
26. See Stanley Wolpert *A New History of India* Oxford: Oxford University Press 2009 pp.375–82.

27 See Cashman *Patrons, Players* pp.48–64.
28 http://www.espncricinfo.com/india/content/player/26223.html Access 17 November 2016.
29 See Steven Lynch 'You're fired' http://www.espncricinfo.com/magazine/content/story/625483.html Posted 18 March 2013, Access 17 November 2016.
30 Ramachandra Guha 'Scoring politically' *The Hindu* 14 October 2001 http://www.thehindu.com/2001/10/14/stories/1314128g.htm Access 17 November 2016.
31 See, for example, Peter Robb *A History of India* Basingstoke: Palgrave 2002 p.212.
32 See, for example, John Roosa 'Passive revolution meets peasant revolution: Indian nationalism and the Telangana revolt' *The Journal of Peasant Studies* Vol.28 No.4 2001 pp.57–94.
33 See Barbara D. Metcalf and Thomas R. Metcalf *A Concise History of India* Cambridge: Cambridge University Press 2006 p.240.
34 Astill *The Great* pp.41–2.
35 The Nawab of Pataudi (as told to Kenneth Wheeler) *Tiger's Tale* London: Stanley Paul 1969 p.52.
36 Guha *A Corner* p.348.
37 Pataudi *Tiger's Tale* p.52.
38 Pataudi *Tiger's Tale* p.65.
39 Astill *The Great* p.48.
40 See Robb *A History* pp.303–4.
41 Metcalf and Metcalf *A Concise History...* p.261.
42 Wolpert *A New History* p.461.
43 Metcalf and Metcalf *A Concise History* p.258.
44 Metcalf and Metcalf *A Concise History* pp.275–7, 281.
45 Mike Marqusee *War Minus the Shooting: A Journey through South Asia during Cricket's World Cup* London: Heinemann 1996 p.165.
46 For example, Robb *A History* p.214.
47 See Perry Anderson *The Indian Ideology* London: Verso 2013.
48 Sugata Bose and Ayesha Jalal *Modern South Asia: History, Culture, Political Economy* London: Routledge 2002 p.227.
49 Robb *A History* p.305.
50 Charu Gupta and Mukul Sharma 'Communal constructions: media reality vs. real reality' *Race and Class* Vol.38 No.1 July–September 1996 pp.1–20, p.2.
51 Metcalf and Metcalf *A Concise History* p.216.
52 Guha *A Corner* pp.371–80.
53 Mihir Bose 'Conflicting loyalties: India–Pakistan cricket relations' in Bateman and Hill (eds.) *The Cambridge Companion to Cricket* pp.203–17, p.204.
54 Quoted in Peter Oborne *Wounded Tiger: A History of Cricket in Pakistan* London: Simon and Schuster 2015 p.84.
55 Abhishek Mukherjee 'Abbas Ali Baig: From Oxford University to a Test debut hundred at age 20' http://www.cricketcountry.com/articles/abbas-ali-baig-from-oxford-university-to-a-test-debut-hundred-at-age-20-24217 Posted 15 June 2016, Access 20 November 2016.
56 Bose 'Conflicting loyalties' p.206.
57 Arunabha Sengupta 'India vs Pakistan: contests amidst conflicts' http://www.cricketcountry.com/articles/india-vs-pakistan-contests-amidst-conflicts-104863 Posted 27 February 2016, Access 20 November 2016.
58 Guha *A Corner* pp.343–9.
59 Bose *A Maidan View* pp.57–8.

106 Cricket and the end of empire

60 See Sonal Bhadoria 'How Sanjay Dutt got caught in web?' http://www.indiatimes.com/news/india/how-did-sanjay-dutt-become-involved-in-the-1993-mumbai-blasts-67595.html Posted 21 March 2013, Access 29 November 2016.
61 Astill *The Great* p.130.
62 Satish Nandgaonkar 'Shiv Sena activists storm BCCI headquarters' *The Hindu* 19 October 2015 http://www.thehindu.com/sport/cricket/shiv-sena-activists-storm-bcci-headquarters/article7779904.ece Access 20 November 2016.
63 Sharda Ugra 'Should Mumbai and Chennai be struck off the international cricket calendar?' http://www.espncricinfo.com/magazine/content/story/931152.html Posted 21 October 2015, Access 20 November 2016.
64 Guha *A Corner* p.405.
65 Marqusee *War Minus* pp.264–6.
66 Marqusee *War Minus* p.164.
67 Satadru Sen 'History without a past: memory and forgetting in Indian cricket' in Stephen Wagg (ed.) *Cricket and National Identity* pp.94–109, p.102.
68 Guha *A Corner* p.329.
69 Bose *A Maidan View* p.15.
70 Marqusee *War Minus* pp.22–4.
71 Marqusee *War Minus* p.14.
72 Guha *A Corner* p.330.
73 Martin Williamson 'How the World Cup became a commercial hit' http://www.espncricinfo.com/wctimeline/content/current/story/824079.html Posted 5 February 2015, Access 21 November 2016.
74 See, in particular, Astill *The Great* pp.74–5 and Marqusee *War Minus* pp.189–90, p.202.
75 Guha *A Corner* p.329.
76 Sharda Ugra 'Cricket's canny iconoclast' [Obituary of Jagmohan Dalmiya] http://www.espncricinfo.com/india/content/story/922183.html Posted 21 September 2015, Access 21 November 2016.
77 Williamson 'How the World Cup became a commercial hit'.
78 Cricinfo Staff 'Nimbus wins telecast rights for Indian cricket' http://www.espncricinfo.com/india/content/story/237563.html Posted 17 February 2006, Access 21 November 2016.
79 Guha *A Corner* p.398.
80 See Mike Marqusee 'Nations for sale' in Rob Steen (ed.) *The New Ball, Volume Four: Imperial Bedrooms* London: Sports Books Direct 2000 pp.11–27, p.25.
81 Scyld Berry 'India beat Pakistan by 76 runs as estimated one billion viewers tune in to World Cup clash' *The Telegraph* http://www.telegraph.co.uk/sport/cricket/cricket-world-cup/11413995/India-beat-Pakistan-by-76-runs-as-estimated-one-billion-viewers-tune-in-to-World-Cup-clash.html Posted 15 February 2015, Access 22 November 2016.
82 'Cricket World Cup 2015: India v Pakistan will be "high-voltage"' http://www.bbc.co.uk/sport/cricket/31469238 Posted 14 February 2015, Access 21 November 2016.
83 Bose *A Maidan View* p.104.
84 Vivek Kamath 'How Mark Mascarenhas redefined celebrity management' http://www.forbesindia.com/article/2013-celebrity-100/how-mark-mascarenhas-redefined-celebrity-management/36751/1 Posted 26 December 2013, Access 22 November 2016.
85 Prashant Kidambi 'Hero, celebrity and icon' pp.195 and 199.
86 Kidambi 'Hero, celebrity' p.200.

87 Quoted by Ramachandra Guha 'Sachin Tendulkar' http://www.espncricinfo.com/wisdenalmanack/content/story/518339.html Posted 2010, Access 22 November 2016.
88 Rahul Tandon 'Sachin Tendulkar: worshipped by Hindus as a living god' http://www.bbc.co.uk/religion/0/24910759 Posted 15 November 2013, Access 22 November 2016.
89 BBC News 'India comedian in trouble over video "mocking" Tendulkar' http://www.bbc.co.uk/news/world-asia-india-36411569 Posted 30 May 2016, Access 22 November 2016.
90 Michael Lind 'The Economist's phony "progressivism"' http://www.salon.com/2012/10/15/the_economist_magazine%E2%80%99s_phony_%E2%80%9Cprogressivism%E2%80%9D/ Posted 15 October 2012, Access 22 November 2016.
91 Astill *The Great* p.55.
92 Sen 'History without a past' p.107.
93 Sen 'History without a past' p.104.
94 Quoted in Astill *The Great* p.53.
95 Marqusee *War Minus* p.268.
96 Arundhati Roy *Capitalism: A Ghost Story* London: Verso 2015 pp.8–9. See also Charlie Smith 'Arundhati Roy explains how corporations run India and why they want Narendra Modi as prime minister' http://www.straight.com/life/616401/arundhati-roy-explains-how-corporations-run-india-and-why-they-want-narendra-modi-prime-minister Posted 30 March 2014, Access 22 November 2016.
97 'Mukesh Ambani is wealthiest Indian cricket team owner, worth $21.2 bn: report' http://www.financialexpress.com/archive/mukesh-ambani-is-wealthiest-indian-cricket-team-owner-worth-212-bn-report/1243082/ Posted 23 April 2014, Access 22 November 2016.

Chapter 7

Cricket in a hard country
Pakistani cricket since 1947

In 2011 the historian and former *Times* correspondent Anatol Lieven published a book called *Pakistan: A Hard Country*.[1] Asked, in a subsequent interview at the Australian National University, to explain the book's title, he replied that Pakistan was a hard country to govern and similarly hard to understand. The phrase had cropped up, he added, in a number of private conversations with Pakistanis – most memorably one with a member of parliament who had told of having to have five people killed the previous year, in retaliation for the murder of his nephew. This had been necessary, the politician explained, because 'this is a hard country'.[2] The first part of this chapter will provide a brief elaboration of this widespread view of Pakistani society, and the remaining sections will relate it to the development of the nation's cricket culture. This latter section will draw in particular on two substantial histories of Pakistani cricket, one by the conservative, but conspicuously open-minded, journalist and historian Peter Oborne[3] and one by Cricinfo writer Osman Samiuddin.[4]

Aside from being widely designated as a hard country, Pakistan is also a young one, having been founded as recently as August 1947. Its survival has frequently been cast in doubt. In 1983 the socialist writer Tariq Ali published a book entitled *Can Pakistan Survive? The Death of a State*[5] and analyses of the country refer routinely to the country's 'long-term challenges'[6] and to the 'traumatic political history and the ongoing crisis of governability'[7] of Pakistan. For over half of its history Pakistan has been governed by military dictatorship and an elected Pakistani government did not complete its term of office until 2013. The country's interlocking political 'challenges' can be explained as follows.

First, Pakistan is the result of an arbitrary partition of India dictated by Britain as the departing imperial power. Under the terms of partition India took 90% of industry, 80% of population (around 390 million at the beginning of 1947) and most of the military. The western and eastern segments of the country were separated by 1,200 miles.[8] While some writers have asserted that Pakistan has a national ideology rooted in Islam[9] there is strong ground for doubting that Islamism, or any other ideology, unites the Pakistani nation. After all, Islamic codes were, to a degree, imposed from above in Pakistan, notably by the Pakistan People's Party administration of Zulfikar Ali Bhutto who in 1977 banned gambling and decreed that Friday, not Sunday, would be the nation's holy day. These reforms were then extended to encompass sharia law by the military dictatorship of General Zia-ul-Haq, who deposed Bhutto in a coup the same year. Local nationalisms have been another factor militating against a national ideology: as Geoff Brown points out, Pakistan was constituted out a number of territories which already had strong cultural and national identities – at partition, there were, for example, six major linguistic groups, among which speakers of Urdu, the new official language, accounted for only 8% of the population.[10] Moreover, Balochistan, one of the provinces of the new Pakistan, was only incorporated by military force in 1948[11] and Bengali nationalism resulted in the secession of East Pakistan to form Bangladesh in 1971. Amid the continued flourishing (and suppression) of these local nationalisms, the maintenance of India as Pakistan's permanent enemy neighbour assumed a vital importance in cohering Pakistani society: as Brown argues, for the Pakistani elite 'the myth of India as a permanent threat is indispensable'.[12] This has two crucial implications for the nation's cricket: (a) outside of the residing international hostility with India, cricket – which now, according to an influential history of the Pakistani game, inspires a genuine enthusiasm across Pakistan's social classes and regions[13] – is a powerful element in an otherwise fractured national identity and (b) cricket matches between India and Pakistan have become commercially and politically potent metaphors for the wider conflict.

Ongoing rivalry with India is but one reason for the existence in Pakistan of a strong and influential military. Another is the Cold War – a war primarily of propaganda and diplomatic manoeuvre between the United States and the Soviet Union (USSR) and their respective allies which lasted from the late 1940s to the late 1980s. Mindful that for much of its early history independent India had had warm relations with the USSR, the United States government was concerned to prevent the entire Indian subcontinent becoming allied to the Soviet Union.[14] As Tariq Ali convincingly argues, Pakistan has, for most of its history, been beholden to US strategic interests[15] and the country has often been analysed through the prism of those strategic interests – for example, one of the most influential writers on Pakistan has been Stephen Philip Cohen, a fellow of the Washington 'think tank', the Brookings Institution, a body very influential in the forming of US government policy.[16]

The Pakistani state is heavily dependent on US funding, much of which returns immediately to the United States to pay defence contractors for military hardware.[17] In 2006 spending on the army and the state bureaucracy, along with debt repayments, accounted for 80% of state spending.[18] Thus, comparatively little is spent on welfare and, as Cohen observes, spending on health, education and social services declined under the martial law imposed by General Zia between 1977 and 1988. Despite acquiring nuclear weapons in 1998, Pakistan remains a very poor country: in 2014 it was ranked 147th out of 188 countries in the United Nations Development Programme Human Development Index.[19] A big factor here is that the Pakistan government has very little tax revenue: as Lieven has noted, only around 1% of Pakistanis pay tax.[20] This increases the burden on Pakistan's poor, 50 million of whom were living in absolute poverty in the early twenty-first century.[21] It also means that, consonant with Lieven's identification of Pakistan as a 'hard country', much power rests with non-state actors. These latter include: the forty wealthy families that, according to a survey in 2007 by *Dawn*, the country's leading newspaper, dominate Pakistani industry and commerce;[22] wealthy landowners; and tribal chieftains – the word 'feudals' often being using to denote the last two groups.[23] In Sindh, wrote Tariq Ali in 2008, 'the old-fashioned feudal landlords . . . continue to administer justice, dominate politics, [and] rule their fiefdoms with an iron hand'.[24] The country runs to a significant degree on patronage. 'The truth is', observed Lieven in 2012, 'that Pakistani politics revolves in large part around politicians' extraction of resources from the state by means of corruption, and their distribution to those politicians' followers through patronage. Radically changing this would mean gutting the existing Pakistani political system like a fish'.[25] Pakistani cricket would scarcely have survived without patronage, much of it from the state.

Pakistan's relationship with the United States became more complicated in 1978 after the Soviet army moved into neighbouring Afghanistan to defend the left-wing government there. The American Central Intelligence Agency (CIA) launched Operation Cyclone, which funded a group of principally non-Afghan Islamist fighters led by Saudi militant Osama bin Laden to drive the Soviet army out. This operation was successful but the Islamists had been motivated by *jihad* (a holy war on unbelievers) and some eventually turned on the United States, in 2001 using hijacked planes to perpetrate attacks on the US Defense Department in Virginia and the World Trade Center in New York.[26] US President George W. Bush now declared a 'war on terror' in which he demanded that Pakistan co-operate – indeed his emissary, Deputy Secretary of State Richard Armitage, threatened Pakistan's military ruler General Pervez Musharraf that the US would bomb Pakistan 'back into the Stone Age' if they did not.[27] This presented Pakistan with an intractable problem. Groups now defined by Western interests as 'terrorists' were in many cases groups in the border regions which the Pakistani state was using as proxies in the ongoing defence against Indian incursion.[28] These self-same groups, however, were a threat to the Pakistani state, especially since traditional tribal elders were being replaced by more militant Islamists.[29] As Stephen P. Cohen observed in 2003, these groups sought revolutionary changes in Pakistan's social and political order:

With little mass support in this deeply Islamic yet still moderate country, radical Islamists have not been able to successfully conduct an Islamic coup to seize the levers of government, and they stand little chance of doing so within the next five years. Beyond that, however, Pakistan's future is uncertain. The political dominance and institutional integrity of the Pakistani army remains the chief reason for the marginality of radical Islamic groups.[30]

Thus, Pakistan must continue to support many of these groups, but, at the same time, keep them at bay. The logic of this situation is that, at most, the army can secure Pakistan's political order but it cannot protect public safety, as was proved in 2009 when gunmen believed to be from Lashkar-e-Taiba (Army of the Righteous) fired on a bus carrying the Sri Lankan cricket team to a Test match in Lahore. Six policemen and two civilians were killed and several of the cricketers injured. Five years earlier, the group had condemned cricket as 'an evil and sinful sport'.[31] As a result of the attack, Bangladesh called off Pakistan's coming visit and New Zealand cancelled its scheduled tour of Pakistan. Since 2009, the Pakistan team has played all its matches abroad.

'When there is no war. . .': Pakistan cricket after partition

We have seen in other chapters – Chapter 2, for instance – that cricket culture in the 1950s was presided over principally by an anglophile elite. As Peter Oborne points out, unlike for other parts of the subcontinent, the British had come to the territory that would become Pakistan through conquest, and not trade. This had engendered considerable hostility, most vividly expressed in an uprising of 1857, known as the 'Indian Mutiny' in Britain, but to many in northern India (including Pakistan's first Test captain, Abdul Hafeez Kardar) as the 'First War of Independence'. Such political unrest had in 1878 prompted the founding, by pragmatic Muslims with British support,[32] of the Mohammedan Anglo-Oriental College at Aligarh in Uttar Pradesh. The college had married Islam to a largely Western higher education and thus produced an anglicised elite.[33] Cricket was part of the curriculum. Comparable institutions included Government College (founded 1864), Aitchison boys' college (1886) and Islamia College (1892); all these colleges were situated in Lahore (with Karachi, one of the two centres of early Pakistani cricket culture) and all produced Pakistani Test cricketers.

As we saw in the previous chapter, the nation of Pakistan was formed in haste and resultant chaos. Amid this chaos the country's cricket in the 1940s and 50s leaned heavily on the anglophile elite trained in these colleges. Understandably they resisted a suggestion from the BCCI official Anthony

De Mello that they continue to play Test cricket under Indian auspices.[34] Instead they hosted the West Indies in November of the following year and the Board of Cricket Control Pakistan (BCCP) was formed in 1949, largely at the instigation of the patrician figure of Alvin Robert Cornelius, a Cambridge–educated legal philosopher (and future Chief Justice) from a landowning family,[35] confidant of the country's founder Mohammad Ali Jinnah and leading light at the Lahore Gymkhana Cricket Club. Pakistan, now with Indian support, was awarded Test status in 1952 and the same year Cornelius founded the Pakistan Eaglets, a national youth team that toured Britain and more locally (Ceylon and Malaya) during the 1950s and early 60s.

The first cricketer to captain Pakistan was, as noted, the Punjabi Abdul Hafeez Kardar. Kardar, politically and culturally, was a man of his time. Born into the Arain landowning tribe, Kardar had the classic social profile: having attended Islamia College and Oxford University he had played cricket in the Ranji Trophy for Northern India and represented India in three Tests. Kardar, like so many of Pakistan's social (and cricket) elite, was an anglophile, having played county cricket for Warwickshire and married the daughter of the club secretary, but he was also a Pakistani nationalist, having acquired a 'post-colonial sensibility'.[36] He led Pakistan to their first Test victory (in Lucknow in 1952) and in 1954 stood proudly on the pavilion balcony at Surrey's Oval ground in acknowledgement of their maiden win over England. Importantly he and others expressed strong indignation when in 1956 a number of touring England players, piqued by several of his decisions, poured a bucket of water over umpire Idris Begh, insisting on an apology for what the England party regarded merely as a prank.[37] (This incident is instructive and Peter Oborne devotes an entire chapter to it in his impressive history.[38] Oborne shows that the incident was taken seriously by the British cricket authorities but with some ambivalence – on the one hand, they were concerned to assert their respect for Pakistani officialdom and offered to bring the England team home in disgrace – but, on the other, there was the private suggestion that the decisions of Pakistani umpires were suspect, due to political pressure. As evidence for this, tour manager Geoffrey Howard pointed to the fact that the chair of the BCCP was a state appointment and that, therefore, cricket in Pakistan was 'under government control'.)[39]

The infrastructure of Pakistani cricket was understandably weak during the 1950s and early 60s. The kinship network, so celebrated by historians such as Lieven, was strongly in evidence. Mohammad Jahangir Khan, captain of North India and another Cambridge graduate, was from a family of cricketers and became a selector for the national side: his nephews Javed Burki (25 Tests 1960–9) and Imran Khan (88 Tests 1971–92) would both captain Pakistan, as would his son Majid (63 Tests 1964–83). Burki recently commented that the Pakistan team of the 1950s was, essentially, the Punjab

University side of 1947.[40] Moreover the patronage system, similarly prominent in Indian cricket, was important in the funding of clubs, tours, training camps[41] and new venues – the latter being in short supply, although a new stadium was opened in Lahore in 1959.

Cricket at the time of partition had a comparatively narrow social and geographical base, being rejected for its British associations, according to Oborne, in the northern Pashtun belt and little practised outside the middle classes of Karachi, Lahore, Rawalpindi and Bahawalpur (where the second Test to be played in Pakistan was staged).[42] Nevertheless the Pakistani public took to Test cricket and there were large and enthusiastic crowds for the first home Test series against India in 1955[43]: all five matches were drawn. This public fervour can be ascribed to two mutually supportive factors – the fact that India were the opposition (in 1952 Kardar had suggested playing India annually)[44] and emergent Pakistani national identity. Politicians of all stripes were increasingly aware of the popularity of cricket: General Ayub Khan, who assumed power in a military coup in 1958 once remarked: 'When war is not on, the best place for the promotion of team spirit is the sports field'.[45] General Khan nevertheless referred to the Pakistan players as 'goondas'[46] (a colloquialism for 'rogues' or 'roughnecks') in need of firm discipline (to be administered by the captain – Kardar or his successor, fast bowler Fazal Mahmood, a senior police officer) and, in this regard, a 'masters and men' culture prevailed in the dressing room, rather as it did in other Test-playing countries, such as England, during the same period.

First-class cricket in Pakistan was somewhat haphazard in the 1950s. The Quaid-e-Azam Trophy was introduced in 1953, chiefly at the instigation of Cornelius. Named for Jinnah ('quaid-e-azam' means 'great leader' in Urdu) and reputedly modelled on the English county championship[47] it initially featured nine teams. Because of the prevalence of patronage and with the lack of a residence qualification, the best players soon gravitated to particular clubs, notably Bahawalpur, who recruited the brothers Hanif Mohammad (55 Tests 1952–69) and Wazir Mohammad (20 Tests 1952–9), members of another notable Pakistani cricketing dynasty, and Sindh, who were funded by the Pir (spiritual leader) of Pagaro.[48] One season (1955–6) saw no first-class cricket at all outside of the Test series against visiting New Zealand, but two years later the Quaid-e-Azam Trophy had swelled to fifteen teams.[49]

Samiuddin describes the 1960s, some domestic growth notwithstanding, as the lost decade of Pakistani cricket. This is for several reasons. First, the make-do-and-mend stewardship of patrician amateurs which had hitherto sustained the nation's cricket was now seen as inadequate: for example, as noted, the team touring England in 1962 was said by its own captain (Javed Burki, 23 at the time, a civil servant and the son of a general who had dismissed the civilian government in 1958)[50] to be 'not good enough' and its manager, Brigadier Haider, a polo enthusiast, knew disconcertingly little about cricket.⁵¹ Second, there was another war with India in 1965 and, third, a war of secession with East Pakistan which culminated in the founding of Bangladesh in 1971 (see Chapter 8). Finally, some of the country's best players, such as Mushtaq Mohammad, were away for years qualifying to play for English counties – Mushtaq for five years (1962–7). Between autumn 1962 and autumn 1964 and again between midsummer 1965 and midsummer 1967, Pakistan played no Test cricket.

There had been clear gains, however: in January 1958 23-year-old Hanif Mohammed had proved his and Pakistan's durability by batting for over sixteen hours to save a Test against a strong West Indies side in Bridgetown, scoring 337 in the process.⁵² This had established a Pakistani alongside the most accomplished batsmen of the Old ('white') Commonwealth (Bradman, Hutton, Hammond . . .) and remains the longest Test innings ever played. Moreover, the growth of radio had begun to popularise the game. Radio Pakistan broadcast from five cities by 1960 and cheap transistor radios brought Test match commentary into myriad homes and public spaces.⁵³ Commentary was for most of the 1960s in English (the favoured language of the Pakistani elite) but Samiuddin argues that the populace at large (including many Urdu speakers, for whom summaries were provided in their native tongue) had a 'phonetic understanding of English'. The game was thus democratised, drawing in males and females alike to the sense of occasion that attended a Test match.⁵⁴

It is also widely argued that the playing of cricket became similarly more democratised in Pakistan during the 1960s and 70s. A big factor here was the state-sponsored television service, instigated by Ayub Khan in 1964 and able to bring Test cricket to most parts of the country by 1969: the first Test to be televised was the First Test against New Zealand in Karachi in October of that year.

Trends begun in the 1960s were accentuated in the 1970s, a decade in which several interlocking political developments in Pakistani cricket stand out.

First, as in India, there was a transition from individual to corporate patronage. In 1971, following the war with East Pakistan and subsequent secession of Bangladesh, the presidency of Pakistan fell to Zulfikar Ali Bhutto, scion of a landowning dynasty in Sindh province and leader of the recently formed Pakistan Peoples Party (PPP). Bhutto immediately embarked on what has been called a 'Nasserite' economic policy, using the state apparatus to stimulate capitalist development,⁵⁵ adopting radical postures and nationalising a range of banks and businesses. Amid mounting financial crisis (brought on in large part by rising oil prices) he also moved to strengthen cultural bonds, increasingly invoking Islam (for example, as we have seen, by banning alcohol in 1977)⁵⁶ and calling for the consolidation of the national cricket team. For the latter task, he conscripted Kardar, already a member of the PPP and a government minister, who now became president of the BCCP. Kardar moved to co-opt banks and other major industries – some nationalised and some (like the mammoth Dawood Group in Karachi and the Lahore-based retailer Servis Industries) not – in the financing of cricket and cricketers. These companies would now not only run teams, but, as in India, they would offer their players careers in commerce.[57]

Second, financial possibilities were in any event expanding for the cricketers of Pakistan, as in other nations. Domestic cricket competition was expanding, with new trophies, including a one-day competition sponsored by Servis, begun in 1974, and, as an ex-county player himself, Kardar was mindful of the career opportunities available in England. Indeed, money became a serious issue in 1976 when, before the scheduled Second Test against New Zealand in Hyderabad six Pakistani players refused to play unless offered better terms. Kardar, like officials in other Test-playing nations in comparable circumstances, assumed the traditional 'I'd-play-for-my-country-for-nothing' position, but Bhutto, recognising commercial realities, overruled him and settled with the players.[58] Tensions escalated the following year when nine Pakistani players were recruited to Kerry Packer's World Series cricket tournament in Australia. Once again the country-versus-commerce arguments were aired and the players concerned were styled as 'Packeristanis' by the cricket press. Kardar suspended the players in question and Pakistan's new military ruler, who had seized power in the country's latest military coup, made a public display of disgust at the Packer enterprise, calling it a prostitution of the game.[59] Nevertheless, realising that the players – no longer, as with Ayub, dismissible as 'goondas' – were vital to the national interest, Zia, like Bhutto before him, overruled Kardar, made peace with Packer and, in January 1978, returned the 'Packeristanis' to the national team.[60] Zia, like previous Pakistani rulers, was keen to boost nationalist feeling by renewing cricket rivalry with India, whom Pakistan had not played for seventeen years.[61] Moreover, despite his claims that the game was being prostituted, the commercialisation of Pakistani cricket increased under Zia and Lt. Gen. Azhar Khan, whom he appointed to run the BCCP. Arif Abbasi, the man charged with commercialising the Pakistani game successfully sought sponsorship from the tobacco industry and Pepsi Cola.[62]

Third, the Pakistani team had now established a credibility and attractiveness in international cricket. While the Test victories in Lucknow (the country's first, in 1952) and the Oval (the first against the imperial power, in 1954) had been important rites of passage, beating Australia at Sydney in 1977 is held by Pakistani cricket's leading historians to be an important coming of age. The manner of the win was important partly in that the Pakistan players learned to respond in kind to the often intimidatory tactics of the Australians by trading one 'sledging' remark for another. As Samiuddin suggests, Pakistan went into the game 'sweet boys' and came out of it 'hardened men', drawing a big crowd as they did so.[63] They played what one writer has called 'vernacular cricket', an expressive game arguably attributable to the widening social base of the nation's cricket .[64]

In practice, this had meant an increased intake of lower-born players, many of them from the Karachi area, which had a large population of Mohajirs (or Muslim Urdu speakers who had migrated from North Indian regions after the creation of Pakistan). These included Hanif Mohammad and his brother Mushtaq (55 Tests 1959–79) the former having accused Kardar of snobbery.[65] In 1973 the 'Oxbridge' elite had still been at the helm: when Pakistan hosted England the two Test captains were Majid Khan and Welshman Tony Lewis, who had been at Cambridge together.[66] Four years later Pakistan's captain was Imran Khan, who represented both the passing of the old era and the ushering in of the new. Imran was Pakistan's first and, arguably, only global celebrity. As Oborne suggests, he had a princely aura without actually being a prince.[67] Certainly, he was well-connected – Javed Burki and Majid Khan (as noted, the son of Jahangir Khan, a founding father of Pakistani cricket) were his cousins – and he was an Oxford graduate, but the Khans, who were Pashtuns, ranked well below the country's social elite and its fabled forty families: Imran's father was a civil engineer and the family home was in the affluent Zaman Park suburb of Lahore.[68] Contrary to his princely bearing and to the patrician ethos promoted by men such as Kardar, Imran had embraced the professionalism and commercialism of the Kerry Packer project and, as a leading 'Packeristani', had refused to play for Pakistan until he was offered more money.[69] In an act symbolic of the coming of a more professional era in Pakistani cricket, Imran dropped his cousin Majid from the Test team in 1982. Kamran Abbasi recently wrote of Majid: 'All grace and fluency, Majid Khan played in the spirit of an English amateur of a bygone era. He had a distant air which sometimes gave the impression that he wasn't really trying.'[70] Imran and Majid did not speak again for twenty-five years.[71]

By the late 1970s cricket had replaced hockey as Pakistan's favourite sport[72] and, in 1984, in another indication of their growing stature in the cricket world Pakistan, jointly with India, was selected to stage the cricket World Cup of 1987.[73]

'They could bowl England out with an orange': Pakistani cricket, racism and diaspora in the global era

Peter Oborne has compared the following attracted by the Pakistan cricket team in the latter part of the twentieth century to the fervour inspired by the Brazilian football team.[74] And, as with the Brazilian footballers, their admirers were scattered well beyond their home country. As a number of academic studies show, Pakistani cricketers became celebrities across the Pakistani diaspora and helped to fashion the identities of a generation of Pakistanis born outside of Pakistan.[75] The team's celebrity grew along with the global media: when Pakistan beat India in the final of the Austral-Asia

Cup in Sharjah in 1986 (with a dramatic six off the final ball) there were an estimated one billion people watching.[76] But the post-Imran period (he played the last of his 88 Tests in 1992) has been scarred by a succession of controversies, the construction of which by the Western media and cricket officialdom has brought (often wholly justified) accusations of racism from the Pakistani cricket fraternity and elsewhere.

As we have seen, English cricketers and management were wont from the early days of Pakistani Test cricket to regard Pakistani umpires as biased. Tension with match officials was high when Pakistan toured England in 1982 and Imran objected to a number of their decisions; when Pakistan returned in 1987 they asked, unsuccessfully, for one umpire, David Constant, to be removed from the panel.[77] The following winter England captain Mike Gatting was involved in a furious on-field row with Pakistani umpire Shakoor Rana during the Second Test at Faisalabad; the England tour was put in jeopardy until the English Test and County Cricket Board ordered Gatting to apologise.[78] Pakistan became the first country to invite neutral umpires to stand in a Test series – against West Indies in 1986.

Beneath the diplomatic courtesies, the racial dimension of these wrangles was inescapable and provided the setting for a kind of post-colonial political theatre in which the former colonial subjects were framed as unreconstructed cheating natives while they in turn charged Britain with continued colonial arrogance. As with the abiding hostilities with India, this theatre strengthened Pakistani identity, at home and abroad, and fired the team with a sense of victimhood.[79] It was also meat and drink to the world's burgeoning and rapacious sports media. The British tabloids, for example, fell eagerly on a remark by England cricketer Ian Botham who, returning injured from a tour of Pakistan in 1984, had told an interviewer that Pakistan was the sort of place that you would send your mother-in-law for a month's holiday.[80] While this crass disparagement was noted in the Pakistani dressing room (when England played Pakistan in the World Cup Final of 1992 in Melbourne and Botham was out without scoring Pakistani player Aamer Sohail is said to have asked Botham 'Who's coming in next? Your mother-in-law?')[81] it was frequently matched by the British press. Oborne records a series of racially charged denunciations of the Pakistan team and their supporters (the latter styled as 'hordes' by David Frith in *Wisden Cricket Monthly*) in the cricket and national press in the late 1980s and early 90s, one writer calling the team 'pariahs'.[82] This commentary took place against a backdrop of racial disadvantage in Britain and a politically cultivated fear of the dark 'enemy within'. In 1978 as Leader of the Opposition, Margaret Thatcher (Prime Minister 1979–90) had set the tone when she had told a TV interviewer:

> If we went on as we are then by the end of the century there would be four million people of the new Commonwealth or Pakistan here. Now, that is an awful lot and I think it means that people are really

rather afraid that this country might be rather swamped by people with a different culture. The British character has done so much for democracy, for law and done so much throughout the world that if there is any fear that it might be swamped, people are going to react and be rather hostile to those coming in.[83]

Pakistani players knew how this political mood played out at street level: Imran Khan, for example, had encountered the phenomenon of 'Paki bashing' in Worcester when he had played for the county in the early 1970s.[84] As a media trope anti-Pakistani rhetoric has been used to fashion three distinct cricket narratives.

First, the Pakistan team was widely depicted once again as cheats – in this case for tampering with the ball during games. In New Zealand in 1990 the Pakistani bowlers Waqar Younis and Wasim Akram achieved what became known in cricket circles as 'reverse swing' – i.e. they made the swing either way in the air – or, alternatively, they persuaded a worn-out cricket ball to behave abnormally. This was a skill rare in the game and was said to have been developed by the Pakistan and Northamptonshire bowler Sarfraz Nawaz (55 Tests 1969–84).[85] During a one-day international at Lord's in 1992, an England player, Allan Lamb, notified the umpires that the ball had been tampered with. The match referee, ex-West Indies Test cricketer Deryck Murray, changed the ball, but refused to say under what rule he had done so. England coach Micky Stewart remarked enigmatically to the press that the ball had been doing strange things and 'I know why'.[86] The majority of the British cricket commentariat made much of this incident and various lurid accounts of Pakistani cheating were written, most notably a full-length book by a leading umpire and a BBC commentator, calling it 'what many believed to be the biggest scandal in modern cricket'.[87] Despite a tempest of tabloid hostility, however, doubt was soon cast on these accusations. Waqar and Wasim both played county cricket and no objection to their bowling had been raised on the circuit;[88] besides, their fellow bowlers had been unable to achieve comparable effects with same ball. Ex-England and Yorkshire cricketer Geoffrey Boycott reminded everyone that Wasim and Waqar were talented bowlers who could bowl out England batsmen 'with an orange'.[89] And, as Chris Rumford has pointed out, in the Ashes series of 2005, when England bowlers Andrew Flintoff and Simon Jones achieved reverse swing they were highly praised.[90] Imran was one of many who argued that attempting to change the condition of the cricket ball was, in any event, as old as the game itself.[91] (The best accounts of the controversy are by Mike Marqusee[92] and the biographer of Wasim and Waqar, John Crace.[93] In 2006 Rabindra Mehta, once a schoolmate of Imran Khan, former club fast bowler and now a NASA scientist based in California, published a detailed scientific explanation of the various forms of swing bowling.[94])

Second, the death of Pakistan's coach, the ex-England cricketer Bob Woolmer, provoked a further rehearsal of cultural stereotypes in the

Western media. Woolmer died in Jamaica. Pakistan had just been eliminated from the World Cup of 2007 by Ireland, an able, but non-Test-playing, team. The following day Woolmer was found dead in his hotel bathroom. Days later the Jamaican police decided that he had been murdered. This was the signal for a sustained bout of 'orientalist'[95] cultural stereotyping of Pakistani society by the British media. A study by researchers Dominic Malcolm, Alan Bairner and Graham Curry shows that it was suggested that: Pakistani players were in fear of death at the hands of 'mobs' of their supporters; that Asian bookmakers, linked to organised crime, the terror group Al Qaeda and/or Saudi jihadist Osama bin Laden were thought to be behind the murder; that the episode was a 'typical Pakistani shambles' characteristic of a society riddled by nepotism and corruption; that Woolmer had been killed with a poison used for assassinations back in Pakistan; that Woolmer had been alienated from his players, who spoke Urdu (which he couldn't understand) and called prayer meetings that clashed with training sessions; and that the players either were, or were influenced by, Islamic fanatics and that a 'fatwa'[96] had been put on Woolmer. These toxic flights of fancy worked to portray Pakistan (a country in the ascendancy in international cricket politics) as dysfunctional and, by implication, England (a nation with diminishing influence in international cricket politics) as superior.[97] (Woolmer, a diabetic in indifferent health, is now widely thought to have died of natural causes. The jury at the inquest on his death returned an open verdict.)

The third area of controversy concerns match-fixing. Although this term encompasses agreements to procure a specific outcome of a sporting encounter, it most commonly refers to 'spot-fixing' – that is, conspiracy, usually with bookmakers, to stage particular (usually minor) incidents during a match, a device to which the game of cricket is ideally suited. Allegations of match-fixing in cricket have grown alongside the increased availability of the game on television and the spread of the internet and online betting platforms, accessible from mobile phones. In the case of the Pakistani cricket team, talk along these lines began around 1980 under the captaincy of Asif Iqbal[98] and Imran Khan has stated that several of his players were approached by bookmakers during the Austral-Asia Cup of 1990 in Sharjah; he dealt with this by betting all the team's money on a Pakistan winning the trophy, which they did.[99] The talk became louder during the captaincy of Salim Malik (1993–5). An official inquiry was launched into match-fixing under High Court Justice Qayyan; the report, submitted in 2000, named Malik as the most culpable and banned him from cricket for life.[100]

Most media attention, however, has centred on incidents during the Fourth Test between England Pakistan at Lord's in August 2010. As a result of an undercover operation by reporters from the British tabloid newspaper the *News of the World* three Pakistani players were found to have accepted money to ensure that no balls were bowled at certain points in the match, thus facilitating lucrative spot-bets. Three of the players – the captain Salman Butt and fast bowlers Mohammad Asif and Mohammad Amir – received prison sentences the following year. This time the British popular press forwent its lexicon of derogatory cultural stereotypes and instead adopted a tone of moral censure and betrayal. The *News of the World*'s sister paper the *Sun* deployed their British Pakistani columnist Anila Baig, who was able to use the word 'we' in her condemnation of the convicted players:

> Salman Butt and Mohammad Asif are said to have dragged their game through the mud. In reality, it's far worse. Cricket is Pakistan's national game – loved by the very young to the very old. People have even delayed prayer times to catch games. You can't help but be carried away by the euphoria of a brilliant game. Knowing how precious it is to so many countrymen – and at the moment there isn't much for Pakistanis to celebrate – these players did the unthinkable. Pakistan has been called a failed state and has always been perilous politically. But with cricket at least we could compete with the rest of the world and hold our heads high.[101]

The citizens of a 'failed state' (among whom the correspondent placed herself), had, in other words, been robbed of one of their few consolations.

Several things, however, must be said in mitigation of the idea that Pakistan is home to the sole, or even the main, perverters of contemporary sport. First, illicit relationships between leading cricketers and bookmakers have been proven in Australia (where ex-Test players Mark Waugh and Shane Warne admitted receiving money from a bookmaker for information supplied over the period 1994–5), in South Africa (with the spectacular public disgrace of Test captain Hansie Cronje in 1996), in India (whose captain Mohammad Azharuddin was banned for life in 2000) and in England (where the Essex bowler Mervyn Westfield received a four-month prison sentence for spot-fixing in 2012). Second, top-class cricket is played by only ten countries, of which Pakistan is among the most populous and enthusiastic, but it is widely asserted that the bookmakers involved in fixing are based India or the United Arab Emirates. Moreover, betting on cricket is illegal in both India and Pakistan so this branch of bookmaking comes inevitably under the ambit of organised crime, thus making players likely to be subject to serious threats if they do not co-operate. Finally, the investigative journalist Declan Hill suggested in 2013 that, if the argument was widened to cover professional sport generally, and football in particular, then match-fixing was now a worldwide and flourishing phenomenon:

> The fixers have operated in Asia, Africa, Latin America, North America and, particularly, Europe. There is now a line of badly affected leagues that is slowly moving west across Europe. Essentially, they dovetail with the former Soviet Empire, so countries like Bulgaria, Poland or

Hungary have all been badly hit. Few football fans in those countries regard their sport with any degree of serious credibility. However, it is not exclusively an ex-Soviet phenomenon – Turkey, Greece and Italy have also been hit with massive corruption scandals. What the current Europol investigation clearly demonstrates is that the line is moving closer to the UK. For example, Germany, Belgium, Switzerland, Austria and Finland have all had scandals linked to fixed matches. This summer Norway had its first taste of the infamy that the fixers can bring to a league when there were suspicious matches in their third division.[102]

Conclusion

The immediate prospects for Pakistan's indigenous cricket culture are not good. As noted, at the time of writing Pakistan has staged no international cricket since the attack on the Sri Lankan team in 2009. The Gaddafi Stadium in Lahore (so named by Prime Minister Bhutto in 1974 in honour of the Libyan Muslim leader Muammar Gaddafi) lies dormant. An initial attempt to launch a Pakistani Super League failed (although it was successfully re-floated in Dubai) and Pakistan-based Pakistani cricket supporters have had to make do with regional cricket and exhibition games against non-Test opposition, such as Kenya, who visited in 2014. The PCCB is losing substantial revenue through its current isolation, but there seems little immediate prospect of it ending.[103] Although they were briefly Number 1 Test side in August 2016, as Oborne observes, Pakistan now play Test cricket in unsupportive settings, such as Dubai, which has no cricket tradition to speak of and where numerous Pakistani guest workers have neither the money nor the time to attend.[104]

Notes

1. Anatol Lieven *Pakistan: A Hard Country* New York: Public Affairs 2011.
2. Anatol Lieven in conversation with Andrew Carr https://www.youtube.com/watch?v=JUIICFHq_wU Posted 6 September 2012, Access 9 December 2016.
3. Peter Oborne *Wounded Tiger: A History of Cricket in Pakistan* London: Simon and Schuster 2015.
4. Osman Samiuddin *The Unquiet Ones: A History of Pakistan Cricket*: Noida, Uttar Pradesh: Harper Sport 2014.
5. Tariq Ali *Can Pakistan Survive? The Death of a State* Harmondsworth: Pelican 1983.
6. Ian Talbot *Pakistan: A New History* London: C. Hurst & Co. 2012 p.243.
7. M.P. Singh and Veena Kukreja in Veena Kukreja and M.P. Singh (eds.) *Pakistan: Democracy, Development and Security Issues* New Delhi: Sage 2006 p.11.
8. Geoff Brown 'Pakistan: on the edge of instability' *International Socialism* No.110 Spring 2006 pp.113–34, p.117.
9. See, for example, M.R. Kazimi *A Concise History of Pakistan* Oxford: Oxford University Press 2009 pp.177–83.
10. Brown 'Pakistan: on the edge' p.117.

11 Geoff Brown 'Pakistan: failing state or neoliberalism in crisis?' *International Socialism* No.150 Spring 2016 pp.143–77, p.155.
12 Brown 'Pakistan: failing state' p.150.
13 See Oborne *Wounded Tiger* pp.398–9.
14 Brown 'Pakistan: failing state' p.144.
15 Tariq Ali *The Duel: Pakistan on the Flight Path of American Power* London: Simon and Schuster 2008.
16 See, for example, Stephen Philip Cohen *The Idea of Pakistan* Washington DC: Brookings Institution Press 2004.
17 For example, in 2015 the Pakistan government concluded 'a $952 million deal [...] for 1,000 Hellfire missiles (made by Lockheed Martin) and 15 Textron TXT 0.98% built AH-1Z Viper attack helicopters' – see Clay Willow 'U.S. companies are making a killing on foreign military sales' http://fortune.com/2015/05/11/foreign-military-sales/ Posted 11 May 2015, Access 12 December 2016.
18 Brown 'Pakistan: on the edge' p.113.
19 See http://hdr.undp.org/en/data Access 12 December 2016.
20 Lieven *Pakistan: A Hard Country* p.12.
21 Brown 'Pakistan: on the edge' p.114.
22 Dilawar Hussain 'People who own greatest amount of wealth' *Dawn* 9 December 2007 http://www.dawn.com/news/279413 Access 12 December 2016.
23 Lieven *Pakistan: A Hard Country* pp.17–19.
24 Tariq Ali *The Duel* p.258.
25 Anatol Lieven 'Pakistan's culture of honourable corruption' *The Guardian* 19 January 2012 https://www.theguardian.com/commentisfree/2012/jan/19/pakistan-culture-honourable-corruption Access 12 December 2016.
26 See, for example, Ben Norton 'We created Islamic extremism: Those blaming Islam for ISIS would have supported Osama bin Laden in the '80s' http://www.salon.com/2015/11/17/we_created_islamic_extremism_those_blaming_islam_for_isis_would_have_supported_osama_bin_laden_in_the_80s/ Posted 17 November 2015, Access 12 December 2016.
27 Suzanne Goldenberg 'Bush threatened to bomb Pakistan, says Musharraf' *The Guardian* 22 September 2006 https://www.theguardian.com/world/2006/sep/22/pakistan.usa Access 12 December 2016.
28 Brown 'Pakistan: failing state' p.156.
29 Tariq Ali *The Duel* pp.249–50.
30 Stephen P. Cohen 'The jihadist threat to Pakistan' https://www.brookings.edu/articles/the-jihadist-threat-to-pakistan/ Posted 1 June 2003, Access 12 December 2016.
31 Amanda Hodge 'Islamists wage war against cricket, "the other religion"' *The Australian* 6 March 2009 http://www.theaustralian.com.au/archive/news/islamists-wage-war-against-cricket/news-story/4c92b129703865c383a2b8430db11f46?nk=508ed827b467284154ceae98b5a87f62-1481562695 Access 12 December 2016. The attack was initially believed to have been mounted by Lashkar-e-Taiba (Army of the Righteous), a Punjab-based terrorist group known to have carried out an attack in Mumbai the previous year. Latterly suspicion fell on Lashkar-e-Jhangvi (Army of Jhangvi), Sunni Muslim terrorists based in Lahore – see Rob Crilly '"Mastermind" behind Sri Lanka cricket team attack arrested' http://www.telegraph.co.uk/news/worldnews/asia/pakistan/9511292/Mastermind-behind-Sri-Lanka-cricket-team-attack-arrested.html Access 12 January 2017.
32 The chief local architect of this initiative was Syed Ahmad bin Muttaqi Khan, an Edinburgh University graduate and empire loyalist. He had financial support

from British administrators such as the Viceroy and Governor General of India Lord Northbrook.
33 Oborne *Wounded Tiger* pp.43–53.
34 Oborne *Wounded Tiger* p.17.
35 Samiuddin *The Unquiet Ones* pp.54–5.
36 Oborne *Wounded Tiger* p.134.
37 See Abhishek Mukherjee 'Abdul Hafeez Kardar: Father of Pakistan Cricket' http://www.cricketcountry.com/articles/abdul-hafeez-kardar-the-father-of-pakistan-cricket-22134 Posted 10 January 2016, Access 15 January 2017.
38 Oborne *Wounded Tiger* Chapter 7 pp.11–132.
39 Oborne *Wounded Tiger* p.130.
40 Samiuddin *The Unquiet Ones* p.134.
41 For example, Makhdoomzada Syed Hasan Mahmood, the Chief Minister of the Bahawalpur in south Punjab, financed a training camp for the Pakistan Test team in 1954 – see Samiuddin *The Unquiet Ones* p.66.
42 Oborne *Wounded Tiger* p.16. Samiuddin reports a thriving club scene in these cities during this period – *The Unquiet Ones* pp.42–6.
43 See Oborne *Wounded Tiger* p.107.
44 Oborne *Wounded Tiger* p.87.
45 Quoted in Oborne *Wounded Tiger* p.156.
46 Samiuddin *The Unquiet Ones* p.114.
47 See Chris Valiotis 'Cricket in "a nation perfectly imagined": identity and tradition in postcolonial Pakistan' in Stephen Wagg (ed.) *Cricket and National Identity in the Postcolonial Age* London: Routledge 2005 pp.110–31, pp.112–13.
48 See Oborne *Wounded Tiger* pp.91–2.
49 Samiuddin *The Unquiet Ones* p.95.
50 Oborne *Wounded Tiger* p.174.
51 Samiuddin *The Unquiet Ones* pp.117–22.
52 Arunabha Sengupta 'Hanif Mohammad's incredible 16-hour effort to save a Test match for Pakistan at Bridgetown' http://www.cricketcountry.com/articles/hanif-mohammad-s-incredible-16-hour-effort-to-save-a-test-match-for-pakistan-at-bridgetown-22312 Posted 8 January 2016, Access 16 January 2017.
53 Oborne *Wounded Tiger* pp.139–40.
54 Samiuddin *The Unquiet Ones* pp.179–82. See also Valiotis 'Cricket in "a nation perfectly imagined"' p.116.
55 See Brown 'Pakistan: failing state' p.148. The term refers to Gamal Abdul Nasser, Arab nationalist president of Egypt from 1956 to 1970.
56 Brown 'Pakistan: failing state' p.149.
57 Oborne *Wounded Tiger* pp.224–8. See also Samiuddin *The Unquiet Ones* pp.216–17.
58 See Oborne *Wounded Tiger* pp.250–2.
59 See Henry Blofeld *The Packer Affair* Newton Abbot: Readers' Union 1979 p.166.
60 See Oborne *Wounded Tiger* pp.262–9. See also David Frith 'World Series Cricket – January 1978' http://www.espncricinfo.com/ci/content/story/321809.html (Undated) Access 19 January 2017.
61 Oborne *Wounded Tiger* pp.269–70.
62 Oborne *Wounded Tiger* pp.442–3.
63 Samiuddin *The Unquiet Ones* p.201.
64 Valiotis 'Cricket in "a nation perfectly imagined"' p.115.
65 See Nadeem F. Paracha 'Pakistan cricket: a class, ethnic and sectarian history' http://www.dawn.com/news/1043800 Posted 19 September 2013, Access 19 January 2017.

66 Oborne *Wounded Tiger* p.237.
67 Oborne *Wounded Tiger* p.287.
68 Christopher Sandford *Imran Khan: The Biography* London: Harper Collins 2009 p.20.
69 Sandford *Imran Khan* p.81.
70 Kamran Abbasi 'Majid Khan' http://www.espncricinfo.com/pakistan/content/player/41919.html Access 20 January 2017.
71 Oborne *Wounded Tiger* p.293.
72 See Oborne *Wounded Tiger* p.441; Samiuddun *The Unquiet Ones* p.325.
73 Samiuddin *The Unquiet Ones* pp.298–302.
74 Oborne *Wounded Tiger* p.290.
75 See, for example, Pnina Werbner '"Our blood is green": cricket, identity and social empowerment among British Pakistanis' in Jeremy MacClancy (ed.) *Sport, Identity and Ethnicity* Oxford: Berg 1996 pp.87–111, and Thomas Michael Walle 'Cricket as "utopian homeland" in the Pakistani diasporic imagination' *South Asian Popular Culture* Volume 11, 2013 pp.301–12.
76 Oborne *Wounded Tiger* pp.312–13.
77 See Martin Williamson 'India's Constant problem' http://www.espncricinfo.com/magazine/content/story/775503.html Posted 30 August 2014, Access 20 January 2017.
78 Gatting's autobiography contains a lengthy defence of his conduct, written by his co-author – see Mike Gatting and Angela Patmore *Leading From the Front* London: Queen Anne Press/ Futura 1989 pp.293–325.
79 Samiuddin *The Unquiet Ones* p.353.
80 Dave Bowler *No Surrender: The Life and Times of Ian Botham* London: Orion 1997 p.108.
81 'When Aamer Sohail rubbed salt in Ian Botham's wounds' http://www.cricketcountry.com/criclife/when-aamer-sohail-rubbed-salt-in-ian-bothams-wounds-496067 Posted 29 October 2014, Access 21 January 2017.
82 Oborne *Wounded Tiger* pp.361–3.
83 Quoted in Jenny Bourne '"May we bring harmony"? Thatcher's legacy on "race"' Institute of Race Relations http://www.irr.org.uk/news/may-we-bring-harmony-thatchers-legacy-on-race/ Posted 11 April 2013, Access 21 January 2017.
84 Sandford *Imran Khan* p.78.
85 'Swing and seam bowling' http://news.bbc.co.uk/sport1/hi/cricket/england/4155734.stm Posted 19 August 2005, Access 21 January 2017.
86 Oborne *Wounded Tiger* p.364.
87 Don Oslear and Jack Bannister *Tampering With Cricket* London: Collins Willow 1996 p.213.
88 John Crace *Wasim and Waqar: Imran's Inheritors* London: Boxtree 1993 p.263.
89 Oborne *Wounded Tiger* pp.365–6; Samiuddin *The Unquiet Ones* p.472.
90 Chris Rumford 'Cricketing controversies: reverse swing, the doosra, and post-western dimensions of cricket's globality' in Chris Rumford and Stephen Wagg (eds.) *Cricket and Globalization* Newcastle: Cambridge Scholars Publishing 2010 pp.270–86, p.275.
91 See Sandford *Imran Khan* p.279.
92 Mike Marqusee *Anyone But England: An Outsider Looks at English Cricket* London: Aurum Press 2005 pp.156–204.
93 Crace *Wasim and Waqar* pp.260–79.
94 Rabindra Mehta 'The science of swing bowling' http://www.espncricinfo.com/magazine/content/story/258645.html Posted 6 September 2006, Access 14 February 2017.

95 The now widely acknowledged concept of 'orientalism' was coined by the Palestinian American academic Edward Said to refer to the prism of condescension through which Western writers have invariably viewed societies of the east: see Edward W. Said *Orientalism* New York: Vintage Books 1979.
96 This word actually means simply a ruling in Islamic law, but was widely used – and used here – to mean a death sentence.
97 See Dominic Malcolm, Alan Bairner and Graham Curry 'Cricket and cultural difference: Bob Woolmer's death and postcolonial relations' in Chris Rumford and Stephen Wagg (eds.) *Cricket and Globalization* Newcastle: Cambridge Scholars Publishing 2010 pp.231–51. See also Dominic Malcolm, Alan Bairner and Graham Curry '"Woolmergate": cricket and the representation of Islam and Muslims in the British press' *Journal of Sport and Social Issues* Vol.34 No.2 May 2010 pp.215–35.
98 See Oborne *Wounded Tiger* p.377.
99 See Sandford *Imran Khan* pp.240–1.
100 The report cam be read at: http://static.cricinfo.com/db/NATIONAL/PAK/NEWS/qayyumreport/qayyum_report.html Access 22 January 2017.
101 Anila Baig 'My view' *Sun* 2 November 2011 https://www.thesun.co.uk/archives/news/880003/pakistan-cricket-stars-face-jail-over-match-fix-scandal/ Access 22 January 2017.
102 Declan Hill 'Match-fixing: how gambling is destroying sport' http://www.bbc.co.uk/sport/football/21333930 Posted 5 February 2013, Access 22 January 2017.
103 See Sajid Sadiq 'Pakistan: Can players and fans dream of the return of cricket to their home country?' http://www.skysports.com/cricket/news/12172/9744896/pakistan-can-players-and-fans-dream-of-the-return-of-cricket-to-their-home-country Posted 5 March 2015, Access 22 January 2017.
104 Oborne *Wounded Tiger* p.495.

Chapter 8

'We rule here, you rule there'
Cricket in East Pakistan and Bangladesh since 1947

As we saw in the last chapter, Pakistan was created in haste and in two sections, over 1,200 miles apart, in 1947. As with the partition of India and Pakistan, the constituting of Pakistan in these two segments proved problematic from the very first and provoked tensions of a variously political, economic and cultural nature. These tensions culminated in civil war and in 1971 the secession of East Pakistan to become Bangladesh. In March of that year, following a meeting between East Pakistan leader Sheikh Mujibur Rahman and Pakistan Peoples Party leader Zulfikar Ali Bhutto (both, at the time, in gaol) Syed Abbas Athar, a journalist on the Pakistani newspaper the *Daily Azad*, had rendered the coming rift with the historic headline 'Idhar Hum, Udhar Tum' – Urdu for 'We Rule Here, You Rule There'.[1] This chapter describes the coming of the rift, the birth and progress of a new nation and the relationship of cricket to these developments.

'When you come back, you'll need a visa': cricket in a divided Pakistan

While friction between the western and eastern segments of Pakistan was clear from the outset, initial controversy centred on religion – Bengal, a major part of East Pakistan, was divided, purportedly, between the perceived Muslim and Hindu areas of that province, provoking immediate inter-communal strife – and language: the Language Movement (or *Bhasha Andolon*, begun in the early 1950s) opposed the designation of Urdu as the official Pakistani language and proposed Bengali instead. There were, however, also underlying economic difficulties. At partition the bulk of resources had gone to India and, within Pakistan, the West, bulwarked by Western (usually military) aid was comfortably the wealthier relation. The eastern part of the country (officially titled East Pakistan in 1956) was largely rural (80% of its labour force worked in agriculture) and principally produced raw materials.[2] Tensions were heightened and public opinion in the east was already turning against Pakistan's founding political party, the Muslim League, when, in 1954, the One Unit programme was introduced.

Under this programme the various provinces making up the western wing of Pakistan were amalgamated into one unit, primarily to save administrative expense,[3] but the scheme, making for a disproportionately large unit in the west, added to the sense of grievance in the east of the country.

This sense of grievance was undoubtedly shared by some of the region's many cricketers. Cricket had been played in Calcutta (now Kolkata), the major city of West Bengal, since the late eighteenth century and a Bengal side had begun competing in the Ranji Trophy in 1935, the year after the competition's inception. Following partition teams from eastern Pakistan competed in the nation's four leagues and an East Pakistan team regularly entered the national Quaid-e-Azam trophy between 1954 and 1968, by which time there was serious political friction between West and East Pakistan. Moreover, Dacca (later Dhaka, the capital of Bangladesh) had staged Pakistan's first home Test match, against India in January 1955. There had been a packed crowd in a stadium assembled in only seven weeks.[4] However, as Oborne notes, no player from East Pakistan was selected to play Test cricket for Pakistan before 1966 – a fact attributed to negligent local governance by some,[5] but to West Pakistani prejudice by many Bengalis.[6]

During the military dictatorship of General Ayub Khan (1958–69) support for the socialist Awami League grew in the east and the league's recurrent demands for autonomy were met with brutal repression. Even Bhutto, a civilian politician, whose power base was in the west, but who enjoyed much credibility on the left, was prepared to see 20,000 East Pakistanis killed to bring the region to heel.[7] Repression grew under Ayub's military successor, Yahya Khan, who, because he was a valued intermediary in their courting of China, was allowed by the United States to wreak further havoc in East Pakistan where the Pakistani army killed an estimated 300,000 people.[8] Yahya Khan was also noticeably slow to provide relief to East Pakistan following Cyclone Bhola which took around 500,000 lives, mainly in Bengal, in 1970.[9]

With growing unrest in its eastern wing the Pakistani government (always closely implicated in the decisions of the Board of Cricket Control Pakistan – BCCP) dictated that more important cricket fixtures be staged in the east of the country – for example, Dacca was given another Test, against England, in 1969.[10] Like the United States, the British government, fearing that the reins of Pakistani government might fall into the hands of the leftish Bhutto, was opposed to independence for East Pakistan and, despite the deaths and general mayhem in the country, the MCC had agreed to send a touring team. A condition had been that they would not have to play in Dacca but this only deepened feelings of grievance in the East and the Second Test was played in Dacca after all. According to one of the England players, fast bowler John Snow, 'that week in Dacca was probably the most nerve-wracking of my life. Day and night we could hear gunfire – some of it only yards from our hotel'.[11] The match passed off without incident, largely because, as another England player, batsman Tom Graveney, recalled, representatives of the students apparently in control of the city had met with the England side before the game and 'guaranteed that there would be no trouble'.[12] (The First and Third Tests, however, were disrupted by rioting. Public assemblies were banned by the military government and protesters used cricket matches to vent their anger.) The Pakistani authorities had also tried to appease the protesters with team selection: for the First Test in Lahore they had picked opening batsman and student leader Aftab Gul Khan while he was on bail for political activities; he also played in the Third Test in Karachi, which was abandoned.[13]

In December 1970 Pakistan held its first General Election. The result showed strong support for Bhutto's PPP in West Pakistan and overwhelming support for the Awami League and its autonomy programme in the East. Indeed there was an overall majority in favour of the League across Pakistan, but the country's military leaders declined to invite the League's leader Sheikh Mujib to form a government. This triggered a mass movement of civil disobedience in East Pakistan and demands for independence, which in turn brought the arrest of Mujib and a ferocious campaign of repression – widely rendered as genocide – in Bengal by the Pakistani army. East Pakistan prevailed, however, with vital military assistance from India, one of whose motives was to dampen the radicalism of the Bangla freedom fighters.[14]

In a further – on the face of it, somewhat feeble – bid to mollify public opinion in East Pakistan in 1970 the BCCP selected Roqibul Hasan, a teenage batsman of modest ability but a known Bengali nationalist, as twelfth man in the Third and final Test against New Zealand at Dacca. The following February, with the country now on the brink of civil war, Hasan was picked to play for a 'Pakistanis' XI against a 'Commonwealth XI' composed of English, Australian and Pakistani cricketers, again in Dacca. Hasan had a map of what would become Bangladesh painted on his bat and informed his teammates that, next time they came to East Pakistan, they would need a visa. Fighting broke out before the game could be concluded and the match was abandoned to the sound of heavy gunfire. There were particular fears for the safety of the players of the Pakistanis XI, now clearly seen as symbols of an occupying power.[15]

Pakistan now undertook a cricket tour of England with the east of the country back home in chaos. Meanwhile Roqibul Hasan, still only 18, was deputed to lead a Bangladesh cricket team-in-exile which played all over India promoting the cause of the emergent nation.[16]

'Whither Bangladesh?' Cricket in a new nation

In 1972 Sheikh Mujibur Rahman was released from prison in order to become Prime Minister of Bangladesh. The Awami League of which he was leader was a broadly socialist and secular movement and Mujib took a number of steps in keeping with this: banks, insurance companies, shipping companies and textile, jute and sugar mills were nationalised and the country was declared a people's republic.[17] But the economic prospects for Bangladesh at this time were not good. The previous December, Dr Henry Kissinger, United States National Security Advisor and one of the most brutal exponents of Western realpolitik, had chaired a meeting of Washington Special Actions Group (WSAG) in the US capital at which the situation in South Asia had been discussed – in particular, the prospect of famine in Bangladesh. State Department official Ural Alexis Johnson had commented 'They'll be an international basket case', to which Kissinger had replied 'But not necessarily our basket case'.[18] Bangladesh did indeed experience famine in 1974, by which time the country's economy was failing and the Awami League riven by internal discord. In a country already ravaged by war an estimated one million more people died in the famine and its effects were exacerbated by the refusal of the US government to provide food aid until Bangladesh stopped exporting jute bags to Cuba.[19] The Awami League government became increasing repressive and Mujib declared a state of emergency. He was assassinated by army officers in 1975.

Cricket had endured amid this traumatic birth of a nation and had, inevitably, been a matter for political contention. The Bangladesh Cricket Board (BCB) was established in 1972 and cricket leagues set up in the two major cities of Dhaka and Chittagong. The club-level Dhaka Metropolis Knockout Tournament was staged in February and March 1973 and the following year a national club championship was founded. (It has never gained first-class status, but ranks with Australian grade cricket and league cricket in England – a respectable standard, by common consent in the international cricket world.) It is said that in 1971 Tajuddin Ahmad, socialist, finance minister and close confidante of Mujib, called for cricket to be scrapped altogether, dismissing it as 'a game of the elite' and a 'bourgeois pursuit', that this led to an angry demonstration at the Bangabandhu national stadium (at the time in an advanced state of disrepair) and that Mujib was subsequently persuaded both to endorse cricket and to promise that no duty would be imposed on imported cricket gear.[20]

Politically, cricket raised two – ultimately intertwined – issues for emergent Bangladesh. First, was it suitable or viable flagship for this new nation? And, second, if cricket were to be promoted as a national sport, could it survive in international competition?

The first question touched a number of subsidiary problems. Clearly Tajuddin Ahmad had raised one: was cricket, historically an elite sport expensive in time, land and other resources, appropriate to culture of a newly minted people's republic? As the socialist dream faded, this issue lost relevance and was replaced by debates about national identity. Cricket had a long history in the region and had already generated strong loyalties and antipathies. It was, first and foremost, the colonial sport and would not have arrived in these parts but for the British incursion. It was also, now, the sport of the recently expelled Pakistani oppressor. Older Bengali Hindus might still cheer for India. Equally, there was the possibility that many older Muslims might, in a formally secular state, still identify with Pakistan as an Islamic nation. Within a diversity of possible reactions to cricket there would be subtle combinations of ethnicity and class. 'Before 1971', wrote Garga Chatterjee recently:

> Cricket was scorned by East Bengalis because it was seen as a game that lighter-skinned sharif elites played. I once heard an anecdote revealing this attitude from a person who was visiting a veteran left-wing trade unionist in Barisal, Bangladesh. The veteran fighter of the masses was irritated by the enthusiasm for cricket among Barisal's youth. 'Amago polapain khyalbe cricket? Cricket khyallbe Hanif Mohammed. (Our boys will play cricket? Cricket is for Hanif Mohammed),' he said. Hanif Mohammed was a legendary cricketer from Jamnagar and then West Pakistan. For the trade unionist, as for many others, cricket and Bengalis were incompatible.[21]

(Hanif wasn't just from West Pakistan. He was middle class – his father ran a hotel.)[22] And, finally, there was the acknowledgement of the popularity of association football in Bangladesh (the Bangladesh Football Federation – BFF – formed the same year as the BCCB) and the sense that football was less expensive to play and more egalitarian in its appeal.

In relation to the second issue – that of credibility in international competition – an important first step was taken by the English cricket writer Robin Marlar. Marlar had a classic cricket establishment profile. Educated at Harrow School and Cambridge University, he had captained Sussex in the English county championship in the late 1950s. Retiring as a player in 1968, he had written an 'opinionated' column on cricket in the British *Sunday Times* and stood as a Conservative candidate in two elections.[23] In 1976 Marlar published an article called 'Whither Bangladesh', calling for this currently detached member of the post-colonial cricket family to be admitted to the fold. He wrote:

> Bangladesh is not a member of the International Cricket Conference. She should be. Bengali cricket is numerically strong. Dacca is a Test match ground fit to rank with any in the world, and if the attraction to Pakistan for playing there in the 50s and 60s was as much concerned with revenue at the gate as encouraging local stars, that in itself was a reflection of the passionate interest in the game. And there have been talented players there, too. Something has to be done to restore the people of the seventh-largest democracy in the world to the international family of cricket.[24]

Marlar had spoken to officials in charge of sport at the Bangladeshi Ministry of Education and had noted the presence there of a Russian delegation who had come to discuss football coaching. Almost certainly noting the Cold War implications of this, Marlar called for India to intervene – 'The only solution seems to me to be for someone from India to go to Dacca and help the Bangladeshis to organise the game in that sad country'[25] – but this read also like a flag flown on behalf of the MCC, still at that time the seat of power in international cricket and the dominant voice in the governing body of world cricket, the International Cricket Conference (ICC).[26] Bangladesh duly applied to join the ICC, who suggested that they invite the MCC to tour Bangladesh: a decision on admitting Bangladesh would hinge on MCC's report on the tour. An MCC team, captained by recently retired Middlesex batsman Ted Clark, duly arrived in the country in December 1976 and in early January 1977 played a Bangladesh XI in front of 40,000 people in Dhaka. The match was drawn. Bangladesh became an associate member of ICC that summer.[27] (Marlar's article is still widely remembered in Bangladeshi cricket circles and is generally noted in the nation's cricket web histories. A writer recently lamented that a copy does not feature in the museum at the new Sher-e-Bangla cricket stadium in Mirpur.)[28]

'The third most historic event in our national life': cricket in Bangladesh in the twenty-first century

In a way that he perhaps did not intend Marlar's article was prophetic. He had looked for Bangladesh to be succoured by the former imperial power – as, indeed, she was – but the greatest boost to Bangladeshi cricket came in the end from India, the emergent economic power in the region, and from what became known in international cricket politics as 'the Asian bloc'.

Associate membership of ICC gave Bangladesh access to what was (and remains) effectively international cricket's second tier – composed of the best of the non-Test-playing countries – which was expanding. They also benefited from a developing regional cricket scene.

In 1979 Bangladesh participated in the first ICC Trophy, held in England, where they beat Fiji and Malaysia, but lost to Canada and Denmark. In 1982, in the second ICC Trophy, again in England, they reached the semi-finals where they lost to Zimbabwe (who were awarded Test status ten years later). In the fourth ICC Trophy, held in the Netherlands, they again reached the semi-finals and again lost to Zimbabwe. These fixtures gave them international experience and facilitated invitations to visit other cricket-playing countries and reciprocal requests to tour Bangladesh. Bangladesh, for example, toured Kenya in 1984 and hosted Denmark in 1990. Politically and commercially, however, the most significant development for the growth of Bangladeshi cricket was the formation of the Asian Cricket Council (ACC) in 1983.

The Asian Cricket Council comprised Bangladesh, India, Malaysia, Pakistan, Singapore, and Sri Lanka and grew out of the burgeoning romance between cricket – particularly one-day cricket – and television on the Asian subcontinent. The council was founded in India and funded by the television revenues now flowing into the Board of Cricket Control India (BCCI) and the further television interest the council itself attracted for its own tournaments. The first of these were the Asia Cup, first staged in 1984 in Sharjah, which would soon become a favourite watering hole for wealthy cricket lovers from India, Pakistan and the Gulf states, and the South East Asia Cup, the first of which was held in Bangladesh, also in 1984. (Bangladesh beat Hong Kong in the final.) Other competitions would follow. Thus, in the late 1980s and 1990s Bangladesh became regular players on the Asian cricket TV circuit, Dhaka and Chittagong became acknowledged international cricket venues and Bangladesh began to become a destination for cricket tourism. Bangladesh also hosted the third Asia Cup in 1988 and the first Under-19 Asia Cup the following year. Ten years later, with crucial support from the BCCI, they were awarded the first 'Mini World Cup' featuring all the Test-playing nations.[29] In 1999 a new first-class format National League was set up. The home and away tournament has divisional teams from Dhaka, Chittagong, Sylhet (in the north east of the country), the port of Khulna (Bangladesh's third largest city), Barisal (in south central Bangladesh) and Rajshahi, a major urban centre in north Bengal. This was all a prelude to the award of Test match status in 2000.

The granting of Test-playing privileges to Bangladesh was understandably the occasion for much public rejoicing in the country. News channels carried film of young, mostly male, celebrants thronging the streets of Dhaka and waving national flags and lighting firecrackers. '"I can't express my joy in words at this happiest hour of the nation," said Prime Minister and avid cricket fan Sheikh Hasina [the daughter of Sheikh Mujib]. "I thank our cricketers who have made it possible."'[30] The president of BCB, entrepreneur and Awami League MP Saber Chowdhury, described the elevation as 'the third most historic event in [Bangladeshi] national life, behind independence and the adoption of a United Nations mother-tongue day commemorating the suppression of the Bengali language under Pakistani rule'.[31] A near-capacity crowd of 40,000 once again turned up to the Bangabandhu Stadium for the country's inaugural Test match in November 2000. Appropriately, it was against India, Indian administrators having been instrumental in Bangladesh's admission to international cricket's high table. A key figure here was the Kolkata businessman Jagmohan Dalmiya, a dominant influence at the BCCI in the 1990s who had become President of the ICC in 1997 and was also a significant presence on the Asian Cricket Council. In 1993 Dalmiya had successfully challenged the monopoly of India's national TV station Doordarshan on coverage of Indian cricket and opened the door for national cricket boards in the region to strike lucrative deals with commercial broadcasters and marketers. For these commercial interests, Asia, with its huge population of cricket enthusiasts, represented an attractive market for soft drinks, replica shirts, mobile phones and the like. Politically, Bangladesh, with an established cricket culture, 130 million inhabitants and a history of war with its cricket-playing neighbour, was a potentially lucrative addition to this market. Moreover, Dalmiya could feel certain that Bangladesh would vote with the emergent 'Asian bloc' on the ICC. He thus, as Sharda Ugra has written, was able to 'ram home the message that the headquarters of world cricket was no longer England and Lord's, but the Asian subcontinent'.[32] When Dalmiya died in 2015 some of the most effusive tributes were paid, predictably, in Bangladesh. Prime Minister Hasina called him 'a true well-wisher of Bangladesh cricket and his death is an irreparable loss to the world cricket'.[33] And Chowdhury reflected:

> There was a lot of doubt about whether the 1998 mini World Cup would be held in Bangladesh because a large part of the country was under water. There was a flood in the country. Dalmiya's support was amazing, in giving us the tournament and then holding on to it.[34]

The following year resentment of Bangladesh's promotion was still smouldering among English commentators: cricket correspondent Scyld Berry of the right-wing *Daily Telegraph* wrote:

> It was through no fault of Bangladesh's cricketers, but of the sport's administrators, that their country was awarded Test status obscenely prematurely. The ICC granted it in 1999 – England at least abstained while the eight other Test countries said yes – on the flimsiest possible playing evidence: Bangladesh had won three of their 35 one-day internationals, two of them against Kenya and Scotland.[35]

And, in 2006, the ex-New Zealand cricketer Martin Crowe fulminated: 'Let's face it – Bangladesh and Zimbabwe are being kept on the international stage for political reasons . . . Talking of politics, why were so few questions raised about the way the Asian subcontinent has taken a stranglehold on World cricket?'[36]

Conclusion: cricket and Bangladesh – a larger resurgence?

Cricket provided a means by which those governing Bangladesh could address problems of national identity, internal dissension and international profile.

On the first count, national identity in Bangladesh has always been, and remains, contested.[37] As Willem van Schendel shows, its political culture has harboured the competing strains of socialism, secularism, democracy, 'vernacular' Bengali cultural nationalism (based on folk traditions – typified by the language movement and more recently called 'mofussilisation'), 'mostanocracy' (rule by racketeers) and radical Islam.[38] Cricket, in which context Bangladesh now resides among the world's top ten nations, provides a basis for sporting national identity which can, if only now and again (i.e. when international tournaments or Test matches are in progress) transcend these serious differences. The World Cup of 2011, co-hosted by Bangladesh, certainly called forth firm statements to this effect. For instance, Kausik Bandyopadhyay wrote in 2013:

> Cricket as a nationalist obsession transcends everything in Bangladesh, binding all in one knot from a rickshaw puller to the prime minister, from a fundamentalist mullah to a westernized IT professional, from a poor farmer's wife to a high society lady or from a Hindu priest to a disgruntled Chakma [an ethnic group found mainly in the Chittagong Hill Tracts of Bangladesh]. More importantly, cricket educates the Bangladeshi youth about nationalist ideology and instils in them a deep emotional attachment towards the nation thus imagined. Performing well or not, nationalism around cricket is not fragile as the other 'invented traditions' are argued to be, since it cuts across affiliations of race, religion, community or ethnicity. The religious fundamentalists and their lay followers, who do not agree with the idea of nationalist ideology, too, seem to have succumbed to the all-pervasive wave of cricketing nationalism in the wake of the World Cup.[39]

Any Bangladeshi government minister reading that would immediately be alive to the possibilities of using cricket fever to mitigate the likelihood of civil strife. After all, analysis of contemporary Bangladesh tends to stress the familiar blend of bad politics and healthy economic growth. For example, two writers on the East Asia Forum, which normally views global developments from the 'business'/investment perspective, wrote in 2016 that:

> Bangladesh's social, economic and political development is one of the great success stories of the past 25 years. But today it is Bangladesh's politically dysfunctional 'battling begums'[40] – Sheikh Hasina of the ruling Awami League (AL) and Khaleda Zia [widow of Ziaur Rahman, Bangladesh's former military ruler] of opposition Bangladesh Nationalist Party (BNP) – that hold the country back. [...] Surveys also show that most Bangladeshis are strongly committed to a moderate strand of Islam and reject violence. The economy has continued to chug along at around 6 per cent growth – with inflation falling, unemployment low and the current account close to balance. Remittance inflows by more than seven million Bangladeshi overseas workers continue to boost rapid spending growth of consumer durables. Rural areas – where

the majority of Bangladesh's 160 million people live – are changing rapidly with improving availability of food, electricity and health care. The agricultural sector is mechanizing and diversifying in response to rising incomes in the cities.[41]

Some, indeed, have been quick to place cricket at the centre of this narrative of growth and progress. When Bangladesh beat both India and Pakistan in successive one-day international series in 2015, Subir Bhaumik suggested this success was:

> A manifestation of the all-round progress that South Asia's youngest nation has made since a US State Department official had sneeringly called it a 'basket case' after its birth in an 'ocean of blood' in 1971. And it is reflective of the enormous self-confidence born out of a powerful language-and-culture driven nationalism playing out on a homogenous demography replete with youth dividend.[42]

What is frequently left out of these accounts is the grim human cost of economic growth, best evidenced in Bangladesh's case by the garment industry, most of which serves Western retail chains, such as Walmart, Gap and Primark. The collapse of the Rana Plaza building in Dhaka which killed 1,129 workers and injured a further 2,500 was symptomatic of a greater gamble with the lives of Bangladeshi workers. 60% of the country's 3,000 garment factories are deemed unsafe.[43] In December 2016 3,500 workers were sacked after asking for their pay (5,300 taka or £54 per month) to be trebled; many of them, along with union leaders, were detained under the Special Powers Act.[44] One might argue that it is brutal governance such as this, rather than political wrangling such as that conducted between 'battling begums', that breeds public discontent and makes the Bangladeshi elite glad of the opportunity to play the cricket card.

The state therefore invests heavily in cricket,[45] although the national game is now amply funded from the commercial sector, chiefly by mobile phone companies – the current sponsor of the Bangladesh team, the Under-19 team and Bangladesh A team is Robi Axiata Limited, the second largest mobile phone network in Bangladesh. They took over in 2015, outbidding another mobile phone company, the previous sponsor Grameenphone.[46] In 2011 Grameenphone were also persuaded by the Bangladesh government to put money into the nation's football.[47] Football, though popular in Bangladesh, cannot bring the country the international profile that, plainly, cricket can. The Bangladesh football team has never risen above 116 in the FIFA rankings (in 1993) and is currently 190th (out of 211).[48]

There's little doubting the genuine and widespread popularity of cricket in Bangladesh. Bandyopadhyay notes the widespread engagement – particularly of women – with the World Cup of 2011 and the vast sales of the Bangladesh team's replica shirts.[49] No doubt partly in anticipation of the increase in cricket visitors the following year, the Bangladesh Tourism Board had been established in 2010 – the same year as the setting up of a professional Twenty20 competition, the National Cricket League – rebranded as the Bangladesh Premier League in 2012. A 75,000-capacity national cricket stadium in under construction in cricket stadium in Purbachal New Town outside Dhaka.

Amid all this commercialism, players in the Bangladesh national team have inevitably become celebrities. However, team captain Mashrafe Mortaza has been anxious to keep cricket celebrity and hyper-nationalism in perspective. In 2016 he invoked the nation's founding ideals:

> I am a cricketer but can I save a life? A doctor can. But no-one claps for the best doctor in the country. [...] They are the stars. The labourers are the stars, they build the country. What have we built using cricket? Can we make even a brick using cricket? Does paddy grow on the cricket field? Those who make courtyards using bricks, make things at factories, grow crops in the fields – they are the stars. What do we do? If I say it very bluntly – we take money, we perform. Like a singer or an actor, we do performing art. Nothing more. The Muktijoddhad [freedom fighters in the war of 1971] didn't face bullets to get money on winning.[50]

Notes

1 See Aatekah Mir-Khan and Sher Khan 'Idhar Hum, Udhar Tum: End of an era in Urdu journalism' [Obituary of Syed Abbas Athar] *The Express Tribune* 7 May 2013 http://tribune.com.pk/story/545477/idhar-hum-udhar-tum-end-of-an-era-in-urdu-journalism/ Access 29 January 2017. The phrase might also translate as 'We stay here, you stay there' or 'We here, you there' although both these versions make less sense in this context.
2 See William van Schendel *A History of Bangladesh* Cambridge: Cambridge University Press pp. 107, 109–15, 133, 135.
3 'Story of Pakistan: West Pakistan established as one unit' http://storyofpakistan.com/west-pakistan-established-as-one-unit/ Access 30 January 2017.
4 Peter Oborne *Wounded Tiger: A History of Cricket in Pakistan* London: Simon and Schuster 2015 p.106.
5 Oborne *Wounded Tiger* p.182.
6 See Shamya Dasgupta 'Bangladesh cricket: scoring on passion, but little else' in Jon Gemmell and Boria Majumdar (eds.) *Cricket, Race and the 2007 World Cup* Abingdon: Routledge 2008 pp.152–71 p.154.
7 Van Schendel *A History* pp.122, 124.
8 For a full account see Gary J. Bass *The Blood Telegram: Nixon, Kissinger, and a Forgotten Genocide* New York, NY: Knopf 2013.
9 See Delwar Hussain 'Pakistan's leaders should heed the lesson of Bangladesh' *Guardian* 15 August 2010 https://www.theguardian.com/commentisfree/2010/aug/15/pakistan-flood-warning Access 30 January 2017.
10 Oborne *Wounded Tiger* p.182.
11 John Snow *Cricket Rebel* London: Hamlym 1976 p.68.

12 Tom Graveney *The Heart of Cricket* London: Arthur Barker 1983 p.63.
13 'Aftab Gul' http://www.espncricinfo.com/pakistan/content/player/38979.html Access 30 January 2017.
14 Van Schendel *A History* p.174–5.
15 Oborne *Wounded Tiger* pp.209–11.
16 Oborne *Wounded Tiger* p.211.
17 Van Schendel *A History* pp.175–6.
18 See Mohammad Rezaul Bari 'The basket case' *Forum/The Daily Star* Vol.3 Issue 3 March 2008 http://archive.thedailystar.net/forum/2008/march/basket.htm Access 31 January 2017.
19 See Olivier Rubin *Democracy and Famine* Abingdon: Routledge 2012 pp.56, 58.
20 See Shamya Dasgupta 'Bangladesh Cricket: Scoring on Passion' pp.155–6.
21 Garga Chatterjee 'Why cricket has been a potent vehicle for nationalism in Bangladesh' *The Field* 3 January 2017 https://thefield.scroll.in/804696/why-cricket-has-been-a-potent-vehicle-for-nationalism-in-bangladesh Access 31 January 2017.
22 See Peter Mason 'Hanif Mohammad obituary' *Guardian* 15 August 2016 https://www.theguardian.com/sport/2016/aug/15/hanif-mohammad-obituary Access 31 January 2017.
23 Steven Lynch 'Robin Marlar' http://www.espncricinfo.com/england/content/player/17328.html Access 31 January 2017.
24 Robin Marlar 'Whither Bangladesh' http://www.espncricinfo.com/cricketer/content/story/135968.html Access 31 January 2017.
25 Marlar 'Whither'.
26 ICC was founded in 1909 as the Imperial Cricket Conference with three members: South Africa, Australia and England.
27 Some information here was taken from http://banglacricket.com/html/History/timeline.php Access 31 January 2017.
28 Ameeruddin Zain 'History not arranged' *The Daily Star* 23 April 2009 http://www.thedailystar.net/news-detail-85214 Access 31 January 2017.
29 'When cricket really was the winner' http://www.espncricinfo.com/wisdenalmanack/content/story/155194.html Access 13 May 2017.
30 'Bangladesh delight at Test status' BBC News http://news.bbc.co.uk/1/hi/world/south_asia/807107.stm Posted 26 June 2000, Access 1 February 2017.
31 Richard Hobson 'The Indians in Bangladesh, 2000–01' http://www.espncricinfo.com/wisdenalmanack/content/story/154207.html Access 1 February 2017.
32 Sharda Ugra 'The President: Jagmohan Dalmiya' in Rob Steen (ed.) *The New Ball, Volume 6: Co-Stars* London: Sports Book Direct 2001 pp.31–49, p.44.
33 Staff Correspondent 'Bangladesh mourn[s] its true friend' http://archive.newagebd.net/160028/bangladesh-mourn-its-true-friend/ Posted 22 September 2015, Access 1 February 2017.
34 Mohammad Isam 'The architect of Asia's rise' [Obituary of Jagmohan Dalmiya] http://phone.espncricinfo.com/india/content/story/922631.html Posted 22 September 2015, Access 1 February 2017.
35 Scyld Berry 'Bangladesh are still paying the price for gaining Test status obscenely prematurely' http://www.telegraph.co.uk/cricket/2016/10/19/bangladesh-are-still-paying-the-price-for-gaining-test-status-ob/ Posted 19 October 2016, Access 1 February 2017.
36 Quoted in Mike Marqusee 'The thump of humbug on willow' *Guardian* 17 July 2006 https://www.theguardian.com/commentisfree/2006/jul/17/disspiritofcricket Access 15 February 2017.
37 Van Schendel *A History* p.267.
38 Van Schendel *A History* See, in particular, Chapter 22, pp.251–67.

39 Kausik Bandyopadhyay 'Cricket as nationalist obsession: ICC World Cup 2011 and Bangladesh as a host nation' *Sport in Society* Vol. 16 No.1 2013 pp.19–32, p.29.
40 Begum – a royal or aristocratic female.
41 Tom Felix Joehnk and Forrest Cookson 'Bangladesh transforms despite its vicious politics' *East Asia Forum* http://www.eastasiaforum.org/2016/01/05/bangladesh-transforms-despite-its-vicious-politics/ Posted 5 January 2016, Access 1 February 2017.
42 Subir Bhaumik 'Cricket victories reflect larger resurgence of Bangladesh' http://opinion.bdnews24.com/2015/06/26/cricket-victories-reflect-larger-resurgence-of-bangladesh/ Posted 25 June 2015, Access 1 February 2017.
43 See Sarah Butler 'Bangladeshi factory deaths spark action among high-street clothing chains' *Guardian* 23 June 2013 https://www.theguardian.com/world/2013/jun/23/rana-plaza-factory-disaster-bangladesh-primark Access 1 February 2017.
44 Michael Safi and agencies in Dhaka 'Bangladesh garment factories sack hundreds after pay protests' *Guardian* 27 December 2016 https://www.theguardian.com/world/2016/dec/27/bangladesh-garment-factories-sack-hundreds-after-pay-protests Access 1 February 2017.
45 Bandyopadhyay 'Cricket as Nationalist Obsession' p.20.
46 Mohammad Isam 'Robi Axiata new Bangladesh team sponsor' http://www.espncricinfo.com/bangladesh/content/story/879507.html Posted 21 May 2015, Access 1 February 2017.
47 James Melik 'Bangladesh football vies with cricket for sponsorship' http://www.bbc.co.uk/news/business-13158011 Posted 29 April 2011, Access 1 February 2017.
48 http://www.fifa.com/fifa-world-ranking/associations/association=ban/men/index.html Access 1 February 2017.
49 Bandyopadhyay 'Cricket as nationalist obsession' p.26.
50 Chatterjee 'Why cricket has been a potent vehicle for nationalism in Bangladesh'.

Chapter 9

After brewing tea for the empire
Cricket in Sri Lanka since 1945

As with a number of other full members of the International Cricket Council – New Zealand, in particular – the history and politics of the Sri Lankan cricket world have, for the most part, been chronicled and discussed by a small number of writers – in this case, two in particular: the prolific Michael Roberts, a Sri Lankan historian, anthropologist and blogger, who retired from the University of Adelaide in 2003, and S.S. Perera, local archivist and author of an exhaustive history of the country's cricket published in the late 1990s by a Colombo insurance company.[1] This chapter draws, inevitably, quite heavily on their work. I should add that, although since the 1980s it has, arguably, become an increasingly important feature of Sri Lankan life, neither mainstream, nor self-professedly innovative, histories of Sri Lanka make much mention of cricket.[2]

Planters at play: cricket in Ceylon

Sri Lanka is an island off the south-east coast of India. Its population (20 million people in 2013) rivals that of Australia, which stands at 23 million. Having earlier been subject variously to Portuguese and Dutch occupation, the island was colonised by Britain in 1815 and, for the duration of the British tenure, and for a while after the granting of independence in 1948, it was known officially (and mostly) as 'Ceylon'. Ceylon had a plantation economy, founded initially on the cultivation of coffee in its central region. Following blight and increased competition from Brazil, tea replaced coffee as the island's staple crop in the late nineteenth century.[3] The tea plantations were usually owned by big British companies, such as Liptons, who bought their first tea plantations in Ceylon in 1890.[4] Cricket was introduced to the island in the early 1830s, principally by coffee planters and army officers.[5] These men founded the first cricket clubs on the island, one of the earliest being the Dimbulla Athletic and Cricket Club (DACC) situated in Radella, in the hill country of Sri Lanka's Central Province, which dates from 1856.[6]

Ceylon cricket, in its first decades, had drawn heavily on the British presence – the British army and the colonial civil service were a source of good cricketers[7] – and thereafter began to prosper with the support of the British imperial cricket elite. The British cricketer and colonial administrator Lord Harris, for example, had called for Australian cricketers to help Ceylonese cricket by visiting the island[8] and a number of teams had duly done so, either as part of a tour of India or to use Colombo as a stopping-off point in a long voyage, usually between England and Australia. Indeed, the first overseas team to visit Ceylon was an All England team, captained by Ivo Bligh – Eton, Cambridge and Kent – in 1882, on their way to Australia. In 1888–9 an English team led by George Vernon (Middlesex and one Test for England) toured Ceylon and India, and played a match against All Ceylon at Kandy, centre of the island's tea trade. In 1890, the Australian team *en route* to England played a game in Colombo. The patrician Lord Hawke, of Yorkshire and England, had brought a team to Ceylon in the winter of 1889–90. He returned in 1892 when DACC hosted a match between a Ceylon Up-Country XI and MCC.[9] (Hawke was a cricket missionary and imperial emissary.[10] Between the winters of 1887–8 and 1911–12 he had undertaken nine foreign tours. In each case the Ceylon trip was part of a wider tour of India.) Clubs were seemingly dependent on the patronage of local or English businessmen – notably Dutch-descended George Vanderspar, a Galle-born millionaire who had played a single match for MCC in 1893, and who on occasion between 1880 and 1912 paid for MCC teams to detour to Ceylon on their way to Australia. Vandespar was an exporter, probably in tea and rubber,[11] and a bowler for the Colombo Cricket Club.

The first overseas tour by a Ceylon cricket team was to India in 1903.[12]

The Ceylon Cricket Association (CCA) had formed in 1922. It was dominated, like all of aspects of Ceylonese life, by members of the islands anglicised elite – figures such as John Rockwood, a Tamil and a physician in the Ceylon Medical Service (CCA's first president), tea broker O.B. Forbes (its first secretary) and Col. E.H. Joseph, manager of Ceylon's *Independent* newspaper and a leading batsman in Ceylon cricket in the 1890s.[13] Joseph was president of the Nondescripts Cricket Club, founded in Colombo in 1888 and, unlike other cricket clubs, not aligned to a particular ethnic group.

Two years later a British coach, ex-Surrey bowler William 'Razor' Smith (then 52) was appointed to the CCA.

In the winter of 1930–1, the Maharaj Kumar of Vizianagram (known in cricket circles as 'Vizzy') had brought an international team to Ceylon that included the England openers Jack Hobbs and Herbert Sutcliffe and the Indian Test player C.K. Nayudu. They had played games in Colombo, Darrawella (another plantation club, founded in 1868) and the south-western city of Galle. Some of these matches were deemed 'first class' – a gesture of approval from the imperial high table at Lord's. (Indeed, during the 1930s, some Ceylonese cricketers were invited to play first-class cricket in India.)[14]

Surrey captain Douglas Jardine had brought his England party to Ceylon in 1932, *en route* for the 'Bodyline' Ashes series of that winter in Australia, and he captained MCC there again the following year. On this second visit the famously high-handed Jardine's masters-and-men demeanour was a sharp reminder of the social distinctions that contoured cricket across the British Empire: in a game against All Ceylon, Jardine refused to continue until spectators who were 'hooting' (presumably, these were lower-born Ceylonese) were removed by police.[15]

In 1934 F.C. 'Derek' de Saram, an eminently anglicised old boy of the elite Royal College in Colombo, had become the first Ceylonese to gain a cricket blue (at Oxford) and in 1938 the island's first inter-club tournament was inaugurated and sponsored by press baron D.R. Wijewardena, owner of Associated Newspapers of Ceylon[16] and later a leading figure in the independence movement on the island.

Recently the political nature of the long-established Sri Lankan cricket clubs was the subject of a sharp, but clarificatory, exchange of words. In 2011 the Sri Lankan novelist Shehan Karunatilaka wrote an article, which was essentially an 'everything-stops-for-cricket' essay about the purportedly redeeming properties of the game in contemporary Sri Lankan life. In the course of the article he observed that:

> Cricket has been a distraction of choice for Sri Lanka since our days of brewing tea for the empire. Back when we were Ceylon. In the 19th century, talent flocked to cricket clubs, christened along racial lines by our divide-and-conquer colonisers: Sinhalese Sports Club, Tamil Union, Moors' Sports Club, Burgher Recreation Club and the perversely titled Nondescripts Cricket Club.[17]

This brought a polite rebuke from Michael Roberts, who offered a more nuanced formulation:

> The cricket clubs in the heyday of British power, say 1858–1931, form a fascinating subject because of the duality of cultural and political currents that they embodied. Along one dimension, they were a medium of Westernization and fostered Anglophilia. Along a parallel dimension, they were fields in which (a) cross-communal comradeship was fostered within the Ceylonese middle class, despite separation into ethnic clubs and (b) Ceylonese patriotism was generated. One outstanding expression of Ceylonese nationalism occurred when the 'Ceylonese' as a team took on the local 'Europeans' in a Test match from 1887 onwards, an annual encounter.[18]

In other words, there were in this period always spaces in which non-elite Ceylonese could form their own institutions; these were freely chosen and contoured by local ethnic identities; and this was compatible with a Jack's-as-good-as-his-master nationalism.[19] As Roberts acknowledges, the British 'heyday' lasted only until the early 1930s, by which time this latter brand of nationalism was, presumably, becoming less viable – indeed, the last Ceylonese v. Europeans game was played in 1933.[20] ('Nondescripts' was one of a number of terms used initially in Victorian England to describe cricket teams with no home ground – 'Wanderers', 'Nomads' and 'I Zingari' were others. A team called the 'Nondescripts' played in London in the 1870s[21] and the Nondescripts of Colombo, founded in 1888, borrowed the name, apparently in this instance to indicate that, unlike other clubs, they were not confined to any ethnic group.) None of this alters the fact that, as Peebles states, the island was governed by an anglicised elite which drew from different racial, ethnic, class and regional groups in Ceylonese society; that British colonial policy primarily benefited 'low country Sinhalese' – that is, those Ceylonese historically more exposed to, and formed by, Western influences, more cosmopolitan and more likely to live in the plains and coastal areas than in the highlands; nor that the ethnic distinctions expressed in the early cricket clubs would become politically more vexatious after independence.

Go back to old times? Sri Lankan cricket, 1945–81

Several factors inform the history of Sri Lankan cricket during this period – among them, the waning of British influence and the search for a Sri Lankan national-identity-in-cricket; the slow establishment of an international presence for the island's team; a national debate over whether or not Sri Lanka should seek, or would merit, Test-playing status; and the need to finance the nation's cricket, whichever route was chosen for that cricket to take.

The question of national identity was made greatly more complex by political developments attending the granting of independence to Ceylon in 1948. Under the new dispensation, official power now passed to the island's anglicised, anglophile elite that had been largely self-governing since 1931; the general election of 1947 was won comfortably by the more right-wing United National Party (UNP), but all parties (including the other main one, the Sri Lanka Freedom Party – SLFP) were drawn from this elite.[22] The same elite would dominate Sri Lankan cricket governance until the 1960s – as Roberts characterises them, 'the Westernised-set drawn from the Christian denominational schools and the Royal-Thomian networks', a reference to the two elite private schools in Colombo, Royal College and St Thomas College. Similarly the presidency of the national cricket board would rest 'in the hands of a few notables from United National Party families'.[23]

In 1946, several of the island's leading cricket clubs – the Sinhalese Sports Club, the Tamil Union Cricket and Athletic Club (both in Colombo) and the Kandy Sports Club – opened their membership to all communities.[24] However, Sri Lankan politics were travelling in the direction of more ethnic division, not less. As Nira Wickramasinghe observes: 'From the time the term "citizen" entered the vocabulary of politics in Sri Lanka, "citizenship", a legal term and the main principle of political legitimacy, has been defined by exclusion'.[25] (Citizenship – always related to notions of blocs of the population whose 'cultures' are rendered as 'bounded and distinct'[26] – has remained a constant subject of Sri Lankan legislation.) Under the Citizenship Acts of 1948 and 1949 many labourers, whose forebears had migrated from India and whose families had been on the island for generations, were made stateless.[27] In the 1950s political parties began to base their pitch to the electorate on issues of Sinhalese culture: there were promises to protect Buddhism (the predominant religion of the Sinhalese) and the Official Language Act No. 33 of 1956 established Sinhalese as the official language, in place of English. This antagonised the Indian-descended Tamil community who lived mostly in the north and east of the country and spoke their own language. Some Sinhalese Buddhists saw themselves as the new emergent elite.[28]

These wrangles would escalate into civil war in 1983. Meanwhile there's little doubt that inter-communal status rivalries of this kind contributed to the disputes that often characterised Ceylonese/ Sri Lankan cricket governance during this period. There was frequent controversy over who should have the captaincy – Perera, for instance, records that Royal College old Boy S.S. 'Sargo' Jayawickrema was the 'thirteenth choice' to lead All Ceylon on a tour of Pakistan in 1950 and a proposed tour of England in 1968 was cancelled four times, team captaincy being one of several apparent bones of contention.[29]

Another key issue concerned expatriate cricketers. If Ceylon was to prosper in international cricket, it followed that they should select Ceylonese who were proven at first-class level. However, when Gamini Goonesena, another Royal College graduate, was selected to captain Ceylon in 1956 there were complaints: Goonesena played for Cambridge University and in the county championship for Nottinghamshire and hadn't been to Ceylon in five years – was this the way, critics asked, to encourage locally based cricketers?[30] In the 1960s similar objections were raised to the selection of Colombo-born county cricketers Dan Piachaud, Stan Jayasinghe and Clive Inman, despite Jayasinghe and Inman leading the Leicestershire batting averages in the 1965 season.[31]

Selection controversies such as these jostled with other, equally pressing, considerations. If these accomplished, expatriate cricketers were to be excluded, who should take their place? And, if (as seemed likely) players of lesser ability were to represent Ceylon, how could the island expect to climb the ladder toward Test-playing status? Indeed, was Test status a viable or worthwhile aspiration? Some answered 'No' to this latter question:

when Ceylon were heavily beaten on a tour of Pakistan in 1966, one local columnist declared the trip 'a terrific waste of money' and another wrote: 'We haven't Test match temperament. Let's go back to old times – and enjoy cricket'.[32] But, for those answering 'Yes', there was the added question of who was to pay for Ceylonese cricket – a question which gained greater urgency at the end of the 1950s, with the departure of most of the leading planter-cricketers.[33] These costs, as elsewhere in the British Empire, had hitherto been borne largely by private patronage. Now, again as elsewhere, they would increasingly be borne by sponsors and by government.

Since the early 1950s, as Perera suggests, the island's cricket had stood at the crossroads. In 1952 Ceylon had established its first indoor coaching school. The following year, the national cricket coach, legendary West Indian all-rounder Learie Constantine, had planned a tour of England – aborted, apparently, partly for lack of funds. 1956 saw the final 'whistle stop' match (against MCC) – teams would no longer drop by to play Ceylon on their way to something more important. But international opposition was vital if Ceylon was to gain access to what was still the Imperial Cricket Conference.[34] Several factors combined to facilitate this access.

First, the MCC took steps toward extending the post-colonial Test-playing family by agreeing to play unofficial 'Tests' in Ceylon. The first of these took place in 1962, when Ceylon lost to an England side captained by Ted Dexter, then captain of the full England side and at the height of his powers as a player. (Perera considers that Ceylon were 'bullied' by the England fast bowlers.)[35]

Second, in 1965, immediately following a tour of India in which Ceylon lost a four-match series 1–3, India sponsored Ceylon to become an associate member of the ICC; Pakistan seconded the nomination. This must be seen as an important milestone in the creation of what would later be known as the 'Asian bloc' vote on the ICC. Prior to the award of Test status in 1981 it's noticeable that Ceylon/ Sri Lanka played most of their international cricket within this bloc: they entertained India in 1974, toured India the following winter, beat Pakistan in the Ali Bhutto Trophy (Bhutto being another statesman seeking to forge Third World political alliances) in 1975 and toured Bangladesh in 1978.

Third, the Ceylon Broadcasting Corporation began covering cricket with Sinhalese commentary in 1967 and this helped to promote interest in the game.[36]

Fourth, the prospect of bringing big-time international cricket to the island was one factor that attracted commercial sponsors. In 1968, in what was seen as a further Test trial, Yorkshire CCC secretary Joe Lister brought a team of Test and leading county cricketers to play Ceylon and the tour was sponsored by Associated Newspapers of Ceylon. The same year Ceylon Tobacco sponsored the island's cricket board.[37]

Fifth, the growth of one-day, limited-overs, cricket from the late 1960s was a boon to a cricket culture that produced more good batsmen than bowlers: in one-day cricket it was less important to bowl sides out in order to win a match.[38] In 1970 the first limited-overs competition was established on the island, sponsored by Browns, a firm founded in Ceylon in the 1870s and now a diverse group of companies. This form of cricket was increasingly tied to television and Sri Lanka's often exciting batsmen made for good viewing. Sri Lanka entered the World Cup of 1975 by invitation and, in the next World Cup of 1979, they beat India, the first time that an associate member of ICC had beaten a full member in the competition.

Sixth, it's possible that, as the cultural hold of the anglicised elite loosened, the country's selectors began to draw from a greater pool of talent. As Roberts put it:

> Though English-speaking, such individuals as Darrel Lieversz, T.C.T. Edwards, A.E. De Silva, Buddy Reid [a St. Thomas old boy, nevertheless], Nihal Gurusinghe and Michael Tissera were unassuming and amiable men. That so many of them gained representative honours for Sri Lanka was due to their talents rather than the power of old boy networks.[39]

(All these players played for Ceylon in the 1960s. They may well have done so as the result of more meritocratic selection, although Lieversz was an old boy of Royal College and Reid – a qualified doctor – Gurusinghe and Tissera were all graduates of St. Thomas College. Moreover, nothing has prevented recurrent criticism of the country's cricket selectors.)

Seventh, the state began to take a greater role. In the mid-1960s there had been objections by socialist members of the Ceylonese parliament that cricketers, previously employed (as in India) in the commercial sector, were now being recruited by state institutions: it was complained that they had not been employed on merit and were being given time off for cricket practice.[40] Moreover, one of the reasons that Ceylon's 'stepping stone' tour of the UK in 1968 had been cancelled had been the government's refusal to finance it.[41] At the time the government had been short of foreign exchange and was maintaining an austerity programme. The Ceylon Communist Party was among those bodies supporting the government's stance. (It's worth remembering that the nation's official title remains 'The Democratic Socialist Republic of Sri Lanka'.) However, after the country became a republic in 1972 the importance of sport – and cricket, in particular – in forging national identity and raising international profile appears to have been recognised. A Ministry of Sports was created immediately and in 1973 a Sports Law was passed establishing sports council. Government funding was provided for the improvement of cricket.[42] In 1979 Sri Lanka won the inaugural ICC Trophy in England and in 1981, following the accession to the presidency of the charismatic UNP politician Gamini Dissanayake, the Board of Control for Cricket in Sri Lanka (BCCSL) had a detailed development plan, promising: new Test venues; public and private sponsorship; an inter-district tournament; trained coaches and a coaching school; an emphasis on three-day cricket; a pool of young players in constant training; and regular games against foreign competition. Thus Dissanayake rejected once and for all the notion of going back to old times and enjoying the game; cricket, he said, 'could be a career for young people and cricket will be an industry'.[43] This was the now-familiar government rhetoric of the elite sport programme, as distinct from the sport-for-all initiatives taken in socialist countries of an earlier era. The same year Sri Lanka were given Test status. When he left the presidency of the BCCSL in 1989 Dissanayake spoke with pride at having gained membership for Sri Lanka of 'the most exclusive club in the world' and reflected: 'We were admitted on the basis that we would do everything to put the cricketing infrastructure of our country right. What we have got, in our country today, is one of the finest cricketing infrastructures in the whole world'.[44] Dissanayake was a wealthy and well-connected politician and, importantly, as Minister of Lands and Land Development, he had piloted the UNP's Accelerated Mahaweli Irrigation and Settlement Project – a plan to build dams and generate hydroelectric power – in the late 1970s. This project had been part-financed by the British government and involved British construction companies and this had perhaps gained Dissanayake some useful contacts in London. (The project was also the cause of further ethnic strife since it took place in areas regarded as Tamil homeland, displacing many Tamils in the process.)[45]

By 1989 leading Sri Lankan cricketers were being contracted to the national board[46] – an arrangement known in Britain as 'central contracts' and not adopted there until 2002.

Life during wartime: Sri Lankan cricket 1981–2015

In general three things dominate the more recent history of Sri Lankan cricket: the long and bitter civil war of 1983–2009; the country's victory in the World Cup of 1996; and the spectacular career of Sri Lankan Tamil spin bowler Muttiah Muralitharan (133 Tests 1992–2010, 800 wickets) who was an intermittent lightning rod for political controversy. This closing section considers each of these matters in turn; the issue of racism and ethnic discrimination (in effect, the same thing) is common to them all.

Consistent with the national plan, a new Test venue was opened at the Asgiriya Grounds in Kandy in 1982 and the Khettarama Stadium (now known as the R. Premadasa[47] International Cricket Stadium) in northern Colombo and the Tyronne Fernando[48] Stadium in Moratuwa (south of

Colombo) were constituted as Test grounds ten years later. (In all Sri Lanka now has eight Test match venues, all in the central or southern areas of the country – five in or near the capital Colombo, two in Kandy and one in Galle on the south-west coast. For much of Sri Lanka's time as a Test-playing nation, the north of the country has been a theatre of war.)

The Sri Lankan civil war on occasion disrupted the conduct of the international fixture list. The principal combatants were the Janatha Vimukthi Peramuna (People's Liberation Front or JVP), who combined leftism with Sinhalese nationalism and opposed both the anglophile elite and the Tamils, and the Liberation Tigers of Tamil Eelam (LTTE) composed of secessionist Tamil fighters.[49] (The latter were defeated in 2009 by government forces, the JVP having adopted parliamentary politics in the early 1990s.) Along with the outbreak of civil war, the 1980s also saw the imposition of neoliberal economic policies in Sri Lanka, manifested among other things in the establishment of so-called Free Trade Zones, in which labour would be cheap and generally not subject to protective legislation.[50] The Tamils (Indian migrants and their descendants), although a diverse social grouping, were already heavily represented among the island's poor. This applied especially to the Estate or Plantation Tamils, many of whom still did not have citizenship rights in the 1980s.[51] Moreover, the ceding of economic policy to 'market forces' made it arguably even more likely that the (ostensibly non-material) questions of culture and ethnicity would remain politically at centre stage.

The LTTE campaign frequently involved the bombing of urban areas, many in Colombo, and sometimes detonated by people wearing suicide belts. These bombings, as was intended, caused some disruption to civilian life, including the international cricket calendar. Between 1987 and 1990 no international cricket was played in Sri Lanka, other Test nations being discouraged by the hostilities – 113 people, for example, had died in the bombing of Colombo's Central Bus Station in 1987. In December 1992 a bomb went off outside a Colombo hotel occupied by the New Zealand cricket team, five of whom then opted to return home; New Zealand provided replacements and the tour continued. Then in January 1996 the LTTE struck at the heart of the country's financial sector by blowing up the Central Bank of Sri Lanka in Colombo, whereupon both Australian and West Indies refused to play their scheduled World Cup matches there.

In the West these withdrawals were generally seen as a common-sense reaction on the part of professional sportspeople to the prospect of playing in a country at war but, as Michael Roberts amply demonstrated, it was not seen as such by many in the Asian subcontinent.

Referring to incidents in Pakistan and Sri Lanka, Roberts argued, first of all, that the predominant Western response was effectively to depoliticise the bombers and render them instead as 'mindless' and 'fanatics'. Such people, presumed to be irrational, could strike against anyone, including innocent cricketers. However, if the bombers were seen as purposeful – which, albeit in a murderous way, they were – then it would be seen that their targets were specific and did *not* include international cricketers.[52]

Second, there were questions of racism – both explicit and implicit – which intertwined with notions of masculinity and professionalism prevailing on the international cricket circuit. As we saw in Chapter 2, 'sledging' – the verbal abuse of an opponent in order to disconcert him – had been increasingly prevalent in international cricket since the 1970s. When Sri Lanka had gained full membership of the ICC in 1981, at least one Western commentator had indulged in a little mild condescension on this issue. Scyld Berry of the British right-wing *Daily Telegraph* had quoted the assistant manager of the Sri Lankan team as saying 'Sludging? What is sludging?' and had added: 'Their gentle manners are perhaps what one might expect from Buddhist cricketers'.[53] Eight years later, in 1989, Sri Lanka had toured Australia and, according to Roberts, had received a great deal of verbal (and some physical) intimidation from the Australian team; nevertheless, the Sri Lankan management had adopted a conciliatory 'We're here to learn' mode. However, when they returned to Australia in 1995, under the captaincy of the pugnacious Arjuna Ranatunga, they were more aggressive – as with the Pakistan team in Sydney in 1977 (see Chapter 7), they felt they had come of age.[54] They were met, according to some accounts, by an even more furious response from the Australians and at one stage Australian fast bowler Glenn McGrath had called Sri Lankan Sanath Jayasuriya a 'black monkey'.[55] McGrath later attempted to rationalise this by suggesting that such remarks were 'now as much a part of the fast bowler's arsenal as his bouncer and yorker'.[56] Years later, and in the wake of the Australian refusal to play in Colombo after the bomb blast of 1996, Roberts reflected: 'These hyperactive, walking, sledging, bullying men-of-steel become wobbly-fish-on-the-beach at the prospect of journeys into the "unknown"'.[57] Quite apart from re-constituting the most unsophisticated street racism as a legitimate part of a fast bowler's 'arsenal', the 'tough guy' white cricket world seemed to Roberts to 'shy away from India, Pakistan, Sri Lanka, Bangladesh. The subcontinent becomes peopled by all sorts of fiendish dangers'.[58] This view was strengthened by Australian captain Mark Taylor's post-tournament remark defending his country's earlier refusal to play in Colombo: 'Put yourselves in our shoes and look at the way we live in Australia compared to the way other people live in the sub-continent'.[59]

These considerations, it can safely be assumed, made Sri Lanka's victory in the World Cup of 1996, when they beat Australia in Lahore, all the sweeter for cricket supporters of the Asian subcontinent. As cricket writer Mike Marqusee reflected: 'India's and Pakistan's elimination had left the sub-continent free to unite behind the Sri Lankans, whose victory offended no one. The result was good for cricket, good for the sub-continent, and a fillip for small nations everywhere'.[60]

Security was not the only issue contributing to the racial undercurrent that characterised dealings in the World Cup of 1996. There had also been ongoing and often bitter controversy over the bowling action of the Sri Lankan spinner Muttiah Muralitharan. Muralitharan had come into the Lankan side in 1992 and in Colombo in March the following year Sri Lanka had beaten England for the first time. The atmosphere on the tour had been 'sour' and England had voiced concerns about the bowling actions of both Muralitharan and his teammate Jayananda Warnaweera, another spinner.[61] Later, on the acrimonious tour of Australia in December 1995, Australian umpire Darrell Hair had no-balled Muralitharan in the second Test at Melbourne.[62] This had led to a political furore in which many of Muralitharan's detractors were white and/or of the political right, the most eminent example being Australian Liberal Party leader John Howard, then in Opposition, whose political philosophy entailed militant opposition to multiculturalism and Aboriginal rights and a punitive policy toward asylum seekers (see Chapter 2). He called Muralitharan a 'chucker'.[63] (Sir Donald Bradman, then in his late 80s and a conservative from a more courtly era, was among Muralitharan's defenders.)[64] Many observers noted with some dismay that Hair had no-balled Muralitharan from the end that he was actually bowling. However, no balls for throwing (that is, straightening his arm in the act of delivery, as distinct from no balls for the misplacement of the foot) are invariably called by the other (square leg) umpire, who has the more appropriate view of the bowler's action. This gave the impression to many of Muralitharan's defenders, in Sri Lanka and elsewhere, that Hair's ruling had been premeditated. Years later Roberts suggested that the bowler's 'bent elbow' and 'rubber wrist' had been seized on by Hair 'and his backers in high places'.[65] In 2007 Marqusee summed up the controversy thus:

> No bowler's action has been as intensively scrutinised as Murali's. Again and again it has been declared within the law. Murali's detractors argue that the law was changed to accommodate him, and that Murali has been spared the rod because of the power of the Asian bloc. They are wrong on both counts. What happened was that in examining Murali's action, experts in human motion (not from the Asian bloc) discovered that many bowlers flex their elbow to some degree at the point of delivery. There was a gap between cricket theory and practice. Just as the precise arrangement of a horse's legs at the trot was undetermined until Edward Muybridge's stop-motion photography in the 1870s, so advancing technology has revealed the complexities of the bowling action as never before. And the definition of a throw appears less clear-cut than was supposed. The authorities responded by revising the laws to allow a degree of flex. This has nothing to do with Murali's feats: the law was changed to reflect new research, not to protect Murali. In retrospect it's clear that, far from enjoying preferential treatment, Murali has been singled out unfairly.[66]

Conclusion: search for the hero

As noted Muralitharan was also, importantly, a Tamil. The Tamil separatist insurgency was defeated in 2009, by which time Muralitharan had become the world's most accomplished international bowler, but the relationship of Sri Lankan Tamils to the nation's cricket team had long since been a troubled one. In 1975, when Sri Lanka had played Australia at the Oval on the World Cup, the match had been disrupted by Tamil demonstrators – Tamils are strongly represented in the Sri Lankan diaspora – claiming that the Lankan team had not been selected on merit, talented Tamil players having been excluded.[67] Decades later, this sentiment lingered. In his article of 2011 Karunatilaka wrote: 'The call-up for international duty continued to elude many Muslim and Tamil cricketers who excelled at club level. Murali was merely the exception that proved the rule'.[68] This, once again, drew a rebuke from Michael Roberts, who pointed to a dearth of Tamils in Sri Lankan first-class cricket.[69] Indeed, Roberts had argued several years earlier that Tamils had been effectively lost to Sri Lankan cricket.[70] One reason for this was in all probability the close identification of cricket with the Sri Lankan state and with Anglo- and Sinhalese elites – a factor that the defeat of 2009 was unlikely to have dispelled.

According to David Fidler and Sumit Ganguly, in the early twenty-first century governments in the global South were beginning to conform to 'Eastphalia', an orthodoxy of governance concocted by the emergent international powers of China and India to rival the Washington consensus.[71] The 'Eastphalia' doctrine, as Chaminda Weerawardhana has pointed out, 'strongly adheres to national sovereignty and non-interference in the internal affairs of states'.[72] According to Weerawardhana, Sri Lankan Tamils remained marginalised, subject to violence and were alleging war crimes had been committed against them by government troops. So far the Sri Lankan government had made little response to these claims:

> Colombo is in a position to channel the course of its international agenda in this manner for two reasons. Firstly, its military victory against an organisation classified in the USA, UK, EU and India as a terrorist outfit has provided it with an increased flexibility in making its domestic and foreign policy decisions. Secondly, the relative international disinterest in the Sri Lankan question and the inclination to view Sri Lanka's ethnic question as a 'past' issue prevent Colombo from facing any international barriers in its course of action. As long as Sri Lanka's policies do not hinder the Delhi-Washington DC consensus, the Rajapaksa[73] regime is unlikely to earn the international community's wrath.[74]

Nevertheless, the government still needed some basis upon which to promote national unity and cricket was a promising place to look – as Karunatilaka remarked: 'In order to live with itself, the nation needs to manufacture more heroes', before noting the 'King Kong-sized billboards' of the Sri Lankan cricket team which lined the streets of Colombo in 2011.[75] Sri Lankan government bodies have made a number of gestures in this regard. In 2010 the Central Provincial Council in Kandy resolved to rename the local Pallekele International Cricket Stadium after Muralitharan. National cricket grounds had already been named after UNP politicians (Premadasa and Fernando) and the following year a cricket stadium named after President Rajapaksa opened in the improbable location of Hambantota, a small town in southern province and Rajapaksa's birthplace. This was part of a wider plan, drawing on Chinese finance and labour, to develop the town as a hub and as the island's second city, whose many constituent parts (port, airport, cinema complex . . .) would be named after Rajapaksa.[76] (The stadium staged little cricket, fell into disuse and became a much-mocked folly, 'strewn with pigeon carcases and pigeon droppings'.)[77] In July 2011 Sri Lankan Test captain Kumar Sangakkara came to Lord's to give the annual Spirit of Cricket Lecture, taking as his topic 'The Spirit of Sri Lanka's Cricket – A celebration of our uniqueness'. In the speech, which is likely to have had prior Sri Lankan government approval, he no doubt warmed his audience by calling cricket 'the most precious heirloom of our British Colonial inheritance' before embarking on a brief history of this inheritance and of the civil strife from which Sri Lanka was now emerging. He told how in 1983 (when he had been 6 years old) his father had sheltered thirty-five Tamils in the family home during a race riot. He talked of developing new 'talent pools' by bringing cricket to the predominantly Tamil areas of north and east Sri Lanka and closed by offering himself as the symbol of a national unity suffused with the mystical healing properties of the game:

> In our cricket you see the character of our people, our history, culture and tradition, our laughter, our joy, our tears and regrets. It is rich in emotion and talent. My responsibility as a Sri Lankan cricketer is to further enrich this beautiful sport, to add to it and enhance it and to leave a richer legacy for other cricketers to follow. I will do that keeping paramount in my mind my Sri Lankan identity: play the game hard and fair and be a voice with which Sri Lanka can speak proudly and positively to the world. My loyalty will be to the ordinary Sri Lankan fan, their 20 million hearts beating collectively as one to our island rhythm and filled with an undying and ever-loyal love for this our game. Fans of different races, castes, ethnicities and religions who together celebrate their diversity by uniting for a common national cause. They are my foundation, they are my family. I will play my cricket for them. Their spirit is the true spirit of cricket. With me are all my people. I am Tamil, Sinhalese, Muslim and Burgher. I am a Buddhist, a Hindu, a follower of Islam and Christianity. I am today, and always, proudly Sri Lankan.[78]

A subsequent article by British cricket writer David Hopps welcomed the talk as '[t]he speech that set free Sri Lanka cricket and glued a troubled nation' and in 2014 Sri Lankan Tamil writer Thiviyanthan Krishnamohan suggested that:

> Kumar Sangakkara may very well become the Imran Khan of Sri Lanka. Right now, Sri Lanka needs a leader under whom Sri Lankans would ardently unite forgetting all differences. There is a leader in Sanga. A leader who could probably open the now closed avenues of Sri Lanka that would aid us in realizing our potential and be the true 'Pearl of the Indian Ocean'.[79]

In 2015 Sangakkara was publicly offered the post of Sri Lanka's High Commissioner in the UK by new President, Maithripala Sirisena of the SLFP.[80]

Others, however, were not persuaded. In 2013, dismissing the 'silver-tongued' Sangakkara, the *Tamil Guardian* called for a sporting boycott of Sri Lanka:

> A clear, moral and principled message must be sent, that Sri Lanka cannot use its cricket team as ambassadors working to conceal the state's on-going systematic violence against the Tamil people. It is only with such determined international action that calls for accountability and justice become more than just empty rhetoric.[81]

Many Sri Lankans, reflecting perhaps on the billboards and the vainglorious aspirations behind such projects as the Mahinda Rajapaksa International Stadium, may have been thinking along the same lines as the Sri Lankan human rights activist who told Mike Marqusee after the World Cup victory in 1996 that the nation's cricket would now lose all its innocence. 'We are a society that apes others', she had said. 'First we aped the English gentry. Now we will start aping the Indian *nouveaux riches*'.[82]

Notes

1 S.S. Perera *The Janashakthi Book of Sri Lanka Cricket 1832–1996* (edited by S. Muthiah) Colombo: Janashakthi Insurance 1999.
2 To take two examples: Patrick Peebles, in his *A History of Sri Lanka* (Westport, CT: Greenwood Press, 2006) observes simply that cricket came to Sri Lanka in the 1830s, that it became popular and that Sri Lanka won the World Cup in 1996 (p.12) and, in her densely argued exploration of the history of Sri Lankan identities, Nira Wickramasinghe (*Sri Lanka in the Modern Age: A History* London: C. Hurst 2014) mentions cricket only in passing – as, for instance, when referring to the murder of a head teacher by Tamil separatists apparently for organising a cricket match between his pupils and Sri Lankan soldiers (p.313).

3 Peebles *A History* p.72.
4 See, for example, Anna Nicholas 'The pioneering ex-pats who put Ceylon tea on the map' http://www.telegraph.co.uk/expat/expatlife/10213779/The-pioneering-expats-who-put-Ceylon-tea-on-the-map.html Posted 2 August 2013, Access 17 February 2017.
5 Perera *The Janashakthi* p.18.
6 Steve A. Morrell 'DACC older than the tea industry celebrates 160 years' http://www.island.lk/index.php?page_cat=article-details&page=article-details&code_title=144928 Posted 8 May 2016, Access 15 February 2017.
7 Perera *The Janashakthi* pp.91–2.
8 Perera *The Janashakthi* p.141.
9 Morrell 'DACC older'.
10 See, for example Dean Allen 'South African cricket and British imperialism' in Dominic Malcolm, Jon Gemmell and Nalin Mehta (eds.) *The Changing Face of Cricket: From Imperial to Global Game* Abingdon: Routledge 2010 pp.34–51.
11 See http://www.genealogy.com/forum/regional/countries/topics/srilanka/2236/ Access 16 February 2017.
12 Perera *The Janashakthi* p.89.
13 See Arnold Wright (ed.) *Twentieth Century Impressions of Ceylon: Its History, People, Commerce, Industries, and Resources* New Delhi: Asian Educational Services 2007 (originally published 1907) p.315.
14 Perera *The Janashakthi* pp.164–6.
15 Perera *The Janashakthi* pp.176–7.
16 Perera *The Janashakthi* p.191.
17 Shehan Karunatilaka 'How cricket saved Sri Lanka' *The Observer* 13 March 2011 https://www.theguardian.com/world/2011/mar/13/how-cricket-saved-sri-lanka Access 17 February 2017.
18 Michael Roberts 'Shehan Karunatilaka blunders into cricket history' *Island Cricket* http://island-cricket.com/columns/michael_roberts/109240203/shehan-karunatilaka-blunders-into-cricket-history Posted 2 May 2011, Access 17 February 2017.
19 A phrase for which I'm indebted to the historian Richard Holt. See his *Sport and the British: A Modern History* Oxford: Oxford University Press 1990 p.232.
20 Perera *The Janashakthi* p.172.
21 See http://www.nomadscc.com/wandering-cricket-clubs Access 17 February 2017.
22 Peebles *A History* pp.97–8.
23 Michael Roberts 'Sri Lanka: the power of cricket and the power in cricket' in Stephen Wagg (ed.) *Cricket and National Identity in the Postcolonial Age* Abingdon: Routledge 2005 pp.132–58, pp.146 and 142.
24 Perera *The Janashakthi* p.226.
25 Wickramasinghe *Sri Lanka in the Modern Age* p.171.
26 See, for example, Nira Wickramasinghe 'Multiculturalism: a view from Sri Lanka' https://www.opendemocracy.net/colonial_multiculturalism.jsp Posted 30 May 2007, Access 20 February 2017.
27 Peebles *A History* p.100.
28 Peebles *A History* pp.106–13.
29 Perera *The Janashakthi* pp.252, 321–6.
30 Perera *The Janashakthi* p.268.
31 Roberts 'Sri Lanka: the power' p.145; Perera *The Janashakthi…* p.298.
32 Perera *The Janashakthi* pp.310–11.
33 Perera *The Janashakthi* pp.283, 287–91.

34 See Perera *The Janashakthi* pp.257, 262–3 and 272.
35 Perera *The Janashakthi* p.296.
36 Roberts 'Sri Lanka: the power' pp.142–3.
37 Perera *The Janashakthi* p.318.
38 Roberts 'Sri Lanka: the power' pp.149–50.
39 Roberts 'Sri Lanka: the power' p. 146.
40 Perera *The Janashakthi* p.316.
41 Perera *The Janashakthi* p.322.
42 Perera *The Janashakthi* p.349.
43 Perera *The Janashakthi* p.394.
44 'Gamini Dissanayake's farewell speech to Sri Lanka Cricket' http://www.island.lk/2009/04/17/sports7.html Access 19 February 2017.
45 Peebles *A History* pp.144–6.
46 Perera *The Janashakthi* p.490.
47 Premadasa, a UNP politician, was Prime Minister of Sri Lanka between 1978 and 1989 and President from 1989 to 1993. He was assassinated by a LTTE suicide bomber in 1994.
48 Fernando, educated at Royal College, Colombo and Oxford University, was another UNP politician. He was Sri Lankan Minister for Foreign Affairs between 2001 and 2004.
49 See Peebles *A History* pp.120, 127–8.
50 See Peebles *A History* pp.142–5, 148.
51 See Wickramasinghe *Sri Lanka in the Modern Age* pp.181–3.
52 Michael Roberts 'Bomb blasts in Pakistan and cricket' in Michael Roberts (ed.) *Essaying Cricket: Sri Lanka and Beyond* Colombo: Vijitha Yapa Publishers 2006 pp.9–13.
53 Quoted in Perera *The Janashakthi* p.396.
54 Michael Roberts 'Arjuna Ranatunga 1' in Roberts (ed.) *Essaying Cricket* pp.131–5, p.135.
55 Michael Roberts 'Racism in cricket? The Lehmann incident' in Roberts (ed.) *Essaying Cricket* pp.21–5, pp.22–3.
56 Michael Roberts 'The grunt, the spit and the snarl in sports' in Roberts (ed.) *Essaying Cricket* pp.96–7, p.97.
57 Michael Roberts 'Faint hearts in cricket, 1' in Roberts (ed.) *Essaying Cricket* pp.14–16, p.14.
58 Michael Roberts 'Faint hearts in cricket, 2' in Roberts (ed.) *Essaying Cricket* pp.17–20, p.17.
59 Quoted in Mike Marqusee *War Minus the Shooting: A Journey Through South Asia During Cricket's World Cup* London: Heinemann 1996 pp.280–1.
60 Marqusee *War Minus* pp.281–2.
61 Perera *The Janashakthi* p.521.
62 The incident can be seen at: https://www.youtube.com/watch?v=pCNHYBAiyiQ Access 21 February 2017.
63 See, for example, Derek Pringle 'Muttiah Muralitharan leaves Test cricket with his legacy still in the air' http://www.telegraph.co.uk/sport/cricket/international/srilanka/7899197/Muttiah-Muralitharan-leaves-Test-cricket-with-his-legacy-still-in-the-air.html Posted 20 July 2010, Access 21 February 2017.
64 See Bernard Whimpress 'Murali's chucking episodes in Australia' in Roberts (ed.) *Essaying Cricket* pp.305–15, p.313.
65 Michael Roberts 'Fundamentalism in cricket: crucifying Muralitharan' in Roberts (ed.) *Essaying Cricket* pp.4–5.

66 Mike Marqusee 'Bend it like Murali' https://www.theguardian.com/commentis free/2007/dec/03/comment.cricket#comment-4396162 Posted 3 December 2007, Access 21 February 2017.
67 Perera *The Janashakthi* p.349.
68 Karunatilaka 'How cricket saved'.
69 Michael Roberts 'Shehan Karunatilaka blunders into ethnicity in Sri Lankan cricket' http://island-cricket.com/columns/michael_roberts/109850208/shehan-karunatilaka-blunders-into-ethnicity-in-sri-lankan-cricket Posted 8 May 2011, Access 21 February 2017.
70 Roberts 'Sri Lanka: the power' p.135.
71 David Fidler and Sumit Ganguly 'India and Eastphalia' *Indiana Journal of Global Legal Studies* Vol. 17 No.1 Article 7 2010 http://www.repository.law.indiana.edu/ijgls/vol17/iss1/7.
72 Chaminda Weerawardhana 'Forgotten woes: Sri Lanka's neoliberal politics' https://www.opendemocracy.net/opensecurity/chaminda-weerawardhana/forgotten-woes-sri-lanka%E2%80%99s-neoliberal-politics Posted 27 September 2013, Access 21 February 2017.
73 Percy 'Mahinda' Rajapaksa, President of Sri Lanka 2005–15.
74 Weerawardhana 'Forgotten woes'.
75 Karunatilaka 'How cricket saved'.
76 See Nirmala Kannangara 'Hambantota white projects eat up economy' *The Sunday Leader* https://www.google.co.uk/search?q=hambantota+white+projects+eat+up&ie=utf-8&oe=utf-8&gws_rd=cr&ei=JVCsWKbqB8KyUbn_kJgL Posted 28 June 2015, Access 21 February 2107.
77 S.R. Pathiravithana 'Political cricket or cricket politics: whatever it is, it stinks like the Sooriyawewa toilet' http://www.sundaytimes.lk/161016/sports/political-cricket-or-cricket-politics-whatever-it-is-it-stinks-like-the-sooriyawewa-toilet-212589.html Posted 16 October 2016, Access 21 February 2017.
78 The speech can be read in full at: http://www.espncricinfo.com/srilanka/content/story/522183.html Access 21 February 2017.
79 Thiviyanthan Krishnamohan 'The other face of Kumar Sangakkara: the man who united Sri Lanka spiritually' https://www.sportskeeda.com/cricket/other-face-kumar-sangkkara-united-sri-lanka-spiritually Posted 27 October 2014, Access 21 February 2017.
80 'Kumar Sangakkara offered a role in politics by Sri Lanka president' http://www.bbc.co.uk/sport/cricket/34042413 Posted 24 August 2015, Access 21 February 2017.
81 'Politics and cricket: stepping up to the crease on Sri Lanka' http://www.tamilguardian.com/content/politics-and-cricket-stepping-crease-sri-lanka Posted 4 April 2013, Access 21 February 2017.
82 Marqusee *War Minus* p.287.

Part II

Cricket in the age of globalisation

The second half of this book relates to globalisation and examines some of the issues that globalisation has raised for the game of cricket. It is in seven chapters.

The first of these (No.10) examines the social and political history of the Ashes series between England and Australia, charting important changes in the meanings of social class and masculinity that these series have carried.

The second (No.11) describes the campaign for one-day cricket, something which took place predominantly in England, but which, once successful, provided the basis for the globalisation of this format of the game.

The third chapter (No.12) is about the changing relationship of the mass media to the game of cricket and it charts the transition from the 'Test Match Special' style of broadcasting (established at the British Broadcasting Corporation in the 1950s) to the more diverse and populist engagement that we see today, wherein many people consume cricket via new media such as their computers and mobile phones.

The fourth chapter (No.13) looks at the spread of women's cricket, something that is unlikely to have taken place without the global movement that was feminism – specifically the so-called 'second wave' of feminism of the late 1950s and early 60s.

Many of those who experience cricket via the new media are below the age of 30 and many of them cannot comprehend a game which lasts for days and may still yield no winner. Their preferred format of cricket is likely therefore to be Twenty20 – the subject of the fifth chapter, No.14. Twenty20 cricket represents the most substantial and important innovation made by the game's administrators to re-fashion cricket in a way that might better reconcile it to contemporary consumer appetites and global media schedules.

The chapter also deals with the development and commercial success of the Twenty20 cricket format and the rise of the Indian Premier League (IPL). The most significant development in cricket governance during the period to be covered by this book is the apparent loss of English hegemony. Two events illustrate this: the move of the International Cricket Council to Dubai (closing its offices at Lord's and its commercial arm in Monaco) in

2005 and the inauguration of the IPL in 2008. In 2010, the US-based Indian academic Amit Gupta described India as 'the epicentre of cricket', a development that he ascribes to three factors: increased television ownership in India, facilitated by new satellite technology; India's winning of the World Cup in 1983; and the opening up of India's economy to multinational corporations in the mid-1980s – cricket provided an appropriate vehicle for the advertising of their consumer products. In 2008 the first season of the IPL was staged. A lucrative, made-for-television event, with a big budget and the full panoply of contemporary marketing techniques, the IPL is seen by many as a vision of cricket's future. It can be seen as the consummation of the ascent of the 'Asian bloc' – much discussed in the first half of the book – in world cricket.

Chapter 15 deals with the rise of technocracy – as a specialist vocabulary, as the appliance of rational techniques and the embrace of the appropriate assumptions – in global cricket: the emergence, in effect, of the 'laptop coach' and his (or her) support team.

The final chapter, No.16, discusses the various attempts to achieve a more full-blooded globalisation of cricket – after all, at the time of writing only ten countries are permitted to play it at the highest level – and discusses the obstacles to these attempts.

Chapter 10

Straight-shooting blokes

Social distinction, masculinity and myth in the Ashes, 1945 to 2015

The Ashes series takes place periodically between the national sides of England and Australia. The female version was inaugurated in 1930 (see Chapter 13); the male is the oldest international cricket event in the world, having been inaugurated in 1882. This chapter examines the latter, charting the changing notions of class, national identity and (almost exclusively white) masculinity that have characterised it since the Second World War. It is a revised and extended version of an article I published in 2012[1] and takes up themes broached initially in Chapter 2.

'Which one of you bastards. . .?' Social class and the Ashes after Bodyline

There's little doubt that the now so widely documented events of the Bodyline series staged in the winter of 1932–3 coloured relations between the Australian and English cricket teams during subsequent decades and that refractions of social class were a clear element in these relations. However, although it had almost no basis in proletarian organisation or radical left politics, there was, as in Rugby League,[2] a shared Britishness between the two sets of players which was not shaken by Bodyline – on the contrary, most Australian cricketers had regarded Bodyline as a betrayal of Britishness. Moreover, in the early 1930s, class was already an issue in the Australian dressing room; sometimes pre-existing resentments there were displaced onto the English and sometimes they were not. Two men in particular – Australian batsman Donald Bradman and Douglas Jardine, England captain in the Bodyline series – had been lightning rods for this ill feeling and had helped thereby to crystallise the typically Australian rendering of social distinction, refracted as it was, then and since, through an apparently egalitarian masculine 'mateship'.

Since before the First World War (and for most of the twentieth century), an abiding issue in the Australian national team was the perceived meanness of the Australian Cricket Board (ACB). In 1912 there had been a serious dispute which had resulted in the Australian team leaving to tour England without six of its leading members and arguments about the restriction of players' rights had rumbled on ever since. Anger among the players was probably heightened by the fact that the Board was composed variously of men from Australia's most established families, its most prestigious colleges and its elite professions and businesses.[3] On the face of it, Bradman had been as aggrieved as any team-mate in the matter of players' rights, having in 1932 been refused permission by the board to write and broadcast on the Test series in which he was due to play. (He had threatened to withdraw from the team.)[4] But Bradman's stand, as was keenly appreciated in the Australian dressing room, was perceived to be not for players' rights as such, but specifically for his own. A volume of literature now attests to Bradman's partial estrangement from his own team, on three grounds. First, Bradman had aspired to join Australia's commercial elite and moved to Adelaide in 1935 to become a stockbroker. He wrote somewhat defensively about this in his autobiography fifteen years later: 'It is wrong for people to think of our large companies in terms of wealthy industrialists when they are, in the main, owned by thousands of shareholders and are a vital necessity to the well-being and democratic progress of our country'.[5] Second, he was both a Protestant and a Mason, making in particular for fractious relations with the Irish-descended 'larrikin'[6] cricketers in the Australian side, such as Jack Fingleton[7] and Bill O'Reilly. 'Don Bradman', O'Reilly said, 'was a teetotaller, ambitious, conservative and meticulous. I was outspoken, gregarious'.[8] This hinted at the third ground for Bradman's unpopularity: he breached the code of mainstream egalitarian middle-Australian masculinity – he was aloof and did not buy a round, swear, back a horse, 'chat up' a young woman or fraternise with the other players. An anonymous team-mate commented that Bradman hadn't spent twopence on the 1930 tour of England.[9] At a party in the 1960s, Vic Richardson, Australian vice-captain in the Bodyline series and another member of the 'larrikin' tendency, was overheard to say to Bradman, 'In England the President [of the MCC] is picked by his friends. If they had that system in Australia, you'd never get a vote, you little cunt.'[10]

Richardson's social class profile was not dissimilar to Bradman's. Both had humble beginnings (Richardson's father was a painter and decorator, Bradman's a carpenter). Both were involved in commerce at some level: Richardson was a salesman, Bradman, aside from his brokerage and journalism, appeared in innumerable advertisements.[11] Both, like most of their cricketing contemporaries, were Empire loyalists: Bradman would accept a knighthood in 1949 and Richardson an OBE in 1954. They both held conservative political views and supported the right-wing Liberal Country League (LCL) in South Australia, Richardson seeking to stand for the LCL in the Federal Division of Kingston, South Adelaide in 1949.[12] But they appeared to be divided, nevertheless, by social class, Bradman, it seems, being defined by his class of aspiration and Richardson by his class of origin – as filtered through the mythically egalitarian mateship that beckoned most Australian males. Bodyline had demonstrated this.

After Bodyline, some Australians were inclined to hold England fast bowler Harold Larwood, a former miner in the Nottinghamshire coalfield, responsible for the Bodyline tactic of 1932–3 (and, indeed the MCC subsequently called on him to apologise to the Australian cricket board for injuries sustained by their players). Douglas Jardine (Winchester and Oxford, the son of a colonial official) published a self-absolving memoir later in 1933, instead blaming Australian crowds for filling the air with 'partisan electricity' and attacking the 'threadbare "humour"' of Australian barrackers.[13] Bradman was reticent about Larwood: when the two met in London in 1948 Bradman was 'courteous but clipped' and didn't mention Bodyline.[14] But Richardson was not. At the height of the controversy, he was quick to identify the upper-class Jardine as the villain of the piece. 'OK', he said to the Australian team, 'which of you bastards called Larwood a bastard instead of this bastard [Jardine]?'[15]

Larwood refused to make an apology and never played Test cricket again. He migrated to Australia in 1950, encouraged by some of his opponents in the Bodyline series such as Jack Fingleton.[16] It seems probable that many Australians saw him as a victim of British Establishment duplicity. He was also seen as a great cricketer: among his admirers was the Swedish Australian fast bowler Ray Lindwall, who had taken to Larwood while watching the Sydney Test of 1932 as an 11-year-old. 'From time to time', wrote Lindwall in 1954, 'I have been told that my action bears resemblance to that of Larwood. That is a real compliment'.[17]

England had come back to tour Australia in 1936. They had lost the Ashes but, in a memoir of ten years later, Wally Hammond, who had played in the Bodyline series, expressed himself pleased that 'happy relations' had been restored: he called it the 'Reconciliation Tour'. However, he was at pains to defend Jardine and, in doing so, pointed up the paradoxical nature of the various metaphors for social class prevailing in the culture of elite cricket at the time. Jardine, he said, had been called 'aloof' and 'supercilious', notably in a book of 1933 called *The Barracker at Bay*.[18] Hammond preferred to see this as Jardine's 'imperturbability, his calmness when things go wrong and equally when they go right, his cold determination to win, neither giving nor seeking quarter'. Australians, he argued, had chosen to render this as 'giving them the colonial', but they had a few cricket captains of their own who fitted this description.[19] Playing coldly and rationally to win was, of course, wholly contrary to the prevailing amateur ethos of the time; these were traits ordinarily ascribed to professionals. Hammond, though, was fully conversant with the ambiguities of social distinction in elite English cricket and, in this regard, he had something in common with Bradman. He had often difficult relations with teammates and was ambitious to cross cricket's social divide: a professional for much of his career, in 1937, at the age of 34, he acquired amateur status. Reflecting later on this transition, he observed, apparently without irony, that, although happy as a professional, 'I had not made very much money'.[20] It also made him eligible for the England captaincy – he was made captain for the Ashes series in England in 1938 and was made captain of his county, Gloucestershire, in 1939. (At this time a strict amateur–professional distinction still obtained in English county cricket. Amateurs and professionals of the same team still changed and ate in separate facilities and every year saw a Gentleman versus Players match.) While the embrace of amateurism might have made him a class traitor in the eyes of some English professionals, in another irony, it boosted his standing in Australia. The Australian journalist Clif Cary recorded that, when Hammond had arrived for the Ashes series of 1946–7, although 'aloof, morose and generally unapproachable' he was cheered everywhere he went because:

> Australians, always opposed to class distinction in sport, appreciated the fact that there was no gulf between him and his professionals [....] the view was general that Hammond would confound certain MCC diehards who had opposed his selection on the grounds that he was an ex-professional, a doubtful after-dinner speaker and unlikely to be a social success.[21]

However, for some England players Hammond represented not the absence of social distinction, but the active embrace of it. On that tour, as England wicketkeeper Godfrey Evans recalled, Hammond had travelled in his own Jaguar car while the rest of the team took the train.[22] 'My only regret', said Denis Compton who also played for England on that tour, 'was the attitude of Wally Hammond, the England captain [. . .] I never got to know Hammond. The professionals were seldom invited to dine with him'.[23]

'We are the real amateurs': social class and the Ashes in the post-war years

In the 1940s and 1950s, the Ashes continued to be a theatre for the rehearsal of class myths prevailing in the cricket cultures of the respective countries, but with some important new inflections. Wartime, and immediate post-war, experiences strengthened the bonds of friendship between the subaltern[24] cricketers in the two countries. In the case of Australia, this category included virtually every player bar Bradman. A number of Australian cricketers had enlisted in the Australian Imperial Force (AIF) during the war and served mostly in the ranks. For example Arthur Morris, who toured England in 1948, spent the war as a private in the transport corps;[25] Keith Miller had been a pilot in the Royal Australian Air Force (RAAF), for a while stationed in England; Ray Lindwall had resigned his job in 1943 (employees of his firm were exempted from military service) in order to join the army;[26] and Lindsay Hassett, Bradman's vice-captain on the Ashes tour of England in 1948, had refused a commission in the AIF in 1940. He later accepted promotion to Sergeant, and then Warrant Officer, only because he was selected to captain Australia in a series of post-war Victory Tests and his opposite number, the upwardly mobile Wally Hammond, was a squadron leader: 'Lindsay', according to his biographer, 'would not budge beyond Warrant Officer II'.[27] Ian Johnson, Hassett's successor, another member of the Australian team to tour England in 1948 and, like Miller, a former pilot in the RAAF, typified an invigorated, if loyal, Australian egalitarianism. Writing in 1957, he noted a more amicable relationship between the two teams, especially during Peter May's captaincy of the England team in the Ashes series of 1956. Nevertheless he asserted that, in general, Australians were better ambassadors than Englishmen, because they 'accept people on their face value'.[28] He went so far as to accuse England player Trevor Bailey (Dulwich College and Cambridge and a prominent figure in the Ashes series in England in 1953) of 'lording it over the "Colonials"' and a 'dour' Len Hutton (England captain in 1953) of discouraging fraternisation between the two sides.[29] Hutton, here, was an important signifier. He was from a small Yorkshire hamlet called Fulneck, near Leeds, and his father was a foreman-joiner and bricklayer; the Huttons were Moravians, a Protestant sect.[30] Yorkshire represented something that Australian sportspeople, in general, liked:[31] it was seen (and often proclaimed by its inhabitants) as a place where people spoke bluntly and, like the Australia that flourished in the national imagination, people there were treated 'on their face value'. The abrasive Yorkshire fast bowler Fred Trueman typified the Yorkshireness to which Australians warmed. Trueman himself wrote with pride of how he had bonded with the barrackers of The Hill at Sydney Cricket Ground on the Ashes tour of 1958 – they'd lined up cans of ale for him to sample[32] – and, in another memoir, judged that 'underneath all their aggression and competitiveness', Australian cricketers were '"bonzer" blokes with whom you could form long-lasting friendships'.[33] Jim Laker, also a Yorkshireman and a veteran of several Ashes series between 1948 and 1959, once wrote that Trueman, who was regularly in trouble with the English cricket authorities, would have '"got by" better as an Australian'.[34] Hutton, though, divided Australians just as he divided Yorkshire people. Hutton certainly professed a love for Australia,[35] but he was socially ambitious in the same way that Bradman and Hammond had been. He tried to modify his Yorkshire accent, moved to live in the South of England and sent his son to private school; in 1956 he became (and remains) the only cricketer from the north of England to be knighted.[36] Aptly, Hutton's boyhood hero had been Douglas Jardine.[37]

Johnson followed these observations to their logical conclusion. The amateur–professional distinction in English cricket, he wrote, 'does seem to savour of humbug'. Australian Test players, he argued, were the true amateurs since they took leave from their jobs and were paid only 'an average of

£A2 10s a day expenses, this excluding hotel bills, travelling and such-like' to cover this 'broken time': 'We are amateurs because none of the Australian touring team lives off cricket. We all have jobs which are our bread and butter, and the majority of our time is spent at those jobs'.[38] The general nature of these jobs did not escape the notice of sympathetic English professionals like Denis Compton, himself the son of a self-employed painter and decorator. While Bradman was a broker, many of his teammates in the late 1940s – men such as Lindsay Hassett, Colin McCool and Arthur Morris – were in less prestigious, lower-middle-class positions such as salesman or commercial traveller.[39] And, if these Australian part-timers were the true amateurs, then, as with Bodyline, English 'gentlemen' certainly did not have a monopoly on 'fair play'. Testimony from or about this period asserts that this Australian or that would neither dispute an umpire's decision, nor seek to profit privately from a mistaken one. According to his biographer, Keith Miller – a hero to succeeding generations of 'larrikin' Australian cricketers – always 'walked', never waiting to be given out.[40] Similarly Ray Lindwall recalled a decision given against Hassett in the Leeds Test of 1948:

> Hassett never shows the slightest disagreement with a decision and when he returned to the dressing-room he sat down quietly and, as he took off his pads, began to look at the television of the Wimbledon Tennis tournament. One of the Australian team watching from the balcony glanced into the room and called out: 'Didn't hit that, did you, Lindsay? I thought it was off your hip'. 'It was', replied Lindsay simply without taking his eyes off the screen.[41]

Bradman, predictably, was a more contentious case. A number of England players of the time cited an incident in the First Test of the 1946–7 series in Brisbane when Bradman appeared to be caught at slip by Jack Ikin off the bowling of Bill Voce. 'I can only suppose', wrote England batsman Bill Edrich, like Compton a *bon viveur* and drinking partner to several of the Australian team, 'that [the umpire] must have thought that the ball hit the ground after leaving the bat; but every English player thought that it never went within nine inches of the grass'.[42] Compton assumed the umpire to have ruled that the ball hadn't hit the bat:

> None of us was in any doubt that Don had got a snick, but the umpire gave it not out. Most of us shrugged and got on with the game, but I recall that our skipper Wally Hammond was absolutely livid. He hardly spoke a civil word to The Don for the rest of the tour, apart from saying heads or tails when they tossed up.[43]

In the Australian dressing room opinion was divided, recalled Lindwall. Some thought it a fair catch, unacknowledged; others that Bradman had 'played down hard on a Yorker. On his return Don said the latter was correct. There could be no doubt about his sincerity'.[44] Lindwall, who liked a drink and a bet and thus, like most of the Australian side of the late 1940s, stood socially apart from Bradman, nevertheless classed him with the other Australian 'true amateurs' in matters of sportsmanship: 'Even when the majority of those watching thought that the umpire had made a mistake, Bradman would return to the dressing-room, sit down quietly to unbuckle his pads and go for his bath without a suggestion of dissatisfaction or disagreement with the ruling'.[45]

Moreover, aside from seeing themselves as keepers of the amateur flame, Australia's cricketers were open in their admiration of the British monarchy. The Australian Ashes squad travelled to London to watch the coronation procession of Queen Elizabeth II in 1953. Jack Fingleton, in Britain to cover the Ashes as a journalist, was in Westminster Abbey for the service: as the newly crowned Queen departed 'to the ringing peals of the Anthem, I thought of England's future unfolding in front of her, and her presence of youthful beauty and majestic bearing the doubts and the tribulations of the future seemed to fade away. And so may it be. God Save and aid Queen Elizabeth!'[46] Ian Johnson described going to Buckingham Palace with Keith Miller in 1956 to receive MBEs in similarly awestruck terms: it was, he said, 'possibly the crowning moment of my sporting life'.[47] The dashing Miller was embraced as a celebrity in post-war London and was on several occasions invited to join Princess Margaret's social circle.[48] This permitted the confident Miller and British dignitaries on occasion to play with British social distinction and, in doing so, to present it as a matter of performance. For example, he befriended Lord Tedder, Marshall of the Royal Air Force and President of Surrey County Cricket Club. At a reception for the Australian players at Windsor Castle in 1948 Tedder pretended to be a waiter:

> With a full tray in his hand, he approached Miller. 'Excuse me, sir,' Tedder said. 'Your tea, sir'. 'Thank you, boy,' Miller replied in an exaggerated pompous English voice to the astonishment of others in the tour group who recognised the illustrious servant. 'Here you are, lad.' Miller gave him a penny. 'Thank you very much, sir,' Tedder said with a deferential tug of his cap as he backed away.[49]

As Miller had found, for the likes of Lord Tedder and Princess Margaret, deference and social distinction – still firmly established in English cricket – were a game, the rules of which might be suspended (or reversed) in private. But, as Miller's fellow professional and close friend Denis Compton observed, 'Miller was never anti-Establishment'.[50]

Given the public condescension of their own cricket authorities and comparing it to typical Australian demeanour, some English people assumed, in the words of Ray Lindwall, that 'everybody is free and easy in Australia, with Jack thinking himself not only as good as his master, but often a sight better . . . [but] Australians can be as stiff and starchy as any others'. Lindwall cited an incident when on the Ashes tour of 1946–7, he, Godfrey Evans and Denis Compton had, on an extremely hot day, been refused admission to an exclusive Sydney golf club for not wearing jackets.[51]

The commercial travellers strike back: markets, media and the Ashes, 1960–80

The period from the late 1950s to the 1970s is one during which the respective social class mythologies of the two cricket cultures intertwined with a range of new factors. At a level of social and economic structure, two things were crucial. One, noted by Tony Collins, was the loosening of the imperial and economic bond between Britain and Australia, as expressed in Britain's application to join the European Common Market in 1961, and the Commonwealth Immigration Act of the following year, which abolished free entry to the UK for Commonwealth citizens.[52] The other was the trend in the Australian economy toward the greater commodification of culture and the image – widely accepted as characteristic of late capitalism and/or the condition of postmodernity. In cricket this was typified by the so-called 'Packer Affair', in which Kerry Packer, a scion of a wealthy Australian media-owning family, staged his own rival tournament to the Ashes during the winter of 1978 and employed most of the world's leading players to do so.[53] At another level, the abolition of the distinction between amateurs and professionals in English cricket and the ongoing financial concerns of the Australian squad, seldom accommodated by their cricket board, were also factors.

In the autumn of 1958 an England team arrived in Australia for the forthcoming Ashes encounters. Ex-player Alec Bedser was travelling with the team as a reporter for the *News of the World*. The England captain, Peter May, who bore the historically typical profile of an England captain (Charterhouse public school, Cambridge University and a job as an insurance broker and underwriter at Lloyd's in the City of London) had requested that press conferences be handled by the tour manager Freddie Brown (another Cambridge blue and veteran of the Bodyline series). He had also asked that there be no questions about the 'Wardle incident' (spin bowler Johnny Wardle had just been sacked by Yorkshire and England for public criticism of his county captain in the *Daily Mail*).[54] Bedser, the son of a bricklayer, a staunch Conservative and May's devoted lieutenant in the Surrey county side, nevertheless thought May's avoidance of the press a mistake; besides, the latter, he said, were no longer interested in cricket 'pure and simple' – 'they were looking for "dressing room" stories and . . . it must be realized that those in cricket are only too willing to accept the publicity they are given. The press therefore are entitled to expect the fullest information and co-operation on all matters of interest affecting the tour'.[55] He also noted that the 'aggressive approach' of Freddie Trueman had made him the most popular England player with Australian crowds.[56] In 1960, the England and Surrey bowler Jim Laker published a second volume of autobiography called *Over to Me*. In it he recounted an altercation he'd had with May, his county and Test captain. May had accused Laker of not trying in a county match. Laker had demanded an apology and May had refused to give one.[57] Laker had then had his honorary membership of both Surrey and the MCC withdrawn and never played either for Surrey or for England again. As one of Laker's biographers observed, these comments (by a professional about an amateur) were 'nothing short of sensational' for the time.[58] But it has to be noted that circumstances now prevailed in which such comments were *allowed* to become sensational. The English popular sports press, conscious of a post-war antipathy towards upper-class high-handedness, were now prepared to publish stories they might have rejected in the 1930s. This was even more the case in Australia. Moreover, as Collins observed, in the 1960s, in the wake of aforementioned political changes, the Australian popular press moved toward a greater disparagement of Britons, with ever more recourse to the derogatory terms 'Pommie' and 'whingeing Poms'.

The distinction between amateurs and professionals in English cricket was abolished in 1962: it had become an embarrassment and its hypocrisies by then widely discussed. In any event the MCC had agreed to stage a one-day cricket competition bearing the name of a sponsor (the Gillette Cup) and a sport which practised formal class division was hardly marketable in an increasingly demotic age. But the cancellation of the gentleman–player divide did not mitigate Australian (or even British) talk of class privilege in English cricket. Quite the opposite: players were now measured against a harsher and more egalitarian yardstick, especially in the Australian dressing room where the 'Pommie' lexicon began to influence Ashes discourse.

The principal focus of this discourse was Ted Dexter. Dexter was the son of a wealthy insurance broker. In his time at Cambridge University (1955–8), where he was registered for a degree in languages, he had not attended a single lecture; he had been the last cricketer to play for Sussex as an amateur and captained England on their Ashes tour of 1962–3. He was nevertheless a technocrat – for example, England batsman Tom Graveney records that, on the outward voyage in 1962, Dexter tried to arrange for Olympic runner Gordon Pirie to provide fitness training for the players (who were horrified);[59] Trueman said that, as a captain, Dexter had 'more theories than Charles Darwin'.[60] Dexter became a successful businessman and, as such, would remain abreast of the times, engaging with proliferating media-related commerce – he later ran a PR company, for example, and wrote a column for the tabloid *Sunday Mirror*. As noted earlier, in 2005 the cricket writer Simon Hughes would describe Dexter, who pioneered the one-day game, as 'the man who shaped modern cricket'.[61] He once declared a Sussex innings closed from Brighton race course – an act of devil-may-care which, had it been committed by Keith Miller, would have secured his legend in larrikin Australia for all time.[62] But Dexter had an almost eighteenth-century aristocratic bearing and, in the emergent anti-Pom perspective of the early 1960s, he was readily rendered as an anachronism in a classless new age. Australians mocked his accent: the story got around, for example, that Dexter had asked the umpire for 'two laigs' [two legs] in a Test match[63] and he had publically denounced the Ashes (an increasingly lucrative media text) as a concept: on tour in 1962 he called the urn 'a bane and a nuisance'.[64] In an emergent press framing of the Ashes, rooted in established national-social class mythology, Dexter emerged as a key symbol: as his biographer noted, in Ted Australia had, in effect, constructed another Jardine.

In this regard Dexter was not helped by the tour arrangements for 1962. On the previous Ashes tour of 1958 the professionals in the England team had been told that they must call their assistant manager Desmond Eagar (ex-captain of Oxford University and Hampshire) 'Mr Eagar', albeit that the Australian team addressed him as 'Des'.[65] In 1962 the England party was managed by the Duke of Norfolk – a figure who, irrespective of his personal bearing, resided at the very top of the English hierarchy of hereditary privilege. This was meat and drink to an Australian press now in a mode of heightened *faux*-egalitarianism. Richie Benaud, Australian captain and a trained journalist, recalled hearing of the Duke's appointment; he immediately called up the Australian popular newspapers and with some relish recited the Duke's full name and title down the phone: 'Bernard Marmaduke Fitzalan Howard, the Sixteenth Duke of Norfolk'.[66]

By the end of the 1960s, however, those cricketers in the England team who carried *both* a biography of hereditary privilege *and* the carefree ethos of the pre-war amateur were a dying breed. The England team at this time was dominated by Raymond Illingworth. Illingworth was the son of a joiner from the small town of Farsley, west of Leeds, a district that had spawned a number of first-class cricketers, including Hutton of nearby Fulneck. His social background was like that of most Yorkshire, and most Australian, cricketers: self-employed working class, ostensibly proletarian but with no connection to organised labour. He'd first played for England in 1958 and was senior professional on the Ashes tour of 1962. He had watched with bemusement as, despite the formal rescinding of the distinction by the MCC, the ex-Oxford and Cambridge men in the team had dined privately with the Duke of Norfolk.[67] Illingworth, however, railed only against the class distinction and not necessarily against its beneficiaries. As his teammate John Snow wrote, Illingworth 'expected professionalism on the field and wanted it off the field as well'.[68] Illingworth admired May for his tough captaincy – May was, he thought, 'quite a hard man' who told the England players to 'get stuck in' – 'Not the sort of attitude one really expected from the public school and university background that he had'.[69] Illingworth, however, expressed open impatience with May's contemporary Colin Cowdrey. Cowdrey had left Oxford in 1954 without sitting for a degree and was married to the daughter of retail magnate Stuart Chiesman, chairman of Kent CCC and High Sheriff of the county; Cowdrey was employed as a meeter-and-greeter PR man in Chiesman's companies.[70] He did not believe in Illingworth's brand of professionalism: on tour, Illingworth recalled, Cowdrey sometimes missed net practice – even when, as Illingworth's vice-captain in 1970–1, he was supposed to be organising it – and once, during the Ashes winter of 1962–3, he had refused to act as twelfth man in a tour match and had, instead, taken his wife to the cinema.[71] The old order, which Cowdrey represented, occasionally disclosed its resentment that more meritocratic figures such as Illingworth were now in the ascendancy: when Illingworth beat her husband to the England captaincy for the 1970–1 Ashes tour, Penny Cowdrey told a newspaper that Colin would have got it 'had he been born in a semi-detached in Bradford'.[72]

In 2009 Illingworth said that he had 'always thought that Australians are actually Yorkshiremen in disguise'; like Hutton, he shared Jardine's belief that 'beating the Australians was far more important than making friends with them'.[73] His opposing captain during the early 1970s, Ian Chappell, was a man of like mind. A BBC correspondent judged the first Ashes series between the two as captains (in Australia in 1970–1) to be 'the most hostile Ashes series since Bodyline, nearly 40 years earlier'.[74] With the all-too-obvious exception of Cowdrey, this was, in effect, the first intra-class Ashes Test series, both teams characterised by masculine aggression, professional competitiveness and an often angry sense of having striven to be where they were. As in 1932–3 the matches were dominated by short-pitched bowling and the men who dispensed it: Dennis Lillee, the son of a long-distance truck driver from Perth, and Sussex's John Snow. Improbably, since fast bowling at Test level was historically a working-class pursuit, Snow was an ex-public schoolboy and the son of a vicar. As we saw, however, he subscribed fully to Illingworth's professionalised code of do-the-business ethics. Lillee, for his part, cited Fred Trueman as an important boyhood influence.[75]

Chappell was the grandson of Vic Richardson and presided over a team which, while honouring the memories of his grandfather Vic's 'great mates' Fingleton, O'Reilly, Keith Miller,[76] and other plain-speaking larrikins, had fully dispensed with the cricket match courtesies of the Hassett era. When captaining Australia against the Combined Universities at Oxford in 1972, for instance, Chappell was asked by the Universities' captain to do up his bootlace, which had come undone; he replied 'You're not doing anything else out here, pal; do it up yourself!'[77] Whereas high-status cricketers like Cowdrey or Bradman had discreet chats with clients or investors, Chappell came from a more aggressive and consumer-oriented part of the capitalist forest. Like previous generations of Australian Test players, he was involved in sales, but, unlike the commercial travellers of the 1940s and 50s, from the early 1960s he had done promotional work, setting up stalls in shopping malls and giving PR advice to consumer-based companies such as travel agencies, Nestlé Australia and the cigarette manufacturers WD and HO Wills – after the Ashes victory of 1974–5 as Ian Chappell Enterprises.[78] Others in Chappell's team had, or coveted, similar jobs. They knew therefore about aggressive marketing and about the sort of money that changed hands in media and advertising circles.

In 1974, however, when England returned to Australia, the Ashes became an anti-Pom melodrama and a metaphor for the decline of the old Jardine elite at Lord's. Illingworth's successor was Mike Denness, a batsman who had difficulty, like most of his team, in batting against fast bowling. Although born in Scotland his captaincy of the southern county of Kent and his persistent politeness gave him an Establishment air. He was no match for an opposition of militant, aggressive new-world professionals and suffered the ignominy of omitting himself from the team for the fourth Test in Sydney. With three England batsmen already nursing fractures to their hands, Colin Cowdrey, now 41, flew out to Australia to bat in the Second Test. Australian fast bowler Jeff Thomson, a plasterer's son and beach bum, had inflicted much of the damage. He describes Cowdrey's appearance on the field of play rather as someone might characterise an exhibit in a post-imperial theme park:

> I had just taken my cap from the umpire when up comes the roly-poly England batsman we call 'Kipper'. And he thrusts out his hand and introduces himself. I must admit it was a bit bizarre. This bloke has just turned up in Australia, Dennis Lillee and I had just dismantled his team in Brisbane and were about to do the same here, and Cowdrey arrives at the crease all smiles and looking for a nice chat in the middle.[79]

Other factors, beside proliferating anti-Pom rhetoric, fired the growing abrasiveness of the Australian team during Ashes encounters of the 1970s. One was a sense of technocracy, fuelled in turn by escalating grievances over money. In the early 1970s Ian Chappell made several representations to the Australian Cricket Board, now chaired by Bradman, and each time his request for increased remuneration was met with a flat 'Can't do that, son'.[80] The Australian players felt their professional status was undermined by their pay rate and they were outraged when the board responded with invocations of the amateurism of the Johnson generation. Soon after ACB secretary Alan Barnes wrote in 1975 that there were '500,000 cricketers who would love to play for Australia for nothing', opening batsman Ian Redpath had grabbed him by the throat and asked 'but how bloody good would they be?' Chappell made clear Redpath had been speaking for the team.[81]

The other factor was the intervention of Kerry Packer in 1977. Packer's one-day cricket tournament had a manifest effect on the social-class dimension of the Ashes. It brought Australian players the substantial fees that they thought they were worth and it undermined what England captain and Packer consultant Tony Greig had called the 'master and servant relationship' in cricket governance.[82] The Australian team had been elevated into that section of the middle class that harboured the emergent professions related to impression management. Packer's made-for-television World Series Cricket had taught them the mechanics of publicity – through a process of Disneyfication[83] they had learned to play characters which were heightened versions of themselves. This gave them social success on something like their own terms: they were now Celebrity Larrikins whose very existence mocked the tight-arsed status consciousness of the country's old Anglophile elite, still personified by Bradman. When these players returned to Test cricket in 1979, two things were evident.

First, with the impression management elite (TV) having won a symbolic victory over the Anglophile elite of old-established business, law and finance (represented by Bradman and the ACB), for the Packer players who returned to the Australian side those who had represented the team in their absence might become objects of contempt. Kim Hughes, the captain, was a case in point. According to his biographer Hughes was derided as a 'golden boy' who happily placed himself in the play-for-love camp. His captaincy was undermined. As Gideon Haigh observed, whereas Ian Chappell was a 'bloke', Hughes was not – despite possessing key 'bloke' signifiers: for instance, he played Australian Rules football as, among others, Vic Richardson had done.[84]

Second, a number of Australian cricketers, in keeping with their greater appreciation of cricket as a TV show, had become increasing conscious of themselves as texts. There had been evidence of this earlier in the decade. Jeff Thomson, another Australian who, as a boy, had drawn inspiration from Fred Trueman,[85] had said in 1974 that he liked to see blood on the pitch. Later he reflected: 'Although it wasn't true that I enjoyed seeing batsman twitching about on the ground and bleeding all over the place after I'd hit them, it probably didn't do my image any harm'.[86] In December 1979 an incident in a Test match at the WACA (Western Australia Cricket Association) ground in Perth crystallised perfectly the re-cast social class mythology of Australia–England cricket encounters. Lillee and his captain, Ian Chappell's younger brother Greg, contrived a memorable scene in the now-established 'Aussie–Pom' melodrama. Lillee came to the crease carrying an aluminium bat. The England captain, Mike Brearley, objected to it, arguing that this bat might damage the match ball. Lillee was asked to change it and a team-mate emerged with a conventional bat. It was refused, whereupon Greg Chappell took the field, apparently to intercede, and Lillee threw the aluminium bat at him. 'People have asked me since', Lillee, who stood to gain a substantial licence fee and royalties from sales of this bat, wrote later, 'why I used it in a Test match – it was a marketing ploy. I'm not ashamed of that'.[87] Chappell's biographer detected a skilful marriage of Jardine-like pragmatism and impression-management in Greg's handling of the incident, noting the captain's pleasure at having his fast bowler thus fired up for the forthcoming England innings and that 'the Poms became the cause of it all'.[88] Brearley, in this regard, was a perfect foil for Lillee's performance of the militant larrikin. He had spent most of the 1960s (1961–8) at Cambridge University and had then captained Middlesex. Although a batsman, he averaged only a little over 20 in Tests and had never scored a Test hundred: an apparent affront to Australian egalitarianism. Commentator and ex-Australian captain Richie Benaud, another Packer consultant, judged Brearley to be 'one of the greatest captains I have seen'.[89] He noted, however, that, when Brearley had become England captain in 1977, 'it was, looking from the outside, almost as though an amateur had returned to the fold in English cricket, not that his views were those of an amateur'.[90] But television, as the Lillee–Chappells axis readily appreciated, centrally involves 'looking from the outside' and, for the purposes of promoting the new aluminium bat to a mass public, Brearley became the effete, 'whingeing Pom', apparently selected for his class position rather than his ability, a snooty conservative blocking resourceful Aussie innovation. Obligingly, six years later, Brearley wrote that the incident had showed 'the uncouth side of Dennis Lillee'.[91] Lillee, for his part, reflected in 2003 that virtually any 'Pom' with whom he had engaged in the public melodrama of Ashes cricket was nevertheless welcome at his table after the performance. The one exception would be the England and Yorkshire batsman Geoffrey Boycott: Lillee had seen Boycott as a private accumulator of runs and individual achievements who, in doing so, had breached the code of Yorkshire and larrikin cricket strivers alike.[92] Boycott had, in effect, been Yorkshire's Bradman.

The Seventies larrikins played with, and bridled at, but did not reject their country's link to the British royal family. In 1972, Dennis Lillee had caused much mirth among the tour party when he greeted the Queen with a cheery 'G'day' at Lord's.[93] On the following tour, in 1975, Australian players such as Ashley Mallett and Jeff Thomson had declared themselves homesick (the Hassett/Miller generation had regarded the UK as home) and had expressed boredom with the sort of formal receptions that Bradman had always relished: Thomson 'was as comfortable at those official functions as a rock star at a sewing class', said his biographer. 'He hated, as most of us did, the utter pretence of it all'.[94] On the 1977 tour Kim Hughes had been the only member of the squad to wear his official green blazer and soon abandoned it in favour of a track suit.[95] When an Australian party arrived back in England for the World Cup of 1979 and were taken to a reception at Buckingham Palace, before entering, tour manager Dave Richards issued the instruction 'No swearing'. Fast bowler Rodney Hogg replied: 'Does that mean we can't say fuck in front of the Queen?'[96] This was larrikin mischief, rather than political critique. Besides, Allan Border, later a huge influence on Australian cricket in the latter part of the twentieth century (156 Tests, captain 1985–94) was at the same reception and spoke of it with awe. He had been very nervous when approached by the Queen but she had put him at his ease; she, he wrote later, was 'a very special lady'.[97]

'On the pitch it's pretty much a war, isn't it?' The Ashes since 1980

The Ashes series in England in 1981, won, improbably, by England, is remembered chiefly for the performances of England all-rounder Ian Botham, whose century in the Third Test at Headingley made possible an unlikely England victory. Botham seemed to have come from somewhere in lower Middle England. His father was an aeronautical engineer with the Westland helicopter company, his mother a nurse. A comprehensive-school boy, with neither a degree nor an obvious regional accent, he was conspicuously a 'bloke', who liked shooting, fishing, a night out and to speak his mind. Perhaps inevitably, Border, a close friend, identified 'a considerable streak of larrikinism' in Botham's makeup and thus tagged him as 'a genuine sort of bloke, a real straight shooter'.[98] Botham had been made England captain the previous year, at the age of 24, but twelve Tests without a win (and perhaps selectors' concern about his 'straight shooting') had provoked his resignation. Brearley was asked to step in and Botham returned to the ranks. There he played without apparent inhibition, adopting, in Brearley's words, 'the sort of approach that would be understood by any village cricketer: let your arms go with the bat and hit the ball as hard as you can [. . .] Blacksmith cricket, one might say'.[99] For many traditionalists, this was the last real glimpse in Ashes cricket of an historic combination: the patrician captain guiding the gifted but undisciplined English yeoman.

This series was also significant for the claims made for it. As the *Daily Mirror* had it the rubber was a 'crazy series that cheered up the nation'.[100] This was an early sighting of what became government policy twenty years later, namely the phasing out by Western governments of 'Sport for All' policies in favour of the funding of elite sportspeople and/or the staging of mega-events.[101] In England this policy was at its most explicit in Game Plan, a policy document issued under the Blair Labour government in 2002, which placed much importance on the 'feelgood factors' generated by national sporting success.[102] These new political priorities were on display after England's home Ashes victory of 2005: the winners appeared on a set of commemorative stamps, were paraded through London in an open-top bus and were awarded MBEs. By the end of the year a box-set of the series issued by Sunset + Vine, the production company covering the series for Channel 4, had sold 635,000 copies, making it the biggest-selling sports DVD of all time.[103] Cricket, however, did not become any more popular as a result.

In the 1980s Allan Border, a working-class captain in the Australian tradition (his father worked as a wool classer and his mother as a shop assistant), sought to maintain the manly camaraderie that had characterised Ashes cricket for much of the century. He wrote in 1986 of the previous year's Ashes series:

> I have never considered friendship or mutual respect among opponents to be a bad thing – so long as the utmost rigour is maintained on the field of play. This, without doubt, was the case in England in 1985. We went down eventually to a better side but, as captain of Australia I can in no way criticise my players on the score of spirit or endeavour.[104]

Border soon abandoned this conviction, however. England's Chris Broad had noted that Border and vice-captain David Boon were 'quiet blokes who said hardly anything on the field'.[105] Soon Border adopted a new hard stance. This:

> Surprised his team-mates as much as it did the England team on the 1989 Ashes tour. 'The contrast was spotted by the Englishmen, not us,' Australian wicketkeeper Ian Healy said. 'It was full-on, a real treat-'em-tough type of attitude.' The atmosphere between the players had been jovial during the losses of 1985 and 1987. 'But in 1989, [David] Gower said that they didn't talk at all at the toss,' said Healy, who saw the shift as a turning point. 'I made a personal choice to have a harder edge as captain, be more stand-offish towards them [the English],' Border said. 'It was a hard thing to do and they all got the shits, but it was all part and parcel of what I wanted to achieve'.[106]

This seemed to represent a marriage between pragmatism and theatre. On the one hand, what had previously been regarded as ungentlemanly conduct became redefined as fierce competitiveness in the 1980s and 'sledging', menacing demeanour and the batsman's helmet, first worn by an Australian in a Test match in 1978 and *de rigueur* by the mid-80s, were recognitions of this 'harder edge'. On the other, the Australian Cricket Board had just embarked on what would be a long sequence of sponsorships by lager and beer brands, beginning with the Brisbane-brewed lager Castlemaine XXXX. Castlemaine's ads had extravagant recourse to the stereotype of the artless, hard-drinking bush ranger and the spectacle of a bunch of glowering, drooping-moustachioed, competitive Aussie male cricketers did no harm to this promotion. Indeed, as observed in Chapter 2, the Australian bowler Merv Hughes (53 Tests 1985–94) may have reinvented himself for a part in this melodrama.

In the time since, this aggressively masculine theatre has been continually revisited. In a vivid illustration of the trajectory of Ashes history since

Bodyline, in the First Test in Brisbane in 2013 Australian captain Michael Clarke was heard to tell England's number 11 batsman James Anderson to 'get ready for a fucking broken arm'. That evening England captain Alastair Cook said matter-of-factly 'On the pitch it's pretty much a war, isn't it?'[107]

After this series a perceptive article by David Rowe of Western Sydney University hinted at how the now 'media-dependent' story of the Ashes was being recycled in Australia with the Pom-bashing melodrama reinterpreted to suit changing political times. In the early twenty-first century this story had the ever-effete Poms eating probiotic yoghurt and mung beans, their competitive instincts choked by 'political correctness', while the macho Aussies rediscovered their 'biff' and capacity to inflict mental disintegration on their whingeing historic adversaries.[108] This narrative is actually an ongoing political construction of Australia itself and it has on-tap support from the millionaire larrikin aristocracy (Border, Ian Chappell, Dennis Lillee and Shane Warne are all prominent members of Australia's cricket commentariat) that pioneered it in the 1980s. Dennis Lillee, for example, was on hand to say after England's Ashes victory in 2005:

> Australia were ambushed by England because way too many people right across the board were living in a comfort zone. Cricket Australia executives, the coach, the manager, the captain and support staff must be all held accountable for this disaster. It's going to take time to digest and ... the first priority is to appoint a captain who can lead from the front.[109]

'Comfort zone' here, as elsewhere, was a metaphor for people lacking the necessary competitive attitudes to life. But, as Rowe observes, 'if these very specific arrangements of the professional cricket match were extended across the nation, the kind of Australia that it represents – macho, malicious and merciless – would soon lose its shine for most of its people'.[110] Indeed, in 2011, in a survey of Australians' participation in sport and recreation, neither cricket nor indeed competitive sport had featured strongly; most Australians preferred to walk, do aerobics, work out at the gym, swim, cycle or go for a run, rather than plot to break the mental resolve of their opponents.[111]

Notes

1 Stephen Wagg 'Class, status and Poms: social distinction, masculinity and the Ashes' *Sport in Society* Vol. 15 No.8 2012 pp.1055–69.
2 Tony Collins 'Australian nationalism and working-class Britishness: the case of Rugby League football'. *History Compass* 3 AU 142 April 2005 pp.1–19.
3 Ric Sissons and Brian Stoddart, *Cricket and Empire: The 1932–33 Bodyline Tour of Australia* London: George Allen & Unwin 1984 pp.86–91.
4 Don Bradman *Farewell to Cricket* London: Hodder and Stoughton 1950 pp.60–1.

5 Bradman *Farewell* p. 94.
6 See, for example, Russell Ward *The Australian Legend* Melbourne: Oxford University Press, 1958.
7 The title of a recent biography of Fingleton actually defines its subject against Bradman. See Greg Growden *Jack Fingleton: The Man Who Stood Up to Bradman* Crow's Nest, New South Wales: Allen and Unwin 2008.
8 Bill O'Reilly *'Tiger' O'Reilly: 60 Years in Cricket* Sydney: Collins 1985 p.54.
9 Brett Hutchins *Don Bradman: Challenging the Myth* Melbourne: Cambridge University Press 2005 p.139.
10 Ashley Mallett, with Ian Chappell, *Hitting Out: The Ian Chappell Story* London: Orion 2006 p.127.
11 Hutchins, *Don Bradman*, pp.81–2.
12 http://en.wikipedia.org/wiki/Vic_Richardson Access 15 April 2011.
13 Douglas Jardine *In Quest of The Ashes* London: Orbis Publishing 1984 (first published in 1933) pp.24, 206.
14 Duncan Hamilton *Harold Larwood* London: Quercus, 2009 p.270.
15 Huw Turbervill 'The Ashes 2010: sledging part and parcel of England v. Australia battles' *The Telegraph*, December 2010 http://www.telegraph.co.uk/sport/cricket/international/theashes/8221316/The-Ashes-2010-sledging-part-and-parcel-of-England-v-Australia-battles.html Access 15 April 2011.
16 Hamilton *Harold Larwood* p.270.
17 Ray Lindwall *Flying Stumps* London: Stanley Paul 1954 pp.19–20.
18 R.T. Corrie *The Barracker at Bay* Melbourne: Keating-Wood, 1933.
19 Walter R. Hammond *Cricket My Destiny* London: Stanley Paul 1946 p.86.
20 Hammond *Cricket My Destiny* p.136.
21 Clif Cary *Cricket Controversy: Test Matches in Australia 1946–1947* London: T. Werner Laurie Ltd. 1948 pp.12–13.
22 Godfrey Evans *The Gloves are Off: A Close-up of Cricket* London: Hodder and Stoughton 1960 p.50.
23 Denis Compton and Bill Edrich *Cricket and All That* Newton Abbott: Readers Union 1979 p.21.
24 The word 'subaltern' is used here principally to mean 'subordinate' and approximates to 'lower middle class'. The word is popularly associated with the postcolonial theorist Gayatri Spivak but its non-military usage originated with Antonio Gramsci: see Stephen Morton 'The subaltern: genealogy of a concept' in *Gayatri Spivak: Ethics, Subalternity and the Critique of Postcolonial Reason* Malden, MA: Polity, 2007 pp.96–97, and Quintin Hoare and Geoffrey Nowell-Smith 'Terminology' in *Selections from the Prison Notebooks* New York: International Publishers 2005 pp. xiii–xiv.
25 http://en.wikipedia.org/wiki/Arthur_Morris Access 19 April 2011.
26 http://en.wikipedia.org/wiki/Ray_Lindwall Access 19 April 2011.
27 R.S. Whitington *The Quiet Australian: The Lindsay Hassett Story* Melbourne: Wren Publishing 1973 p.7.
28 Ian Johnson *Cricket at the Crossroads* London: Cassell and Company 1957 p.104.
29 Johnson *Cricket at the Crossroads* pp.105, 107.
30 Gerald How *Len Hutton: The Biography* London: Mandarin, 1990 pp.1–3.
31 See Collins, 'Australian nationalism and working-class Britishness'.
32 Fred Trueman *Ball of Fire* London: J.M. Dent & Sons 1976 p.81.
33 Fred Trueman *As It Was* Basingstoke: Macmillan 2004 p.222.
34 Jim Laker *Spinning Round the World* London: Frederick Muller 1957 p.93.
35 Len Hutton *Cricket is My Life* London: Hutchinson 1951 p.201.

36 England Test cricketer Ian Botham, who was knighted in 2007, was born on the Wirral in Cheshire in 1955. Although this makes him a northerner by birth, and although he finished his county cricket career at Durham (1992–3), Botham went to school in Somerset and played most of his county cricket there (1974–86). He also played for the midland county of Worcestershire (1987–91). He was never a signifier of Northern-ness in the manner of, say, Hutton, Illingworth or Trueman.
37 Howat *Len Hutton* p.165.
38 Johnson *Cricket at the Crossroads* pp.110, 112.
39 Denis Compton *Playing for England* London: Sampson Low, Marston and Co. 1948 pp.128–9, 132.
40 Roland Perry *Keith Miller: The Life of a Great All-Rounder* London: Aurum Press 2005 p.141.
41 Lindwall *Flying Stumps* p.117.
42 W.J. Edrich *Cricket Heritage* London: Stanley Paul 1949 p.126.
43 Norman Giller *Denis Compton* London: Andre Deutsch 1997 p.140–1.
44 Lindwall *Flying Stumps* p.39.
45 Lindwall *Flying Stumps* p.77.
46 J.H. Fingleton *The Ashes Crown the Year: A Coronation Cricket Diary* London: Collins, 1954 p.92.
47 Johnson *Cricket at the Crossroads* p.204.
48 Perry *Keith Miller* pp.230–2.
49 Perry *Keith Miller* p.245.
50 Compton and Edrich *Cricket and All That* p.128.
51 Lindwall *Flying Stumps* p.44.
52 Collins, 'Australian nationalism and working-class Britishness' pp.12–14.
53 For a perceptive analysis see David L. Andrews and Andrew G. Grainger 'The "Packer Affair" and the early marriage of television and sport' in Stephen Wagg (ed.) *Myths and Milestones in the History of Sport* Basingstoke: Palgrave Macmillan, 2011 pp.239–61; the best account by a journalist is Gideon Haigh *The Cricket War: The Inside Story of Kerry Packer's World Series Cricket* Melbourne: Melbourne University Press 2007.
54 Alec Bedser *May's Men in Australia* London: Stanley Paul 1959 pp.3, 15–16.
55 Bedser *May's Men* p.196.
56 Bedser *May's Men* p.207.
57 Jim Laker *Over to Me* London: Frederick Muller 1960 pp.12–16.
58 Don Mosey *Laker: Portrait of a Legend* London: Queen Anne Press, 1989 p.90.
59 Tom Graveney *The Heart of Cricket* London: Arthur Barker 1983 p.72.
60 Trueman *As It Was* p.281.
61 Simon Hughes 'From La Scala to Lord's: a life lived to the full' *The Telegraph* 18 May 2005 http://www.telegraph.co.uk/sport/columnists/simon-hughes/2359793/From-La-Scala-to-Lords-a-life-lived-to-the-full.html Access 22 April 2011.
62 http://en.wikipedia.org/wiki/Ted_Dexter Access 22 April 2011.
63 Story retailed in Alan Lee *Lord Ted: The Dexter Enigma* London: Vista 1996 p.53 and Ted Dexter, *Ted Dexter Declares: An Autobiography* London: Stanley Paul 1966 p.48. In Dexter's version the story had come back to him as 'one laig'.
64 Dexter *Ted Dexter Declares* p.101.
65 Laker *Over to Me* p.76.
66 Richie Benaud *On Reflection* London: Fontana 1985 p.302.
67 Raymond Illingworth, with Don Mosey *Yorkshire and Back* London: Queen Anne Press 1980 p.62.

68 John Snow *Cricket Rebel: An Autobiography* London: Hamlyn Publishing 1976 p.81.
69 Illingworth *Yorkshire and Back* p.63.
70 Ivo Tennant *The Cowdreys: Portrait of a Cricketing Family* London: Simon & Schuster 1990 p.51.
71 Illingworth *Yorkshire and Back* pp.63–4.
72 Tennant *The Cowdreys* p.94. This was also indicative of Mrs Cowdrey's lofty world view: there were, after all, plenty of homes in Britain that might be thought inferior to a semi-detached house in Bradford.
73 Martin Johnson 'Ray Illingworth urges England to "give the Aussies nowt"' 31 May 2009 http://www.timesonline.co.uk/tol/sport/cricket/article6394952.ece Access 22 April 2011.
74 http://news.bbc.co.uk/sport1/hi/cricket/8073686.stm Access 23 April 2011.
75 Dennis Lillee *Menace: The Autobiography* London: Headline 2003 p.24.
76 Mallett and Chappell *Hitting Out..* pp.124, 191–2.
77 Mallett and Chappell *Hitting Out* p.4.
78 Mallett and Chappell *Hitting Out* pp.25, 99–100.
79 Ashley Mallett *Thommo Speaks Out: The Authorised Biography of Jeff Thomson* Crow's Nest, New South Wales: 2009 p.92.
80 Mallett *Thommo* pp.121–7.
81 Mallett *Thommo* p.101.
82 Mallett *Thommo* p.110.
83 Alan Bryman *The Disneyization of Society* London: Sage 2004.
84 Christian Ryan *Golden Boy: Kim Hughes and the Bad Old Days of Australian Cricket* London: Allen & Unwin 2009 pp.23, 169, 38, 143, 63.
85 Mallett *Thommo* p.22, 109–10.
86 Mallett, *Thommo* p.63.
87 Lillee *Menace* p.152.
88 Adrian McGregor *Greg Chappell* Sydney: William Collins 1985 p.180.
89 Benaud *On Reflection* p.37.
90 Benaud *On Reflection* p.39.
91 Mike Brearley *The Art of Captaincy* London: Hodder and Stoughton 1985 p.250.
92 Lillee *Menace* pp.254–9.
93 Mallett and Chappell *Hitting Out* p.66.
94 Mallett *Thommo* p.112.
95 Ryan *Golden Boy* p.52.
96 Ryan *Golden Boy* p.237.
97 Allan Border *Allan Border: An Autobiography* London: Methuen 1987 p.218.
98 Border *Allan Border* p.162.
99 Mike Brearley '"Ian Botham's Ashes": the myths, the legends and me' *The Guardian* 2 July 2011 https://www.theguardian.com/sport/blog/2011/jul/02/ian-botham-ashes-1981-mike-brearley Access 26 April 2017.
100 'A crazy series that cheered up the nation' http://www.mirror.co.uk/sport/cricket/ashes-1981-a-crazy-series-that-cheered-405230 Posted 28 January 2012, Access 26 April 2017.
101 See, for example, Jonathan Grix and Fiona Carmichael 'Why do governments invest in elite sport? A polemic' *International Journal of Sport Policy and Politics* Vol.4 No.1 2012 pp.73–90.
102 Dept. of Culture, Media and Sport 'Game Plan: a strategy for delivering Government's sport and physical activity objectives' 2002 www.gamesmonitor.org.uk/files/game_plan_report.pdf access 28 April 2017.

103 Andy Bull '2005 and all that: an alternative history of the greatest Ashes' *The Guardian* 6 July 2015 https://www.theguardian.com/sport/2015/jul/06/2005-alternative-history-greatest-ashes Access 28 April 2017.
104 Border *Allan Border* p.164.
105 Gideon Haigh *Sphere of Influence* London: Simon and Schuster 2011 p.263.
106 David Sygall 'Savour dominance: Border' *The Age* 9 January 2005 http://www.theage.com.au/news/Cricket/Savour-dominance-Border/2005/01/08/1104832358959.html Access 28 April 2017.
107 Andy Wilson 'Ashes: Alastair Cook ready for "war" after Clarke's "broken arm" sledge' *The Guardian* 24 November 2013 https://www.theguardian.com/sport/2013/nov/24/ashes-alastair-cook-war-clarke-broken-arm-sledge Access 28 April 2017.
108 See David Rowe 'The Ashes: Australian masculinity reborn amid English tumult' *The Conversation* 10 December 2013 http://theconversation.com/the-ashes-australian-masculinity-reborn-amid-english-tumult-21265 Access 29 April 2017.
109 Colin Crompton 'Sack Ponting and let Warne lead Australia, declares Lillee' *The Independent* 14 September 2005 http://www.independent.co.uk/sport/cricket/sack-ponting-and-let-warne-lead-australia-declares-lillee-312683.html?amp Access 29 April 2017.
110 Rowe 'The Ashes'.
111 See http://www.abs.gov.au/AUSSTATS/abs@.nsf/Lookup/4102.0Main+Features30Jun+2011 Access 29 April 2017.

Chapter 11

'Everyone seemed to be "with it"'

Cricket politics and the coming of the one-day game, 1940–1970[1]

The term 'one-day cricket' is a metaphor. In a literal sense, one-day cricket is commonplace and as old as the game itself; indeed most recreational cricketers have, as players, known no other kind. More importantly, one-day cricket has historically characterised the northern leagues, vital signifiers of class and region in the culture of the English game, not to mention women's cricket, which had flourished in several countries between the World Wars.[2] However, in the decades that followed the Second World War the term 'one-day cricket' had a more specific meaning and a greater import. It referred to cricket matches that would be limited not only by time, but by structure (a specified number of overs), thus taking a crucial aspect of the encounter beyond the control of the two team captains, and it meant that the contest would, by the end of the day, have produced a winner: honours could no longer be even. It also meant a challenge to the prevailing economic order of cricket and to its traditional pattern of governance. This chapter explores these issues historically. It will argue that a number of factors contributed to the entrenchment of one-day cricket, initially in England, in the 1960s. These included: the relative decline in financial and political power of the British aristocracy; a corresponding fall in the annual revenue of the English county cricket clubs; the growth in influence in ruling circles of the elites of what the American sociologist Alvin Gouldner called 'impression management';[3] the politicisation and enhanced bargaining power of professional county cricketers; material changes in the consumer market for cigarettes; and what can be assumed to have been new attitudes to leisure and sport on the part of sections of the English public.

'Plenty to play and enough to watch': English cricket during the Second World War

Not surprisingly, given its historic purchase on national identity, cricket was maintained during the Second World War and it thrived, principally in its one-day form. *Wisden* of 1940, reporting on the season of 1939, in the latter stages of which war had been declared, warmed to the idea of one-day cricket and neatly weaved together notions of the one-day format, the war effort, the game's traditions and the stout yeomen of England in their villages:

> There is only one solution of the question [of maintaining county cricket], unless beyond expectation but not hope, peace returns early, and that is the improvising of one-day matches whenever and wherever possible, in the same spirit that has moved villagers to come out from under the yew-tree and bowl in the place of Tom looking after the calf and bat for Johnson delivering a telegram, and be d——d to the score and the points and the Cup! There will be plenty to play and enough to watch such games. Many would delight to see again a few early-Edwardian drives and a late-Victorian pull or two. And if most of the pence taken at the gate should go to help a greater cause than cricket, so much the better.[4]

This enthusiasm was maintained into the following year when R. C. Robertson-Glasgow observed in *Wisden* that 'Essex, always enterprising, had arranged a long programme of one-day matches for 1940, but early in the summer the County was declared a Defence Area, which stopped teams from travelling into restricted parts. Six matches were played, and won; and a profit of some £60 was made in the season' and that the elite school Eton College had beaten traditional rival Harrow 'by one wicket in an unofficial one-day match at Harrow. It was a finish which, in old days at Lord's, might have induced a frenzy of umbrella-cracking'.[5] In 1942, however, there was a stern and somewhat high-handed rebuke for anyone supposing that one-day cricket could be more than a temporary diversion in a time of national emergency:

> These one-day matches have given such good entertainment, where at one time little or none had been expected, that some critics have urged their retention as a regular process for the first-class County Championship in peace time. I do not agree with this view. Those who urge it most strongly would, I believe, be the earliest to tire of the experiment. The new clockwork monkey in the nursery, which waves its arms and waggles its head, delights for a few short hours or days. But the children soon return to the older, if more sedate toys, the tried companions in the familiar cupboard. The faults of the three-day match are not few, but the objections to a one-day County Championship are overwhelming. There is a false analogy drawn from modern sports that all spectators are in a hurry, and that, therefore, all games-players should be in a hurry too. Cricketers and cricket-watchers are not made like that. There will always be found those who understand no batting except that which keeps the ball far, high, and often [...] Such spectators

are, frankly, not wanted at County cricket. They would do better to stay at home and write to the newspapers about it. For first-class cricket is a subtle as well as a strenuous game. It is a thing of leisure, albeit of leisure to-day not easily found or arranged; a three-act play, not a slapstick turn. And, in practical detail, such one-day matches would be farces, though not of the sort intended by their promoters.

'Cricket fostered in such an academy', he added, 'would be ill-prepared to face the Australians in England, let alone in the timeless Tests abroad'.[6]

There's little doubt that Robertson-Glasgow, an ex-Oxford Blue who'd played for Somerset and covered cricket for the *Daily Telegraph*, was expressing the view prevalent among English cricket's high command. Here the now-familiar argument that one-day cricket would fail to nurture the skills necessary to maintain the England team was used to bulwark a more fundamental contention: that cricket was essentially high culture and, as such, belonged to people who appreciated such things. It was like classical music, therefore, and, when peace returned, people wanting something cruder and with a bit more rhythm should stay away from it. Note, also, the prophetic reference to 'a thing of leisure, albeit of leisure to-day not easily found or arranged': the Second World War was, arguably, a watershed in the decline of Britain's leisured elite.

In *Wisden* of 1943, an anonymous writer (almost certainly Robertson-Glasgow once again) noted that 'the first season of County cricket after the war will be given over to experiments, without any set championship' and that three-, two-, and one-day match formats would be considered. While he judged that majority opinion at the county clubs would favour three days, he preferred the two-day option, reasoning that it might salvage traditional forms of sociability in the face of a populist surge toward one-day cricket:

> Here is a basis for good cricket, good watching, with enough of leisure surely to satisfy officials, umpires, scorers and ground staff, and to give the County teams the chance of reasonable travel and of playing local sides, with the enjoyment of those social pleasures without which any game is only half a game.

It would also 'satisfy the discerning public'.[7] The writer, however, made clear that a major concession to modernity should be part of the new settlement: the distinction between amateurs and professionals should be abandoned, the hour being 'ripe, indeed over-ripe, for the sweeping away of anachronisms and the exploding of humbug'.[8] This did not appeal to the principal proponents of two-day cricket (the committees of Sussex and Lancashire county cricket clubs), however, since part of their rationale for this arrangement was the '[g]reater possibility of amateurs being able to play, especially in week-end matches'.[9]

But little prospect of moving to two-day cricket – despite a widespread acknowledgement that county takings were poor on the third day of matches – was held out at the meeting at Lord's of the Advisory County Cricket Committee in December 1942, a report of whose proceedings was carried in the same edition of *Wisden*. The meeting was dominated by two archetypal figures in the history of the governance of English cricket; Sir Stanley Jackson and Sir Pelham ('Plum') Warner. Jackson, educated at Harrow and Trinity College, Cambridge, was by then 72; he had played for the university and for Yorkshire, been a Conservative minister and Governor of Bengal. Warner (Rugby School and Oriel College, Oxford), an ex- Middlesex and England captain and manager of the England team during the controversial 'Bodyline' tour of 1932, was 69. Both men were firmly for the retention of three-day cricket at county level. 'Interfere,' Jackson said, 'with the implements of the game and you are taking upon yourself a great responsibility, for what may be possible in one class of cricket may be unsuitable in another class of cricket'.[10] Warner was more emphatic, citing, like Robertson-Glasgow, the cerebral nature and inviolability of cricket as culture:

> I can see nothing wrong with modern cricket, except there are too many counties and some wickets are over-prepared and over-doped. Do not be led away by the call for brightening cricket. It is a leisurely, intricate game of skill. We live in an age of speed and people are apt to think that cricket must be speeded up; but my experience is that it is not necessary to have fast scoring to have interesting cricket. I do not wish to see anything better than two fine batsmen opposed to two first-class bowlers, backed up by good fielding; then the number of runs scored in an hour is unimportant.[11]

Sussex, meanwhile, had drawn back from the proposal of a shorter (two-day) game, now arguing that, whatever the format, the mystical properties of cricket captaincy would continue to determine whether a first-class match engaged its spectators:

> When the Sussex members reviewed the position at their annual meeting, it was emphasised that the number of days allotted to a match cannot make a deal of difference to the attractiveness of the cricket unless it is played in the proper spirit, which depends upon the captains. Here is the crux of the problem. The destiny of the County Championship lies in the hands of the County Committees and the captains who hold the reins during the summer months. When all is said and done the Eleven is a reflex of its leader.[12]

Two years later, with peace imminent, *Wisden* rebuked reformers for their folly:

> While the fate of the world was being determined, English cricket was the scene of an interesting little battle, which ended in the rout of the hustlers and the triumph of conservatism over the heresy that progress and speed are synonymous. The defeat of the *soi-disant* [so-called] progressives, with their programme of one-day and time-limited matches for first-class cricket, was a certainty so long as the issue of debate rested with the majority opinion of practising cricketers. In truth, it was an easy victory, as their opponents for the most part consisted of a few honest, if deluded, zealots, a few showmen, always ready for any change that might bring them into the light of publicity, and a few columnists, who instinctively hammer tradition.[13]

Likewise the New South Wales Cricket Association was reminded that one-day cricket should be seen only as a temporary wartime arrangement:

> The New South Wales C.A. experimented for a time with one afternoon games. This, naturally, suited the Serviceman on a fleeting visit, and the more audacious tactics of the batsmen seeking runs quickly pleased the onlookers who sought relief from their burdens and craved excitement as a counter to worry and anxiety. The matches attracted splendid crowds, but it would be foolish to say that they did – or could – produce or develop real cricketers. Actually there was a suspicion that a game of skill was being converted into a vaudeville exhibition, and though cricket must be entertaining, it can achieve that without sacrificing the dignity of craftsmanship to the hurly-burly of crude utilitarianism. Still, as a war-time measure the move was justified.[14]

Moreover, this confident rejection of reform was bathed in an explicit anti-commercialism:

> The cricket reformers should be more honest about their aims. They talk much about improving cricket, in the same way that some talk about improving the breed of race-horses. But what they are really talking about is money. They are not considering the art and technique of the game. They speak as financiers, not craftsmen. To them faster, faster means richer, richer. They believe that one-day cricket would mean more spectators. I believe it would empty the grounds as surely as the rain.[15]

English cricket, historically, had always been run – and for a little while longer would continue to be run – by men who had money, but disdained the talk of money. These men were, in the main, drawn from the landed classes, the City of London and the top professions; in general, they were rentier capitalist landowners and/or the providers of prestigious services. Around such men had been fashioned the cult of the 'gentleman', the ethos of which drew on the pre-capitalist heritage of the English aristocrat. As the historians Cain and Hopkins put it:

> A gentleman required income, and preferably sizeable wealth, but he was not to be sullied by the acquisitive process any more than he was to be corrupted by the power that leadership entailed. In an order dominated by gentlemanly norms, production was held in low repute. Working directly for money, as opposed to making it from a distance, was associated with dependence and cultural inferiority.[16]

A pother of suggested alterations: the 1950s and cricket's clash with modernity

Eric Midwinter has noted that the Second World War (like the First) produced 'a pother [a fuss] of suggested alterations' to English cricket.[17] A number of these suggested alterations were a direct challenge to this gentlemanly ethos, of which cricket was one of the chief public manifestations. By the beginning of the 1960s several of the alterations would have been made, thus inaugurating what Mike Marqusee termed 'cricket's clash with modernity'.[18]

Warner and Jackson were both steeped in this gentlemanly ethos. Warner had been born in Trinidad, the son of a colonial administrator (his father was the island's Attorney General); Jackson's people were comparative newcomers to the Establishment, his father having inherited the family leather business in Leeds and been created the first Baron Allerton. Together they typified an Englishness that, in the words of the historian Martin J. Wiener, did not feel comfortable with 'progress'.[19] They were essentially guardians of a mythological game – one that stood historically above the market, which, again to quote Marqusee, belonged to 'an earlier, less predatory, less money-minded age' and one that had 'come to represent the English Pastoral, the dream of an unchanging natural society in which all conflicts are magically resolved'.[20] In their governance, they were direct counterparts of the Conservative Party, whose leadership was still determined behind the closed doors of a gentleman's club, and not discussed by the wider membership. Besides, as the historian Ross McKibbin noted, in 1945, the 7,000 members of the MCC, 'the institutional centre of English cricket . . . were as unrepresentative of the national polity as any society could be'.[21] Of Warner, his granddaughter recalled in 2004, 'it seemed that the sphere of cricket and the power of England existed in some deep relation to each other, and made Plum at the MCC the King's sporting counterpart'.[22]

Outside of the two-day format, the principal alterations being proposed were one-day (and, specifically, limited-overs) cricket; a knock-out competition; and an end to what one *Wisden* writer had called the 'humbug' of the amateur–professional divide. The Advisory Committee of 1942 baulked at all these proposals and they were shelved until a meeting of the same committee in 1957, by which time the political and financial winds begun to change direction. Warner later acknowledged that the one-day games of the early 1940s had been popular:

> The public took to these, and cricket enjoyed a boom. The number of close finishes was a great attraction, as the side batting first generally left its opponents, if enterprising cricket was played, to make the runs necessary for victory, and time after time a thrilling finish was seen. The most exciting, though typical of many, was the finish to the British Empire Eleven v. the Buccaneers match, played on May 30, 1942.[23]

But this passage contains two clues to the dismissal of one-day cricket after the war. One was the stress laid upon 'enterprising cricket', wherein, once again, captains of the right stuff (that's to say, 'gentlemen') would make the necessarily courageous decisions. But peacetime one-day cricket was predicated on stipulated equalities: each team would be given the same allocation – of time, say, or overs – and there could therefore be no declarations: this tampered unduly with the captaincy mystique central to the prevailing ethos. The other was the fact that the popular wartime games had not been county matches and the MCC would not countenance any change that threatened the hegemony of the county system, entrenched since the late nineteenth century and self-evidently their power base.

Similar fears underlay the rejection of a cup competition. As a number of writers have observed, this idea had been around, unconsummated, in English cricket since the 1870s.[24] But, in the 1940s, the traditionalists would still only consider a contest played over three days, which had no overs restriction and in which a draw remained a possible outcome: indeed, it was also envisaged that, were the final to be drawn, the trophy would be shared.[25] A three-day contest which carried the possibility of a replay of the same duration would play havoc with the county fixture list and was easily discounted.

If the prevailing format of county cricket were to be maintained it followed that its key predicate, the amateur–professional distinction, would also remain. It stayed and, indeed, was affirmed, albeit with the proviso that amateurs could receive 'broken time' payments (to cover lost earnings) for overseas tours, by an MCC committee chaired by the Duke of Norfolk in 1958.[26]

With the pre-war structures of the county game intact, the MCC appealed simply for a 'dynamic attitude' to be adopted by players, who should 'aim for victory from the first ball'.[27]

Various factors conspired to defeat the hopes of Warner and others to keep cricket as it had been before 1939. Some of these factors had been foreseen within Warner's own rarefied social circle. Sir Home Gordon, for example, was a gentleman publisher who in 1906 had inherited a baronetcy originated by Charles the First. Gordon predicted (correctly) that cricket would thrive immediately after the war, but that a slump would follow.[28] He counselled the MCC, unsuccessfully, not to forget how during wartime one-day cricket had made spectators 'thrilled over close finishes'.[29]

The chief precipitate of change, when it came in the early 1960s, was the falling attendances at county matches. This may indeed have been partly due to the cricket public's longing for these exciting close finishes, the often-dreary three-day game having, for the most part, failed to deliver them. It may also have had to do with full employment in Britain throughout the 1950s and with the diversification of leisure options available to British people. But it must also have been related to changes in the way county clubs had in previous eras been underwritten. After all, it can only have been retired people, the unemployed, shift workers, children on school holidays, wealthy brokers and the like with flexible working hours and those of independent means who had ever been able to attend a whole three-day match. 'The average man – highly important at the turnstiles – could not hope to see a game the whole way through', wrote the cricket historian Derek Birley later, 'even if he himself was prepared to stick it out for three days'.[30] Counties had been able to keep costs low arguably, first, because players were on low wages and dependent on wealthy patrons within their clubs to find them work in the winter and on retirement and, second, because members of the county elite would regularly subsidise them. As the writer Geoffrey Moorhouse put it, unless the Australian team had been touring and drawn big crowds, the counties could expect to make a loss on the season:

> It was then that county secretaries thanked providence and the English caste system for endowing them with a Duke or Earl as county president. Derbyshire's secretary [from 1908 to 1953] Will Taylor, knew that he could rely on a phone call from the Duke of Devonshire towards the end of October, by which time he would have done his annual sums. 'Now then, Taylor,' the voice on the line from Chatsworth would say, 'what's the damage this time?'[31]

While in the 1950s conditions for professional cricketers remained largely on the semi-feudal basis they had had before the war – virtually all counties, for example, insisted where possible on amateur captains – the financial affairs of the county clubs and their patrons were beginning to disintegrate. Whereas in the euphoric post-war season of 1946 2.3 million people had attended first-class cricket matches and virtually sustained that figure the following year, by the end of the 1950s attendances were down to 1 million. In 1963 attendances had sunk further to 700,000.[32] Moreover, the accustomed sources of financial sustenance (and amateur cricketers) were drying up.

As Marqusee observed: 'The old rentier section of the upper classes – the backbone of empire and county cricket – had been squeezed by higher taxes and rising wages. In 1929, there were 205 amateur players in county cricket. In 1959, there were only thirty nine'.[33] Members of the aristocracy were now contemplating turning their homes into commercial ventures – the Duke of Bedford, for example, opened his country estate at Woburn Abbey to the public in 1955[34] – and an estimated 300 stately homes were demolished during the 1950s.[35] Moreover, landowners had been slipping steadily down the national status hierarchy: as the sociologist John Scott noted in the early 1980s, land ownership had ceased to be a necessary qualification for a barony in the early 1900s and, in the economic sector, this title now tended to be bestowed on captains of industry; and, by the 1950s, the majority of peerages were being awarded to former MPs.[36]

The Conservative Party reflected the important changes taking place in the upper echelons of British society. The 'gentlemen' and the landed interest still dominated the leadership – Tory leaders between 1945 and 1964 (Churchill, Eden, Macmillan and Douglas-Home) all had aristocratic families or links. But successive post-war general elections had sent an increasing number of new Tory MPs to Westminster who were drawn from business – some, notably, from the emergent elites of impression management: advertising, broadcasting and public relations. Many of these new backbenchers began to exert influence within the party and were instrumental in the successful campaign for commercial television which culminated in the Television Act of 1954.[37] Not only were the party establishment, like their counterparts at Lord's, generally unsympathetic to advertising and consumer-related commerce, but some of them could not see the merits of television: Prime Minister Winston Churchill had asked indignantly, 'Why do we need this peep show?'[38]

English cricket and the 'peep show'

The post-war flourishing of television, advertising and PR had a number of clear implications for English cricket, whose elite was now slowly recognising that it was in crisis.

First, although advertisers had been using leading sportsmen to showcase their wares since the nineteenth century – the adoption in the early 1880s of the swimmer Capt. Matthew Webb by the match manufacturers Bryant and May is an early example – the culture inhabited by pre-war English cricketers had, by definition, been unconducive to mass advertising. It had been self-evidently a culture of masters and men. For gentleman amateurs, styled, as we have seen, as 'above the market', this would have been a vulgar and unthinkable breach of their code: an exception was Dr W.G. Grace, always a maverick among amateurs, who advertised Colmans Mustard in 1890.[39] Professionals, even if they were permitted to advertise products, seldom had the necessary glamour. There were exceptions. For instance, Jack Hobbs, the premier professional batsman of the pre-war period (Surrey 1905–34, England 1908–30) was a quiet, modest man, widely regarded as 'the professional who batted like an amateur'.[40] His saintly standing in English cricket brought him a number of advertising contracts, including one for cigarettes, in spite of a public admission that he, personally, kept 'well away from them'.[41] Len Hutton, the professional who dominated English batting in the immediate post-war period, was a similarly diffident personality, famously concerned to obliterate his working-class, Yorkshire origins. Hutton endorsed a new Slazenger cricket bat in 1950[42] and also appeared in an advert for Raleigh bicycles around the same time.[43] But the move to a more full-blooded commercial exploitation of cricketers, making celebrities out of them in a way that transcended their work as sportspeople, had begun with the Middlesex and England batsman Denis Compton. Compton, the son, as previously noted, of a self-employed painter and decorator from north London, conspicuously lacked the deferential traits of previous generations of professionals. He batted with the devil-may-care attitude that, in conventional wisdom, could only be expressed by amateurs and, off the field, he typified a post-war egalitarianism and *joie de vivre*. Like his Australian friend and counterpart, Keith Miller, he liked a drink, a day at the races and the company of women.[44] In the winter of 1948, Compton, then 30 and touring South Africa with England, had showed journalist Reg Hayter a suitcase he had full of unanswered letters from the public. 'Many', remembered Hayter, 'were fan letters, particularly from women and young girls, requesting signed autographs, but also among them were requests for him to open shops, write newspaper and magazine columns, put his name to books and give after-dinner and club talks'.[45] Hayter, typical of a burgeoning number of reporters in the 1940s and 50s happy to broker such deals, introduced Compton to the agent and sometime journalist Bagenal Harvey, who, in turn, procured a nine-year contract for the cricketer advertising the men's hair product Brylcreem. Men such as Harvey could see the growing market potential of sportsmen as individuals and they, with the help of recently elected Conservative MPs, moved politically against any obstruction to the realising of that potential. Harvey and Philip Goodhart, who became Tory MP for Beckenham in 1957, worked with the Professional Footballers' Association in the late 1950s to campaign for the removal of the players' maximum wage restriction, abolished in 1961,[46] and regarded cricket's restrictive practices and sleepy three-day games with similar impatience. There needed to be a more appropriate setting for the dash of players such as Compton.

Second, a more contemporary commercial philosophy began to be expressed within the Lord's inner circle. Two figures, in particular, represented this political tendency. Ted Dexter was an ideal bridge between the game's patricians, such as Warner, and the new social and political world of publicity. The son, as observed in Chapter 1, of a wealthy insurance broker, he had attended Radley public school and Cambridge University, leaving the latter in 1958 without having shown any interest in academic study. He had been made captain of Sussex in 1960 – he was a personal friend of the Duke of Norfolk, the Sussex president – and of England in 1962. He became openly bored with county cricket and frequently went to the races while matches in which he was playing (and captaining his team) were still in progress. Dexter was a flamboyant batsman and autocratic in his captaincy, which gained him the nickname 'Lord Ted'. This pre-meritocratic eighteenth-century disposition, however, was wedded to a mid-twentieth-century commercial acumen wholly in keeping with the new political currents in the Conservative Party; he became a journalist on the tabloid *Sunday Mirror* and developed a number of media-related businesses, including his own PR agency.[47] With county attendances dwindling, Dexter threw his weight behind the idea of a one-day competition, based on the long-shelved knock-out principle, and this was approved at Lord's in December of 1961. The competition, doubtless to the consternation of the Jackson–Warner faction, would have a sponsor – the Gillette razor company. 'Dexter', wrote his biographer, 'had identified the public appeal of one-day cricket even before the Gillette Cup came along'.[48] One of Dexter's Sussex team recalled that 'over the years [Ted] lost interest in county cricket. The Gillette was a different matter, though. He was full of enthusiasm and ideas when it came to the one-day games'.[49] Cricket commentator Simon Hughes has called Dexter, perhaps extravagantly, 'the man who shaped modern cricket'.[50] (Dexter's Sussex won the first two Gillette tournaments, in 1963 and 1964.)

The other important figure was Mike Turner, who had become secretary of Leicestershire County Cricket Club in 1960 at the age of 26. Leicester was a typically bourgeois town, based on hosiery and light engineering. Its ties to the landed gentry were fewer and less lucrative and the county had developed other sources of revenue, such as a pools competition; it was also, at Turner's instigation, one of the first counties to put advertising boards, symbols of vulgar commerce to cricket's gentlemanly elite, around the county's Grace Road ground.[51] Turner, another strong believer in the commercial promise of the one-day format, staged the first one-day knock-out competition – the Midland Counties Knock-Out Cup (contested by Leicestershire, Northamptonshire, Derbyshire and Nottinghamshire) – at Leicester in 1962; it was deemed a success (the local paper reported it as 'Champagne Cricket')[52] and, effectively a dry run for the Gillette Cup the following year. (Later, in 1966, Turner introduced Sunday cricket at Leicestershire, having carefully negotiated the matter with the Bishop of Leicester.[53] One-day cricket was often proposed for Sundays and religious objections had, historically, been another obstacle to its introduction.)[54]

The first Gillette Cup Final in September 1963 was declared a success by leading commentators, many of whom might have been regarded hitherto as traditionalists on the question of one-day cricket. For instance, the patrician E.W. Swanton, a reliable mouthpiece for current orthodoxy at Lord's, wrote:

> Nothing is better to see than the ball hit hard and often when the conditions allow; but this 'instant cricket' is very far from being a gimmick and there is a place in it for all the arts of cricket, most of which are subtle ones. That is why the day was so enjoyable, not only for the patriots with their banners and their rosettes 'up for the Cup', but for the practising cricketers, past and present, of all ages and types, who seemed to form the bulk of the crowd. Everyone seemed to be 'with it'.[55]

Thus one-day cricket, this brash and long-resisted newcomer, was finally assimilated by the game's elite. The distinction between amateurs and professionals had been dispensed with the year before – a precondition, surely, for the attracting of sponsors: a game still clinging to its Victorian social hierarchy would very likely have deterred consumers in an increasingly egalitarian post-war world. The editor of *Wisden*, Norman Preston, was puzzled as to the MCC's apparent *volte face*. After all, the MCC had affirmed the professional–amateur divide only four years earlier. 'By doing away with the amateur', he wrote, 'cricket is in danger of losing the spirit of freedom and gaiety which the best amateur players brought to the game'.[56]

Third, a growing number of people (Bagenal Harvey, Dexter and Turner among them, along with a range of agents, journalists and commentators) were aware of how attractive, given the right circumstances, cricket, as a game and as a motif, could be to advertisers. Cricket was new to this sort of transaction, but Gillette was not. An American company, founded in 1895, it had funded sport in some way since 1910 and in 1939 had sponsored the US baseball World Series.[57] Gillette now sought to support something recognisably English in order to stimulate sales. The deal for the Gillette Cup was brokered by a PR company with the suggestion for a commercially sponsored competition being put by MCC assistant secretary James Dunbar, the argument in favour of both one-day cricket and advertising having now been won within English cricket's governing coterie. Interestingly, some Gillette executives were worried lest sponsorship be thought to sully this venerable game and thus visit bad publicity upon their razors.[58] But the opposite proved to be (and, arguably, has remained) the case: cricket's apparently timeless, pastoral and commercially uncontaminated aura was very lucrative for the companies that purchased a stake in it. The key case in point here was the tobacco industry.

According to one writer, significant price competition in the cigarette industry had ended in the 1920s; since then, tobacco companies had, in effect, been selling not cigarettes, but ideas of cigarettes – with the concomitant emphasis upon advertising.[59] The quest to associate cigarettes with seductive ideas was given a greater urgency by medical research identifying smoking as the chief cause of lung cancer. This was affirmed by the report of the Surgeon General of the United States in 1964[60] and the 1969 edition of the authoritative *Springer Handbook of Special Pathology*, published in Germany, devoted twenty-five pages to the now medically accepted link between smoking and carcinoma of the lung.[61] This, of course, made the image of cigarettes more important than ever. Cricket was clearly attractive in this regard: companies sponsoring cricket could be seen to be supporting a vital piece of national heritage and, at the same time, to be borrowing cricket's healthy, pastoral and civilised aura. This symbiosis, however, would depend on television coverage and such coverage would, in turn, have to entail regular one-day cricket. Only the one-day game attracted the necessary audiences, three-day cricket being a minority interest and Test matches still regarded as sacrosanct (English Test cricket did not engage a sponsor until 1978).

Thus, in the wake of the inaugural Gillette Cup Final, the Bagenal Harvey Organisation (Harvey now operating at the heart of an expanding sport–media–commerce nexus) laid on a series of Sunday afternoon cricket matches, featuring popular Test stars from the 1950s such as Compton, Godfrey Evans, Jim Laker and Tom Graveney, all of whom were Harvey's clients. Dexter, along with overseas stars not currently engaged in Test cricket, often featured. Harvey also arranged for the matches to be seen on BBC Television and for the games to be sponsored by the tobacco company Rothmans. His all-star side, constituted as the Rothmans International Cavaliers, usually played a county side. Rothmans, at the time controlled by the South African Rembrandt Group, one of six multinational corporations dominating the global tobacco market, sold more than 60% of their cigarettes in Europe, as well as having a big share of the market in New Zealand and Australia, both cricket-playing countries.[62] The Cavaliers' games continued through the 1960s and proved popular: crowds regularly topped 10,000 – an extraordinary turnout, given the parlous state of attendances for the three-day county game.[63]

The Cavaliers' matches ran successfully to the end of the 1960s but dwindled, amid some acrimony, after 1969. By then the MCC had appointed another assistant secretary (Jack Bailey, ex-Oxford University and Essex, taken on in 1967) specifically responsible for press, public relations and business[64] and had resolved to run its own one-day Sunday league, sponsored by John Player, part of the Imperial Tobacco Group, another of the six major multinationals. In establishing the Player League the MCC seems to have moved to reassert its hegemony and in the process, quite ostentatiously, to have bitten the hand that had fed it. In March of 1969 it was announced that no player registered to an English county (including the Minor Counties) or a first-class Australian club could take part in a televised match not arranged through the Test and County Cricket Board or the MCC Council. All the Cavaliers' matches were to have been offered to ITV as a package, thus rivalling the Player League which would go out on BBC2. 'The game has enough anxieties', lamented leading cricket writer John Arlott, 'without internal strife between its main authority and the only organisation which has succeeded in making money from it in modern times'.[65] The Cavalier project collapsed and Rothmans withdrew their support. Gates for the Player League doubled between 1969 and 1976 and BCC2's viewing figures quadrupled during the same period.[66] In 1971 the MCC set up another one-day knock-out tournament, this time sponsored by the cigarette brand Benson and Hedges, then owned by another tobacco multinational, the Gallaher Group; the deal was brokered by West Nally, a sports marketing company set up by Patrick Nally, a marketing specialist and BBC cricket commentator Peter West, who, along with other BBC voices, had read Gillette commercials on Radio Luxemburg in the 1950s.[67]

Conclusion: 'the pleasantest possible people'

The MCC, having broken bread with the elite *nouveau* of impression managers, were clearly anxious now that the tail should not wag the dog. The gentleman faction of the English ruling class wished, despite recent necessary compromises, to continue to administer the national game on their own terms. This, in part, meant maintaining one-day cricket in its place, thus reassuring the MCC membership that this whole new enterprise was being handled with the utmost discretion. After all, many members clung to the view that it was fun – a boost to morale in wartime (as Warner had acknowledged) and now something to enliven a Sunday afternoon – but it was not the real thing. As late as 1970, in the wake of the first season of the John Player League, *Wisden* editor Norman Preston could still argue that the one-day game was 'instant cricket and an instant success', but that it should never become a substitute for genuine first-class cricket.[68] Similarly Sir Brian Batsford, publisher and, until that year, Conservative MP for Ealing South, wrote to *The Times* in June of 1974 to complain that 'the enjoyment of cricket, especially on television, is now marred by advertising. [. . .] Is there no authority in the world of cricket, of advertising or of government which can halt this steady deterioration in our standards?'[69] Many of cricket's elite liked the trappings of one-day cricket perhaps no better than English aristocrats enjoyed car-loads of day trippers picnicking in the grounds of their stately homes; they certainly wanted the new arrangements to be designed as far as possible on their terms.

But this issue had a far more important dimension. The historic English rite of cricket was now a lucrative brand, but could only remain so as long as it was not *seen* as a brand. Once again, the sponsors were buying not cricket, but an *idea* – the idea being of a civilised, gentlemanly English pursuit which had always placed itself above the tumult of politics and naked commerce. This brand could only be protected while the 'gentlemen' ran cricket and kept the publicists and advertisers at arm's length. Otherwise, not only would too many people be demanding a piece of the pie, but cricket could easily acquire that curse of the latter half of the twentieth century – a 'bad image'. Small wonder then that Lord's began in the late 1960s to re-establish social distance between themselves and Bagenal Harvey's operation. In his autobiography Jack Bailey recalled Rothmans Cavaliers in disparaging terms, claiming that, although individual clubs had done well out of their match against the Cavaliers, the 'larger interests' of cricket had 'benefited hardly at all'.[70] Moreover, Lord's were doubtful of the 'seemliness' of allowing one-day cricket to be shown on commercial television.[71] The commercial station London Weekend Television was actually awarded the rights to show the Gillette Cup of 1968, but Bailey was somewhat put out to be told by LWT's John Bromley and Jimmy Hill, when they came to Lord's to negotiate, that they were clients of the Bagenal Harvey Organisation: 'in the circumstances there seemed no reason why this should make any difference', reflected Bailey testily, adding that relations with Harvey had become 'somewhat strained'.[72] In the event, adverts and the scheduled David Frost show prevented viewers from seeing a tense finish and the result of the game (won by Warwickshire) was announced later.[73] This seems to have been a remarkably symbolic and instructive political-cultural moment, demonstrating exactly what the MCC wished now to avoid. Not only had the cerebral game of cricket (Warner's 'leisurely, intricate game of skill', albeit in condensed form) been shorn of its subtlety by commercial breaks, but viewers had been robbed of the game's climax by a TV talk show. David Frost was a TV celebrity and entrepreneur and a standard-bearer of the new impression management elite with which Lord's had, however reluctantly, now to deal; Lord's of course represented older elites and the writer Kitty Muggeridge probably spoke for many MCC members when she observed that the *arriviste* Frost had 'risen without trace'.[74] So Lord's would now tread carefully in the marketing of one-day cricket, dealing where possible with businesses and intermediaries more like themselves. Cricket returned to the BBC – a non-commercial institution with a similar claim on national heritage to cricket itself – and in seven years' time the first cricket World Cup would be staged in England, its sponsorship safely in the hands of the Prudential Assurance Company, established in the mid-nineteenth century in the City of London and esteemed provider of financial services. Reflecting later on the contracts with Benson and Hedges and Prudential, Bailey said:

> For all these sponsorship deals we were blessed with the pleasantest possible people to deal with, who understood that we would do everything in our power to promote their names through the media and on the grounds where their competitions were played, but that all

other arrangements were in the hands of the individual clubs. And the cricket format was in the hands of the cricket authorities. It all worked remarkably well.[75]

Thus, with some justification, Bailey and the other MCC mandarins saw themselves moving skilfully with the times, identifying and absorbing new political and commercial realities and allowing executives from tobacco corporations, insurance companies and advertising intermittent access to their inner circle. These, after all, were 'the pleasantest possible people to deal with' and at Lord's, subject to these minor modifications, the cricket governance of the English gentlemen would endure. But history shows that the genie was now out of the bottle. In Australia the first domestic one-day competition – the Australasian Knock-out Competition, which incorporated one New Zealand side and was sponsored by the Vehicle & General insurance company– was inaugurated in 1969. (Vehicle & General were replaced in 1971 by Coca Cola.) In the Caribbean the inter-island one-day competition the Banks Trophy began in 1972. The same year, the equivalent Deodhar Trophy (named after Dinkar Balwant Deodhar, 1892–1993, former Indian cricketer and Vice President of the BCCI) was launched in India. And in South Africa in 1981 the Benson and Hedges cigarette brand sponsored the domestic one-day tournament. The first cricket World Cup, based on the one-day format, would be held in 1975. The deliberations at Lord's would follow their own logic. The 'Packer moment' of World Series Cricket in Australia in 1977 would be a foretaste of the decline of British cricket dominance. The now-licenced one-day cricket format was tied to television and to sponsorship. The future of cricket power therefore lay with the countries that could offer the biggest TV audiences for cricket and the biggest markets – for insurance, for cigarettes, for soft drinks and, in time, for mobile phones. These audiences and markets, as we saw in earlier chapters, lay neither in England nor the white dominions, but on the Asian subcontinent.

Notes

1 This chapter is a revised and extended version of an article of the same name first published in *Sport in Society* Vol.16. No.1 2013 pp.5–18.
2 See Judy Threlfall-Sykes 'A history of English women's cricket, 1880–1939' Doctoral Thesis, De Montfort University, 2015.
3 Alvin W. Gouldner *The Coming Crisis of Western Sociology* London: Heinemann 1971 p.382.
4 'The War and cricket' *Wisden* February 1940 http://www.espncricinfo.com/ci/content/story/151855.html Access 13 May 2017.
5 R.C. Robertson-Glasgow 'Notes on the season' *Wisden* February 1941 http://www.espncricinfo.com/ci/content/story/151866.html Access 13 May 2017.
6 'Unwanted spectators' *Wisden* February 1941 http://www.espncricinfo.com/ci/content/story/151869.html Access 13 May 2017.

7 'Post-war cricket' *Wisden* January 1943 http://www.espncricinfo.com/ci/content/story/151872.html Access 13 May 2017.
8 'Professionals and amateurs' *Wisden* January 1943 http://www.espncricinfo.com/ci/content/story/151872.html Access 13 May 2017.
9 'Scheme for two-day matches' (proposed by Sussex CCC) *Wisden* 1943 http://www.espncricinfo.com/ci/content/story/151873.html Access 13 May 2017.
10 'Planning post-war cricket' *Wisden* 1944 http://www.espncricinfo.com/ci/content/story/151873.html Access 13 May 2017.
11 'Planning post-war cricket'.
12 'Planning post-war cricket'.
13 'Views and values' *Wisden* 1945 http://www.espncricinfo.com/ci/content/story/152858.html Access 13 May 2017.
14 'Australian survey' *Wisden* 1945 http://www.espncricinfo.com/ci/content/story/152859.html Access 13 May 2017.
15 'Views and values'.
16 P.J. Cain and A.G. Hopkins *British Imperialism: Innovation and Expansion* London: Longman 1993 p.23.
17 Eric Midwinter *The Lost Seasons: Cricket in Wartime 1939–45* London: Methuen 1987 p.154.
18 Mike Marqusee *Anyone But England: Cricket, Race and Class* London: Two Heads 1998 p.117.
19 Martin J. Wiener *English Culture and the Decline of the Industrial Spirit 1850–1980* Cambridge: Cambridge University Press 1981 p.5.
20 Mike Marqusee Anyone But England: An Outsider Looks at English Cricket London: Aurum Press 2005 pp.70–1.
21 Ross McKibbin *Classes and Cultures: England 1918–1951* Oxford: Oxford University Press 1998 p.339.
22 Marina Warner 'My grandfather, Plum' *Guardian* 11 June 2004 http://www.guardian.co.uk/books/2004/jun/11/sportandleisure.cricket Access 5 February 2012.
23 Sir Pelham Warner *Lord's 1787–1945* London: George G. Harrap 1946 p.246.
24 See, for example, Midwinter *The Lost Seasons* p.161; Jim Laker *One Day Cricket* London: B.T. Batsford 1977 p.25.
25 Midwinter *The Lost Seasons* pp.161–2.
26 See Marqusee *Anyone But England* (1998) p.118.
27 Eric Midwinter *Brylcreem Summer: The 1947 Cricket Season* London: Kingswood Press 1991 p.9.
28 Quoted in Midwinter *The Lost Seasons* pp.153–4.
29 Quoted in Midwinter *Brylcreem Summers* p.7.
30 Derek Birley *The Willow Wand: Some Cricket Myths Explored* London: Aurum Press 2000 p.149.
31 Geoffrey Moorhouse *Lord's* London: Hodder and Stoughton 1983 p.135.
32 Figures for 1946 and 1960 see Marqusee *Anyone But England* (1998) p.115; figure for 1947 see Laker *One Day Cricket* p.11; figure for 1963 see Moorhouse *Lord's* p.135.
33 Marqusee *Anyone But England* (1998) p.118.
34 John, Duke of Bedford *A Silver-Plated Spoon* London: Cassell and Co. 1959 p.202.
35 Giles Worsley 'Country houses – the lost legacy' *The Telegraph* 15 June 2002 http://www.telegraph.co.uk/culture/art/3578853/Country-houses-the-lost-legacy.html Access 6 February 2012.
36 John Scott *The Upper Classes: Property and Privilege in Britain* London: Macmillan 1982 p.155.

37 H.H. Wilson *Pressure Group* London: Secker and Warburg 1961. See in particular pp.81–3.
38 Asa Briggs *Sound and Vision* Oxford: Oxford University Press 1979 p.424; quoted in Colin Seymour-Ure 'The Prime Minister and the public: managing media relations' in Donald Shell and Richard Hodder-Williams (eds.) *Churchill to Major: The Prime Ministership Since 1945* London: Hurst and Co. 1995 p.189.
39 http://www.lordprice.co.uk/SPCT1017.html Access 7 February 2012. No longer available.
40 See http://www.espncricinfo.com/england/content/player/14225.html Access 14 May 2017. The remark is usually attributed to Sir Neville Cardus, doyen of Establishment cricket writers, or to Sir Pelham Warner.
41 Leo McKinstry *Jack Hobbs: England's Finest Cricketer* London: Yellow Jersey Press 2011 p.16.
42 Gerald Howat *Len Hutton: The Biography* London: Mandarin 1990 p.88.
43 Simon Briggs 'A hundred years of sport and advertising' *The Telegraph* 26 February 2008 http://www.telegraph.co.uk/sport/othersports/2292796/A-hundred-years-of-sport-and-advertising.html Access 14 May 2017.
44 Norman Giller *Denis Compton* London: Andre Deutsch 1997 pp.91–9.
45 Ibid. pp.154–7. See also Tim Heald *Denis Compton* London: Pavilion Books 1994 pp.142–4.
46 Stephen Wagg *The Football World: A Contemporary Social History* Brighton: Harvester Press 1984 pp.117–18.
47 Simon Hughes 'From La Scala to Lord's: a life lived to the full' *The Telegraph* 18 May 2005 http://www.telegraph.co.uk/sport/columnists/simonhughes/2359793/From-La-Scala-to-Lords-a-life-lived-to-the-full.html Access 14 May 2017.
48 Alan Lee *Lord Ted* London: Vista 1996 p.71.
49 Lee *Lord Ted* p.75.
50 Simon Hughes 'From La Scala'.
51 I've discussed Turner's stewardship of Leicestershire in more detail: see Stephen Wagg '"The four-day game doesn't pay the bills" Leicestershire, 2010–11: a case study in the contemporary political economy of county cricket' *Sport in Society* Vol.4 No.10 December 2011 pp.1407–20.
52 Tim Murray 'Turner fears for the future of "saturated" Twenty20' *Leicester Mercury* 29 May 2009 p.45.
53 Denis Lambert *The History of Leicestershire County Cricket Club* London: Christopher Helm 1992 p.5.
54 In *The Cricketer Annual* of 1944, A.J. Holmes had suggested that one way to accommodate professional Sunday cricket might be to make it inclusive of an open-air service – see Midwinter *The Lost Seasons* p.164.
55 E.W. Swanton *As I Said at the Time* (edited by George Plumptre) London: Unwin Hyman 1986 p.286.
56 Norman Peston 'Disappearance of the amateur' *Wisden* 1963 http://www.espncricinfo.com/ci/content/story/152769.html Access 14 May 2017.
57 Gordon Ross *The Gillette Cup: 1963 to 1980* London: Queen Anne Press 1981 p.11.
58 Ibid. pp.12–13.
59 Simon Chapman *Great Expectorations: Advertising and the Tobacco Industry* London: Comedia 1986 p.12.
60 Peter Taylor *Smoke Ring: The Politics of Tobacco* London: The Bodley Head 1984 p.31.
61 Hanspeter Witschi 'A short history of lung cancer' *Toxicological Sciences* Vol.64 No.1 2001 pp.4–6 http://toxsci.oxfordjournals.org/content/64/1/4.full Access 14 May 2017.

62 Taylor *Smoke Ring* p.35.
63 Laker *One Day Cricket* p.36.
64 Jack Bailey *Conflicts in Cricket* London: The Kingswood Press 1989 p.26.
65 John Arlott 'Stupid, damaging, unnecessary' *The Guardian* 25 March 1969. Reproduced in David Rayvern Allen (ed.) *Arlott on Cricket* London: Fontana/Collins 1985 p.20.
66 Laker *One Day Cricket* p.43.
67 Ibid. p.53; Peter West *Flannelled Fool and Muddied Oaf* London: W.H. Allen 1986 p.86.
68 *Wisden* 1970 http://www.espncricinfo.com/ci/content/story/155957.html?years=1970 Access 14 May 2017.
69 Marcus Williams (ed.) *The Way to Lord's: Cricketing Letters to 'The Times'* London: Fontana/Collins 1984 p.123.
70 Bailey *Conflicts* p.34.
71 Bailey *Conflicts* p.35.
72 Bailey *Conflicts* p.35.
73 Bailey *Conflicts* pp.35–6.
74 See Peter Guttridge 'Those choice words that say "I hate you"' *The Independent* 26 January 1996 http://www.independent.co.uk/life-style/those-choice-words-that-say-i-hate-you-1325795.html Access 14 May 2017.
75 Bailey *Conflicts* p.44.

Chapter 12

'Paint a picture, and keep it the right way up'

Cricket and the mass media 1945–2015

This chapter charts the changing and complex relationship between cricket and the mass media. As with most of the other chapters, it covers the period between the 1940s and the time of writing, although it takes brief note of earlier times. In doing so it tries to take account not only of the range of mass media (print media, radio, television and internet-related services), but also of attendant notions of social class, politics and culture which were always inherent, and sometimes explicit, in the media engagement with cricket. Given cricket's historic links to the British Empire, a good deal of the opening sections of the chapter are necessarily about English media and about their representation of the game.

Test cricket and 'the big funerals': cricket, media and the British Establishment, 1945 to 1975

By the twentieth century, cricket reporting in the British newspapers was long established and stretched back into the 1700s – the time when the first rules of the game had been laid down, principally to provide the basis upon which gentlemen could make wagers. By 1945 cricket print journalism consisted, in the main, of providing scorecards and describing the main events of the day's play. In addition, as with other sports in the 1940s and 50s, some cricket writers would, usually without attribution, ghost-write autobiographies for leading cricketers, many of them published by the London sport book publisher Stanley Paul.[1] Generally speaking, before the 1950s the newspapers did not concern themselves with off-the-field controversy – there were exceptions, certainly, one being the dispute over the Yorkshire captaincy in 1927, covered extensively in the *Yorkshire Post*[2] – or with the lives of players away from the game. Among those cricket writers who sought to go beyond bare description, the most influential was Neville Cardus of the *Manchester Guardian*. Cardus, who also wrote on classical music, was prone to render cricket matches as epics and his favourite players as heroes. In his accounts of Lancashire and Yorkshire matches, for instance, the players became quirky characters in a Northern myth world, speaking dialect as if in a novel by the Yorkshire writer J.B. Priestley.[3] Toward the end of his life Cardus acknowledged that he had used some licence in his writing. In 1974, by then in his late 80s, he responded to a remark by a BBC correspondent that the game now lacked characters:

> I sympathise with him in his searching for characters in our first-class cricket at the moment. Frankly, I think they are there, present embryonically. Emmott Robinson, Rhodes and Herbert Sutcliffe,[4] were not actually the rounded 'characters' looming large in my accounts of Lancashire versus Yorkshire matches. They provided me with merely the raw material, so to say; my histrionic pen provided the rest. I have often told, in print, of a wet morning at Leeds, a Yorkshire versus Lancashire match. The sun came forth hot and sumptuous. At half-past two Rhodes and Robinson went out to inspect the wicket, I with them. Rhodes pressed a finger into the soft turf, saying, 'Emmott, it'll be "sticky" at four o'clock.' 'No, Wilfred, half-past.' I put words into his mouth that God intended him to utter.[5]

The 'merrie England' perspective through which Cardus described the game expressed his insistence that cricket was not only an art form but one which expressed the uniqueness of the English people.[6] 'It is far more than a game, this cricket', he wrote in 1946. 'It somehow holds the mirror up to English nature'.[7] Cardus was then 58 and had long since become convinced that, with an emergent welfare state, the game and, thus, the mirror had lost their sparkle. In his autobiography, published in 1947, he reflected:

> Between 1926 and 1936 our cricket in the lump was as stereotyped as the council houses and flats and ribbon roads which more and more month by month symbolised the post-war England. Whatever the occasion, England against Australia, or Eton against Harrow, the procedure was much the same – safety first […] each side afraid of a sportsman's gesture.[8]

Cardus still has his admirers. 'If you wish to understand the significance of Neville Cardus', said cricket writer Scyld Berry in 2010:

> take the agency report of any cricket match. 'On the first day the home side scored 268 for 5, the highlight being a century by so-and-so with two sixes and nine fours. The stand-out bowler was X, who took 4 for 65' etc. Cardus put in what agency reports left out. He introduced the crowd, the atmosphere, the ambience of a cricket match, the personalities involved. He made the match come alive.[9]

In the decades immediately following the Second World War, however, Cardus' brand of romantic hyperbole carried less and less conviction.

'To the irreverent 1970s', observed cricket historian Derek Birley, Cardus' writing could seem 'merely bogus' and, at its worst, 'like advertising copy. He exploits the nostalgic, white-on-green, rustic bliss, dreaming spires and village inn images that can be relied upon to evoke deep and satisfying emotions in cricket-lovers, just as a television commercial exploits sex or greed'.[10] But if, in general, the cricket press had less recourse to Cardus' style of writing, a kindred spirit could be found in John Arlott, who began commentating on cricket for the BBC in 1946. Of life in Southampton during the Second World War, Arlott recalled: 'Still in summer there was cricket, cricket known now with a new understanding; illuminated above all by reading Cardus'.[11]

Both Cardus and Arlott wrote for the *Guardian*, the voice of British liberalism, but, among the British broadsheets, it is the right-wing *Daily Telegraph* that is widely held to have spoken to, and for, the majority of British cricket enthusiasts. For much of the second half of the twentieth century cricket writing at the *Telegraph* was dominated by E.W. ('Jim') Swanton,[12] who joined the paper in 1946. Swanton's prose was more measured than Cardus' and, unlike Cardus, he was an Establishment insider, with ready access to the game's, and the country's, ruling elite: when touring to watch England play he was usually a guest in the mansions of governor-generals.[13]

A patrician and, like most members of the English cricket elite, an imperialist, Swanton always supported – and, on occasion, tried to restore – the political status quo. For example, following the England tour of West Indies in the winter of 1953–4, which was marked by anti-colonial unrest,[14] he gladly accepted an invitation two years later to bring a team to the Caribbean to try to restore harmonious relations.[15] Fourteen years later, in 1968, doubtless sensing the new, post-colonial cultural racism that was now in play in British politics, he wrote an indignant letter to Conservative house journal *The Spectator* condemning the recent racist anti-immigration speech of ex-Tory minister Enoch Powell: 'If "Enoch" knew what passions he was about to unleash, he was guilty of an act that was the complete negation of patriotism', stated Swanton. 'It is possibly more charitable to suppose that his frothy speech was a bid for future political power which, pray God, he may never achieve'.[16] The same year he did his best, as an MCC loyalist, but one who found apartheid abhorrent, to mediate in the controversy surrounding the exclusion of Basil D'Oliveira from the England team to tour South Africa (see Chapter 1).[17]

Swanton wielded considerable influence over English cricket writing since he was also editorial director of *The Cricketer* magazine. In this capacity and that of elder statesman-cricket correspondent, Swanton presided over a platoon of eminent males with shared social background and ways of thinking: Christopher Martin-Jenkins, then 22 and an old boy of Marlborough public school and a Cambridge graduate, was recruited to edit *The Cricketer* in 1967 straight from the May ball at a Cambridge college and was delighted to find that two Harrow old boys had an office on the same corridor.[18] When Swanton retired from the *Telegraph* in 1975 he was succeeded by Michael Melford (Charterhouse and Oxford), whom Martin-Jenkins described as 'a shrewd observer of the game, loyal to the establishment'.[19] Assuming himself to be as one with the cricket nation, in 2013 Martin-Jenkins described a county cricket ground on a May morning in the 1980s thus:

> Most are men but there are women too, usually in charge of a picnic bag. Already the thermos has been opened for a first cup of coffee. On their menfolk panamas outnumber floppy white sun-hats. Everyone has a newspaper. For the great majority of them it is the *Daily Telegraph*. Each of them is cheerfully scrutinising one of the cricket pages.[20]

In 2011 journalist and academic Rob Steen wrote of the cricket media:

> Newspapers remain the one constant. Read a discursive day's report in the *Daily Telegraph* or the *Sydney Morning Herald* and it will not differ markedly from those of half a century, even a century ago. There is a greater informality of language, yes [...] but to read the magisterial E.W. Swanton in the *Telegraph* during the 1950s was not an altogether dissimilar experience to reading the endlessly fair-minded Christopher Martin-Jenkins in the 1990s. Both were better-informed, closer to the seats of power than their rivals.[21]

Along with Oxford graduate John Woodcock, cricket correspondent for *The Times* (from 1954 to 1988) these writers functioned as an unofficial mouthpiece for Lord's. Needless to say they would all vehemently oppose Kerry Packer's World Series Cricket project of 1977. When the controversy broke Woodcock suggested that Packer's chief recruiter, South African-born ex-England captain Tony Greig, was, after all, not an Englishman 'through and through'; Christopher Martin-Jenkins judged this remark to be 'spot on, in that Greig did not feel that deep loyalty to the established order of English cricket that would have prevented him from – in essence – following Mammon rather than honour'.[22]

Swanton also frequently broadcast on cricket for the BBC. Ball-by-ball commentary of cricket matches dated back to 1922 when ex-cricketer Len Watt had reported on a game from the Sydney Cricket Ground in Australia. BBC commentaries had begun in 1927. The first broadcast was by ex-Essex player Rev. Frank Gillingham (Dulwich College and Durham University) reporting from Leyton. Gillingham continued to do the occasional commentary but is said to have infuriated BBC Director General Lord Reith (and, doubtless, Lord's) when he spent a rain break at The Oval reading out the various advertisements he could see from his commentary position.[23]

The commentators themselves had been recruited quite casually, often from among sport-loving Oxbridge graduates known to BBC management. Teddy Wakelam (Marlborough and Cambridge), who, beginning in 1927, had covered several sports, including cricket, for the BBC, had been selected via a phone call from a man asking if he was the same Wakelam who played rugby for Harlequins (a leading London club); if so, could he come to the BBC for an interview.[24] In 1946 Brian Johnston (Eton and Oxford) received a similar call from future Conservative minister Ian Orr-Ewing (Harrow and Oxford) then in charge of Outside Broadcasts at the BBC. Orr-Ewing reminded Johnston of the cricket they'd played together before the Second World War; would he therefore like to commentate on cricket for the BBC's nascent television service?[25] Peter West, like Johnston an ex-serviceman and a public school old boy, was taken on as a commentator in 1947, following a chance meeting with the legendary sportsman C.B. Fry at Taunton cricket ground; Fry was working for the *Sunday Graphic* and West phoned his copy through for him.[26] Socially and politically the odd one out among the early BBC cricket commentators was Arlott. Arlott had worked initially as a policeman in his native Hampshire and had come to the BBC as a poetry specialist. He was asked to do radio commentary on the England–India Test matches of 1946 but his strong Hampshire accent caused consternation among the corporation's administrators. Fellow commentator Robert Hudson (who had been to Shrewsbury, one of England's nine most prestigious public schools,[27] and the London School of Economics) said 'My God, no one with an accent like that will ever get anywhere'.[28] Seymour de Lotbiniere (Eton and Cambridge), BBC's new head of Outside Broadcasts, told Arlott bluntly 'while I think you have a vulgar voice, you have a compensatingly interesting mind'.[29] As an ex-grammar-school boy, a supporter of the Liberal Party and a lover of the arts with a distinctive regional accent Arlott stood somewhat apart from what was otherwise both an upper-middle-class gentleman's club and the journalistic arm of Lord's governance. Arlott's view of cricket also differed from theirs. They saw it as a rite of sporting Englishness conducted amicably between the natural rulers of England and their loyal subjects, at home and abroad. Arlott was closer to Cardus: for him, cricket was not sport, but folk culture – a kind of people's poetry.[30]

Reith had been conscious that the BBC's monopoly '"had the effect of "making the nation as one man"' and resolved that its mission should be to 'inform, educate and entertain'.[31] In the early years of the BBC this had seemed to imply both a diversity of sports and a diversity within a sport. For instance, Christopher Martin-Jenkins describes how in 1936 the BBC covered well over a dozen sports, including 'even darts and pigeon racing' (note the 'even' in regard to two unequivocally working-class sports). In the case of cricket, all levels of the game were initially considered – one feature in 1937 was 'Three Aspects of Cricket' with alternating reports from a working man's club game, a league fixture and a county match.[32] During the 1940s and 50s, however, the primacy of first-class and, in particular, Test match cricket – and, thus, of the MCC – seems to have been quietly reasserted. As Marqusee wrote, Test cricket and its administrators were like the royal family – above politics and 'the disinterested embodiment of national and imperial destinies'.[33] Indeed cricket and royal broadcasts were sometimes entrusted to the same 'safe pairs of hands'. Early cricket commentator Howard Marshall (Haileybury and Oxford) had covered the coronation of King George VI in 1937 for BBC radio and when Peter West commentated on his first Test match for BBC television in 1952, Anthony Craxton was producer – 'He did it right through the 1950s', recalled West. 'He did the big funerals, the Coronation and Royal weddings'.[34] Ball-by-ball commentary on England's home Test matches was instituted in 1957 and went out on the Third Programme – the radio channel devoted to high culture (chiefly classical music) and broadcasting hitherto only in the evenings.

Across the BBC's radio and television commentary teams during the 1940s and 50s the patrician voices of Swanton, Johnston, West and others predominated,[35] with Arlott – a kind of artist-in-residence and token man-of-the-people – the sole anomaly. Moreover, the culture of management continued to be that of the imagined public school or Oxbridge college – a jovial, male and generally unreflecting environment whose inhabitants addressed each other by their surnames, adjusted, as in public schools, to add the letters 'e', 'r' and 's' to the end of them. 'Though a true blue Conservative with a very capital "C" "Tukers" had a flair for good broadcasting ideas', enthused Christopher Martin-Jenkins of Michael Tuke-Hastings, producer of the BBC's *Test Match Special* from its inception in 1957 to 1973.[36]

The commentary provided by this team was generally matter-of-fact and succinct. The advice of Yorkshire and England veteran Wilfred Rhodes to Robert Hudson – 'Paint a picture and keep it the right way up'[37] – seems to have been a benchmark for the radio commentators. But threats to the post-public-school idyll were soon apparent; some of them had important long-term implications for cricket's relationship with the media.

First, there were private objections to John Arlott's poetic flights of fancy. Australian Broadcasting Corporation (ABC) commentator Alan McGilvray, who had captained New South Wales in Australian state cricket and who would join the commentary team when Australia toured the UK, did not share the widespread admiration for Arlott's commentary.[38] McGilvray became angry that Arlott 'didn't give the score or the card. I mentioned this to him and he said "Who wants the score? I'm not interested in the score?"'[39] Here was one of the first glimpses of an alternative way of rendering cricket, with greater emphasis placed on drawing the audience in, not to the game's history or its myths, but to the action itself.

McGilvray thus raised a second bone of contention – the growing feeling that cricket should be rendered by people who had played it at first-class level, as the BBC team had not. BBC producer Nick Hunter said: 'You cannot criticize the best players in the world if you are [just] a club cricketer. You haven't got the right to'.[40] In 1956 this thinking had prompted the appointment as a summariser of Australian ex-Test batsman Jack Fingleton and, two years later, of Denis Compton, who had just retired from Test cricket. It also likely lay behind the transfer of Swanton (in 1967) and Johnston (in 1969) to radio. Former Australian captain Richie Benaud became the first ex-Test cricketer to commentate (as opposed to summarise) in 1964; Jim Laker was the first England Test cricketer to do so, in 1969.[41] Two important considerations flow from this. One was that, since by the 1960s the British Empire had largely been dismantled and the English cricket team was correspondingly struggling to hold its own, more criticism of them could now be expected – better that it should come from an authoritative voice, one who had been there and done it. The other was that, in the longer term, the most influential voices of cricket would be technical ones, introducing an audience to the game's mysteries; they were more likely to be ahistorical and less likely to be upper class, or even English.

Third, with the birth of Independent Television (ITV) in 1955, the BBC now had a rival for broadcast cricket. ITV bid more money than BBC to show the Ashes series of 1956; BBC got the contract, but perhaps partly because their offer was for three years (ITV's was for one) and because ITV could not then be viewed throughout the UK[42] – thus affirming the BBC as continuing guardian of 'the national interest'. Although rivalry with ITV was never fully to develop, BBC would now have to consider their audience and its preferences in ways that had not hitherto been the case. For many of this audience the BBC style was too formal. Always mindful of prevailing opinion at Lord's, however, in 1950 the BBC team had to consider a complaint from MCC President Sir Pelham Warner that the use of players' first names in commentary was 'undignified'.[43] On the other hand, they also had to admit that the commentary of Rex Alston, who retired in 1964, was rather 'schoolmasterly'.

Fourth, there was the matter of 'race'. While none of the team would likely have considered themselves racists and certainly none of them publicly endorsed South Africa's apartheid system, they nevertheless supported MCC policy of playing Test cricket against white South Africa. Except for John Arlott. South Africa's state racism had become an issue in the international sport world in the 1960s and South Africa had been expelled from the Olympic Games of 1964 in Tokyo. But Arlott, as we saw in Chapter 3, had called the South African government as 'predominantly a Nazi one' in a radio programme as long ago as 1950. 'We had shouting arguments about South Africa – he felt deeply about that, and I felt the other way', said Brian Johnston.[44]

Fifth, there were early hints that the gentlemen who peopled the worlds of cricket and of the BBC would now be fair game for journalists of the

206 Cricket in the age of globalisation

popular press seeking salacious stories about the private lives of well-known individuals. In an improbable foretaste of what would become common coin twenty years later, in 1964, having been on holiday in Majorca with BBC colleague Peter Dimmock, their wives and other friends, and gone for nude swim at midnight, Peter West found himself several weeks later answering a call from the *News of the World*, asking him to confirm that this was the case. The paper ran it as their second story and a number of dailies followed suit the next day.[45] Dimmock, who successfully denied everything, and West, who did not, had a right to expect that as vaguely Establishment figures their private lives would have been kept out of the public domain. In the early 1960s, in the wake of two series of the BBC television satire programme *That Was the Week That Was* (1962–3) and 'Profumo Affair' of 1963, this was clearly an outdated expectation.

Losing that fuddy-duddy image? Cricket, media and markets 1975 to 2015

With forty years of hindsight, the most significant development in the relationship between cricket and the mass media since 1945 seems to have been the so-called 'Packer Affair' of 1977 in Australia, briefly discussed in Chapter 2. This affair had a range of ramifications which will be described in this section.

First, as we saw in relation to the campaign for one-day cricket (in the previous chapter), since the 1950s the rising elites of impression management (media, advertising, PR . . .) had gained increasing cultural and economic influence in the Western world. In England, while the influence of these elites was being felt in industry and the Conservative Party, the old wealth at the MCC thought that they could maintain this influence – perceived as commercial vulgarity – at arm's length: they had consented to sponsored competition, but only on what they felt were their terms. In Australia, the Anglophile elite that had dominated the country's cricket (and politics) was more intransigent and it faced stiffer opposition in a country where commercial broadcasting was longer established. Once the Australian Broadcasting Corporation (ABC) had rejected a substantial offer for coverage of the forthcoming Test series from Kerry Packer's Channel Nine, Packer resolved, and had the wherewithal, to run his own tournament. In the process of setting up this tournament, cricket and television, in effect, became conjoined: instead of television being allowed simply to relay an independently staged event to an audience, television devised the event and the circumstances of its transmission.

Interestingly, BBC broadcasters were sympathetic to the Packer approach and one, cricket producer David Kenning, acted as consultant to the project. Packer used a camera behind both wickets and, in all, eight cameras (rising, later, to thirteen) at each match, more than double what was then customary;

an interviewer was deployed to speak to each batsman on his way onto and off the field of play; and in 1978 microphones were placed on the pitch so that the TV audience could hear players talk.[46] From now on, cricket-watchers, and especially those who had first encountered cricket in the late 1970s, would likely measure the game against the Packer version and, since that time, a series of innovations have deepened the involvement of television in the transaction of the cricket match itself. Stump microphones have been common since 1990, but probably the most decisive intervention came in 1992, with the introduction in a Test between South Africa and India of a third umpire, using television replays for adjudication, to whom the on-field umpires could refer for a verdict. In 2008 the third umpire was given the power to overturn decisions taken on the field. Meanwhile more and more analytic technology has been adopted in cricket broadcasts: in 1995 the BskyB satellite channel deployed slow-motion replays and a device called Spinvision to show the rotation of the ball in flight; the Snickometer system, a sound-detection technology for judging if the ball had hit the bat, was developed in the mid-1990s and adopted by Britain's Channel 4; in 2001, for the England v. Pakistan Test at Lord's, Channel 4 also introduced Hawkeye, a device that could track the trajectory of balls in flight, and thus assess whether or not a ball would have hit the wicket. Hot Spot, yet another detecting tool, this time involving infra-red cameras, was first adopted by Channel Nine in Australia for the Ashes series of 2006–7.[47] Now, in top level televised cricket, the game was often paused while TV considered an umpiring decision; the verdict would now usually be relayed to spectators, either in the crowd or watching on TV, via an on-site screen. As writer Jim Melly could reflect in 1996: 'The line between reporting cricket and becoming part of the game was finally crossed with the introduction of the third umpire'.[48]

Other aspects of the Packer package were also readily adopted by cricket boards around the world, including (crucially) the commercial primacy of limited-overs cricket, coloured clothing, day-night matches (to fit more easily with spectators' typical work-leisure timetables) and a different coloured ball – white or pink. Packer, much reviled at the time by the old elites in England and Australia and their spokespeople, had set cricket on a trajectory, during which the label 'Made in England' would be steadily stripped from it and replaced by one reading 'Developed for television'.

The second major effect of the Packer episode was that it deepened the acceptance in the commanding heights of English cricket that the game over which they presided could no longer be seen simply as a taken-for-granted fundament of an undifferentiated English identity. In 1992 the Chief Executive of the Test and County Cricket Board (TCCB), former Warwickshire and England wicketkeeper A.C. Smith (King Edwards School, Birmingham and Oxford) felt the need to justify once again awarding the contract for live television broadcasts to the BBC: they had made a good offer, he said, and, besides, 'we couldn't ignore the community as a whole'.[49] By now, though, many people in the world where sport and media met were arguing that there was no such thing as 'the community as a whole'; there were now only niche markets. Thus, in 1996 the TCCB became streamlined as the England and Wales Cricket Board (ECB) and its new chair, as we saw in Chapter 1, was Lord MacLaurin. The appointment of MacLaurin, an old boy of Malvern public school who had nevertheless not been to university and only played Minor Counties cricket, was a recognition both of the new business imperatives and of the admission to the Lord's inner circle of another previously disparaged elite: retail – he had been chairman of Tesco supermarkets and would shortly become chairman of Vodafone. The BBC had lost their rights to show England Test matches two years later, giving way to Channel 4.

Several things are important to note about the move to Channel 4. In 1998 it had been broadcasting for only sixteen years. It was a commercial broadcaster with a specific public service remit: to demonstrate innovation, experiment and creativity and to cater to cultural minorities. At the time in media circles it was associated with the youth market; it had shown little previous interest in sport. Channel 4 appointed Sybil Ruscoe, who had worked mainly for BBC Radio One (a predominantly music channel also aimed mainly at the young) to be the first woman to present cricket on television. They also engaged Richie Benaud, widely regarded as the cricket commentator with the most credibility, who, it was hoped, would bring most BBC cricket viewers with him. Channel 4 now promised to 'revolutionise TV coverage of cricket'[50] and journalist Jason Deans commented that the ECB was now anxious 'to ditch the sport's fuddy-duddy image and gagging to get its hands on the youthful, female, multi-cultural values associated with Channel 4'.[51]

This may have been so, but the Channel 4 contract was short-lived and there seems little doubt that a longer game was being played. Satellite and cable television were now available on subscription in Britain (and elsewhere) having been licensed by the last Conservative administration of Margaret Thatcher in 1989. Under the terms of a further Broadcasting Act in 1996, passed by the Conservative government of John Major, the Secretary of State for Culture, Media and Sport had been empowered to 'list' sport events deemed to be of national significance, so that the rights to show them could not be sold to subscription-only channels. English Test cricket was so listed. The ECB, however, were now dependent on television revenue – in 1995, for the first time, they had received more money from broadcasters than in gate receipts[52] – and they had engaged Westminster Strategy, a lobbying firm, to campaign against this ruling. Chris Smith, culture minister in the freshly-installed Labour administration of Tony Blair, had obliged.[53] Crucially, the deal of 1998 gave *all bar one* of the home Tests between 1999 and 2002 to Channel 4; the other went to the satellite channel Sky Sports.

In 2004 the ECB was said to be split, some favouring renewal of this contract and some preferring now to award all live television rights to Sky. The latter faction won the argument: satellite television could not promise bigger audiences, but they could pay more money – a key consideration for the financially beleaguered county cricket clubs.[54] In return Lord's could offer Sky the prestige of televising this historic gentleman's game. Sky were given four years' exclusive live coverage of England home Test matches (along with one-day, Twenty20 and women's internationals as well as county cricket) from 2006; live access via terrestrial television to England cricket matches therefore ceased. Highlights were to appear on Channel 5, a terrestrial entertainment channel only launched in 1997, between 7.15 and 8 o'clock in the evening. David Morgan, MacLaurin's successor at the ECB, was aware that, with A.C. Smith's notion of 'the community as a whole' now receding, the board were negotiating a difficult moment in the relationship between cricket and nation. 'We understand that the decision to place all live cricket coverage on satellite and cable television is an emotive issue for some people', he said. 'We have made an agreement that will offer the highlights package to a peak time audience. Five will broadcast highlights from 7.15-8.00pm, a time which is the most popular slot for TV viewing for children and a time when an average of 21 million people watch television'.[55]

Critics were quick to point out that the majority of this admittedly large audience were watching popular soap operas at that time. The mention of children was significant, both sides arguing that, with cricket dwindling in state schools, they were trying to safeguard the game for future generations – the ECB with money, the proponents of the free-to-air argument with the greater opportunity to see it played. Former England captain Alec Stewart argued: 'Young girls and boys should be able to see cricket without having to pay for it. The ECB have to look at the whole picture. They may be getting a big cheque but, long-term, English cricket will suffer'.[56] A counter argument, however, dated back to the Packer innovations: in 1985 Richie Benaud had claimed an upsurge in interest in cricket in Australia since the introduction of World Series Cricket and that television should be seen as a the prime mover in cricket's future and rising generations' knowledge of the game should not be taken for granted:

> Parents and children who had no interest in the game have seen the night matches televised from the Sydney Cricket Ground, and day matches from other grounds, and have been instantly intrigued. When the matches come to their own state they have been keen to go and watch and, from this point of view, the clicking turnstiles have been complementary.[57]

Sky television has held its exclusive rights to England internationals ever since and, for Test cricket, the innovative presentation pioneered by Britain's

Channel 4 has been lost. The Sky commentary box, in keeping with the doctrine enunciated decades earlier by Nick Hunter, is full of ex-professional cricketers, mostly men who captained England in the 1980s and 90s. The Global Cricket Corporation, a lesser-known arm of the News International media empire, had a five-year contract for the global broadcasting and marketing rights to all ICC events between 2003 and 2007, including the World Cups of those years.

The third identifiable consequence of the Packer moment was the rise of cricket, and cricket-related, celebrity. Test cricketers had for a long time been celebrities of a kind. They had been noted for representing the nation and for their sporting prowess. From time to time this celebrity had been merchandised in a small way, through a 'ghosted' autobiography, perhaps, or the endorsement of cricket equipment. On occasion they had lent their name to products in general usage – as with W.G. Grace's advertisement for Colman's mustard in the 1890s, Jack Hobbs' endorsement of Quaker Oats and cigarettes[58] and Denis Compton's association with Brylcreem hair lotion in the 1940s.[59] Even the venerated John Arlott, who had seemed to stand for art rather than commerce, had appeared in advertisements for tobacco, beer, biscuits and lawnmowers.[60] And, as noted in the previous chapter, BBC commentator Peter West was partner in a PR agency which in the late 1960s had brokered sponsorship deals between Lord's and leading cigarette manufacturers.[61]

But this had been small scale and press interest in the private lives of cricketers had been scant: for example, the many extramarital affairs of Gloucestershire and England captain Wally Hammond (85 Tests 1927–47) had been ignored by the popular newspapers and did not come to light until a biography of Hammond was published over thirty years after his death.[62] The approach of Channel Nine production team, however, had been based on notions of consumer sovereignty. Not only were they now, effectively, in a television show; with microphones everywhere, the cricketers, were placed under the surveillance of their public.

Some cricketers, therefore, now became celebrities in the postmodern sense – people 'known for being known' and 'living news items'.[63] The sociologist Chris Rojek has suggested that late twentieth- and early twenty-first-century celebrity is driven by the PR and other media industries[64] and in this regard Ian Botham is an illustrative case study. A prodigious and bumptious cricketer, Botham made his Test debut for England in 1978 and, despite a liking for raucous nights out and a known distaste for decorum, was given the England captaincy in 1980. He lost it very soon but remained in the team and was the star of England's improbable victory in the home Ashes series of 1981. This heightened his celebrity and he gained much currency as a news item. In 1983 right-wing tabloid the *Sun* printed a story headlined BOTHAM IN NEW YEAR'S EVE BRAWL WITH AUSSIE TEST STAR. Botham already had a contract with the *Sun* for a ghosted column and a friend advised him to withdraw from it: 'My attitude, however, was that the money was good and that no one took the tabloids seriously anyway'.[65] Botham's response shows a pragmatic acceptance of life as a text, divorced not only from his trade (cricket) but, if necessary, from himself: the paper was simply buying the use of his name. Botham, 62 at the time of writing, has been an intermittent news item ever since and generated seven autobiographies or quasi-autobiographies between 1982 and 2011. His experience is typical of leading cricket figures in the postmodern media world. 'Before Botham', wrote Melly, 'cricketers were generally left alone by the tabloid press. After Botham, cricket could never be free of them'.[66]

A warped intelligence? A new cricket culture?

One significance of this pursuit, by British and other tabloids, of information on the non-cricket lives of cricketers was that it revealed new patterns of taste and consumption. In the 1960s the more far-sighted among the MCC leadership had recognised that cricket would now be consumed differently in different markets. In the 1980s and 90s a similar realisation seems to have taken place at the BBC with regard to radio commentary.

As we have noted, the BBC began ball-by-ball radio commentary of England Test matches in 1957, the programme being given the title *Test Match Special* (*TMS*). At the time of the launch of World Series Cricket in the late 1970s some of the principal voices in the *TMS* commentary box belonged to Christopher Martin-Jenkins, Brian Johnston (Eton and Oxford), Henry Blofeld (Eton and Cambridge) and ex-Essex and England all-rounder Trevor Bailey (Dulwich College and Cambridge, 61 Tests 1949–59). They took their place alongside the veteran Arlott, who would retire in 1980. The (still) predominant presence of upper-middle-class males had been leavened in 1974 by the addition of ex-Yorkshire and England fast bowler Fred Trueman (67 Tests 1952–65) and Yorkshire journalist Don Mosey. With the exception of Arlott they all held conservative views and, together, constituted a kind of Upper and Lower Middle England of the airwaves. Mosey spiced this up with some public status-anxious resentment of his higher-born colleagues. Of Martin-Jenkins he wrote in 1991: 'I had heard of children being born with a silver spoon in the mouth but for Chris to walk so easily into the cricket correspondent's post[67] with relatively little experience smacked of being born with a diamond-encrusted golden spoon thrust well down the throat'.[68] Mosey, who retired that year, judged that 'towards the end of the 1980s [. . .] the TMS honeymoon with the columnists had ended' and that now the team was a shambles akin to *Monty Python's Flying Circus*' Upper Class Twit of the Year sketch.[69] But what the traditionalist Mosey regarded as a shambles was, in effect, a means of defining *TMS* in the new, increasingly diverse cricket-media market. Instead of downplaying the 'silver spoon' aura of the broadcast, it was accentuated, so that *TMS* became a boarding-school caricature, wherein each commentator, regardless of objective social background, was given a surname ending in 'ers' ('Johnners', 'Durders', 'Tuffers', 'Aggers' and so on), feeble jokes were exchanged and female listeners of a certain age encouraged to bake cakes for the commentators to eat – cakes from home being another emblem of boarding-school life. These became trademarks and helped identify *TMS* as *faux* traditional in the post-Packer age of satellite TV, the internet and the phone app. Nothing illustrated this better than the 'leg over' incident of 1991 in which, commentating on an incident in which Ian Botham disturbed his wicket with his leg, Brian Johnston giggled uncontrollably at Jonathan Agnew's observation that Botham in the end 'couldn't get his leg over'.[70] Perceived as a gaffe at the time, the incident rapidly became the motif for a commentary team now identified with cheery, permanent immaturity.

This was most vividly demonstrated in the person of Brian Johnston, born in 1912 the son of a wealthy City coffee merchant, who drew on his upper-class background (aside from his Eton and Oxford education Johnston was godfather to the daughter of Conservative Prime Minister and Scottish laird Sir Alec Douglas-Home)[71] and his years in BBC Light Entertainment to create the playful ambience of *TMS*. 'Johnners widened the audience for *TMS* dramatically with his jokes, terrible puns and, of course, the chocolate cakes', wrote ex- Leicestershire and England bowler Agnew ('Aggers'), who joined the team in 1991.[72]

The implied politics of Johnston's commentary will probably have been more noticeable to listeners abroad than in the UK. Ramachandra Guha wrote recently:

> For Indian males, the BBC [...] meant *Test Match Special*. We loved the gravelly tones of John Arlott and the growly tones of Fred Trueman, although Brian Johnston irritated us with his aimless banter and his manifest Little Englandism. (I still recall how, during the 1976 England–West Indies series, a short ball from Holding or Roberts was routinely described as 'a nasty one', but a short ball from Willis or Old as 'a splendid bouncer').[73]

But for the inhabitants of Little England the 'aimless banter' is almost certainly what they liked best and Johnston's death in 1994 brought a host of tributes and volumes of remembrance, including *Brian Johnston: The Authorised Biography*; *Summers Will Never be the Same*; *Johnners – The Life Of Brian*; *A Delicious Slice of Johnners*; *Another Slice of Johnners*; *A Further Slice of Johnners*; *An Evening With Johnners*; *Brian Johnston: Letters Home 1926–1945*; and *Thanks, Johnners: An Affectionate Tribute to a Broadcasting Legend*.[74] Many of these were compiled by Johnston's eldest son for an evidently devoted readership.

These 'Johnners' tributes prompt two comparisons. First, they are reminiscent of the tributes and posthumous biography devoted to the comedian Eric Morecambe, who died ten years earlier. Both Morecambe and Johnston represented a time of greater certainty, when both cricket and comedy were seen as unproblematic and were relayed as such to the nation – the Morecambe and Wise Christmas Show was a national event, drawing 28 million viewers in 1977, and BBC had cricket to themselves until the 1990s. At the time of their respective deaths both comedy and cricket had fragmented into niche markets. Second, the death three years later of Princess Diana would draw forth emotions similar to those evoked by Johnners. Diana and Johnston were both drawn from a social class known for its emotional reticence. One explanation for the huge outpouring of public grief that followed Diana's death was that she had talked publicly about her emotional difficulties in the face of rejection by the stiff upper lips of the British royal family. The jovial Johnston had, correspondingly, taken the severity and condescension out of the upper-class voice and replaced it with intimations of mischief and eternal childhood – a far cry from Sir Pelham Warner's suggestion in 1950 (made four years after Johnston's first cricket commentary) that commentators should use only players' surnames, because first names were 'undignified'. For many, Johnners made surnames fun. Jack Williams, a leading authority on cricket and broadcasting, has convincingly argued that Johnston's influence in this field has lasted longer than John Arlott's.[75]

TMS enthusiastically writes its own history, nurtures its own myths and is a self-declared 'national treasure'. As with the passing of Brian Johnston, it has been the launch-pad for a host of books: Peter Baxter, producer of *TMS* between 1973 and 2007, alone has produced at least five.[76]

It should be added that *TMS* has influenced other cricket broadcasters around the world – for example, the leading cricket writer Matthew Engel recently suggested that *TMS* 'yanked Australian commentary away from its old solemnity'.[77] Moreover, some *TMS* commentators found that, far from being banished as old hat, new possibilities of global cricket celebrity were opening up for them. For instance, his northern accent and often harsh criticisms of players might have made ex-Yorkshire and England batsman Geoffrey Boycott (108 Tests 1964–82) who made his first *TMS* broadcast in 1995, unsuited to the self-conscious, boys' boarding-school ambience being cultivated for the programme. But Boycott proved hugely popular as a broadcaster with Indian cricket audiences for whom his Yorkshire pronunciations, since they were new to Indian ears more used to English public-school diction, were perceived as subversive and, in a sense, post-colonial. Indian boys were heard in the streets of Mumbai and Kolkata deriding each other's shots as 'roobish'.[78]

But it's also clear that other cricket consumers began in the 1990s to define themselves against *Test Match Special*. This was principally on two grounds, both spelled out in a book of 1996 announcing 'the new cricket culture'.[79] First, there were those for whom, despite the best efforts of Johnners and *TMS*, the mainstream cricket media still represented an unacceptable up-tightness. Pointing to the recent forming of a 'Barmy Army' of England cricket supporters,[80] for whom *TMS* commentators had quickly showed their disdain,[81] Ian McQuillin informed the cricket authorities that the youngish audience they were now seeking 'while liberal and intelligent, aren't ashamed to admit that they enjoy shagging and getting pissed' and, moreover, 'have no inherent respect for the establishment'.[82] A similar mood was abroad in Australia and supported the career of comedian Billy Birmingham (see also Chapter 2), who between 1984 and 2006 used an alter ego called 'The Third Man' to perform unsparing parodies of all the Channel Nine cricket commentators.[83] An honourable exception was made for the *Guardian* journalist Matthew Engel, then 45, who was identified as 'the first to write about the game in a language and style that made it seem part of the late twentieth century'.[84]

The other objection was more straightforwardly political: a fanzine called *Sticky Wicket* had emerged in 1989 in which it was pointed out that the BBC employed a commentary team, at least seven of whose members 'gave varying degrees of support to the breaking of the sporting boycott of South Africa'.[85] This expressed a wider resentment that, with Arlott an honourable exception, the voices which spoke for and about cricket had come overwhelmingly from the political right. This resentment was at least partially assuaged in 1994 with the first publication of Mike Marqusee's book *Anyone But England*.[86] The book was a political history of English cricket, something for which there was no obvious precedent. The book was widely praised, but Establishment spokespeople were grudging and clearly offended. Swanton wrote of Marqusee's 'warped intelligence' and Martin-Jenkins, while also acknowledging the author's intelligence, was 'uneasy about the way he has a go at just about everything cricketers hold dear'.[87]

There were several other fanzines, including *Johnny Miller 96 Not Out*, also founded in 1989, the irreverent humour of which persuaded several counties to ban it from their club shops. It sold around one third of its print run of 28,000 and disappeared in the late 1990s.[88] Greater success, however, befell *Test Match Sofa*.

The people who devised *Test Match Sofa* availed themselves both of the new consumer attitudes to cricket and of the media technology now available to those wishing either to transmit or receive cricket news. The internet was now a crucial consideration for those concerned with broadcasting cricket: as Owen Gibson pointed out in 2004, 'Under European Union competition guidelines designed to encourage new media companies, the TV rights cannot be awarded until the internet and mobile phone contracts have been agreed'.[89] Indeed, as Barrie Axford and Richard Huggins observed in 2010, by the early twenty-first century, we were living in the age of the 'telemediatization' of cricket: while there were now comparatively few large TV audiences for sport there was nevertheless a variety of other ways in which cricket could be consumed – ways that made the consumer more central. This might mean receiving cricket news or match transmissions on a phone, a home computer or a tablet; blogging or tweeting about cricket; 'friending' cricketers on Facebook; or going to a game, listening to commentary on *TMS*, while receiving replays, Hawkeye pictures, third umpire verdicts and statistical information from a screen and waving '4' and '6' placards (distributed by the TV companies) for the cameras.[90] (As we have seen in previous chapters, the biggest markets for the new, telemediatised cricket were now in Asia.) *Test Match Sofa*, the brainchild of young entrepreneurs Daniel Norcross and Tom Clark, began broadcasting in 2009 from a terraced house in south London, covering the Ashes series of that year. It provided commentary using Sky television pictures and streamed it over the internet. It followed the logic of consumer sovereignty by excluding experts. As per the 'new cricket culture' there was swearing, irreverent humour and acknowledged partiality; listeners contacted the commentators during the broadcast via Twitter. *Sofa* was immediately welcomed in the liberal *Guardian*, whose blogger Barney Ronay wrote that 'suddenly any lingering yearnings for Aggers and Tuffers were being flushed away by a thoroughly cleansing draught of the kind of spiky, unaffected, deeply personal bile only the internet can offer'.[91] *Wisden India* called it 'a glorious rollercoaster ride through a day's play'.[92] 'Rather than conventional broadcasting, with a number of experts lecturing their audience, what we are creating is a bunch of people talking to each other', said Clark in 2010.[93] By now the demographic identified loosely as 'the new cricket culture' was considered important enough to prompt the improbable purchase of *Test Match Sofa* by *The Cricketer* magazine in 2012. *The Cricketer* had been founded by Sir Pelham Warner. It numbered E.W. Swanton and Christopher Martin-Jenkins among its past editors and had always been the organ of cricket's Establishment. But this Establishment was now politically divided between its traditionalists and those who followed MacLaurin and others in trying dislodge the game's fabled fuddy-duddy image. Predictably, there was an outcry from the established commentators of *Test Match Special*. Jonathan Agnew resigned from the board of the magazine and in *The Times* Christopher Martin-Jenkins wrote: 'The thought of having to listen to the predators who purport to be producing commentaries from sofa or armchair without paying a penny to the England and Wales Cricket Board for the rights, is too ghastly to contemplate. The sooner they are nailed and swept offline, the better'.[94] In 2013, in another unprecedented development, *The Cricketer* sued the ECB when Andrew Miller, then the magazine's editor, was banned from Test matches by the board after he tweeted from the press box during the Ashes series that people should listen to *Sofa*.[95]

Test Match Sofa stopped broadcasting in 2014 after what is reputed to have been strong behind-the-scenes pressure from Lord's and other broadcasters, but a virtually identical operation – called *Guerilla Cricket* – began almost straightaway. *Guerrilla Cricket* drew a glowing endorsement from Conservative organ *The Spectator*, whose correspondent told readers to 'join the revolution to save cricket' and to 'expect music, drinking, occasional swearing, masses of interaction with fans and plenty of jingles'.[96] And Mezzy Jez, a blogger at Pointless Beauty: The Magic of Cricket similarly identified in *Guerrilla Cricket* what seemed now to be a successful – even mandatory – combination: 'an absolute passion for cricket, an extremely affable nature, a willingness to divulge pretty well every personal secret, a good sense of humour, and a healthy disrespect for the cricket establishment'.[97]

Conclusion: democratising cricket?

The press and audience reception accorded to *Test Match Sofa* and *Guerrilla Cricket* is instructive. Certainly these initiatives met the mood of the rising generation of cricket lovers – a generation for whom the various social media are a taken-for-granted fact of life. While previous generations were sat relishing John Arlott's salty prose or chuckling with Johnners, today's cricket listeners are trending on Twitter. 'The mainstream commentaries build a brick wall between themselves and their audiences', said Nigel Walker of *Guerrilla Cricket* in 2016. 'They don't really want a two-way flow of information'. 'What alternative commentary does is democratise cricket', said someone from White Line Wireless, another alternative commentary stream.[98] While talk of democracy can be overstated, several things are clear from the successful intervention of the streamers and their sofas. First, that while national audiences for cricket talk may be dwindling – except in India and Pakistan – global and transnational audiences can still be substantial. Second, there must be a greater recognition of the diversity and more relaxed social codes of younger cricket audiences. Indeed the door of mythic boys' club *Test Match Special* has been recently been opened wide enough to admit women (since 2014 ex-Test cricketers Isa Guha and Ebony Rainford Brent and career sport journalist Alison Mitchell have joined the team) and *Test Match Sofa* founder Daniel Norcross in 2016. Third, the relationship with the audience must be interactive.

    The latter consideration is at the heart of the success of web company Cricinfo. Like *Test Match Sofa*, Cricinfo was begun by young enthusiasts and its success has been based on recognition of these market trends. It originated in the early 1990s among a group of expatriate (mainly Indian) cricket enthusiasts based in US universities who wished to receive or transmit cricket information – updates, scorecards, results – over the internet. They progressed to live commentary, which tends to be close to *Test Match Special* in its ambience, but has other important dimensions, such as Cricinfo Mobile, a service launched in 2006 that includes Cricinfo Genie, 'which delivers live ball-by-ball simulations of games, and

3D, live three-dimensional animation'.[99] In 2008 it introduced 'Page 2 – a humour and satire section – and Chatterbox, an interactive match-time chat between readers and the site's writers'.[100] In 2013 it announced 'new ventures in social and interactive media with the launch of the fan microsite The Stands; a social-media scorecard, Match Companion; and The Cordon, an enhanced blogs section'.[101] Along the way, understandably, it began to attract global advertisers – Cable & Wireless (based in London), Intel (California) and Titan watches (an Indian brand) – and established a base in India in 1999. Cricinfo sponsored the Women's World Cup of 2000 and the English county championship and women's Ashes series of the following year: thus it repeated the circularity pioneered by Packer: it sponsored what it was reporting. For the semi-final of the World Cup of 2011, between India and Pakistan, it recorded 6.5 million unique users.[102] By 2007, what had begun as the internet project of a bunch of expat cricket and computer nerds had been bought by US cable and satellite sports channel ESPN, which is in turn owned jointly by Disney and the Hearst Corporation.[103]

The morals to be drawn from this commercial triumph are, first, that – as we have said – consumers now participate in cricket media, rather than simply receiving them. Second, in the cricket world, the global media elite has become the new 'Establishment'. The old elite that regarded itself as stewards of an historic and English game was wealthy primarily through land and high finance. It now plays second fiddle to the elite it once scorned – the commercial *arrivistes* of the information and impression management industries.

Whether, in a world where fewer and fewer schools play cricket, this elite can sustain the game of cricket in the longer term is uncertain. Perhaps Richie Benaud was right and the Packer television revolution of 1977 and subsequent televising and other media renditions have been the shot in the arm that cricket needed. There are those, however, who will with sympathise with Charles Randall, who wrote in 2014:

> BBC Television seems to have a unique vision of school sport in the summer. It goes like this. Primary school head teacher: 'Now, children, it's time for sport. My car is in the car park; see how quickly you can change the tyres. After that, you can run round and round the playground one after the other shouting brrrm, brrrm.' The BBC public service broadcasters have continued to spend a fortune on Formula One and have screened no cricket since 1998. Our national summer sport, an activity in clubs and schools for many thousands of children, is ignored in favour of motor racing. As Giles Clarke, chairman of the ECB, once asked in exasperation: 'How many schools "play" Formula One?'[104]

Notes

1. Founded in 1906, liquidated in 1927, resurrected in 1928. Since 1989 part of Random Century.
2. See, for example, Alan Hill *Herbert Sutcliffe: Cricket Maestro* Stroud: Stadia 2007 pp.104–16.
3. As, for example, in his novel *The Good Companions*, first published in 1929.
4. All three played for Yorkshire; Robinson from 1919 to 1931, Wilfred Rhodes from 1898 until 1930 and Herbert Sutcliffe from 1919 to 1945.
5. See Swaranjeet Singh 'Cricket writer par excellence – the incomparable Neville Cardus' http://www.cricketweb.net/cricket-writer-par-excellence-the-incomparable-neville-cardus/ Posted 8 January 2010, Access 30 March 2017.
6. Assertions of this kind were not unusual. Similar claims, for example, were made by Welsh nationalist historians – see David L. Andrews 'Welsh indigenous! and British imperial? Welsh rugby, culture, and society 1890–1914' *Journal of Sport History* Vol.18 No.3 pp.335–49.
7. Neville Cardus *English Cricket* London: Collins 1946 p.9.
8. Neville Cardus *Autobiography* London: Collins p.198.
9. Scyld Berry 'Neville Cardus' writing' http://www.espncricinfo.com/magazine/content/story/451653.html Posted 13 March 2010, Access 29 March 2017.
10. Derek Birley *The Willow Wand: Some Cricket Myths Explored* London: Aurum Press 2000 p.205. For a taste of Cardus' writing see Neville Cardus *Cardus in the Covers* London: Queen Anne Press 1990. For an account of Cardus' life, see Christopher Brookes *His Own Man: The Life of Neville Cardus* London: Methuen 1985.
11. John Arlott *Basingstoke Boy: The Autobiography* London: Willow Books 1990 p.94.
12. See Chapter 1.
13. As observed by Brian Johnston *It's Been a Lot of Fun: An Autobiography* London: Star Books 1974 p.167.
14. See, for example, Alex Bannister *Cricket Cauldron: With Hutton in the Caribbean* London: Pavilion Books 1990.
15. E.W. Swanton *Sort of a Cricket Person* London: Collins 1972 p.247.
16. See David Rayvern Allen *E.W. Swanton: A Celebration of his Life and Work* London: Metro Publishing 1996 pp.187–8.
17. See Peter Oborne *Basil D'Oliveira Cricket and Conspiracy: The Untold Story* London: Time Warner Books 2005 pp.214–15.
18. Christopher Martin-Jenkins *CMJ: A Cricketing Life* London: Simon and Schuster 2013 pp.79–80. One of the Old Harrovians was Bimby Holt: http://www.telegraph.co.uk/news/obituaries/1340257/Bimby-Holt.html Posted 12 September 2001, Access 29 March 2017.
19. Martin-Jenkins *CMJ* p.199.
20. Martin-Jenkins *CMJ* p.198.
21. Rob Steen 'Writing the modern game' in Anthony Bateman and Jeffrey Hill (eds.) *The Cambridge Companion to Cricket* Cambridge: Cambridge University Press 2011 pp.238–53, p.249.
22. Martin-Jenkins *CMJ* p.224.
23. Martin Williamson 'Frank Gillingham' http://www.espncricinfo.com/england/content/player/13376.html Access 31 March 2017.
24. Christopher Martin-Jenkins *Ball by Ball: The Story of Cricket Broadcasting* London: Grafton Books 1990 p.20.
25. Johnston *It's Been* p.89.

26 Peter West *Flannelled Fool and Muddied Oaf* London: Star Books 1987 pp.43–4.
27 The nine were the subject of the Clarendon Report of 1864. The other schools were Eton, Winchester, Harrow, Rugby, Charterhouse, Westminster, St Pauls and Merchant Taylors.
28 David Rayvern Allen *Arlott: The Authorised Biography* London: Harper Collins 1996 p.289.
29 Arlott *Basingstoke* p.136.
30 Rayvern Allen *Arlott* p.291.
31 Charlotte Higgins *This New Noise: The Extraordinary Birth and Troubled Life of the BBC* London: Guardian Books/Faber & Faber 2015 pp.9 and 37. Higgins was quoting from *Broadcast over Britain*, Reith's book of 1924.
32 Martin-Jenkins *Ball by Ball* p.53.
33 Mike Marqusee *Anyone But England: An Outsider Looks at English Cricket* London: Aurum Press 2005 pp.74–5.
34 Quoted in Chris Broad and Daniel Waddell *...And Welcome to the Highlights: 61 Years of BBC TV Cricket* London: BBC Worldwide 1999 p.40.
35 Jack Williams *Cricket and Broadcasting* Manchester: Manchester University Press 2011 p.89.
36 Martin-Jenkins *Ball by Ball* p.94.
37 Martin-Jenkins *Ball by Ball* p.101.
38 MacGilvray retired from *Test Match Special* in 1985, five years after Arlott.
39 Rayvern Allen *Arlott* p.292.
40 Broad and Waddell *...And Welcome* p.95.
41 Williams *Cricket and Broadcasting* p.89.
42 Williams *Cricket and Broadcasting* p.17.
43 Williams *Cricket and Broadcasting* p.63.
44 Rayvern Allen *Arlott* p.294.
45 West *Flannelled Fool* pp.82–4.
46 See Gideon Haigh *The Cricket War: The Inside Story of Kerry Packer's World Series Cricket* Melbourne: Text Publishing 2001 pp.103–4, 173.
47 For an overview, see Williams *Cricket and Broadcasting* pp.81–5.
48 Jim Melly 'Cricket 2000: how the media reinvented the game' in Alastair McLellan (ed.) *Nothing Sacred: The New Cricket Culture* London: Two Heads Publishing 1996 pp.146–64, p.148.
49 Quoted in Williams *Cricket and Broadcasting* p.29.
50 'Channel Four wins rights to home Tests' http://news.bbc.co.uk/1/hi/sport/cricket/194168.stm Posted 16 October 1998, Access 2 April 2017.
51 In *Broadcast* magazine 23 October 1998. Quoted in Williams *Cricket and Broadcasting* p.29.
52 Williams *Cricket and Broadcasting* p.137.
53 See Jennifer Whitehead *PR Week* 6 November 1998 http://www.prweek.com/article/93418/campaigns-tv-triumph-english-cricket—-lobbying Access 2 April 2017.
54 See Owen Gibson 'Board split as Sky seeks TV exclusive' *The Guardian* 14 December 2004 https://www.theguardian.com/media/2004/dec/14/sport.cricket Access 2 April 2017.
55 'BSkyB lands England Test coverage' http://news.bbc.co.uk/sport1/hi/cricket/4097137.stm Posted 15 December 2004, Access 2 April 2017.
56 'BSkyB lands England Test coverage'.
57 Richie Benaud *On Reflection* London: Fontana 1985 p.106.
58 Leo McKinstry *Jack Hobbs: England's Finest Cricketer* London: Yellow Jersey Press 2011 p.16.

59 See Simon Briggs 'A hundred years of sport and advertising' http://www.telegraph.co.uk/sport/othersports/2292796/A-hundred-years-of-sport-and-advertising.html Posted 26 February 2008, Access 2 April 2017.
60 Rayvern Allen *Arlott* p.283.
61 West *Flannelled Fool* p.86.
62 David Foot *Wally Hammond: The Reasons Why* London: Robson Books 1996. See in particular pp.171–85.
63 The first phrase is thought to have originated with the American writer Daniel J. Boorstin and developed in his book *The Image* Harmondsworth: Penguin 1962. The second must be credited to Dick Hebdige and can be found in his 'The Kray twins: A study of a system of closure' Stencilled Occasional Paper: Centre of Contemporary Cultural Studies, University of Birmingham 1974 p.5.
64 A bedrock assumption of his two books: Chris Rojek *Celebrity* London: Reaktion Books 2001 and Chris Rojek *Fame Attack: The Inflation of Celebrity and its Consequences* London: Bloomsbury Academic 2012.
65 Ian Botham and Peter Hayter *Botham: My Autobiography* London: Collins Willow 1994 p.162.
66 'Cricket 2000' p.156.
67 Martin-Jenkins, then 28, had become BBC cricket correspondent in 1973, following the retirement of Brian Johnston.
68 Don Mosey *The Alderman's Tale: An Autobiography* London: Weidenfeld and Nicolson 1991 p.114.
69 Mosey *The Alderman's Tale* pp.131 and 177. The sketch can be seen at: https://www.youtube.com/watch?v=TSqkdcT25ss Access 3 April 2017.
70 This can be heard at https://www.youtube.com/watch?v=KsVTpX7LdZQ Access 3 April 2017.
71 Johnston *It's Been* p.147.
72 Jonathan Agnew *Over to You, Aggers: A Cricketing Odyssey* London: Vista 1998 p.55.
73 Ramachandra Guha 'As an Indian fan of the BBC, I can tell you why it matters' *The Guardian* 16 July 2015 https://www.theguardian.com/commentisfree/2015/jul/16/indian-bbc-cricket-beatles-world-service Access 24 April 2017.
74 Tim Heald *Brian Johnston: The Authorised Biography* London: Methuen 1995; Christopher Martin-Jenkins and Pat Gibson (eds.) *Summers Will Never be the Same: A Tribute to Brian Johnston* London: Partridge Press 1994; Barry Johnston *Johnners – The Life Of Brian* London: Hodder 2004; Barry Johnston (ed.) *A Delicious Slice of Johnners* London: Virgin Books 2001; Barry Johnston (ed.) *Another Slice of Johnners* London: Virgin Book 2001; *A Further Slice of Johnners* London: Virgin Books 2003; *An Evening With Johnners* (audio CD) London: Hodder & Stoughton 2000; Barry Johnston (ed.) *Brian Johnston: Letters Home 1926–1945* London: Orion 1999; and Jonathan Agnew *Thanks, Johnners: An Affectionate Tribute to a Broadcasting Legend* London: Harper Collins 2011.
75 Williams *Cricket and Broadcasting* p.72.
76 Peter Baxter (ed.) *Test Match Special* London: Queen Anne Press 1981; Peter Baxter (ed.) *From Brisbane to Karachi with the Test Match Special Team* London: Queen Anne Press 1988; Peter Baxter (ed.) *Test Match Special: 50 Not Out: The Official History of a National Sporting Treasure* London: BBC Books 2007; Peter Baxter *Inside the Box: My Life with Test Match Special* London: Aurum Press 2010; Peter Baxter *Can Anyone Hear Me?: Testing Times with Test Match Special on Tour* London: Icon Books 2013.

77 Matthew Engel 'From Alston to Zaltzman, 60 years of Test Match Special remembered' http://www.telegraph.co.uk/cricket/2017/04/03/alston-zaltzman-60-years-test-match-special-remembered-wisden/ Posted and access 3 April 2017.
78 See Stephen Wagg 'Muck or nettles: men, masculinity and myth' in Stephen Wagg and Dave Russell (eds.) *Sporting Heroes of the North* Newcastle-upon-Tyne: Northumbria Press 2010 pp.1–29.
79 McLellan (ed.) *Nothing Sacred*.
80 It came together for the Ashes tour of Australia in the winter of 1994–5. See http://www.barmyarmy.com/about/ Access 3 April 2017.
81 Ian McQuillin 'Who's afraid of the Barmy Army?' in McLellan (ed.) *Nothing Sacred* pp.37–54, p.45.
82 Ibid. p.38.
83 See http://www.the12thman.com/store/ Access 4 April 2017.
84 McLellan (ed.) *Nothing Sacred* p.166.
85 McLellan (ed.) *Nothing Sacred* p.205.
86 Mike Marqusee *Anyone But England: Cricket and the National Malaise* London: Verso 1994.
87 See p.3 of the third edition – Mike Marqusee *Anyone But England: An Outsider...*
88 See Charles Oulton 'Old guard says "out" to cheeky cricket fanzine' *The Independent* 23 July 1994 http://www.independent.co.uk/news/uk/home-news/old-guard-says-out-to-cheeky-cricket-fanzine-1415868.html Access 3 April 2017.
89 Gibson 'Board split as Sky seeks TV exclusive'.
90 Barrie Axford and Richard Huggins 'The Telemediatization of Cricket: Commerce, Connectivity and Culture' in Chris Rumford and Stephen Wagg (eds.) *Cricket and Globalization* Newcastle-upon-Tyne: Cambridge Scholars Publishing 2010 pp.122–49.
91 Barney Ronay 'Test Match Sofa – it is TMS couched in chumminess' *The Guardian* 31 July 2009 https://www.theguardian.com/sport/2009/jul/31/test-match-sofa-review Access 4 April 2017.
92 Gary Naylor 'Why Test Match Sofa matters' http://www.wisdenindia.com/cricket-article/test-match-sofa-matters/33258 Posted 3 November 2012, Access 4 April 2017.
93 Andrew Miller 'A different kind of commentary' http://www.espncricinfo.com/magazine/content/story/480852.html Posted 11 October 2010, Access 4 April 2017.
94 Quoted in Jonathan Harwood 'BBC's angry Agnew lashes out at cricket rival Test Match Sofa' http://www.theweek.co.uk/cricket/49875/bbc%E2%80%99s-angry-agnew-lashes-out-cricket-rival-test-match-sofa Posted 1 November 2012, Access 4 April 2017.
95 PA Media Lawyer 'English cricket governing body "unlawful" in trying to freeze out sofa-based Test commentary team' *Press Gazette* 9 August 2013 http://www.pressgazette.co.uk/english-cricket-governing-body-unlawful-trying-freeze-out-sofa-based-test-commentary-team/ Access 4 April 2017 .
96 Justin Marozzi 'Join the revolution to save cricket!' *The Spectator* 29 July 2015 https://blogs.spectator.co.uk/2015/07/join-the-revolution-to-save-cricket/ Access 4 April 2017.
97 Mezzy Jez 'Guerillas in the Night' https://messyjez.wordpress.com/author/messyjez/ Posted 12 February 2016, Access 4 April 2017.

98 Both quotations taken from Angikaar Choudhury 'How social media has changed the way cricket fans consume the game' Posted 8 April 2016, updated 3 January 2017, Access 4 April 2017.
 99 Rachna Shetty 'The first two decades' http://www.espncricinfo.com/cricinfoat20/content/site/cricinfoat20/timeline.html Undated, Access 4 April 2017.
100 Rachna Shetty 'The first'.
101 Rachna Shetty 'The first'.
102 Rachna Shetty 'The first'.
103 Jemima Kiss 'ESPN buys Cricinfo website' *The Guardian* 11 June 2007 https://www.theguardian.com/media/2007/jun/11/digitalmedia.sport Access 4 April 2017
104 Charles Randall 'BBC must share responsibility for club cricket 'decline' http://www.club-cricket.co.uk/news/details/485 Posted 3 December 2014, Access 4 April 2017.

Chapter 13

Women's cricket
The feminism that dared not speak its name: a brief history

Women have played cricket for as long as men have but, in a sport that has generated a huge literature, the history of the women's game has been chronicled a good deal less than the men's. To take some examples, Derek Birley's copious social history of English cricket makes only one reference to women's cricket;[1] *A Corner of a Foreign Field*, Ramachandra Guha's impressive disquisition on Indian cricket, mentions women, but only once as cricketers (when Lord Harris promotes a game between a team of European women and one of European men in 1890);[2] and Harte and Whimpress's (otherwise exhaustive) *A History of Australian Cricket* does not refer to Australian women's cricket at all in over 800 pages.[3] Moreover, much that has been written about the female game would likely cause the progressively minded reader to wince. Sometimes comment has been hostile, telling women to leave cricket to the men; at times it has been flatly condescending and silly; at other times there has been excessive recourse to tired phrases such as 'the fair sex' or 'bowling a maiden over' while even plainly sympathetic accounts of women's cricket have insisted on titles such as *Fair Play*[4] or *Skirting the Boundary*[5] which seemed still to frame female cricketers as Other and/or as novelties, rather than simply as cricketers; and cricketing women have often been at pains to disavow any feminist intent in their embrace of the game – despite the fact that their very project entails the pursuit of some version of gender equality, feminism's defining characteristic. This chapter analyses this fitful progress of women's cricket, a branch of the game which, at the time of writing, is, arguably, thriving as never before. Happily, recent academic work shows that women's cricket is no longer, to borrow Sheila Rowbotham's noted phrase, 'hidden from history'[6] and the chapter draws in particular on the excellent recent doctoral work of two historians, Judy Threlfall-Sykes[7] and Rafaelle Nicholson.[8]

'Half afraid of ridicule': women's cricket before the 1950s

As with the male game women's cricket dated back at least to the eighteenth century when from time to time teams of women played cricket on village greens across the south of England. For example, in a now widely cited match in late summer 1745 a game was played at Gosden Common, near Guildford, between the women of two Surrey villages, Bramley and Hambledon, in which 'the girls bowled, batted, ran and catched as well as most men could do'. Such events were popular in Surrey, Sussex and Hampshire and were often staged between married women and unmarried.[9] And – once again, as with the male game – women's cricket had been played at the country houses of the English aristocracy and gentry, notably by the White Heather Club (founded in 1887) whose members were wealthy Yorkshire women.[10] However, the most powerful impetus to the spread of women's cricket in the nineteenth century had been the movement to promote physical activity for females and the subsequent incorporation of games into the curricula of girls' elite boarding schools. Scholars have made clear, not only that this development took place in defiance of considerable medical opposition, but that the case for women's sport and exercise was made on the basis of conservative ideology – specifically, that it would make for fitter women who would then produce more and healthier babies.[11] This was an especially important consideration in a late Victorian society anxious to staff an expanding empire: the rationale, as historian Richard Holt put it, had been in the form of a question: 'How could the sons be strong if their mothers were weak?'[12] Prominent female educators of the late Victorian period had, in addition to swimming and gymnastics, favoured team sports. Thus, as Holt observes, the girls attending prestigious schools such as Roedean and Wycombe Abbey 'were encouraged to play hockey, tennis and even cricket'.[13] The word 'even' here may denote special difficulty: cricket had a unique and mythical place in the culture of the country's male establishment and, for female cricketers, these gentlemen's acceptance would likely be yet more grudging than that accorded to, say, female tennis players. Sport for women had therefore developed in a largely separate sphere, administered by the emergent profession of the games mistress and often fiercely policed so that it did not become a vehicle for any kind of feminist emancipation or furtherance of the 'New Woman' ideal.[14] Under the influence of the Swedish physical educationist Martina Bergman-Österberg, women-only physical education colleges began to be founded, beginning with Hampstead College in 1885. These colleges, and the subsequent pursuit of sport by ex-boarding-school girls at Oxford and Cambridge, had brought about what Nicholson calls the 'circular movement of physical training college graduates and Oxbridge educated mistresses into the public schools'.[15] For much of the twentieth century this circular movement would be the source of a large number of prominent English women cricketers, Dartford College (Madam Bergman-Österberg having transferred her Hampstead College to this Kent town in 1895) being a prominent example.

The inheritors of this college tradition, in alliance with upper-, middle- and lower-middle-class enthusiasts had dominated women's cricket during the period between the World Wars, having formed the Women's Cricket Association (WCA) in 1926.

The WCA was chaired initially by Mrs Patrick Heron-Maxwell, who had a large estate in Kent and had organised the Women's Land Army there during the First World War.[16] Its membership had been predominantly young, unmarried, educated privately or at selective secondary school[17] and resident in the South East or Midland regions of the UK – although it had a presence also in Yorkshire and Lancashire. It had excluded men, except as honorary members and, as an organisation, the WCA had cultivated a femininity of a very specific kind, based on an often oppressive notion of female decorum and an equally uncompromising embrace of the amateur ethic – the latter a key means by which the WCA had sought to define women's cricket against the male game.

A chief proponent of this code had been Marjorie Pollard (1899–1982), a regular writer in *Women's Cricket* magazine and the WCA's principal ideologue. Pollard had defended what was essentially a position of deference to the male game with some venom. Writing in 1934, in a book edited by England men's captain Douglas Jardine, Pollard had insisted on the separate nature of women's cricket:

> No one tried to bowl terribly fast; no one tried to lift the ball out of the ground. We realised that we could play cricket but it would have to be a cricket of our own. We did not want to play like men; we wanted to play women's cricket – and we have kept to that severely.[18]

And, in *Cricket for Women and Girls*, her influential book of the same year, she had rejected the notion that cricket should teach its players 'the game of life': 'Games – and especially such games as cricket – should not, I feel, be mixed up with sentimentalism, hypocrisy and cant. Why, then, do we play cricket? Because we like it.'[19] After an end-of-the-season game featuring WCA luminaries in 1931 she had written: 'It would be a thousand pities if anything even suggestive of earnestness, or concern about the result, ever crept into this happy-go-lucky affair'.[20] This purportedly amateur spirit should also be expressed on the body – WCA players had been given a strict dress code entailing divided skirts and white socks and should never wear trousers (for Pollard, the ultimate symbol of masculinity)[21] – and in in 1936, ten years after many young women on either side of the Atlantic had happily been dancing the Charleston, Pollard had fulminated against the sight of bare knees in women's cricket.[22] It followed that, for the WCA magic circle, mixed cricket was unthinkable. Pollard stated: 'it is sound and sane to realise from the start that men and women cannot play team games together or against each other'.[23]

For the WCA competitiveness was coded as masculine and, when county associations for women's cricket had formed in the early 1930s, the WCA had urged that their fixtures be described as 'county association matches' to avoid comparison with the men's county championship.[24] However, competitiveness was also regarded as a working-class trait.[25] Women's cricket, based mainly on works teams, had flourished in Yorkshire[26] and Lancashire between the World Wars and much of it had been played in evening leagues. Many of the clubs and leagues involved had come together in 1934 to form the England Women's Cricket Federation (EWCF). The EWCF had been run by men, with the aim of using women's cricket to promote the men's game; its teams and players were competitive and disdained any strict dress code – some players wore trousers in matches.[27] Relations between the two organisations had been tense – the WCA, after all, repudiated competitive cricket – but, paradoxically, some leagues sought (and were allowed) to affiliate to the WCA, as with the Manchester Cricket League, formed in 1939.[28] The WCA ethos notwithstanding, the Manchester Cricket League, did, after all, play women's cricket. Besides which, WCA controlled access to Test cricket and there had been accusations of Southern bias in selection for the England team.

Test cricket had brought the first international outing for the WCA and its governing doctrines. The first women's Test matches had been played between Australia and England in 1934 in circumstances which affirmed the class identity of the WCA. The Australia and New Zealand women's cricket associations had invited England to tour, offering hospitality but asking that England meet their own travel costs. This automatically confined the tour largely to the women of means who already dominated the WCA. Moreover, once the tour began, England players had been 'surprised to learn that women's cricket in Australia had transformed from the exclusive game of private school girls, to being played in state schools, factories, businesses and working-class suburbs' and that a number of their hosts found them snobbish – something that caused them some surprise.[29]

When the Australians had visited the UK in 1937 the WCA had made what was perceived as a gesture toward northern cricket by selecting Mona Greenwood of Brighouse (West Yorkshire) for the Second Test at Blackpool and the third at the Oval.[30] But, in issues of perceived snobbery and class bias, the severe gender politics of the WCA often trumped other considerations: neither working-class nor Australasian cricketers were comfortable with the restrictive dress code the WCA continued to expect. For example, as Threlfall-Sykes notes:

> In 1936, affiliated members, Betty and Barbara Peden overthrew the requirement of the WCA to wear stockings with their accompanying, inconvenient suspender belts. Betty persuaded club members to change to wearing knee-high hose (legally still stockings) while their superiors Mrs Heron-Maxwell and Miss [Vera] Cox [the secretary] were away for the summer holidays. It was noted by Betty that 'the furious elders reacted as if they were ruining the whole image of cricket'.[31]

It's worth noting that the Peden sisters, from New South Wales, were figures of manifest middle-class respectability: the daughters of Sir John Beverley Peden, professor of law at Sydney University, Barbara was a qualified architect and Betty, who captained Australia, a Girl Guide Commissioner.[32] Nevertheless the WCA leadership continued its ascetic policies on cricket apparel well into the 1950s with England captain Molly Hide (1913–95), a farmer with 200 acres of land in Surrey, often their chief advocate. In 1945 'the Executive Committee amended the rules to allow for "shorts", the length – not shorter than four inches from the ground when kneeling – was still carefully controlled, and knee length socks were required wear'; some time later, at one game Hide accused a member of her Surrey team of being 'improperly dressed' for having the 'wrong' colour hair grip.[33] And, at the Annual General Meeting of the WCA in 1954, Hide spoke of 'the dangers of allowing members to wear caps . . . [she] hoped the meeting would realise how harmful their wearing would be to the prestige of the Association'.[34] For the WCA leadership, caps, like trousers, signified the male game, thus sullying their preferred version of femininity, and the WCA asked the New Zealand side touring the UK in the summer of 1954 not to wear them.[35] If anything, the years of rationing and 'austerity' in the 1950s seemed to accentuate the middle-class nature of women's cricket, since the WCA continued to insist on clothing that many players could no longer afford.[36] In 1976 the WCA instruction on apparel still read: 'Official WCA teams must play in white. Uniform: divided skirt or pleated shorts, which must not be less than five inches and not more than eight inches above the ground when kneeling; skirt; jersey; knee-length socks. Headgear: only cricket hats or eye-shades may be worn'.[37]

'I love women and I love cricket': women's cricket and the quest for financial support, 1960s–1990s

It's widely argued, and accepted, that the strict sartorial discipline and equally stern embrace of 'happy-go-lucky', uncompetitive cricket professed by the WCA had a material basis: the organisation had few sources of income and was ever-anxious not to antagonise the MCC hierarchy, whose attitude toward women's cricket, given their gentlemanly evasions, was often difficult to read. They had also, like the MCC themselves, to operate on political terrain that was in flux and growing in its complexity. This complexity derived from factors discussed in previous chapters such as decolonisation and the growing (and half-acknowledged) dependence of cricket on the London's impression management elite (television, PR, advertising), previously dismissed as vulgar. To this could be added the increased role of government in the governance and promotion of sport. A central figure in shaping the future of women's cricket in the latter half of the twentieth century was England captain and businesswoman Rachael Heyhoe Flint

(1939–2017), who understood these new imperatives at least as well as the WCA, with whom she was often in conflict.

As he recalled in 1976, during a charity match in Kent in 1963 BBC cricket commentator Brian Johnston had asked ex-England men's captain Len Hutton what he thought of women's cricket. Hutton's now quite widely shared reply was 'It's just like a man trying to knit, isn't it?'[38] Johnston was known to support women's cricket and Hutton seems from this remark to have thought it quaint, but both the question and the answer in this exchange are indicative of the place of women's cricket in British society at the time. The very fact that a question such as Johnston's could be asked in the early 1960s showed how marginal the women's game remained. (At this historical juncture, could he equally have asked, say, what Hutton thought of women doctors? Or women teachers? Or women tennis players?) And Hutton's response was, ultimately, a tenable summary: cricket, after all, was still socially constructed as a male activity and knitting as a female one. Women cricketers were seen as guests in an essentially male space – a perception which the WCA's presentation of self had scarcely challenged. For their part the administrators of the WCA could not easily judge the nature or extent of their welcome in that male space. Ex-England cricketer and future President of MCC Sir Colin Cowdrey expressed the ambiguity of approach of the game's male hierarchy to women's cricket very well when he wrote in 1976: 'for years there has been enormous goodwill between us – and may we be forgiven for not letting the ladies into Lord's'.[39] The task of women's cricketers was to convert this 'enormous goodwill'[40] into harder currency and meanwhile to seek alternative sources of funding. In the short term they had no reason to be optimistic: women would not be admitted to MCC membership until 1998.

In the 1940s and 50s, as we have seen, the WCA was still devoutly amateur, middle class and wedded – albeit in the face of mounting opposition from its membership – to an outmoded dress code. It staged few matches for paying spectators and possessed no ground of its own. This latter consideration strengthened its historic dependence for playing space on the facilities of private schools (thus doing little to mitigate its middle-class image) and the generosity of the county cricket clubs. Like the male game, it was also largely imperialist. For example in 1949, leading member Netta Rheinberg, on tour in Australia, had confided to her diary that the dominion players had needed a lecture on the correct spirit of cricket:

> We have tried our best here to instil into the Aussies the advantage of playing cricket merely for the love of the game, as it is done in England, and not for points altogether as is the case throughout Australia. This competitive spirit leads to jealousy and rivalries and personal animosities which are unknown in England.[41]

Nor was there much questioning of white privilege – Rheinberg exulted in the availability of black servants ('One claps one's hands and there they are') while staying over in Ceylon *en route* to Australia[42] – or of racist practices: for example, in recounting the cancellation of a WCA tour to South Africa in 1968, Rachael Heyhoe Flint says merely that 'the British Labour government, who had given a grant to the England touring team to help towards their travel costs, stepped in and suggested that the visit should be cancelled. This was a shattering disappointment to the South African Association who had worked hard to raise the necessary finance'.[43] There was, pointedly, no mention of South Africa's apartheid system of state racism, by then the subject of global controversy, or of the fact that in South Africa England would have been playing all-white opposition, as dictated by that system. If women's cricket was to expand, nationally or internationally, then in time these dominant attitudes to class, 'race' and gender would have to be modified. National associations, after all, were keen to arrange further Test matches and formed the International Women's Cricket Council (initially composed of the all-white quintet of England, Australia, New Zealand, the Netherlands and South Africa) in 1958. These countries continued to play Test matches when finances permitted.

At home, the WCA's policy of, in effect, confining membership to women with the desired attitudes came under increasing strain. Funded principally by subscriptions (affiliations went up between 1945 and 1955 and many league teams were now allowed to join, although trophies were still frowned upon),[44] subventions from the MCC, donations and fundraising events. The WCA had also begun to apply to the Ministry of Education for grant aid, an option that had been created by the Physical Training and Recreation Act of 1937 and the (resulting) Women's Team Games Board.[45] After the Second World War government concern for sport had increased in the wake of the Wolfenden Report of 1960 which had placed an emphasis on sport development.[46] In 1969, at a time when their fortunes were again declining,[47] the WCA were obliged to produce a five-year plan as a condition of further grant aid. This included a range of junior competitions and, four years earlier, a national knock-out competition had been established causing the WCA to abandon its objection to trophies in 1966.[48] Evidence of more growth was the condition of a further three-year grant in 1974.[49]

Now accepting the necessity of growth and of sponsorship,[50] the WCA established a Publicity Sub-Committee in 1968, appointed its first Public Relations Officer (an honorary post) in 1970 and took on its first full-time National Development Officer the following year. Meanwhile, with its historic ideological architecture now apparently crumbling, the WCA now found that the political initiative in developing women's cricket had passed to someone acting largely outside their authority – Rachael Heyhoe Flint.

Heyhoe Flint was the daughter of PE teachers and, initially, a PE teacher herself – it was a familiar occupation in women's cricket. She played her first game for England in 1960 and captained the side between 1966 and 1978. A Conservative with an entrepreneurial bent and a flair for publicity, she relished her place in what she called 'the friendly and exciting world of sport, media and promotion'[51] and promoted women's cricket, often via her own burgeoning career as a journalist, television personality and after-dinner speaker. Her evangelism and visibility led to the award on an MBE in 1972.

Like most of her fellow players Heyhoe resented the trivialisation of women's cricket, but she herself was at pains to trivialise feminism, and was known for her disavowal of it. Her challenge to male supremacy in cricket, she wrote in 1978, 'doesn't mean that I'm Women's Lib. – far from it, because I value that bit of underwear they rush out and burn each week with a matinee on Wednesdays. I, too, believe in strong support'.[52] The notion of bra-burning feminists was a myth concocted by the right-wing popular press on both sides of the Atlantic.[53] This cartoon version of feminism was shared by a number of Heyhoe's team-mates[54] and was, in a sense, a modernisation of the WCA's historic deference to male authority. She and others could distance themselves from that word's more radical implications. After all, Heyhoe routinely appealed for donations from big businesses, many or most of whom would be engaged in the exploitation of cheap female labour. An expressed disdain for 'Women's Lib' allowed Heyhoe to be seen simply as a supplicant and gung-ho enthusiast, rather than as a troublemaker or a political radical.

Heyhoe was hard at work canvassing business support for a WCA tour of Australia and New Zealand in 1968 when an invitation to visit Jamaica was relayed to the WCA by Jamaican coach Derief Taylor, who had played county cricket for Warwickshire (1948–50). She approached Sir Charles Hayward, a stockbroker and industrialist who ran the Firth Cleveland group of companies and was well known in her native Wolverhampton. Hayward referred her to his equally wealthy son Jack who, who resided in the Bahamas and was known as 'Union Jack' for his love of the British Empire and his financial support of British causes.[55] 'Union Jack' immediately agreed to finance England's tour of the Caribbean, the cricket generating much public enthusiasm on the islands,[56] and Hayward funded further events: in 1971, on a return visit to Jamaica, England won a three-match Test series 1–0, and Trinidad and Tobago won the Jack Hayward Trophy in a triangular series involving both England and Jamaica.

He also agreed to donate £40,000 (over half a million pounds at today's rates) to the staging of a women cricketers' World Cup in the UK in 1973. When asked why he had made such a substantial outlay he replied: 'It's quite simple. I love women, and I love cricket – and what could be better than have the two rolled together'.[57]

This was perhaps a mixed blessing for women's cricket. The Hayward money boosted the international game and the profile of the women's game.

But it was also in a sense retrograde. Caribbean women's cricket was already modernised. As Tony Cozier observed, in the 1960s '[t]he Jamaica association's league and limited-overs competitions, as well as the teams, were sponsored, a concept before its time'.[58] By contrast, English women's cricket now depended largely on patronage – a means of subsistence now phased out in the men's game in India and, for that matter, in England. Moreover, the patronage came from a single patron who could not be expected to reach into his pockets indefinitely.

Hayward, in any event, cancelled his patronage of the WCA in 1978 in the wake of their sacking of Heyhoe, both as captain and as a player, the previous year. This dismissal, which is covered in detail in the first three chapters of Heyhoe's memoir,[59] published soon after Hayward's withdrawal, seems certain to have been made on non-cricketing grounds: her successor, Cheshire cricketer Mary Pilling, was a year older and less experienced and Heyhoe had a Test batting average of 46, having the year before scored 179 not out against Australia at the Oval. Heyhoe Flint seems to have paid the price for a jovial remark made to a sports journalist to the effect that, if the MCC would not allow a women's match to be played at Lord's she would take them to the Equal Opportunities Commission (established the previous year under the Sex Discrimination Act). The remark became public and she then learned that the WCA had been negotiating privately with MCC over the staging of such a match.[60]

There is a political irony here: Heyhoe Flint had fallen from grace for accidentally raising the spectre of 'Women's Lib' – the one cause that she and most other WCA members had sought always to disavow. (Indeed, as late as 1996 a WCA newsletter would insist that 'Women's cricket is not a vehicle for women's rights, nor should it be'.)[61] The WCA's sacking of Heyhoe Flint represented a gamble – that 'softly softly' diplomacy with Lord's officials (who, according to Cowdrey, harboured 'enormous goodwill' toward them) would serve them better than Heyhoe Flint's public campaigning. But, either way, women's cricket was, and would long remain, in a politically weak position, as a credit/debit examination of women's cricket in the twenty or so years that followed the Heyhoe Flint affair suggests.

On the credit side, international women's cricket was gaining public profile and beginning to attract sponsors. The tour of England by India women in 1986, for example, was sponsored by Uni-Vite, known principally for their slimming products. Uni-Vite were doubtless hoping to profit from the 1980s pursuit of fitness among women (the first Jane Fonda Workout video had been issued four years earlier), although their investment seemed to assume a predominantly female audience for the tour – by no means a safe bet.[62] There was also Kwik cricket, a modified indoor version of the game, devised in Australia in 1984 to combat the decreasing access of children to cricket in schools and launched in the UK in 1988 under the sponsorship of the Milk Marketing Board. Kwik cricket was open equally to boys and girls. 'By 1998, 374,000 primary school girls and 83,000 secondary school girls were participating in Kwik Cricket, and *The Cricketer* reported that 51% of primary schools and 67% of secondary schools were now offering this form of cricket to their pupils'.[63]

Set against this the WCA lost its centre of excellence in Bedford in 1977; through lack of support it was unable to undertake an international tour between 1979 and 1984; barring one match (broadcast by Channel Four in 1987) no women's cricket was shown on British television between 1980 and 1992; and a host of companies declined to sponsor the women's World Cup of 1993.[64]

Despite public interest (the World Cup Final of 1993 attracted 4,500 spectators)[65] and the evangelising benefits of Kwik cricket, women's cricket in the UK lacked elements vital to the sustenance of late twentieth century sport. It had had comparatively little presence in British state schools and, having been dominated by middle-class women who preferred to play recreationally and in seclusion, it had, as noted, rarely been played before paying spectators. Its purchase on the national imagination was therefore comparatively slight and, thus, it attracted little interest from television companies. (In another irony, the possibility of ITV televising a match at Lord's in 1976, which was being negotiated for the WCA by Heyhoe Flint, was lost when the WCA were found to have themselves been negotiating with BBC, unbeknown to Heyhoe Flint.[66]) The absence of television deterred sponsors. Moreover, women's cricket did not carry the same historic myths that the male game did, the aura of which sponsors were so anxious to acquire.

In the 1990s, according to Nicholson, financially the Test and County Cricket Board were 'propping up' the WCA.[67]

But such assistance was not accompanied by any substantial shift in the attitude toward women on the part of the MCC: women could still not be admitted to membership, the one exception being the Queen, who was the club's patron. Rachael Heyhoe Flint applied for membership in 1991, with the support of male members such as the aforementioned Brian Johnston, 'Union Jack' Hayward and wealthy lyricist Tim Rice. The application was refused by a substantial majority (over 70% were opposed) and in February 1998 a similar application was turned down, this time for lack of the required two-thirds majority – 56% of members had now been in favour.[68] The following month *The Independent* reported: 'Theresa Harrild, a receptionist at the ECB, won her industrial tribunal action after claiming that her bosses bullied her into having an abortion but then sacked her anyway. Attitudes at the board were deeply sexist, she said, with female cricketers referred to as lesbians'.[69] Less than a year later a third vote produced a 70% vote in favour of admitting women and ten eminent women cricketers, including Heyhoe Flint, were given honorary membership.

Rachael Heyhoe Flint died in 2017 and amid many public tributes there was a tendency to see her retrospectively as having singlehandedly battered down the doors to the male citadel of English cricket. One journalist wrote

'Heyhoe Flint succeeded, in part, because she knew how to charm the men who made the decision'.[70] This seems a mistaken judgement, not merely for its doubtful assumption that social change can be achieved simply by an individual female deploying 'womanly wiles' in her dealings with male decision-makers. Heyhoe Flint's charm had been of no avail a few months earlier. What the MCC hierarchy had realised was that a new political wind had begun to blow – one that would open up new cricketing possibilities for women all over the world.

In May 1997 a Labour government had been elected in the UK. It had proclaimed itself as 'New Labour', a shorthand way of saying that it accepted the basic 'free market' principles in the name of which the preceding Conservative administrations of Margaret Thatcher and John Major had governed. They also made clear, however, their embrace of equal opportunities and identity politics (including anti-sexism). In August 1998 new Prime Minister Tony Blair and Sports Minister Tony Banks had both criticised the MCC's exclusion of women and it was immediately clear to Lord's that their men-only stance would jeopardise future funding. 'Jubilant committee members last night said that good sense had prevailed', reported *The Independent*:

> Although it has been suggested that the club may have been more worried about losing out on National Lottery money than about upsetting women's sensibilities. Chris Rea, the MCC's head of marketing and public affairs, tactlessly admitted that the decision had been commercially inspired: 'The overriding question is, are we a gentleman's club or are we a cricket club? We are a cricket club. No sponsors want to be involved with an organisation whose image is elitist, fuddy-duddy and old-fartish'.[71]

Sisters doing it for themselves? Women's cricket and globalisation

The disclaimers of feminism are still being made – when asked in a recent interview if she was a feminist, former England captain Charlotte Edwards (debut 1995) replied 'No not really. Not really at all. I'm not like that . . . I just love cricket'[72] – but there can be little doubt that, however obliquely at times, women's cricket has benefited from the historic campaigns fought by feminists. However much or little pragmatism was entailed in MCC's decision it could scarcely have come about without the influence of feminism on political common sense. That is not to deny that the advancement of women's cricket has come at a price. In the watershed year of 1998 the English WCA was absorbed into the England and Wales Cricket Board; the consensus among observers of women's cricket is that, while the women's game gained resources (money, good pitches . . .) they lost representation.[73]

This merger was part of a global pattern. In 2005 the International Women's Cricket Council (IWCC) merged with the International Cricket Council (ICC). Never a very influential body (they met[74] rarely and supervised occasional Test matches, which were privately funded; subsequent World Cup tournaments were often in jeopardy through lack of money)[75] and they had never had more than thirteen members at any one time. Importantly they had lost the Caribbean island associations in 1978. Mergers have also meant that more and more female cricketers have been obliged to present themselves according to the demands of sponsors and attendant PR advisors. This, in turn, has often meant selecting the most physically attractive players for interview and swimwear photoshoots – a sexualisation that women's cricket administrators strove for seventy-five years to prevent.

Equally, while in a neoliberal age class inequalities and the possibility of the redistribution of wealth have ceased to be a priority in international political dealings, the 'empowerment' of women has not. Very often corporate grants fund sport programmes for young women to facilitate wider social change via this empowerment. 'In many countries', said Lakshmi Puri, UN Assistant Secretary-General and Women Deputy Executive Director, recently:

> It has been recognized that sport can be a force to amplify women's voices and tear down gender barriers and discrimination. Women in sport defy the misperception that they are weak or incapable. Every time they clear a hurdle or kick a ball, demonstrating not only physical strength, but also leadership and strategic thinking, they take a step towards gender equality.[76]

Women's cricket has also gained from the widespread redefinition of sport at state level, where recreational, 'sport-for-all' policies have been downplayed in favour of an emphasis on elite performance.[77] More and more nations are concerned to maintain a profile in international competition. Here a successful women's cricket team – especially in formerly British territories – is a doubly piquant prospect, being both a feminist and a post-colonial statement. Nowhere is this more the case than in South Africa where, as we saw in Chapter 3, extreme economic inequalities endure, but where black people have been freed from apartheid – a system, in effect, of internal colonisation.

This section concludes with a brief review of how these issues have played out in some of the countries where women's cricket is, or is becoming, established.

Empowerment: 'banter, dance, laughter, conversations . . .'

In matters of female empowerment, it's important to remember that initiatives to promote women's cricket have been taken by female enthusiasts themselves, sometimes before the word 'empowerment' entered the international political lexicon. Heyhoe Flint had her equivalents in the Global South. Women's cricket in the Caribbean, for example, developed in the 1960s at the instigation of Jamaican campaigners such as businesswoman Monica Taylor, the first president of the Jamaican Women's Cricket Association, and Sally Kennedy, who procured some of the first sponsorship for women's cricket, from companies such as Canada Dry, who lent their name to trophies and clubs.[78] They invited England to tour in 1970, an invitation initially refused by the WCA.[79] Similarly, Aloo Bamjee and her husband were prominent in the setting up of Albees, Mumbai's first women's cricket club, in 1969[80] and the launch of the Sri Lankan WCA in 1997, in the wake of the Sri Lankan men's World Cup win the previous year, owed much to the work of Gwen Herath, who became its president. And, in Pakistan, much pioneering work was done by the Karachi-born sisters Shaiza and Sharmeen Khan, who learned their cricket in England in the 1980s and who put together a Pakistani women's team to play New Zealand and Australia in 1997. All these women had cultural and/or economic capital – Herath, for instance, was a former actress, a successful novelist and the wife of a government minister[81] and the Khans' father ran a successful carpet business which financed their endeavours[82] – but they invariably tapped into strong grass roots support. By the early 1970s, for instance, there was a flourishing women's cricket association on several Caribbean islands – there were eleven teams on Tobago alone[83] – and five of them (Jamaica, Barbados, St. Lucia, Grenada and Trinidad & Tobago) formed the Caribbean Women's Cricket Federation in 1973. In India women had been playing cricket since the 1950s[84] and were welcoming touring parties from the mid-1970s – Australia Under-25s in 1975 and West Indies the following year. Both teams played in trousers.[85]

In more recent times, as we have noted, empowerment has become a narrative 'top-down' concept in projects and promotions run by governments, governing bodies, non-governmental organisations (NGOs) and corporate sponsors. This works at various levels and in different contexts. At one level the purpose is plainly ideological: women cricketers are deployed as a means of suggesting that the key to a better society is greater gender equality and the combating of female disadvantage. Promotion of the Women's World Cup of 2017, which began the previous autumn, made this quite explicit. The promotion strategy was called 'Who Runs the World?' Lizzy Pollot, associate creative director at HSE Cake (the PR agency who had devised the campaign), said in October 2016: 'For us the climate was right for a truly empowered campaign. We already have a woman Prime Minister and by the end of next month, we may well have a woman President in the US too'.[86]

Pepsi, who in recent years have launched a number of 'empowering women' initiatives,[87] also sponsored the ICC's Development Programme.[88]

At another level, these policies provide sponsored mobility – now a feature of first-class cricket across the world – whereby, in the absence of routine access to cricket (such as a place in school curricula) empowerment projects double as talent-identification schemes via which to uncover gifted individuals, whose skills are then honed by coaches. Once again the clearest examples of this are from the Global South. In Pakistan in 2005 the Pakistan Cricket Board (PCB), having belatedly wrested control of the country's women's cricket operation from the Khan sisters, ran a Fair Play for Girls campaign jointly with Unicef; in September that year, in conjunction with the campaign, 12,000 girls watched a match between two women's teams in Lahore.[89] Mark Seacombe's recent account of the lives of Bangladeshi cricketers Chumki Akter and Ismat Ara is another case in point. These young women, he says, were rescued from extreme poverty, Akter in Dhaka and Ara in a rural district that had no electricity, no running water and no cars. They were placed in a charity by an NGO and encouraged to play cricket by the charity's organiser, Pat Kerr. Kerr said:

> Ismat had no sense of personal discipline. She didn't bother with school work and was quite disruptive. But from day one she was good at cricket and her school work began to improve almost straight away. [...] Now the world opens up in front of her. This cricket is not a trivial thing! Even the girls who are not playing are enthused by it. It's an amazing empowerment vehicle – something they can be proud of. But can you imagine how they would feel if a girl from here was playing in the national team? Can you imagine that? YES!'

Ismat met England men's player Jos Buttler, who told her 'I look forward to seeing you on television'.[90]

A third example is in England, where a number of top players have emerged through the Chance to Shine charity which has employed many of them as ambassadors since 2008. Members of the England women's cricket squad have had professional contracts since 2014.

These various schemes are undeniably progressive, although the rags-to-riches/empowerment stories they generate are untypical and cannot be said substantially to combat the poverty or disadvantage from which individual young female cricketers have often been rescued. They are also empowering in ways of less interest to sponsors. For instance, Pakistani women cricketers have had to contend with the various restrictions promoted in the name of Islam by a succession of right-wing politicians (see Chapter 7) – until 2003 women playing sport in public was virtually unknown in Pakistan and, in North West Frontier Province a ban on males coaching female teams wasn't lifted until 2005.[91] On tour in India in 2016 it seemed clear that cricket had kindled in the Pakistan team the sort of happy-go-lucky conviviality and freedom from male constraint to which the English WCA always claimed to aspire. Cricinfo reporter Shanshank Kishore met the team in Delhi for the Women's World T20 tournament in 2016:

All along, there's leg-pulling, banter, dance, laughter, conversations, *chai*,[92] and more. Above all, the camaraderie within the squad is one of a happy family. [...]The camaraderie and warmth is visible not just on the field, but also in little things like choosing of seats in the bus, controlling of playlists, and bowling order at the nets. Unlike the men, there is no weight of history, no chaos, no talks of having to beat India at any cost. Pakistan Women have beaten India Women twice at ICC events. There are no talks of being cornered tigers, no pressure of expectations or reputations to live up to. The team knows while they are no world beaters, they are out to have fun and make the most of the exposure and opportunity to play on the big stage, on live television. While they look to win, they are also sensible enough to understand a loss isn't the end of the world, as cricket, for most, was almost an afterthought, not because they didn't like the game, but because circumstances forced them to rethink. Some took the game like fish to water; other developed their love in the quest to 'do something different'.[93]

Ethnic identity and social inclusion: 'a true picture of multiculturalism'?

These are two further concepts central to the political vocabulary of the neoliberal era. While it is clear that women's cricket has not been free of racism (any more than male cricket has) women's cricket has, especially in twenty-first century, been inclusive of ethnic minorities and has even in some cases been regarded as a flagship for multiculturalism. This has been a matter both of important political statement and, on occasion, of the scarcity of cricket talent available.

As we have seen, the English women's cricket team has been dominated historically by white, middle-class players. In recent times the team has featured only two women from ethnic minorities: Ebony-Jewel Rainford-Brent, born in London to Barbadian immigrant parents in 1983 and Isa Guha (b.1985), a Buckinghamshire player of Bengali descent. Rainford-Brent represented England between 2001 and 2010 and was one of the first Chance to Shine ambassadors in 2008; Guha's England Test career spanned 2002 to 2010. They were the first Afro-Caribbean woman and the first Asian woman, respectively, to play cricket for England. Both now work in the cricket media.

In Australia, as we have seen, migrants and Indigenous groups have experienced hostility and discrimination and the country has been self-satirised as 'a nation of blow-ins' (see Chapter 2). Ethnic minorities have not been well represented in Australian women's cricket, although there were two early examples. Spin bowler Peggy Antonio, the dark-skinned daughter of a Chilean migrant dock worker, had made her debut against England at Brisbane in 1934 and became the first Australian woman to take a wicket in a Test match. She worked in a shoe factory and money had to be raised for her to tour England in 1937. She was often compared to leg spinner Clarrie Grimmett, who played for Australia between 1925 and 1936. And in 1958, Faith Thomas, a nurse of Indigenous background, opened the bowling against England in the Third Test of the Ashes in 1958. It was her only cap. She said in 2016: 'I always say that I hold two records. I think I'm still the fastest woman bowler ever. And I think I also might have been the biggest flash in the pan ever'.[94] At the time of writing 19-year-old Ashleigh Gardner was expected to become only the second Indigenous woman to play for the Australian first team, having already represented Australia A and captained the first Indigenous Australian women's cricket team on their tour to India in 2016.[95] The same year Cricket Australia announced:

> A record 1,311,184 people played cricket across Australia in 2015–16, an 8.5 per cent increase on 2014–15 – placing cricket at No.1 as the current top participation sport in Australia. Women's cricket at the highest level went from strength to strength last summer with the success of the Women's Big Bash League and that success is being reflected at grassroots level, where participation reached record figures in 2015–16, growing nine per cent to 314,936 players. Overall, 24 per cent of all cricketers in Australia are female, with 581 girls and women's teams playing traditional, 11-a-side cricket at clubs across the county.[96]

In top-level West Indies women's cricket a white face is rare and is likely to belong to one of the support staff – but, as Beckles argued in 1998[97] (and as we saw in Chapter 5), West Indies male cricket became a nationalist project and a Trojan horse for independence. Whites were selected only as captains, a practice phased out in the face of political protest in 1960, and the last white player of outstanding talent to turn out for West Indies was George Challenor on a tour of England in 1923.[98] The only white male cricketer to represent West Indies in recent times was Australian-born Brendan Nash, who qualified through his Jamaican father and played 21 Tests for West Indies between 2008 and 2011. Women's cricket has followed this pattern. The West Indies women's cricket squad for the ICC World T20 in 2016 were all of African or Asian descent.[99]

South Africa, the cricket country with the history of the most institutionalised racism, appears to have the most multiracial team in international women's cricket. Of the fourteen players selected to tour Bangladesh in January 2017 at least five were of black or Asian heritage. This ethnic distribution should be judged against the factors discussed in Chapter 3 – on the one hand, the determination of African National Congress (ANC) government to establish racial quotas and, on the other, poverty among black South Africans and the suppression of their cricket. Most women's cricket in South Africa is played in Gauteng, a highly urbanised province, site of the capital Johannesburg and the country's economic hub.[100]

Canada, a country with an uneven cricket history, has used the idea of a multicultural nation as a means to boost their women's cricket project. Alison Korn wrote in the *Toronto Sun* in 2010:

> The Canadian team is a true picture of multiculturalism, with 11 nationalities represented on the squad. A lot of them learned the game where they were born. 'Pakistan, India, Kenya, Australia, West Indies, Sri Lanka, they're coming from all over,' Canadian head coach George Codrington said. 'Coming to Canada, not knowing that there is women's cricket here, no real grassroots, that poses problems. There's nothing to draw from. We're really relying on the immigrants coming to the country. They only know about the men. We have a few who are Canadian-born and they learned it in the schools.' Codrington wants to get the word out to female cricket players – and softball players, since the sports are similar – that Canada has a national women's cricket team. It has existed since 2006.[101]

We now turn to the question of the degree of acceptance that women's cricket had achieved by the early twenty-first century.

Credibility: unsung heroes?

It's now over half a century since Len Hutton characterised women's cricket as akin to teaching a man to knit. Today the concept of women's cricket is fully established and, come to that, the notion of males knitting is gaining credence: there is a website at which men who knit can share their experiences[102] and in 2014 an article in the right-wing *Daily Telegraph* asked 'Men's knitting: is it "the new yoga"?'[103]

Women's cricket is no longer a novelty. It has broad, tacit acceptance. The debate now is over the degree to which it is acknowledged – measured by the resources allocated to it, by its public visibility, by the prestige accorded to it and by the nature and frequency of the opportunities it is given. There is strong evidence that it is still being short-changed in these areas.

In 2015 Kathy Gyngell wrote the following on the website *The Conservative Home*:

> If people dared be honest they'd admit that neither women's football, nor cricket nor rugby, has any takers – apart from the lasses who tog up to play. Without the bullying BBC and every other feminised outfit pushing it down our throats, no one would be talking about it. But never fear, the feminist front of women's sport more than makes up for its lack of fans. I have had had it up to here – to drowning point – frankly. First, we had women's cricket paraded before us on the sports spot on BBC Radio 4's Today programme all summer long. Even Sky

> Sports was at it, devoting precious sports minutes to inane coverage of a wimmin's [sic] Ashes in Australia. Who cared? No one! I don't know what the cricket-loving chaps thought but I was ready to scream.[104]

This illustrated two things about the political landscape in which women's cricket was now transacted. First, that cartoon versions of feminism were still in play, especially when coupled to the popular right-wing canard 'political correctness' – Gyngell's article was entitled 'Spare us the PC drive to plaster feeble women's sport all over TV'. Second, that, in public discussion, watching sport was often presumed to be more important than playing it. For women's cricket, the second consideration was a greater threat than the first.

Since most people watch sport via the mass media, elite women's cricket depends for its progress substantially on television and the access of women's cricket to television has, once again, been limited. The first tournament of women's cricket to be shown live on television in Pakistan was the Shaheed Mohtarma Benazir Bhutto Women's Cricket Challenge Trophy in Lahore in 2013.[105] The whole of the 2015 Ashes series between England Women and Australia Women was covered by the BSkyB satellite channel. However, in 2016 South African journalist Antoinette Muller could write:

> On Friday night, South Africa completed a historic feat. For the first time they beat England in a T20. It was a significant achievement for a side which had just turned professional two years ago. Yet, you wouldn't know that the match had even happened if you glanced at mainstream media. Of course, we are not talking about the men here: South Africa has a women's cricket team that's making strides but you would never know.[106]

Lack of television deters sponsors and sparse crowds can deter television, crowd shots now being almost as important as the play itself in the televising of contemporary sport.

A good audience would not be a new development for women cricketers. The three Tests played by England women in Australia in 1934 drew crowds of 9,000, 12,000 and 13,000 respectively[107] and they played before 6,000 people at Sabina Park, Jamaica, in 1970. Recent indications are that women's cricket, especially in the Twenty20 format, can draw both big crowds and TV audiences. In Australia in 2016 a match in the Rebel Women's Big Bash League had 400,000 viewers.

> In the competition's debut on Network Ten's main channel, a record average of 372,000 viewers tuned in, reaching a high of 439,000, to see the Melbourne Renegades' thrilling final-over victory against cross-town rivals the Stars at the MCG [Melbourne Cricket Ground] [...] Almost 13,000 fans were also inside the MCG by the end of the match.[108]

(Women's T20 matches are often staged immediately before men's games, although they aren't always well publicised.) And, during the Women's T20 World Cup in India in 2016 30,000 people came to the Feroz Shah Kotla Stadium in Delhi to watch New Zealand play England.[109]

ICC now tend to sell television rights to male and female tournaments as a package, which will likely increase interest in women's cricket. Meanwhile, many female cricketers and male sympathisers argue that national cricket associations have continued to marginalise women's cricket. In 2015 writer Geoff Lemon took the three main associations (India, Australia and England) to task on this issue:

> National players fund their own training while officials haggle over match fees [...] After decades of women organising their own matches on next-to-no funding, the three richest national boards are whimpering about the bill. You know, the boards that are signing broadcast deals worth billions, running lucrative T20 leagues and scooping the biggest serve of ICC revenue on to their own plates. Yet they claim non-profit status and tax exemptions on the grounds of growing the game, and the national service they provide in doing so.[110]

And the following year the *New Zealand Herald* reported: 'Moves are afoot to raise the profile, playing and governance numbers, on the back of a report, *Women and Cricket, Cricket and Women*, slamming New Zealand Cricket's treatment of the women's game since the old New Zealand Women's Cricket Council merged under the NZC umbrella'. Suzie Bates, captain of the White Ferns, the New Zealand women's cricket team, commented: 'Initially when I heard the report was being done, I rolled my eyes and thought "here we go again" [. . .] This is the first time I have seen some positive change.'[111]

As to prestige and recognition, this has begun slowly to come the way of women cricketers. The ICC instituted a Women's Cricketer of the Year award in 2012 and two England players – Clare Taylor in 2009 and Charlotte Edwards in 2014 – were named among the *Wisden* cricketers of the year. In 2014 Belinda Clark, who had captained Australia between 1994 and 2005, was inducted into the country's Cricket Hall of Fame, followed in 2017 by the late Betty Wilson (11 Tests 1948–58). Clark and Wilson now have awards (made to domestic female cricketers) named after them.

In the case of West Indies, while in 2016 the writer Vaneisa Baksh argued powerfully the 'boorish proposition to the television reporter Mel McLaughlin in early January' that year made by batsman Chris Gayle showed him to be no more than a 'mindless soldier in the vulgar battle of chauvinism' in Caribbean cricket culture,[112] this has not prevented growing recognition of the region's women cricketers. In 2011, former West Indies fast bowler Colin Croft wrote on the Kaieteur News website:

> Simply comparing the input and success of West Indies Women cricket teams to those of their male counterparts seems like cheese to chalk. West Indies men have been way behind in achievement. So, with this in mind, I say, now, […] that West Indies Women's Cricket team, collectively, is my Caribbean Sports Person and Sports Team too, of 2011.[113]

The West Indies women's captain, Jamaican Stafanie Taylor, now enjoys a global reputation in the cricket world as a big-hitting batter and, like a number of international women's cricketers, has invitations to play in Australia and New Zealand. And in 2017 Antiguan lawyer Verlyn Faustin became the first female Chief Operating Officer of the West Indies Cricket Board.

The quest to be accepted as cricketers is not made easier by the PR strategies, mentioned earlier, that boards, sponsors and agents now prescribe for female cricketers. These, as Nicholson observes, usually entail the selection of the most physically attractive players for interviews and photoshoots and the wearing of designer outfits and slim-fit playing kit that emphasise femininity, as with those designed for the England team by sponsors Adidas in 2008.[114] Having beaten Bangladesh in 2015, to take another example, the Pakistani women's team was taken to a photo-shoot at which they modelled a kurta-trouser set with a 'simple, feminine look' designed for them by the Al Karam studio in Karachi.[115]

The reputations that female cricketers have acquired and the salaries they have earned have in large part derived from playing the shorter formats of cricket, which attracts the crowds and the sponsors. As Alun Hardman pointed out in 2017:

> Heyhoe Flint had an England career that spanned 19 years (1960–1979), during which time she was awarded 22 test caps and played 23 one-day international matches. The recently retired England captain, Charlotte Edwards likewise had a 19-year England career between 1996 and 2015 and achieved 23 test caps, but – as a sign of the times – she played 171 one-day international matches and 95 T20s.[116]

For most elite cricketers Test matches are the ultimate arena for honing and displaying their skills. Leading women cricketers have endorsed this view: '[Mignon] Du Preez [of South Africa], [Australian] Meg Lanning, Charlotte Edwards, [India's] Mithali Raj: captains line up to tell the media that Test cricket is the biggie as far as they, and their teams, are concerned'.[117] However, there is a reluctance to stage Tests for women. Between August 2007 and July 2014 the only Tests played by women were one-off Ashes games between England and Australia.[118] Clare Connor of the ECB noted the Australian board's unwillingness to consider staging more than that: 'Cricket Australia have said they don't see it as a viable format to grow the game from a commercial perspective, profile perspective, participation perspective. They don't think it's going to be appealing to young girls or to women to follow it and take up the sport as a consequence'. Tests, said Connor, were 'hanging by a thread'.[119] 'I am often left wondering', wrote Raf Nicholson:

> Why, if amateur cricketing bodies could afford to stage Test series, it is such a big deal for the multi-million-dollar-making enterprises that are modern-day cricket boards to stump up the cash to do so? [...] if we let women's Test cricket die, you can bet that men's Test cricket won't be far behind. England, Australia and New Zealand Women have all been playing Test cricket far longer than men's teams from Pakistan and Sri Lanka. The triumph of commercialism would surely spell the death knell for some men's Test encounters, even if the men's Ashes were to survive.[120]

Conclusion: 'I see no reason why a woman couldn't say, "I want to play men's cricket"'

One answer to Nicholson's question is that the amateur bodies who sustained cricket in the past were largely male and had access to considerable wealth, usually derived from land and high finance. When that was not enough they broke bread with commercial capital – the supermarkets, the soft drinks manufacturers and the mobile phone companies. Their central concern is profit. Women's cricket at the highest level is now professional and it must pay its way. In England, unlike the men's team, elite women cricketers are, on the whole, not privately educated.[121] As Kath Woodward suggested in 2014:

> [England] Women cricketers acknowledge the huge support which many have gained from the *Chance to Shine* programme. It's an admirable initiative, but it sees women lumped in with deprived areas as if women's sport were either a worthy cause or a troublesome problem that requires intervention. This charitable discourse and the classification of women as a disadvantaged group still haunts sport, so the move to professionalism in cricket is a watershed.[122]

The urgency of this statement was soon clear. A few weeks later women's empowerment was apparently forgotten when the ICC cancelled the Americas Women's Championship for cricket – part of the Pepsi-sponsored development programme; the cancellation was described as 'a business decision'.[123]

If, however, women's cricket thrives as many hope, it may face another important decision – whether or not, at the elite level, to press for the mixed, sex-blind cricket already available to children.[124] In 2015 Geoff Lemon wrote: 'it's not like women must aspire to play like men. As with so many sports, women play a subtly different game, the same field and equipment met with varied rhythms and strategies'.[125] The same year English wicketkeeper Sarah Taylor became the first woman to play Australian grade cricket. What she told the press arguably constituted the worst nightmare of Marjorie Pollard and the WCA:

> I see no reason why a woman couldn't say, 'I want to play men's cricket' and keep going with it. I hope it does push the boundaries. I'm too far into my career now to start changing but there will be some girls who will try and keep going in the male game. I do hope it happens – it'll be good for women and good for the game. If you're trained to play against the guys, you never know what you can do.[126]

Notes

1 Derek Birley *A Social History of English Cricket* London: Aurum Press 2003 p.352.
2 Ramachandra Guha *A Corner of a Foreign Field: The Indian History of a British Sport* London: Picador 2003 p.57.
3 Chris Harte, with Bernard Whimpress *A History of Australian Cricket* London: Andre Deutsch 2003.
4 Rachael Heyhoe Flint and Netta Rheinberg *Fair Play: The Story of Women's Cricket* London: Angus and Robertson 1976.
5 Isabelle Duncan *Skirting the Boundary: A History of Women's Cricket* London: The Robson Press 2013.
6 Sheila Rowbotham *Hidden From History: 300 Years of Women's Oppression and the Fight Against It* London: Pluto Press 1977.
7 Judy Threlfall-Sykes 'A history of English women's cricket, 1880–1939' Doctoral thesis De Montfort University 2015.
8 Rafaelle Nicholson '"Like a man trying to knit"? : Women's cricket in Britain, 1945–2000' Doctoral thesis Queen Mary University of London 2015.
9 'The first ever women's cricket match takes place' http://www.telegraph.co.uk/only-in-britain/first-recorded-womens-cricket-match/ Posted 26 July 2016, Access 13 March 2017. Originally reported in the *Reading Mercury* 26 July 1745.
10 Threlfall-Sykes 'A history' pp.65–6.
11 See, for example, Jennifer Hargreaves *Sporting Females: Critical Issues in the History and Sociology of Women's Sports* London: Routledge 1994 pp.44–6, 70. For the most detailed examination of the late nineteenth-century campaign for women's sport, see Kathleen McCrone *Sport and the Physical Emancipation of English Women, 1870–1914* London: Routledge 1988.
12 Richard Holt *Sport and the British: A Modern History* Oxford: Clarendon Press 1990 p.117. Quoted in Threlfall-Sykes 'A history' p.25.
13 Holt *Sport and the British* p.120.
14 Holt *Sport and the British* pp.119–122.
15 Nicholson 'Like a man' p.20.
16 Threlfall-Sykes 'A history' p.100.
17 Jack Williams *Cricket and England: A Cultural and Social History of the Interwar Years* London: Frank Cass 1999 pp.95 and 100.

18 Marjorie Pollard 'Women's cricket' in D. R. Jardine *Cricket: How to Succeed* London: Evan Brothers 1934 p.30. Quoted in Threlfall-Sykes 'A history' p.109.
19 Marjorie Pollard *Cricket for Women and Girls* London: Pollard Publications 1934 pp.13–14. Quoted in Threlfall-Sykes 'A history' p.110.
20 Quoted in Heyhoe Flint and Rheinberg *Fair Play* p.37.
21 Pollard said that women cricketers should never be 'so garbed'. See Pollard *Cricket for Women* p.21. Quoted in Williams *Cricket and England* p.97.
22 In an editorial in *Women's Cricket*. Quoted in Williams *Cricket and England* p.103.
23 Pollard *Cricket for Women* pp.16–17. Quoted in Williams *Cricket and England* p.99.
24 See Threlfall-Sykes 'A history' pp.104–8.
25 See Threlfall-Sykes 'A history' p.29.
26 Peter J. Davies' study of women's cricket in the West Yorkshire town of Brighouse in the 1930s shows how, condescending male commentary aside, that the women's game was well established in the area during this period. See Peter J. Davies 'Bowling maidens over: 1931 and the beginnings of women's cricket in a Yorkshire town' *Sport in History* Vol.28 No.2 June 2008 pp.280–98.
27 A photograph of the Yorkshire women's team featured in Jack Williams' *Cricket and England* shows several players wearing trousers. The image is between pages 108 and 109.
28 Williams *Cricket and England* p.96.
29 Threlfall-Sykes 'A history' pp.164–5.
30 Heyhoe Flint and Rheinberg *Fair Play* p.44.
31 Threlfall-Sykes 'A history' pp.131–2.
32 http://adb.anu.edu.au/biography/peden-margaret-elizabeth-maynard-8009 Access 14 March 2017.
33 Nicholson 'Like a man' p.55.
34 Nicholson 'Like a man' p.56.
35 Heyhoe Flint and Rheinberg *Fair Play* p.87.
36 Nicholson 'Like a man' p.57.
37 Heyhoe Flint and Rheinberg *Fair Play* p.89.
38 Brian Johnston 'Foreword' of Heyhoe Flint and Rheinberg *Fair Play* p.9.
39 Colin Cowdrey 'Foreword' of Heyhoe Flint and Rheinberg *Fair Play* p.11.
40 Nicholson lists a number of leading male cricket figures who spoke up for women's cricket in the years that followed the Second World War – see 'Like a man' pp.58–9.
41 Netta Rheinberg tour diary, 17 February 1949, WCA Archive, Lancashire. Quoted in Nicholson 'Like a man' p.61.
42 Netta Rheinberg tour diary, 1 November 1948, WCA Archive, Lancashire. Quoted in Nicholson 'Like a man' p.51.
43 Heyhoe Flint and Rheinberg *Fair Play* p.105.
44 Nicholson 'Like a man' pp.45 and 64.
45 Threlfall-Sykes 'A history…' p.28.
46 See Richard Holt and Tony Mason *Sport in Britain 1945–2000* Oxford: Blackwell 2000 p.150.
47 Nicholson 'Like a man' p.91.
48 Nicholson 'Like a man' pp.105–6.
49 Heyhoe Flint and Rheinberg *Fair Play* p.81.
50 Nicholson 'Like a man' p.112.
51 Rachael Heyhoe Flint *Heyhoe!* London: Pelham Books 1978 p.13.
52 Heyhoe Flint *Heyhoe!* p.14.

53 See, for example, Jennifer Lee 'Feminism has a bra-burning myth problem' http://time.com/2853184/feminism-has-a-bra-burning-myth-problem/ Posted 12 July 2014; access 16 March 2017.
54 See Nicholson 'Like a man' pp.148–9, 161.
55 See Phil Shaw 'Sir Jack Hayward: Businessman who gave generously to British causes and transformed the fortunes of his local football club, Wolves [obituary]' *The Independent* 15 January 2015 http://www.independent.co.uk/news/people/sir-jack-hayward-businessman-who-gave-generously-to-british-causes-and-transformed-the-fortunes-of-9978702.html Access 16 March 2017.
56 Heyhoe Flint and Rheinberg *Fair Play* p.75.
57 Heyhoe Flint *Heyhoe!* p.116.
58 Tony Cozier 'The rise of the West Indies women's team' http://www.espncricinfo.com/magazine/content/story/999313.html Posted 17 April 2016 Access 16 March 2017.
59 Heyhoe Flint *Heyhoe!* pp.17–46.
60 Heyhoe Flint *Heyhoe!* pp.37–9.
61 Nicholson 'Like a man' p.260.
62 'All the research tells us that more men watch women's cricket...', said ECB head of women's cricket Clare Connor in 2016. See Seb Joseph 'England women's cricket chief Clare Connor unveils bold plan to take the sport mainstream' http://www.thedrum.com/news/2016/12/06/england-women-s-cricket-chief-clare-connor-unveils-bold-plan-take-the-sport Posted 6 December 2016, Access 20 March 2017.
63 Nicholson 'Like a man' pp229–30.
64 See Nicholson 'Like a man' pp.211, 199–200, 221–2.
65 Nicholson 'Like a man' p.221.
66 Heyhoe Flint *Heyhoe!* pp.40–1.
67 Nicholson 'Like a man' p.271.
68 'MCC vote on allowing women to become members (24 Feb 1998)' http://www.espncricinfo.com/ci/content/story/75248.html Access 17 March 2017.
69 Cole Moreton 'It's hardly cricket' *The Independent* 15 March 1998 http://www.independent.co.uk/life-style/its-hardly-cricket-1150496.html Access 17 March 2017.
70 Andy Bull 'Rachael Heyhoe Flint: The reluctant feminist who could talk Lord's language' *The Guardian* 24 January 2017 https://www.theguardian.com/sport/2017/jan/24/heyhoe-flint-womens-cricket-lords-mcc Access 17 March 2017.
71 Cathy Comerford 'After 200 years, MCC finally votes to admit women' *The Independent* 28 September 1998. An account of the three votes can be found in Duncan *Skirting...* pp.241–56.
72 Nicholson 'Like a man' p.260.
73 See Philippa Velija, Aarti Ratna and Anne Flintoff 'Women at the wicket: the development of women's cricket in England and overseas' in Chris Rumford and Stephen Wagg (eds.) *Cricket and Globalization* Newcastle Upon Tyne: Cambridge Scholars Publishing 2010 pp.103–21, pp.113–17; Raf Nicholson 'Where are the women on England cricket's power list?' http://phone.espncricinfo.com/blogs/content/story/1063539.html?source=home;objects=1062062,1063539,1064155,1064156,1063969 Posted 30 October 2016, Access 18 March 2017.
74 The (sparse) minutes of their occasional meetings can be read at: http://www.womenscrickethistory.org/History/iwcc.html Access 19 March 2017.
75 See, for example, Abhishek Mukherjee 'Australia women lift 1978 World Cup – the tournament which was almost called off' http://www.cricketcountry.com/articles/australia-women-lift-1978-world-cup-the-tournament-which-was-almost-calld-off-85737 Posted 13 January 2016, Access 18 March 2017.

76 http://www.unwomen.org/en/news/stories/2016/2/lakshmi-puri-speech-at-value-of-hosting-mega-sport-event Posted 16 February 2016, Access 17 March 2017.
77 In Britain this priority was affirmed in Game Plan, the government policy document of 2002.
78 Hilary McD. Beckles *The History of West Indies Cricket Volume 1: The Age of Nationalism* Kingston, Jamaica: University of West Indies Press/London: Pluto Press 1998 p.123.
79 'Cricket mourns pioneer Rachael Heyhoe Flint' https://www.pressreader.com/uk/the-daily-telegraph/20170119/281479276118119 Posted 19 January 2017, Access 19 March 2017.
80 Sidhanta Patnaik 'Women's cricket in India: a progressive journey' http://www.alloutcricket.com/features/womens-cricket-in-india-a-progressive-journey Posted 13th August 2014, Access 19 March 2017.
81 Her husband Herald was Sri Lankan Foreign Minister between 1991 and 1993.
82 For a good account of these endeavours, and of official opposition to them, see Peter Oborne *Wounded Tiger: A History of Cricket in Pakistan* London: Simon and Schuster 2014 pp.423–33.
83 Heyhoe Flint and Rheinberg *Fair Play* p.109.
84 Heyhoe Flint and Rheinberg *Fair Play* p.111.
85 Shubangi Kulkarni 'The history of Indian women's cricket' http://www.espncricinfo.com/ci/content/story/94140.html Posted 8 September 2000, Access 21 March 2017.
86 Tony Connelly 'International Cricket Council launches empowering campaign for women's World Cup 2017' http://www.thedrum.com/news/2016/10/10/international-cricket-council-launches-empowering-campaign-womens-world-cup-2017 Posted 10 October 2016, Access 19 March 2017.
87 See, for instance, 'PepsiCo elevates women's empowerment discussion in the Middle East' (Press Release) http://www.pepsico.com/live/pressrelease/pepsico-elevates-womens-empowerment-discussion-in-the-middle-east05222013 Posted 22 May 2017; 'PepsiCo and FUNDES launch "Women With Purpose" program to empower women Across Latin America' (Press Release) http://www.pepsico.com/live/pressrelease/pepsico-and-fundes-launch-women-with-purpose-program-to-empower-women-across-latin-america Posted 22 January 2017, Access 19 March 2017.
88 'Pepsi ICC Best Overall Development award won by Cricket Scotland' http://www.icc-europe.org/newsdetails.php?newsId=23653_1390543020 Posted 24 January 2014, Access 19 March 2017.
89 See Jonathan Dyson 'Now Pakistan's women start to show their class' *The Guardian* 18 December 2005.
90 Mark Seacombe 'Breaking boundaries: Bangladesh's women cricketers' *The Observer* 4 December 1947 https://www.theguardian.com/sport/2016/dec/04/breaking-boundaries-bangladesh-women-cricketers-charity Access 19 March 2017.
91 Dyson 'Now Pakistan's women'.
92 Tea, sometimes made with spices.
93 Shashank Kishore 'A window into Pakistan Women's bonhomie' http://www.espncricinfo.com/icc-womens-world-twenty20-2016/content/story/988177.html Posted 23 March 2016, Access 19 March 2017.
94 Russell Jackson 'Aboriginal cricket pioneer Faith Thomas: "I'm still the fastest woman bowler ever"' *The Guardian* 22 December 2016 https://www.theguardian.com/sport/2016/dec/23/aboriginal-cricket-pioneer-faith-thomas-im-still-the-fastest-woman-bowler-ever Access 19 March 2017.

95 Sam Ferris 'Indigenous teenager set for historic first' http://www.cricket.com.au/news/ashleigh-gardner-first-indigenous-woman-cricket-faith-thomas-australia-southern-stars-wbbl/2017-01-31 Posted 31 January 2017, Access 19 March 2017.
96 'Cricket becomes Australia's No.1 participation sport' http://www.cricket.com.au/news/cricket-australia-census-participation-numbers-women-men-children-james-sutherland/2016-08-23 Posted 23 August 2016, Access19 March 2017.
97 Beckles *The Age of Nationalism* p.133.
98 See Andy Bull 'The forgotten story of … white West Indian cricketers' *The Guardian* 2 February 2009 https://www.theguardian.com/sport/blog/2009/feb/02/forgotten-story-of-white-west-indian-cricket Access 19 March 2017.
99 http://www.icc-cricket.com/world-t20/teams/women/west-indies Access 19 March 2017.
100 http://www.southafrica.net/za/en/articles/entry/article-southafrica.net-womens-cricket Access 20 March 2017.
101 Alison Korn 'Team Canada on lookout for women cricketers' *Toronto Sun* 15 July 2010 http://www.torontosun.com/sports/columnists/alison_korn/2010/07/15/14729616.html Access 20 March 2017.
102 http://www.menwhoknit.com/ Access 20 March 2017.
103 Theo Merz 'Men's knitting: is it "the new yoga"?' *Daily Telegraph* 9 January 2014 http://www.telegraph.co.uk/men/thinking-man/10552983/Mens-knitting-is-it-the-new-yoga.html Access 20 March 2017.
104 Kathy Gyngell 'Spare us the PC drive to plaster feeble women's sport all over TV' http://www.conservativewoman.co.uk/kathy-gyngell-spare-us-the-pc-drive-to-plaster-feeble-womens-sport-all-over-tv/ Posted 30 October 2015, Access 20 March 2017.
105 'Breakthrough moment for Pakistan women's cricket' *Dawn* 8 March 2013.
106 Antoinette Muller 'Women's cricket: the name of the media game is inequality' *Daily Maverick* 21 February 2016 https://www.dailymaverick.co.za/article/2016-02-21-womens-cricket-the-name-of-the-media-game-is-inequality/#.WNAIP5NcphY Access 20 March 2017.
107 Tanya Aldred 'England's women cricketers still the unsung heroes' *Daily Telegraph* 14 January 2014 http://www.telegraph.co.uk/sport/cricket/international/theashes/10572040/Englands-women-cricketers-still-the-unsung-heroes.html Access 20 March 2017.
108 'Women's Big Bash a ratings hit' http://www.cricket.com.au/news/womens-big-bash-league-attendance-mcg-television-ratings-broadcast-melbourne-derby/2016-01-03 Posted 3 January 2016, Access 20 March 2017.
109 Supriya Nair 'Women's cricket scores a resounding win in India' *Financial Times* 1 April 2016 https://www.ft.com/content/1eaa43b0-f75a-11e5-96db-fc683b5e52db Access 20 March 2017.
110 Geoff Lemon 'Cricket should stop treating women as second-class citizens' *The Guardian* 18 June 2015 https://www.theguardian.com/sport/the-nightwatchman/2015/jun/18/womens-cricket-second-class-citizens-embarrassing Access 20 March 2017.
111 David Leggat 'Suzie Bates and the state of women's cricket' http://www.nzherald.co.nz/sport/news/article.cfm?c_id=4&objectid=11746635 Posted 11 November 2016, Access 20 March 2017.
112 Vaneisa Baksh 'Inside sexism' *The Cricket Monthly* April 2016 http://www.thecricketmonthly.com/story/984051/inside-sexism Access 20 March 2017.

113 Colin E.H. Croft 'West Indies women cricketers are Caribbean's sports personalities for 2011!' http://www.kaieteurnewsonline.com/2011/12/29/%E2%80%9Cwest-indies-women-cricketers-are-caribbean%E2%80%99s-sports-personalities-for-2011%E2%80%9D/ Posted 29 December 2011, Access 20 March 2017.
114 Nicholson 'Like a man' p.288.
115 See 'Pakistan women's cricket team gets stylish with off-duty kurtas' https://images.dawn.com/news/1174033 Access 20 March 2017.
116 Alun Hardman 'Rachael Heyhoe Flint blazed a trail for women's cricket, but change comes slowly to the "gentleman's game"' *The Conversation* http://theconversation.com/rachael-heyhoe-flint-blazed-a-trail-for-womens-cricket-but-change-comes-slowly-to-the-gentlemans-game-71636 Posted 21 January 2017, Access 21 March 2017.
117 Raf Nicholson 'Why cricket needs women's Tests' http://www.espncricinfo.com/blogs/content/story/804999.html Posted 28 November 2014, Access 21 March 2017.
118 Nicholson 'Why cricket'.
119 Melinda Farrell 'Tests "hanging by a thread" – Connor' http://www.espncricinfo.com/women/content/story/772609.html Posted 20 August 2014, Access 21 March 2017.
120 Nicholson 'Why cricket'.
121 Hardman 'Rachael Heyhoe Flint blazed'.
122 Kath Woodward 'Professional era means women's cricket is no longer about charity' *The Conversation* Posted 18 February 2014, Access 21 March 2017.
123 Nadia T. Gruny 'International Cricket Council axes Americas women's cricket' http://www.huffingtonpost.com/nadia-t-gruny/icc-americas-womens-cricket_b_5490232.html Posted 13 July 2014, Access 21 March 2017.
124 Hardman 'Rachael Heyhoe Flint blazed'.
125 Lemon 'Cricket should stop'.
126 Tim Wigmore 'England wicketkeeper Sarah Taylor on making the grade in the men's game' *The Independent* 16 December 2015; http://www.independent.co.uk/sport/cricket/england-wicketkeeper-sarah-taylor-on-making-the-grade-in-the-mens-game-a6776291.html Access 21 March 2017.

Chapter 14

Remove the gunk in the middle...
The coming of Twenty20 and the Indian Premier League

This chapter charts the emergence in the early twenty-first century of a new, shorter format of cricket, now known universally as 'Twenty20'. It explores the politics of this emergence and discusses the establishment and significance of Twenty20's most visible and lucrative manifestation – the Indian Premier League (IPL), established in 2008. The first section of the chapter draws extensively on the work of Martyn Hindley, whose book is probably the only one to try to account for the emergence of the format.

'Some people thought you needed a shirt and tie': the birth of Twenty20

As has been asserted, intermittently, in this book, part of the paradox of cricket, and of the dilemma that faces those who administer it, is that the game must trade on, but at the same time mitigate, its history and tradition. By the beginning of the twenty-first century the ship of cricket, intermittently in commercial crisis since the 1960s, was still taking in water. Moreover, given its shrinking audience and its disappearance from the curricula of many schools, there were huge swathes of people, even in the Test-playing countries, who were either unfamiliar with cricket or who could not fathom its attractions as a spectacle. Twenty20 emerged principally out of an address of this situation. Initially, however, in a development that underlined cricket's now-sealed dependence on television, the new format was prompted by a gap in the satellite TV schedules. In 1995 Martin Crowe, a retired New Zealand Test cricketer, learned that Sky television, concerned that they would lose newly recruited viewers at the end of the rugby season, was looking for some cricket to broadcast through the summer.[1] Crowe devised a shortened and otherwise modified version of the game and called it Cricket Max.[2] Cricket Max immediately created some interest in New Zealand, attracting crowds of over 5,000 people, as well as the Caribbean. A Max Cup was staged in 1997. Crowe, however, judged Cricket Max 'too contrived' and New Zealand journalist Joseph Romanos suggested that the format only survived as long as it did because Sky didn't have the rights to screen any conventional cricket.[3]

Another slimmed-down version of the game – the Super 8, in which teams of eight competed over a similarly shortened time period – was developed in Australia in the mid-1990s, received the endorsement of fast bowling icon Dennis Lillee and was tried out there and in Malaysia.[4] It did not gain sufficient media or commercial traction but is still practised at youth level in several countries.

In 2001, anxious once again about the recurrent problem of falling attendances, the ECB funded a consumer survey. 'We spent £200,000, which was considered to be a lot of money for something like this', said Stuart Robertson, ECB marketing manager at the time:

> We tried to identify who was coming to cricket matches but, more importantly, who wasn't and why. There was a significant decline in attendances across the board and we had to do something about it. We came up with something that we hoped would appeal to people who were cash-rich but time-poor.[5]

The conclusions of the survey were, according to Robertson, that cricket was seen as a matter for middle-aged, middle-class white males and carried little appeal for 16- to 34-year-olds, women, children or ethnic minorities. Such was the impression of the game's exclusiveness that 'some people were under the impression that you had to be a member to watch cricket or be seconded or go in a shirt and tie'.[6]

Sky television were closely involved in the subsequent development of the Twenty20 format,[7] which would consist of two innings of twenty overs, one each side – a match, in other words, that could be transacted in around four hours. The English counties voted 11–7 in favour of adopting Twenty20 and it replaced the 50-over Benson and Hedges Cup in 2003: 50-over cricket, seen in the 1960s as cricket's commercial salvation, was now being seen in some quarters as boring and outmoded.

The principle embodied in Twenty20 has been to retain the elements of cricket which people are known to like (the striking of boundaries, cards labelled '4' and '6' to wave for the cameras, the taking of wickets, the emergence of a winner . . .) and eliminate those that they were known to find frustrating – chiefly, the long periods (usually in the middle of a one-day or a longer match – the 'crap bits', as Crowe called them at one stage)[8] when, at least to the uninitiated, little of significance seems to happening. These elements were then blended with other, non-cricket elements which were also known to be popular – music (sometimes provided by live bands), speed-dating, bar extensions, interviews with members of the crowd, hot tubs and so on.[9] Teams in England were given names intended to more attractive than their formal county designations. Some of these drew on local tradition – 'Kent Spitfires', for example, recalled the air engagements of the Battle of Britain in 1940, much of which had taken place over Kent, and 'Nottinghamshire Outlaws' traded on the legend of

Robin Hood; others ('Hampshire Hawks', 'Sussex Sharks'...) seemed to be straightforward reinventions. An early game between Hampshire Hawks and Sussex Sharks drew a heartening gate (8,500) but a huffy response from the local paper the *Southern Daily Echo*, which condemned the 'Americanisms' entailed in the event.[10]

Twenty20 was soon popular in all the major cricket-playing countries although some, inevitably, harboured doubts about its long-term viability. For instance, Richard Boock of the *New Zealand Herald* wrote wryly:

> The Twenty20 contest, launched as the possible new face of popular cricket, was almost lost in the sea of dress-up and music, and it would be no surprise if it was eventually reduced to Eleven11, then Seven7 and finally Zero0. The suggestion is that in time, the players could just come to the entrance of the tunnel, wave briefly to the cameras, and then let the crowd get on with the real business of having a party.[11]

A decade on, however, Martin Crowe was confident of the format's future: 'Let's see the one-day game settle into 40-over mode. Remove the gunk in the middle, keep it simple, stupid, and hey presto, every captain will be positive about the format that is still the life blood of our fine game'.[12]

Several years later there seemed little ground for doubting Crowe's optimism. National Twenty20 competitions had been instituted across, and beyond, the established cricket world. By 2017 there were Twenty20 cricket competitions in all the Test-playing countries. Banks were prominent as sponsors in Pakistan (where, at one time or another, eleven T20 competitions had been staged between 2004 and 2017) and fast food chains in Australasia: in New Zealand, where a national T20 competition was inaugurated in 2005 Georgie Pie (a New Zealand fast food company, based in Auckland) assumed sponsorship of what was now called the Super Smash in 2014, McDonalds taking over two years later, and the Kentucky Fried Chicken (KFC) brand endorsed Australia's Big Bash from its inception in 2005. Moreover there were T20 competitions in Kenya, Brazil, Canada, Hong Kong, Afghanistan, Nepal, Malaysia, the United Arab Emirates, the Netherlands, Scotland and Ireland. In most cases women's competitions ran parallel to men's. Team names across most of these countries seemed to have been drawn from an adventure playbook – some invoking the world of predatory and/or male animals (Sharks, Eagles, Cobras, Lions, Wolves, Tigers, Stallions, Stags...), others the historic imagery of combat (Warriors, Knights, Titans, Gladiators...). Another raft of arguably more gender-neutral names, such as Heat, Hurricanes, Thunder, Lightning and Scorchers, called up extreme weather conditions. This dramatic nomenclature is thought to suit the excitement-seeking spectator and the television audience – all or most of the T20 competitions are televised – and is favoured in other sports such as rugby and quasi-sports like wrestling.

Who wants to be a millionaire? The rise of the Indian Premier League

Although the commercial success of Twenty20 cricket is not guaranteed – for example, in 2015 in New Zealand the final of the McDonalds Super Smash at the Yarrow Stadium in New Plymouth attracted few spectators[13] – it soon became clear to a number of entrepreneurs that Twenty20 cricket could be very lucrative. The format was welcomed by many cricketers, partly because most of them were used to performing before crowds far smaller than those attracted to T20: Leicestershire bowler Charles Dagnall probably spoke for many players when he said that T20 'made all the days playing in front of ten men and a dog worthwhile'.[14] (This ironic crowd estimate is common in first-class cricket circles and is often pitched even lower. In his memoir of 1999, the ECB's Lord MacLaurin had it down to *two* men and a dog.[15]) The first Twenty20 international was held in Auckland between New Zealand and Australia in February 2005 and the ICC staged the first Twenty20 World Cup (won, significantly, by India) in South Africa two years later. Before long, T20 matches in several countries were drawing over 20,000 spectators: in 2016 average attendances at Australia's Big Bash stood at over 28,000, the Bangladesh Premier League approaching 22,000, the Caribbean Premier League 8,300 and England's T20 Blast 6,500[16] – all figures far exceeding the turnout for domestic three- or four-day cricket in any of these countries. Financially, it seems clear, the cricket administrators in these nations had rapidly become dependent on their participation in T20 tournaments. The stewards of English county cricket, dogged by money worries for much or most of its recent history, were the leading example of this.

However, from the outset, the television rights, advertising and sponsorship generated by Twenty20 cricket made it possible for cricketers to be offered salaries to play T20 that were on scale that no other cricket employment could match, or even approach. This clearly posed threats to existing arrangements in cricket's global labour market: specifically, the loyalty to their national boards of professional cricketers who excelled at the T20 format would now be tested and many of these players would likely become what Chris Rumford described as 'portfolio players', opting to be global cricketers for hire rather than representing their national sides.[17]

The emergence of Twenty20 cricket as the game's key commercial resource brought about what has been widely described as global cricket's second 'Packer moment'. In 2007 plans were announced for an 'Indian Cricket League' (ICL). As with Packer's World Series Cricket project ICL was a private affair which would constitute a showcase for established cricketers recruited from around the world and, again like Packer's tournament, it appeared to have been provoked by a dispute over television rights. The proprietors of Zee TV, a satellite and cable television station based in Mumbai and owned by the Essel Group, one of India's leading business houses, was said to be put out by its failure, despite making the highest bid, to secure the broadcasting rights to Indian cricket.[18] It attracted West Indian Brian Lara, who had retired from Test cricket the previous year, and a number of established cricketers from England (English county players stood to earn £50,000 for three weeks' work),[19] Pakistan, South Africa and New Zealand and the venture had recruited Packer's lieutenant Tony Greig as a board member. Indian cricket hero Kapil Dev, now head of the India's National Cricket Academy in Bangalore resigned his job and he too threw in his lot with ICL. Cricinfo's Siddhartha Vaidyanathan noted that the ICL camp were 'upbeat' ahead of the launch, promising that Bollywood actresses, pop stars and the winners of Sa Re Ga Ma Pa (a musical reality TV show popular in India since 1995) would be appearing. However, as Vaidyanathan noted, the venue – the Tau Devi Lal stadium in Panchkula (in Haryana, northern India) – was 'too small – almost like one used for college games – and the outfield dangerously patchy'.[20] This was because the Board of Cricket Control in India (BCCI) had moved swiftly to safeguard its own project – the Indian Premier League, then in preparation and inaugurated the following year – and forbidden the ICL access to the cricket grounds under its jurisdiction. This was despite an undertaking by West Bengal sports minister Subhash Chakraborty in August 2007 that ICL could use the iconic Eden Gardens in Kolkota.[21] As a result ICL matches were confined to four grounds.[22]

Cricket boards around the world worked similarly to deny legitimacy to the ICL. In July 2008 James Sutherland, chief executive of Cricket Australia, stated: 'We have made clear our position in respect to the ICL from the start. We don't support competitions that are not properly authorised by the home body and we wouldn't support that in our country'.[23] Two months later, thirteen players from Bangladesh, who had entered a team in the ICL as the 'Dhaka Warriors' were banned for ten years by the Bangladesh Cricket Board 'in the interests of Bangladesh cricket'.[24] In England, the ECB's initial policy was to ask counties to persuade their players not to play in the ICL. However, Warwickshire and ex-Test batsman Darren Maddy, one of the first four county cricketers to sign for ICL, received support both from his county and the Professional Cricketers Association.[25] A year later the ECB stated that any player now joining the ICL would be banned from county cricket.[26] It has been suggested, however, that the desire to assuage any ill feeling among the England players may have tempted the ECB themselves into a further Packer-esque scheme devised in the Caribbean.

The Stanford Super Series was devised by Allen Stanford, an American billionaire, resident in the US Virgin Islands but with significant economic interests on the island of Antigua, where he was accommodated by the right-wing prime minister Lester Bird.[27] In June 2008 Stanford announced a US$100 million investment in a series of T20 matches that would take place over the coming five years. The central feature of this series would be five

T20 matches between England and a Caribbean team styled as the 'Stanford All-Stars XI'. These matches would be played for a prize of $20 million; the winner, in a stark evocation of neoliberal economics, would take all: the winning players would receive $1 million each, the rest being divided among squad players, management and the England and West Indies cricket boards. The cricket writer and academic Rob Steen suggested that the ECB had seen Stanford as an ally against the BCCI, participation in his series being an attempt to prevent England players making themselves available for the Indian Premier League.[28] Cricinfo reported the somewhat disingenuous remarks of Giles Clarke, the chairman of the ECB, who appeared to confirm this view, while trying to deny it. Clarke:

> Brushed aside suggestions the deal was pandering to the players in light of the distractions offered by the IPL. 'I'm not seeing a great deal of worry in the dressing room about finances and we are not trying to appease them,' he said. 'It gives them a chance to perform under pressure and to make money beyond the dreams of some of their predecessors'.[29]

The enterprise foundered within months, for two principal reasons. First, it rapidly developed into a vulgar self-promotion on the part of Stanford: he owned the ground in which the matches were staged and it was named after him; he had access to the players' dressing rooms and he was filmed with the wife of one of the England players on his knee. This reflected badly on the ECB, still trading on what remained of Lord's' gentlemanly aura.[30] Second, doubts had soon been raised about Stanford's probity and the stability of his business empire: he was jailed for fraud in the United States in 2012.

Through the wreckage of the ICL (which was wound up after two seasons in 2009) and the Stanford debacle strode the (IPL), a tournament cooked to broadly the same recipe as the ICL but one which, unlike them, enjoyed the full support of the BCCI (which had, apparently, hounded its rival to destruction), a range of sponsors and advertisers and the bulk of India's business elite.

The IPL was founded in 2008. It was, once again, a private commercial undertaking based on the franchise system employed in Major League Baseball in the United States. As in the US, each franchise gave access to a team domiciled nominally in one of eight designated cities or territories, at the outset these being Bangalore, Punjab (based in Mohali), Chennai, Hyderabad, Mumbai, Delhi, Kolkata and Rajasthan (whose team, the Royals, played in Jaipur). The first auction, in 2008, grossed $723.59 million and distributed the teams among the big beasts of India's burgeoning corporate sector. As *The Times of India* recalled:

> The Mumbai franchise owned by Mukesh Ambani's Reliance Industries Limited (RIL) was the most expensive franchise – fetching $111.9 million closely followed by Vijay Mallya's United Breweries which paid

$111.6 million for the Bangalore franchise. Media house Deccan Chronicle won the Hyderabad chapter of the IPL for $107 million, while India Cements' Chennai franchise cost $91 million. Bollywood also made its presence felt with two of its leading stars bagging the ownership of their respective teams – Shah Rukh Khan and Juhi Chawla's Red Chillies Entertainment buying out Kolkata for $75.09, while Preity Zinta and her beau Ness Wadia bought the Mohali team for $76 million.[31]

The names of the teams, once again, seemed to have been taken randomly from an international sports branding catalogue: mediaeval myth ('Kings', 'Royals', 'Knight Riders' . . .) jostled with the merely alliterative ('Delhi Daredevils') and the less than imaginative ('Mumbai Indians').

The ownership of cricket teams by commercial companies was nothing new in India, but the IPL was more than that: it was a flagship for India's status as an emergent power on the world economic stage and a celebration of the 'free market' policies adopted by Indian governments in the late 1980s and early 1990s (see Chapter 6).

Political opinion of the IPL among cricket observers, both at home and abroad, was sharply divided.

Among those voicing approval was the Indian academic Boria Majumdar. The IPL, he wrote in 2009, signalled the 'decolonisation of Indian cricket' and established India as a (he could, perhaps, have said 'the') cricket superpower. Nor could one quarrel with the argument that the IPL was popular: it played to packed houses while conventional domestic cricket, such as the Ranji Trophy, was of comparatively little interest, either to the public or to the sport media. The IPL, he suggested, was an example of 'atypical globalisation' in which, for a change, the West looked to the East.[32] US-based Indian scholar Amit Gupta wrote a similarly strong endorsement. For too long the West had dominated international sport, he argued: the Empire, and latterly Commonwealth, Games had invariably been hosted by 'Western' (i.e. white) nations and, through consideration of time zones and TV audiences, the USA had been awarded the Olympics three times in twelve years.[33] During the 1950s and 60s India had been disparaged as a destination by other Test-playing nations, who have grumbled about the food and the hygiene. Now India had thrown off the shackles of a 'socialist-style economy' and was thriving. Specialised TV networks had created a global market for sports and the Indian subcontinent, with over a billion cricket enthusiasts, constituted a huge swathe of that market. India, along with other non-Western nations[34] were now assuming their seats at the top table. So long as the administrators of the IPL could deal with the problems of security and corruption its success was assured.[35]

In any case, many cricket-lovers would be opposed to the IPL on principle. As Indian writer Ajeyo Basu observed: 'For purists, the glamorous, cash-rich tournament is very anathema of what the game of cricket has traditionally stood for – gentlemen in white flannels toiling away at the five-day version, not for any material reward, but purely for the love of the game'. Nevertheless the 'IPL's update on the staid colonial game of cricket – faster, bigger-hitting and consumer-orientated – reflects the sensibilities of India's new middle class millions, who pack the stadiums every night to watch the short season'.[36]

However, cogent (and not so cogent) criticism of IPL could not be reduced to a longing for the 'gentlemen in white flannels'.

One issue here with a range of political implications was the use of cheerleaders. This was the importation of an American mode of presentation – indeed, a troupe of cheerleaders was on loan to the IPL from the US National Football League team, the Washington Redskins (a name, incidentally, thought offensive by many Native Americans)[37] – and thus flew in the face of any claim for the IPL that it was a celebration of Indian culture. Strong criticism here came from the political left: 'This is not our culture', said Sudeep Banerjee, student leader of Forward Bloc, a leftist party that joined a protest outside Eden Gardens against the employment of cheerleaders. 'If the IPL is so hell bent on promoting entertainment to the audience, then why don't they promote our classical dances which showcase Indian culture? Also, it can be dubbed as nothing but exploitation of women.'[38] The latter argument was strengthened when it became known that impoverished young female 'wannabes' were also being brought from Eastern Europe. 'In a league where salaries are in crores, they get paid a pittance', wrote Yogesh Pawar in 2013:

> And half of this goes to the 'madam'. But the IPL's cheerleaders keep coming back to titillate India. Last month, a few of them protested topless outside the Indian embassy in Kiev: Delhi was restricting visas for young women from former Soviet states […] A minibus arrives to take the girls for a party at a well-known beachfront five-star hotel in the suburbs. At the party, Kurylenko [the madam] and Anna Vaslavsky, one of her girls, meet a well-known honcho from a corporate major that owns an IPL team. Though it's only an offer to mingle with baraatis [guests of the bride] during a wedding at a Lonavla resort [near Mumbai], both women are excited that this gig could open up many more doors for them. [Kurylenko] says her girls are usually paid around Rs 1,200 for a shoot. She asked for Rs 3,000 per girl for the wedding, but reduced it when the client haggled on the condition that he bear the expense of hiring traditional ghaagra-cholis [traditional skirt-blouse ensembles] and matching jewellery.[39]

Predictably, the far-right Shiv Sena also objected to the cheerleaders. They 'bring obscenity to the game of cricket which is watched by all members of a family', said a Shiv Sena politician. The cheerleaders were issued with less revealing outfits as a result.[40]

Another important area of critique concentrated on the claims for IPL as a consummation of free market endeavour. The problem here, according to the writer Mike Marqusee, a seasoned and sympathetic watcher of Indian cricket, was that the IPL market was not free at all. On the contrary, 'the IPL provides a heavily protected environment for the franchises' and:

> Just as the financial speculators were exposed in the end as dependent on the public purse, so the IPL franchises are dependent on cricket's vast non-profit sector – for grounds and facilities, players and umpires. For their foreign stars, they're dependent on international cricket. Since it's a six-week event, there's little incentive for owners to invest in any wider development. And it can only ever be a six-week event.[41]

Moreover, it emerged in 2012 that the BCCI was preventing Indian cricketers from playing T20 in other countries. On top of which:

> The BCCI has done its best to ensure that Indian involvement in domestic Twenty20 matches is restricted to the IPL. Its principle is a simple protection of its assets in order to ensure no rival league will be able to lure their players away with larger pay-cheques. It has used the IPL's clout – 10% of the overseas cricketers' IPL contracts is directed to their boards – to ensure a diplomatic silence over the one-way traffic.[42]

Not only did this seem like a restraint of trade, and thus contrary to 'free market' principles; it pointed to multiple conflicts of interest. Gideon Haigh, for example, observed the 'phoniness' of ex-Test players Ravi Shastri and Sunil Gavaskar, who were both IPL commissioners, acting as TV commentators during IPL matches and 'getting high on their own supply'.[43] But in 2010 there was evidence of more perturbing conflicts of interest when allegations of corporate malfeasance on a grand scale in the IPL brought down the league's principal founder, Lalit Modi, a tobacco and media mogul and leading light in the right-wing Bharatiya Janata Party (BJP). Marqusee identified the charges and their implications:

> It's the private franchising that created the morass that's now under investigation. Among the allegations are bribery, kickbacks, insider trading, tax evasion, money laundering, offshore tax scams and violations of foreign exchange regulations. Behind all these manoeuvres lies a tangle of conflicts of interest, with IPL and BCCI officials and their relatives financially involved in the private franchises and the broadcasting-rights holders. It's a web that involves government ministers, the CEOs of some of India biggest corporations, media powers and Bollywood stars. Despite the recent revelations, there's little indication things will change. All those vying for power in Indian cricket share

the same assumptions and the same methods and not a few of the same cronies. Modi's successor Chirayu Amin – chairman of pharmaceutical giant Alembic and former president of the Federation of Indian Chambers of Commerce and Industry – promises a more disciplined and cautious approach but his model for cricket's future is no different from Modi's. In selling the franchises, the BCCI was licensing exclusive groups of investors to exploit the common cricket market for private profit. That was problematic from the outset. Under private ownership, management is less hedged in by non-commercial concerns, such as ensuring wider access to facilities; they have neither a mandate for, nor an interest in, promoting the welfare of the game as a whole.[44]

For Marqusee, the tycoons of the Indian Premier League were neither saving nor revolutionising cricket; they were looting it. Three years later Ramachandra Guha, Indian cricket's most eloquent biographer, put it thus:

As I watched the tournament unfold, I saw also that it was deeply divisive in a sociological sense. It was a tamasha [grand show] for the rich and upwardly mobile living in the cities of southern and western India. Rural and small town India were largely left out, as were the most populous states. That Uttar Pradesh and Madhya Pradesh, both of whom have excellent Ranji Trophy records, had no IPL team between them, while Maharashtra had two, was symptomatic of the tournament's identification with the powerful and the moneyed. The entire structure of the IPL was a denial of the rights of equal citizenship that a truly 'national' game should promote. The IPL is representative of the worst sides of Indian capitalism and Indian society. Corrupt and cronyist, it has also promoted chamchagiri [sycophancy] and compliance. [...] What is to be done now? The vested interests are asking for such token measures as the legalisation of betting and the resignation of the odd official. In truth, far more radical steps are called for. The IPL should be disbanded.[45]

(In 2013 Modi was found guilty on eight charges by the BCCI and banned for life, although he was re-elected as the President of Rajasthan Cricket Association, his power base, the following year. He currently lives in exile in London. There has been no significant change in the governance of the IPL.)

Conclusion: bright lights, big city?

In 2014, after receiving a loan of £20 million from Birmingham City Council for the rebuilding of their pavilion, Warwickshire County Cricket Club agreed to change the name of their T20 team to 'Birmingham Bears'. The bear had been the county's symbol for many years, but the dropping of 'Warwickshire' annoyed some of the club's members.[46] Nevertheless it was a sign of the times. Short, festive, televised and floodlit games between teams based in cities seemed now to be a proven commercial formula across several sports and, three years later, the ECB announced its own city-based franchise tournament, to begin in 2020. ECB chief executive Tom Harrison was said to have 'spent time in the US meeting Facebook and Twitter, discussing both marketing and their streaming options for the sport online, while also picking the brains of officials at Major League Baseball, the NBA [National Basketball Association] and the NFL [National Football League]'.[47] The ECB, who would own the eight proposed teams, hoped, of course, to generate significant revenue to sustain the other forms of cricket under their governance. But sociologists Thomas Fletcher and Dominic Malcolm immediately warned:

> City-based Twenty20 will attract a new, younger audience, but perhaps they will be attracted for different reasons. Twenty20 packs stadiums drawn by cricket's global superstars, but there is little evidence that it has the capacity to sustain audiences across the sport's longer formats. You cannot breathe economic life into Test cricket by selling the audience something else so, at best, these latest plans create the need for further tinkering and, at worst, plant the seeds of Test cricket's future demise.[48]

Notes

1. Martyn Hindley *Crash! Bang! Wallop! Twenty20: A History of the Brief Game* Studley, Warks: Know the Score Books 2008 p.10.
2. The rules of Cricket Max can be found at: 'Cricket Max – the game invented by Martin Crowe (02 Feb 1996)' http://www.espncricinfo.com/ci/content/story/67577.html Access 29 April 2017.
3. Hindley *Crash!* pp.12, 15 and 17.
4. http://static.espncricinfo.com/db/ARCHIVE/1998-99/OTHERS+ICC/AUS_SUPER-8S/AUS_SUPER-8S_OCT1998_ANNOUNCEMENT.html Posted 25 April 1998, Access 3 May 2017.
5. Paul Newman 'Meet the man who invented Twenty20 cricket – the man missing out on millions' *MailOnline* 11 June 2008 http://www.dailymail.co.uk/sport/cricket/article-1025831/Meet-man-invented-Twenty20-cricket—man-missing-millions.html Access 29 April 2017.
6. Hindley *Crash!* pp.21–2.
7. Hindley *Crash!* p.23.
8. Hindley *Crash!* p.9.
9. Hindley *Crash!* pp.42–3.
10. Hindley *Crash!* p.30.
11. Richard Boock 'Cricket: it may not be real cricket, but it's fun' http://www.nzherald.co.nz/sport/news/article.cfm?c_id=4&objectid=10111584 Posted 18 February 2005, Access 29 April 2017.
12. Martin Crowe 'Forty overs is one-day cricket's future' http://www.espncricinfo.com/magazine/content/story/713821.html Posted 31 January 2014, Access 29 April 2017.

13 Mark Geenty 'NZC launches review into Twenty20 competition as fans stay away again' http://www.stuff.co.nz/sport/cricket/75263918/nzc-launches-review-into-twenty20-competition-as-fans-stay-away-again Posted 18 December 2015, Access 30 April 2017.
14 Hindley *Crash!* p.51.
15 Ian MacLaurin *Tiger by the Tail: A Life in Business from Tesco to Test Cricket* London: Macmillan 1999 p.189.
16 Scyld Berry 'Crowd-pleasing T20 format is vital to the game's future' http://www.telegraph.co.uk/cricket/2016/07/26/crowd-pleasing-t20-format-is-vital-to-the-games-future/ Posted 26 July 2016, Access 1 May 2017.
17 Chris Rumford 'Twenty20, global disembedding, and the rise of the "portfolio player"' *Sport in Society* Vol.14 No.10 2011 pp.1358–68.
18 Cricinfo Staff 'Everything you wanted to know about the ICL' http://www.espncricinfo.com/icl/content/story/310677.html No precise date, 2007, Access 1 May 2017.
19 Cricinfo Staff 'Everything'.
20 Siddhartha Vaidyanathan 'ICL camp upbeat ahead of launch' http://www.espncricinfo.com/icl/content/story/322651.html Posted 28 November 2007, Access 1 May 2017.
21 *Times of India* 'ICL can use Eden Gardens' http://timesofindia.indiatimes.com/sports/sri-lanka-in-india/top-stories/ICL-can-use-Eden-Gardens/articleshow/2305476.cms Posted 23 August 2007, Access 1 May 2017.
22 In addition to the one mentioned, these were the Lal Bahadur Shastri Stadium in Hyderabad, the Sardar Vallabhbhai Patel Stadium in Ahmedabad and the Tau Devi Lal Stadium in Gurgaon, another city in Haryana.
23 Ajay S. Shankar 'Australia spells out tough stand on ICL' http://www.espncricinfo.com/ci-icc/content/story/359749.html Posted 4 July 2008, Access 1 May 2017.
24 Ajay S. Shankar 'Bangladesh bans ICL recruits for 10 years' http://www.espncricinfo.com/bangladesh/content/story/370016.html Posted 17 September 2008, Access 1 May 2017.
25 'Maddy unworried by India threats' http://news.bbc.co.uk/sport1/hi/cricket/7100860.stm Posted 18 November 2007, Access 1 May 2017.
26 Scyld Berry 'Indian Cricket League seeking former England players for unofficial World Cup' http://www.telegraph.co.uk/sport/cricket/international/india/2695883/indian-Cricket-League-seeking-former-England-players-for-unofficial-World-Cup-Cricket.html Posted 6 September 2008, Access 1 May 2017.
27 See Andy Bull 'Warning signs showed Stanford empire was built on 'threats and innuendos"' *The Guardian* 20 February 2009 https://www.theguardian.com/sport/2009/feb/20/allen-stanford-profile1 Access 1 May 2017.
28 Rob Steen 'Acronym wars: the economics and Indianisation of contemporary cricket' in Chris Rumford and Stephen Wagg (eds.) *Cricket and Globalization* Newcastle-upon-Tyne: Cambridge Scholars Publishing 2010 pp.84–102, p.85.
29 Cricinfo Staff 'Stanford reveals US$100 million deal' http://www.espncricinfo.com/england/content/story/354348.html Posted 11 June 2008, Access 1 May 2017.
30 Cricinfo Staff 'ECB under fire as players go cold on Stanford' http://www.espncricinfo.com/stanfordtwenty20/content/story/375957.html Posted 30 October 2008, Access 1 May 2017.
31 'Indian Premier League: how it all started' http://timesofindia.indiatimes.com/ipl-history/Indian-Premier-League-How-it-all-started/articleshow/19337875.cms Posted 2 April 2013, Access 1 May 2017.

32 Boria Majumdar 'The Indian Premier League and world cricket' in Anthony Bateman and Jeffrey Hill (eds.) *The Cambridge Companion to Cricket* Cambridge: Cambridge University Press 2009 pp.173–86, pp.173–4 and 176.
33 The Winter Games at Lake Placid in 1980 and the Summer Games at Los Angeles in 1984 and Atlanta in 1996.
34 Often in public discourse called the BRICS – an acronym for Brazil, Russia, India, China and South Africa.
35 Amit Gupta 'India: the epicentre of cricket?' in Rumford and Wagg (eds.) *Cricket and Globalization* pp.41–59.
36 Ajeyo Basu 'Ugly side of IPL' http://www.dailypioneer.com/sunday-edition/foray/sports/ugly-side-of-ipl.html Posted 19 May 2013, Access 2 May 2017.
37 See, for example, Tim Hill 'Washington's "Redskins" name dealt serious blow by federal judge's ruling' *The Guardian* 8 July 2015 https://www.theguardian.com/sport/2015/jul/08/washington-redskins-team-name-native-americans-ruling Access 15 May 2017.
38 Jeremy Page 'Indian Premier League cheerleaders told to cover up and tone down' http://www.planetsrk.com/community/threads/cheerleaders-told-to-cover-up-and-tone-down.11226/ Posted 29 April 2008, Access 2 May 2017.
39 Yogesh Pawar 'Dancing for their lives for Rs5,000 a match' http://www.dnaindia.com/india/report-dancing-for-their-lives-for-rs5000-a-match-1818258 Posted 3 April 2013, Access 2 May 2017.
40 Page 'Indian Premier League cheerleaders told to cover up'.
41 Mike Marqusee 'IPL points to a bleak future for cricket' *The Guardian* 12 March 2010 https://www.theguardian.com/commentisfree/2010/mar/12/indian-premier-league-just-not-cricket Access 2 May 2017.
42 Sharda Ugra 'Why Indians don't play in foreign T20 tournaments' http://www.espncricinfo.com/india/content/story/570934.html Posted 3 July 2012, Access 2 May 2017.
43 Gideon Haigh *Sphere of Influence: Writings on Cricket and its Discontents* London: Simon and Schuster 2011 p.307.
44 Mike Marqusee 'IPL's dark side of neoliberal dream' *The Guardian* 9 May 2010.
45 Ramachandra Guha 'The serpent in the garden' http://www.espncricinfo.com/magazine/content/story/638602.html Posted 1 June 2013, Access 4 May 2017.
46 Brian Halford 'Warwickshire's T20 "Birmingham Bears" name is confirmed' *Birmingham Mail* 25 February 2014 http://www.birminghammail.co.uk/sport/cricket/warwickshires-t20-birmingham-bears-name-6745754 Access 3 May 2017.
47 Ali Martin 'ECB starts process for new T20 format but county official reveals "gun to head" tactics' *The Guardian* 28 March 2017 https://www.theguardian.com/sport/2017/mar/28/ecb-broadcasters-facebook-twitter-new-t20-tournament-rights-cricket Access 3 May 2017.
48 Thomas Fletcher and Dominic Malcolm 'Cricket: more Twenty20 may sow seeds of demise for the quintessential English game' *The Conversation* http://theconversation.com/cricket-more-twenty20-may-sow-seeds-of-demise-for-the-quintessential-english-game-75520 Posted 6 April 2017, Access 3 May 2017.

Chapter 15

Have you made this team great, or have they made you?
Cricket, coaching and globalisation

This chapter discusses the emergence of technocratic ideas in the cricket world – ideas, that's to say, of the game as an area of expertise. It concentrates on the emergence to greater prominence of the cricket coach. Its central arguments are: that the word 'coach' has, at the highest level, come to mean less 'the person who imparts technical instruction' and more 'the person responsible – and accountable – for team performance'; that the growing acceptance of this notion has challenged and, thus, provoked often strong argument over traditional ideas of masculinity and national identity in cricket. The chapter draws on an article I wrote in 2000[1] and on work I did in collaboration with the Indian cricket writer Sharda Ugra, first published in 2009.[2]

'If you have read such historical novels as *Ivanhoe* . . .' Cricket instruction in the pre-computer age

Coaching in cricket has a long history. In the thirty or more years that followed the Second World War cricket coaching seemed to maintain much of its pre-war character: it was steeped in ideologies of class and ethnicity and it was seen as a common sequel to a career in first-class cricket. Coaches were usually working-class ex-professional cricketers employed at private schools or, as in the case of the ex-Surrey and England bowler Alf Gover (1908–2001), running their own coaching school: Gover ran an indoor coaching school in South London, founded in 1928 by fellow Surrey and England cricketers, Andy Sandham and Herbert Strudwick, between 1938 and 1989. Coaches, by and large, prepared young cricketers by explaining basic technique: for example, in his obituary of Gover in 2001, Mike Selvey wrote: 'His technical expertise was immense, but his bread and butter were the basics'.[3] This technique was assumed to be correct on tacitly rational grounds – although science was never mentioned, the way of playing cricket that was taught was regarded as optimal and value free: everybody, for example, should be taught to play with 'a straight bat'. Gover's pupils included many future Test players from overseas[4] and many young cricketers in the British colonies were taught by ex-county professionals.

This orthodoxy of cricket technique was overlaid by a corresponding orthodoxy of social class. In this perspective, the conduct of cricket matches was the responsibility of the team captains and the leadership qualities and much of the tactical acumen required for cricket was thought simply to reside in men of the right stuff. In 1904 the Lancashire and England amateur A.G. Steel (educated at Marlborough public school) had written:

> Few professional cricketers (it is a well-known fact) make good captains; we have hardly seen a match played where a professional cricketer was captain of either side, in which he was not guilty of some very palpable blunders [...] Amateurs always have made, and always will make, the best captains; and this is only natural. An educated mind, with a logical power of reasoning, will always treat every subject better than one comparatively untaught.[5]

In practice although the counties persisted in the appointment of amateur captains they often lacked either these mythical qualities of governance or the requisite cricket skills, or both. Myles Kenyon, for example, a future High Sheriff of Lancashire who took over the captaincy of that county in 1919, hadn't played first-class cricket before[6] and Boer war veteran Major Arthur Lupton was made captain of Yorkshire in 1925, despite a very modest record and not having played for the county since 1908. Amateur captains, therefore, had often been dependent for advice on the subaltern figure of the senior professional.

Coaching manuals of the time had specific advice on captaincy. The widespread expectation was that cricket captains at all levels would be from middle-class backgrounds or above. For example, in *Schoolboy Cricket*, his instruction manual of 1952, Rayleigh G. Strutt assumes that its readership will be 'going on to their Public Schools or Grammar Schools'.[7] (Strutt himself was headmaster of a private preparatory school.) Captaincy, Strutt stated, should combine the will to win with a chivalric code: 'If you have read such historical novels as *Ivanhoe*, *Sir Nigel* or *The White Company*, you will remember that in the Age of Chivalry the Knights would have a good dinner together before going out to a jousting [. . .] where they would do their best to kill one another'. 'There is not very much of that spirit left in the modern world', he continued, 'but it can, and does, survive on the cricket field. Long may it do so'.[8] This was an accurate rendition of the MCC ethos. Chapter 1 of the *MCC Cricket Coaching Book*, first issued the same year and reprinted regularly through the 1950s and 60s, is called 'The Spirit of the Game'. It begins thus:

> Cricket is, in a sense, warfare in miniature and a cricket match should be fought out by both sides with all the resources of spirit and technique at their command. At the same time it should always be a recreation, a game to be played not only to written laws but in harmony of an unwritten code of chivalry and good temper.[9]

This ethos had anchored the historic divide between amateurs and professionals, the argument being that professional cricketers, dependent on the game for their livelihoods, could not play the game in the necessary spirit – a spirit thought to be possessed only by high-born gentlemen of independent means. It was also, in essence, the ethos of the British Empire in which subject peoples labored under the purportedly benevolent guidance of colonial administrators.[10] Broadly speaking at this time the other Test-playing countries all subscribed to the MCC's 'spirit of cricket': Australian cricket was dominated by an Anglophile elite, Indian teams were led by English-educated patricians and West Indies insisted on a white captain, of English or European descent.

Captaincy retained – even enhanced – its importance after the abolition of the amateur status in 1963, but, in English cricket, the notion of a gentleman captain with inherent leadership qualities had steadily receded. As suggested in Chapter 10, its last significant incarnation was Mike Brearley's captaincy of England in the Ashes series of 1981. In qualification, it should be added that Brearley, while a Cambridge graduate picked for his captaincy rather than his cricket skills, was beginning to acquire the aura of a psychologist, thus signifying science rather than breeding.

The emergence of the coach as technocrat is attributable to at least two factors: the rise of sport science and the growing need for accountability in an increasingly media-dependent sport. The narrative of the rise of the professional coach is paralleled in other sports, notably football, and runs roughly thus: a new, no-nonsense broom sweeps away the lazy old order and establishes a fresh regime, based on hard work. For instance, this is how *Guardian* journalist Paul Coupar recently described Micky Stewart, who became the England team's first full-time coach in 1986:

> Stewart's work-ethic gave England a sense of purpose not seen for years. He found them in blazers, with methods which had barely changed since the 1950s, and left them in tracksuits. A former professional with Charlton Athletic as well as Surrey, Stewart, 'knew what it was to prepare thoroughly' according to his first captain, Mike Gatting. David Gower was bored by the new physical jerks.[11]

Stewart, who did the job from 1986 to 1992, and his immediate successors, Keith Fletcher (1992–5), Raymond Illingworth (1995–6) and David Lloyd

(1996–9), were all seasoned professionals who had captained county sides only because the embargo on professional captains had, effectively, been lifted in 1963. They represented the moving of the subalterns to centre stage. They were hired for their accumulated wisdom as professional cricketers and to assume a public accountability in the face of the increasingly derisive cricket media. When Stewart retired in 1992, one valedictory article judged him almost solely on this count:

> Away from the environment of the on-the-record quote, Stewart is an honest, relaxed and friendly man, who enjoys a drink with individual journalists. When he was team manager with Surrey, he never failed to spend time in the press-box volunteering information, but a series of bad experiences, not to mention a close friendship with the former England football manager, Bobby Robson, has taught him not to go swimming in alligator-infested waters. 'I'm aware of the newspapers, but I try not to read them,' Stewart said. 'Some of the more scurrilous stuff leaves me feeling terribly hurt – not for myself, but for the image of cricket'.[12]

Similarly, David Lloyd, who became England coach four years later, reflected in his autobiography:

> It did not take long. By the time 1997 was a few days old, my honeymoon period in the job was well and truly over. I was being lampooned in the newspapers and my conduct in the aftermath of a Test match had earned me some sensational headlines and an official reprimand from my bosses. On top of all this, the England team had been castigated as useless for failing to beat the newest of Test-playing nations and as graceless for failing to exhibit the true spirit of touring.[13]

This testimony from the early England team coaches is telling in several ways. Cricket was the definitively imperial sport and the largely unsuccessful England cricket teams of the 1980s and 90s became a symbol of post-imperial, national decline. England's cricket elite were now happy to devolve responsibility for failure both to beat the former subject nations and to uphold the unworldly 'spirit of cricket' to their non-commissioned officers. These NCOs would have to face the flak fired by a scornful national tabloid press and receive official censure if they faltered. Sponsors – now central to the successful administration of first-class cricket – would also expect resignations in the event of failure on the field.

Other cricket countries had meanwhile defined themselves against MCC orthodoxy. West Indies had first appointed a black captain for a full Test series in 1960. Later their star batsman Vivian Richards (121 Tests 1974–91, batting average 50) had challenged the conventional wisdom of the 'straight bat' and called his autobiography *Hitting Across the Line*.[14] Australian cricketers had abandoned their gentlemanly Anglophile amateur code in favour of a militant larrikinism. Indian cricketers too were wont to perceive their brand of cricket as intrinsically Indian. For instance, Ramachandra Guha asserted as recently as 2008 that India had a special relationship to cricket, judging it to be 'a game that privileges wrist-work rather than size or physical fitness; to be small and stocky is not always a disadvantage. Thus, Indians can compete with the rest of the world. Its slow pace and uninterrupted structure of play suits Indians'.[15]

'Subjects ranging from Hulk Hogan to the Bee Gees': the rise and implications of the 'laptop coach'

There is now an itinerant cadre of laptop coaches, who transcend nationality and ply their trade on the global cricket circuit: two out of England's last three coaches have been from Zimbabwe; ex-Australian captain Greg Chappell coached India between 2005 and 2007 (a case study for this chapter), Englishman Bob Woolmer coached Pakistan from 2004 until his death in 2007, and so on. To a degree, coaches, like football managers, have become a paradigm within which the results of cricket matches and series are explained. This operates at the level of individual culpability, as when a coach is asked to step aside following a string of defeats. By the twenty-first century this responsibility was increasingly being devolved to one of an international cadre of experts, wholly comfortable with the expectations placed upon them. New Zealander John Wright, who accepted the post of coach and manager at Kent County Cricket Club in 1997, wrote in 2006: 'As a coach my sole focus was on winning cricket matches. The Kent County Cricket Club exists to win cricket matches, which pleases its fans and satisfies its sponsors'.[16]

By the 1990s, the necessity of such appointments was accepted across the global cricket market and it is possible to make a number of observations about these appointments in the time since.

First, initially most countries selected coaches from within their own cricket cultures. Between 1994 and 2015, for instance, South Africa had taken on eight national coaches, only one of whom had been born outside of South Africa – Bob Woolmer, an Englishman who had migrated to South Africa after retiring as a player. West Indies' first three national coaches were Rohan Kanhai (1992–5), Andy Roberts (1996) and Malcolm Marshall (1996–9) – all ex-West Indies Test players of the highest class and thus able to command respect. The first seven Indian national coaches, over a ten-year period (1990–2000) were, similarly, all ex-Indian Test cricketers. This seemed to reflect the same assumptions as in England – that there was now a need for an accountable figurehead; that accumulated cricket wisdom could be passed by on its possessors to the next generation; and that there were discrete national cricket cultures, fully comprehensible only to insiders.

Second, in the early twenty-first century, this pattern began to break up and a group of acknowledged international experts began to emerge. These coaches – the Sri Lankan Australian Dav Whatmore, New Zealander John Wright, Zimbabwean Duncan Fletcher, South African Mickey Arthur, England's Bob Woolmer and Australians John Buchanan and Trevor Bayliss were examples – were defined primarily by their coaching reputations; their first-class playing careers, although Woolmer had played 19 Tests, had not been especially distinguished. They worked to comparatively short contracts and had each coached a number of nations and other teams. There was soon strong demand for their services: in 2000, for example, Woolmer was offered a salary of £250,000 per year, flights for his family and a house in Colombo to become Sri Lanka's national coach.[17]

Third, they all represented 'the West' (Whatmore, a Sri Lankan by birth, had migrated to Australia in 1962 at the age of 8). While these coaches worked in Asia and the Caribbean – Arthur and Woolmer for Pakistan; Whatmore for Sri Lanka, Bangladesh and Pakistan; Wright and Fletcher for India; Australian John Dyson for Sri Lanka and West Indies; Bayliss for Sri Lanka and Pakistan – no national coach travelled in the opposite direction. So far the national coaches of England, Australia, South Africa and New Zealand have been whites, recruited either from one of those countries, or Zimbabwe: England had Duncan Fletcher (1999–2007), fellow Zimbabwean Andy Flower (2009–14) and appointed Australian Trevor Bayliss in 2015; UK-born South African Tim Nielsen coached Australia from 2007 to 2011 and was succeeded by Arthur; and so on.

Fourth, coaching has become more in demand and more specialised, with appointments for specific formats (Tests, one-day internationals or T20) or specialisms – batting, bowling, fielding or keeping wicket.

The centrality of coaching (and other specialist advice), however, has not been achieved without dispute. In the Caribbean, for example, a debate raged over the appliance of science as a way to retrieve West Indies' faltering position in world cricket. For instance, Hilary Beckles of the University of West Indies defied local traditionalism by calling in 1998 for an academy to be set up providing coaching and strategic planning.[18] Likewise leading Caribbean writer Tim Hector conceded the need for science, if only in combination with the radical nationalist spirit which characterised the West Indies' most successful cricket years.[19]

Elsewhere there was angry opposition and a sense that prevailing notions of gender and nation in the cricket world were being undermined. Australia was a case in point. In 1999 the Australian board appointed 46-year-old Queenslander John Buchanan, who had played only seven first-class cricket matches, as their chief coach. Buchanan's regime was soon rendered as a media melodrama in which a deluded, word-mongering theorist peddling science confronted a sceptical hyper-masculine opposition, schooled in the university of cricket life, the latter invariably represented by spin bowler

Shane Warne (145 Tests 1992–2007, 708 wickets). Jo Harman wrote in 2015 that Buchanan:

> Set about introducing a whole new coaching philosophy to the Australian dressing room and while captain Steve Waugh and later Ricky Ponting were ardent followers, Warne was not. Data analysis and fitness were two of the central tenets of the new regime and Warne just couldn't see the point. For Warne, a lager-guzzling larrikin whose phenomenal natural talent made his rise to super-stardom inevitable, these were unnecessary complications. Cricket had always been about having a laugh, gobbing off at a batsman, getting him out and then sinking a cold one. But for Buchanan, who'd worked his way up to the top coaching job in Australia despite having no playing career to speak of, they were absolutely integral to success. Coaching to Buchanan meant more than batting, bowling and fielding; it meant broadening the horizons of his players and developing them as human beings. He encouraged his players to deliver lectures and recite poetry in the dressing room to build self-confidence, with subjects ranging from Hulk Hogan to the Bee Gees. The English press dubbed Buchanan the 'Wacky Professor' after a team-briefing document was leaked during the 2001 Ashes that drew on the teachings of fifth Century Chinese warlord Sun Tzu. [...] The bad-blood started to coagulate when Warne was allegedly overheard at a charity do saying: 'These boot camps are a big waste of time ... after a bit I just turned to the coach and said: "I'm weak as piss, I hate your guts and I want to go home. You're a dickhead"'.[20]

Retired Indian spin bowler Bishan Bedi was also outspoken in defence of the old order: at the Wisden International Awards of 2003 he was asked to present a special achievement award for the Australian team to Buchanan. Before doing so he said to Buchanan, 'Tell us, John, have you made this Australian team great, or have they made you?'[21] In the cricket media and beyond Buchanan continued to be a test case for the new coaching: was he 'a complete fraud or a cricketing mastermind'?[22]

Australian Greg Chappell's tenure as coach of India between 2005 and 2007 provides another illustrative case study both of this conflict and of the commercial dimensions of the coaching phenomenon in a neoliberal world.

Different hats, different thinking: coaching and culture clash

Greg Chappell, former captain of Australia and a member of that country's first cricketing family, was appointed coach to the Indian cricket team in May of 2005. As an accomplished Test cricketer he carried evident credibility; nor, since he was succeeding John Wright, was he India's first Western coach.

The Indian cricket team has only had a coach since 1989, when Bishan Bedi was employed to coach the team on its tour of New Zealand. As noted, the first seven men to take the job were all Indians: Bedi (1990–1), Abbas Ali Baig (manager, Australia tour 1991–2), Ajit Wadekar (1992–6), Sandeep Patil (1996), Madan Lal (1996–7), Anshuman Gaekwad (1997–9) and Kapil Dev (1999–2001). After Kapil had departed, implicated in a scandal over match-fixing, leading Indian players who had played on the English county circuit had lobbied for the post to go to New Zealander John Wright. He was appointed, ahead, it is rumoured, of Chappell and Geoff Marsh, both Australians.[23] As things stood (and as they remain), all the 'Eastern' international cricket teams had 'Western' coaches: Chappell, the Englishman Bob Woolmer at Pakistan, Australian Tom Moody, who coached Sri Lanka, and Dav Whatmore who was in charge of Bangladesh. It was difficult to dismiss this as coincidence, particularly since, as we saw, no 'Western' national cricket sides were tutored by 'Eastern' coaches. West Indies currently had an all-Australian coaching team of four, headed by Bennett King. King, appointed in 2004 and the first non-Caribbean to have the job, had never played first-class cricket. When Mickey Arthur was appointed in 2005 to coach his own national side of South Africa, Moody, Marsh and fellow Australian Steve Waugh are said to have been in the frame.[24]

Chappell carried broadly the same philosophy as Buchanan and was a cardinal example of a growing trend. One of the factors said to have persuaded the appointment panel to take him on is Chappell's presentation on the theme of 'Commitment to excellence'.[25] In mid-July 2005, two months into the new regime, *The Hindu* reported from Bangalore on Chappell's 'first formal interaction as coach with the Indian players', which had taken the form of a 'cricket skills camp'. This report appeared beneath the headline 'Chappell asks players to make their own destiny'[26] – on reflection, a powerful and heterodox request in a culture still at least partly wedded to the notion that destiny is given and not achieved. The first decisive step toward excellence and destiny had apparently been taken under the tutelage of Shiva Subramaniam of Tata Consultancy Services, here described as 'among the world's 20 master teachers of the Edward de Bono method', de Bono being a Maltese psychologist whose notion of 'lateral thinking' had been commercially successful in the business world. This method was said to have given the players 'tools for thinking'. 'You have tools for cutting vegetables', Shiva informed a sceptical media contingent, 'you have tools for communicating but we don't have tools for thinking'. These tools for thinking were imparted via de Bono's 'coloured hat' principle:

> The five hats, white hat for information, yellow hat for benefits, black hats for problems, green hat for creativity and red hat for feelings and the last hat is the blue hat which controls my thinking. Which tells me to go from one hat to another. Essentially, we are talking about tools for thinking.[27]

At this press conference Chappell intervened to support his de Bono expert: 'The tools help in organised thinking, so that, in team sessions, we can get the players focussed on speaking about the same subject, rather than talking at cross purposes'.[28] Another leading paper, the *Deccan Herald*, underlined Chappell's emphasis on 'mind games', continuing: 'the Aussie then admitted that de Bono will play a huge part in Team India's prospects in the coming season'.[29]

Two months later there was a substantial public *contretemps* between the coach and the team captain Sourav Ganguly. Ganguly, the son of a wealthy Kolkata family had, according to various cricket web pages, been nicknamed 'Bengal Tiger' and 'Prince of Calcutta' by his team-mates and 'Lord Snooty' by his opponents.[30] Chappell was reported to have said that Ganguly was 'mentally and physically unfit to lead the team' and that his 'attitude and outlook are not ideal'. He was also said to be 'miffed that the Indian captain did not follow the fitness regimen prescribed, and most of the time uses the false pretext of injury to exempt himself'.[31] Already, by late September, this was being described as 'the Sourav Ganguly–Greg Chappell saga' and Chappell had sent a lengthy email to the Board of Cricket Control India (BCCI) explaining his position. In it the coach claimed that Ganguly had been 'struggling as a player'. 'I also told him that his state of mind was fragile and it showed in the way that he made decisions on and off the field in relation to the team, especially team selection'. Chappell stated: 'Greg King [the team's trainer]'s reports continue to show Sourav as the person who does the least fitness and training work based on the criterion that has been developed by the support staff to monitor the work load of all the players'. He concludes: 'It is time that all players were treated with fairness and equity and that good behaviours and attitudes are rewarded at the selection table rather than punished'. The mail was signed 'Greg Chappell MBE'.[32] Ganguly was omitted from the Indian team the following month.

Chappell's assistant, Ian Frazer, a specialist in biomechanics and thus, to the traditionally-minded, a signifier of intrusive sport science, now announced that the (BCCI) 'have to come to terms fast with making "hard decisions" when it came to a player's retirement', relating this to the market reforms India had undergone in the previous two decades. He added: 'Indians, despite their diverse cultural background, had the ability to make such hard decisions. "Indians have entered the business world, they are in the global market where they make decisions every day. It is a natural consequence. It can be done, and done professionally"'.[33]

Meanwhile Chappell's email rapidly became public, as did Ganguly's lengthy rebuttal of its claims. In *India Today* beneath the headline 'Recipe for DISASTER' Sharda Ugra announced an 'uneasy truce'. 'He hears you out but sometimes you feel he is not listening to you', a member of the Indian team had told her. 'Chappell has made it known that the anxiety he sees in the team is an exercise in weaning the weak from the strong'.[34]

However, the article closed with a commentary by ex-Indian Test cricketer Sanjay Manjrekar. 'What would have been really sad', wrote Manjrekar:

> Was if Chappell had headed home. [...] That would have meant that we as a nation would have made a strong statement: that India was not a place for a man on a mission who wanted to make a difference and was willing to speak his mind at the risk of losing a highly lucrative job. That would have been a tragic portrayal of our country [...] If Chappell succeeds, India will go to the next level.[35]

Two months later Chappell told the same publication:

> The disciplines of what it takes to be successful are universal; it does not matter what environment you are in. we have obviously had to massage them [the players] to fit into a different culture. I mean Indians are not as used to the straightforward. We have had to speak more slowly for the boys to understand our accent.[36]

In January, 2006 the *Indian Express* web site reported that Indian opening batsman Virender Sehwag had been engaging in a 'simple schoolyard exercise devised to test and sharpen reflexes – But Ian Frazer, Team India's biomechanist has a more respectable name for it: Repositioning, or "neural stimuli"'.[37] The following June Chappell was interviewed for *Indian Express* by Ajay S. Shankar, who asked him the definitely leading questions: 'Have you ever encountered a clash of cultures during your stint? In India there's always a lot of sentiment attached to team selection, how have you handled that?' Chappell did not blink:

> No differently from any time in the past. I think honesty is the best policy. You need to deal with the truth if you want to be successful at this level. You have to be honest with yourself, you have to be honest with your teammates. I think, as coach, I have to be honest with the players. I don't know any other way, and that's the way I am going to be. I think, so far, the players have understood that and have respected it.[38]

In mid-October 2006, the Indian paper *The Tribune* reported from New Delhi that Kapil Dev, recently appointed chair of the National Cricket Academy, did not know what the role entailed, thus calling into question BCCI claims of an enhanced professionalism at the commanding heights of Indian cricket. Dev turned on Chappell:

> Chappell's methods foreign to Indians
> Former captain Kapil Dev today expressed his disapproval of the policy of continuous experimentation with the composition and strategies of the Indian team, saying Indian players performed better when

their place in the side was secure. 'Indians are not very comfortable with uncertainty. They need to be sure of their spot in the team to instill confidence in them,' the World Cup-winning captain said. He attributed this factor to the culture and the general upbringing provided in the country. 'We need our base to be strong. We are brought up that way. Even in other walks of life, Indians were not very amenable to change,' Kapil said. 'We don't change our bases readily for better jobs and higher salary. We want to stay close to home,' he said.[39]

On 25 November *Indian Express* reported that politicians were now baying for Chappell's head, but that BCCI 'top guns' were considering asking him to stay on beyond the World Cup of 2007.[40] In December the *Calcutta Times* discussed the 'flak' that Chappell had drawn during his eighteen months in the job. Among the opinions solicited was that of former India opener and BJP (the right-wing Bharatiya Janata Party – otherwise known as the Hindu Nationalist Party) MP, Chetan Chauhan, who was:

> Not yet ready to label foreign coaches as unsuccessful. 'It is too early to say that. Performance of the players is also a factor. The coaches have to be given a free hand and their strategy has to be right. One big problem with foreign coaches is that they haven't seen domestic cricket and are not accustomed to Indian conditions. Apart from the language and tradition of the country, the cricket culture is also very different. Here, the media and the public are hysteric, there is tremendous pressure, there are pressure groups in administration too,' says the former selector. Chauhan goes on to make a point: 'Chappell is a great player but his experiments have boomeranged. In Australia and England the players are mentally very mature and independent. But that is not the case in India. Some of the players are not yet ready for international cricket. The chopping and changing policy has not yielded results.'[41]

Chappell ended the year still defending himself against criticism, resorting once again, like many spokespeople in this ongoing controversy, to a comparison of ethnicities. 'I'm an Australian', he told reporters, 'we are used to being blunt, saying things as they are. We can continue to be fine with each other after that too. In India, maybe people take it as a slight and don't forget it easily'.[42]

It was telling that, in 2007, with Chappell's contract about to expire, the BCCI sounded out Buchanan as his replacement.[43]

The Chappell furore and of the trend for Eastern cricket nations to seek Western coaches clearly raised questions about cricket and globalisation and the politics of what was, in effect, the new cricket coaching.

First of all, there were, perhaps inevitably, post-colonial elements in the discourse over Chappell. Pranay Daryanani of the *Merinews* web site, for instance, compared the 'anti-Chappell' refrain to the angry reception Indians gave to Sir John Simon's commission on Indian governance which sat in 1942. Disparaged as 'Guru Greg' he had been met, observed Daryanani, with burnt effigies and 'Chappell, go back' placards everywhere he went.[44] There is, ultimately, some substance to the notion of Chappell and his entourage as some kind of neo-colonial flagship.

Second, the wrangle over Chappell and his modus operandi had been replete with ethnic stereotyping, but the picture here had been complex and no clear-cut case can be made for an orientalist discourse: Chappell did not, in other words, essentialise – that is, attribute fixed characteristics to – Indian cricket. To be sure, well-meaning, but intellectually unreliable generalisations about Indian cricket were not hard to find in the international cricket world. The writer and commentator Simon Hughes, for example, wrote in 2000:

> The more I thought about it, the more I realised that Indian driving was like their cricket. Their batting was cheeky, pushy, risky, there was a general absence of braking. It was erratic and balls, like cars, had a habit of shooting off at odd angles. The hullabaloo their fielders made as they swarmed round the bat was no different to the chaos and commotion on the roads. In fact the rules about horning and appealing were identical.[45]

Broadly speaking, Greg Chappell had resisted such Kipling-esque stereotyping, in general arguing simply that Indian players must not be afraid of change or bear grudges. This had applied even when he was posed pointedly leading questions about a 'clash of cultures'. The racial/ethnic generalisations in this chapter of Indian cricket history were at least as likely to come from Chappell's critics, whether Indians like Chetan Chauhan (England players are 'mentally very mature', Indian players are not) and Kapil Dev, or from Chappell's own country. Indeed the most full-hearted denunciation both of Chappell's methods and of the rush to appoint Western coaches came from ex-Australian captain and national coach Bobby Simpson. In his 'Cricket Corner' column on the Sport Star web site Simpson argued:

> The Indian selectors and Greg Chappell seem to be trying to change Indian cricket to fit in with their theory of how the game, and in particular one-day cricket, should be played. While more theories abound today than ever before, cricket is still a simple game that is only made more difficult by well meaning theorists. My whole theory on coaching the cricketers is based on improving the natural talents of the players and the culture of their game. Almost every country has its natural way of playing the game. Australia are different to England. South Africa and New Zealand are different to Australia and more like England.

The Asian countries are similar to each other, but have slightly different ways of using their incredibly flexible wrists while batting. The West Indies have their own individual style, and thank goodness, this is what makes them so different and exciting than the other countries. Unfortunately, the globalisation of world cricket and the predominance of clipboard, biomechanical and scientific coaching have tended to muddle the natural skills of the players. Equally unfortunate is that Australia seem to be the heartbeat of this movement and the Australian coaches now all the rage with Tom Moody (Sri Lanka), Greg Chappell (India) and Bennett King (West Indies). Fellow clipboard Englishman Bob Woolmer coaches Pakistan. What worries me greatly is that in their desire for change and their faith in the so-called scientific approach, they will destroy the naturalness and culture of cricket in these lands. Everybody now wants to jump the Australian bandwagon. (Emphasis added.)[46]

Hughes' and Simpson's observations, though well meant, would certainly have had Edward Said[47] reaching for his revolver. But, doubtful references to flexible wrists aside, Simpson's article recognised something which was at the heart of the Chappell project, and of the appointment of similar coaches in similar situations elsewhere is the international cricket world: that it was about the attempted dismantling of national cricket cultures or the passage, to adopt Hilary Beckles' terms in relation to Caribbean cricket, from the nationalist phase of development to the age of globalisation.[48] This transition had caused anguish in the West Indies, where writers such as Tim Hector had sought to reconcile Caribbean cricket to science and modernity while maintaining it as a site of nationalist struggle.[49] In India, as Ugra had pointed out, the minds of the national cricket team had similarly drifted on from thoughts of independence and national self realisation and 'the symbolic undoing of colonial history is no longer a priority'.[50]

International cricket, especially given the growth in the importance of one-day and Twenty20 cricket over the last thirty years, is a continuous, all-year-round affair. India's players, like comparable players of other countries, spend less and less time in their own countries and communities and more and more time on the international circuit. When they are in India, the Indian team have the status of celebrities – when he came to India, Chappell likened them to the Beatles[51] – and that status was, naturally, contingent on their performance as players. It's worth remembering that India's first foreign/western coach (John Wright in 2001) was appointed at the instigation of several of the Indian players, who knew him from the English county circuit. The aspirations of the players – to maintain and improve their performances on the international stage – married with those of the BCCI. As we saw in Chapter 6, the Indian cricket team – as opposed to cricket generally in the regions and localities of the country – was massively popular culture in India and, since the early 1990s, its matches had been opened up to the commercial media. Here, and in the stadia, it commanded huge audiences, but as Ugra noted, 'the end result in favour or against the national team began to occupy the mind of the spectator, especially the one newly arrived to the game, to a greater extent than the quality of the cricket played [. . .] the cricket match has become a barometer of national self-worth'.[52] And the now-prevalent forms of cricket allow no draws.

This is where Chappell, or somebody like him, came in. The people that now ran India, and Indian cricket, did not have unduly flexible wrists, nor were they congenitally incapable of driving a car in a straight line. They managed business empires embracing breweries, call centres, finance companies, film studios and computer businesses and the like. And, as with all Indian governments of the previous twenty-five years, they were fierce advocates of neoliberal economic policies, privatisation and the global capitalist economy. In this context, cricket had become important in two ways.

First, like cinema, it was a bridge between the country's elite and the masses – a purportedly shared national treasure and, like the nuclear bomb, a visible means by which, provided the team did well, Indians might feel good about themselves in a globalised world: along with a thriving Indian team, the imminent Indian Premier League would become the most obvious manifestation – and consummation – of this objective. Secondly, though, cricket was a ready vehicle for the ideology of neoliberalism itself and a means to the imparting of the stark disciplines that characterised the global marketplace. In his analysis of 'reality TV' sociologist Nick Couldry revived a notion originally proffered by the historian E.P. Thompson, namely that 'every shift in economic organization [. . .] requires new disciplines, new incentives, and a new human nature'.[53] Like 'Reality TV', also by then a key element in Indian popular culture, the Indian cricket team was becoming a theatre for neoliberal truths. The players in this theatre were coming under increased surveillance and must handle their 'workloads', they were 'flexible' and would be laid off when their efficiency as economic units had diminished, they must clear their minds (perhaps, with the enigmatic assistance of Edward de Bono) of unnecessary cultural baggage. As Couldry observes, neoliberalism 'legitimates the market and de-legitimates the social'.[54] Indeed, as we saw, Ian Frazer, Chappell's right-hand man, had said as much when calling for the laying-off of cricketers past their best: 'Indians have entered the business world', he had said, 'they are in the global market where they make decisions every day. It is a natural consequence'. Corroboration had come from leading Indian spokespeople such as Manjrekar, who already spoke the restricted code of the global marketplace with its deadpan allusions to 'making a difference' and 'going to the next level'.

There was a sense in which these disciplines had had to come from outside the country. Chappell became a bringer of 'truths' and 'realities' defined outside of an India still weaning itself off the planned economy and the postcolonial nationalism of Nehru's Congress Party. And while he dispensed these new disciplines Chappell would run the gauntlet of a populist media, comparing him to previous white invaders and accusing him of tampering with the Indian psyche.

The business of coaching: the new coach as entrepreneur

But Chappell also related to the global marketplace on his own account. He had a reputation derived from his gifted batsmanship, his captaincy of Australia and as author of the most pragmatic act in modern cricket history – when, as captain of Australia in a one-day international against New Zealand at the Melbourne Cricket Ground in February of 1981, he had ordered his brother Trevor to bowl the final ball of the game underarm, so that New Zealand, needing six, could not win. Moreover, as an Australian he is a leading representative of an aggressively competitive and successful national sport culture, within an equally aggressive, marketised economy. Chappell had the attitudes to match, being characterised by his biographer as 'a true conservatism – conservation fine, but who paid for it?; erotica OK, pornography no; was Aboriginal rights back-door apartheid?; export uranium and retain the nuclear alliance'. Chappell was associated with the right-wing Nationalist party and, in the early 1980s, was briefly rumoured to be going into politics.[55] Chappell stayed with cricket but he undoubtedly saw, and wished to exploit, the market possibilities of a modernising 'guru coach' in a cricket-crazy and increasingly entrepreneurial society. Sunil Khilnani has described the emergence in India of a 'highly internationalised and entrepreneurial class – many with qualifications from America', the migration to India of foreign capital and multinational companies like Hewlett Packard in the 1990s and the corresponding growth of cities like Bombay and Bangalore as the leading centres of 'Non Resident India'.[56] This rising entrepreneurial and cosmopolitan class, with its globalised cultural horizons and aspirations, was likely to provide a lucrative market for *The Chappell Way*, a training programme devised by Chappell and marketed via the Australian International Sports Academy (AISA) and an Indian marketing agency called The Flea:

> In India, The Flea has been appointed official affiliates of AISA (Australian International Sports Academy). This programme is open to all boys between the ages 12 to 20 years, who wish to improve their game and learn what our national team is learning.
> The Flea is also marketing AISA's coaching programmes for the Web and mobile phones.
> *The Chappell Way* is a two-week programme that is meant to teach specialist skills to the participants, as well as inculcate a love for cricket. The training module takes into account a participant's individual

strengths and weaknesses and hone them to perfection with personalized attention.

'We are proud to be associated with Greg Chappell and AISA and we hope to help them realize their vision of tapping the potential of talented youngsters all across India,' says Sunil Shibad, Director, The Flea.

Headquartered in Mumbai, with associates in Houston, St Louis, Brisbane and Pune, The Flea, India's first and only non-traditional marketing communication agency, is already carrying out viral and buzz marketing campaigns for clients such as Himalayan Natural Mineral Water, matrisearch.com, Idea Cellular, fropper.com, Jopasana Wildlife Conservation and Tain Construction. With AISA and *The Chappell Way*, the Flea is now entering the field of sports marketing.'[57]

Frazer and Chappell were partners in *The Chappell Way*. Tony Dell of AISA told India's *The Telegraph* 'Right now our focus is largely India. The growing spending power of the middle class there is a big draw. And having Chappell there is a passport for us'.[58] The article continued:

'My friends who go to Shivaji Park for cricket coaching told me about it. Sounds great. They are not asking for any previous cricketing record and there is no selection process involved. They say it is one's interest in the game and willingness to learn that counts,' said Shamit Shah, a student of an elite Mumbai school.

The camp, to which the first batch of students went in November, involves running, swimming, games and cricket training sessions peppered with sightseeing and lectures. With Chappell in India, most of the actual training is left to John Buchanan, the coach of the Australian team, and Ian Healy, the former Australian wicketkeeper.

For those that don't want to go all the way to Australia, *The Chappell Way* might soon come to India. 'We are hoping to start Greg Chappell Clinics in various schools and sports academies across India from June. There is talk also of an AISA team touring India, playing and conducting Chappell Way Clinics,' said Dell.

The first such 'clinic' will be in Bangalore's Jain Academy of Sporting Excellence, run by R. Chenraj Jain. The fee hasn't been fixed yet.

Also in the pipeline is a reality TV show, from which the winner will get an all-expenses paid trip to Australia for *The Chappell Way* package, which Shibad describes as 'Greg's personally researched and patented mode of training'.

'Though *The Chappell Way* is generally brought to young cricketers through CD-ROMs and online interactive sessions, the Indian coach has designed a special in situ programme in Australia specifically for Indians. It shows his commitment towards India,' Shibad said.

The online programme is not available for Indians.

'The programme has been researched for the past five years using footage of all the great batting and bowling performances. A lot of this has been slowed down and analysed to see what makes these players great. This is the basis of the cricket programme brought to India by some of Australia's best coaches and communicators, people that have helped make Australia a great cricketing nation,' he said. Cricket academies in Mumbai charge between Rs 60,000 and Rs 80,000 for a two-month summer package, compared with two weeks in *The Chappell Way*.

For many youngsters hoping to sign up for the India coach's package, there's also the trip to Australia to look forward to, not counting the brag value among peers.

'My dad has promised to send me for the programme during summer vacations. I am in the process of getting all the details. They have tied up with Qantas and the airline is giving discounted air fares to students going for *The Chappell Way* programme,' says Ayub Bandookwala, 15.[59]

This is another key characteristic of life in the global economy – the commercially strategic presentation of self, using one's life, achievements and personal 'philosophy' as a purported navigational aid between newly enriched middle-class children and the dreams (cricket greatness, meeting/being coached by a celebrity . . .) now held out to them. In another example of this, for twenty-five years, from its inception in 1987 to 2012, ex-Australian fast bowler Dennis Lillee ran the MRF Pace Foundation in Chennai, trading on Lillee's reputation as a player, forged in the 1970s (70 Tests 1971–84, 355 wickets) and on India's fabled shortage of indigenous pace bowling resources. He was succeeded by fellow Australian Glenn McGrath (124 Tests 1993–2007, 563 wickets).[60]

The presence of eminent ex-cricketers in the coaching and commentating market sometimes made for friction with the coaches who had never played cricket at a high level: they threatened the credibility of ex-Test captains as consultants. It's perhaps not a coincidence that Greg Chappell's elder brother Ian, another ex-Australian captain and, like Warne, now one of a legion of ex-larrikin pundits on the Australian cricket scene, became a strident critic of coaching. 'I've often stated: "An international coach is something the Australian team travels in around England."', he said in 2015. 'While I haven't changed my opinion in the intervening years, coaches are now a way of life in international cricket'.[61]

In 2016 the international coaching scene produced probably its most piquant controversy to date. For their tour of Sri Lanka the Australian Cricket Board hired Lankan national bowling hero Muttiah Muralitharan as bowling coach. When Sri Lanka were all out for 117 on the first day of the First Test, there were accusations that Murali was a traitor to the Sri Lankan cause. Sri Lanka Cricket president Thilanga Sumathipala pointed out that back in the 1990s Australians had been among the most vociferous critics of Murali's bowling action: 'Professionally it is OK for Murali to coach any foreign team, but the irony is that he is supporting Australia which tried to get him out of cricket'.[62]

Conclusion: 'there are just not enough players thinking about cricket'

At the highest level the new coaching represents a conjoining of sport, science and business. Coaches are now part of the routine explanation of success and failure in cricket, something that was established in other sports – such as football, where virtually all explanations are channelled through the football manager – a generation earlier. In cricket, this role, historically, was ascribed to the captain. Now first-class cricket is transacted like any other form of commerce and is acquiring a vocabulary to match. For example, when 33-year-old Andrew McDonald, another of the new school of Australian coaches, became head coach of the English county of Leicestershire in 2014, he recruited as captain a fellow Australian, who he said possessed 'a serious skill-set'.[63] There was talk in the local press about changes to the 'coaching structure' and the activities of the 'backroom staff' and McDonald himself took the title 'Elite Performance Director'. This vocabulary would have been unthinkable in most cricket domains before the 1990s. Some cricketers have clearly welcomed it as an extra dimension of their professionalism and several cricket coaches have started taking clients for their problem-solving services from a wider public. In 2005, for example, ex-county cricketer and sport psychologist Jeremy Snape set up a company called 'Sporting Edge' which, according to its website, 'is a high performance consultancy that helps business leaders, elite teams and global organisations stay ahead of the game'.[64] Similarly, South African Paddy Upton, coach to T20 teams in the IPL and Australia's Big Bash League, also works as a consultant and has 'successfully coached a variety of elite sport and business teams and individuals to take their game to even greater heights'.[65] Nevertheless it is still contested, often being seen as an affront to common sense and individual initiative, and players could always be found to echo the scepticism about 'new wave' cricket coaching expressed in Australia by Warne and Ian Chappell. Recently, for example, England players Kevin Pietersen and Graeme Swann agreed that 'England have become too reliant on computer analysis to tell them what to do'.[66] And in 2013 ex-England captain Michael Vaughan (whose coach in the Ashes victory of 2005, Duncan Fletcher, was awarded an OBE in 2005, along with the players) wrote of England's Ashes defeat in 2013: 'There are just not enough players thinking about cricket. It appears that too many of the tactics and strategies are being delivered to them by an analyst sat at a computer given the lack of "cricket thought" out in the middle with the bat, ball and field settings'.[67] England took a squad of eighteeen to play the Ashes Tests of 2013 and the same number of support staff.

Notes

1 Stephen Wagg '"Time, gentlemen, please": the decline of amateur captaincy in English county cricket' in *Contemporary British History* Vol.14 No.2 Summer 2000 pp.31–59.
2 Stephen Wagg and Sharda Ugra 'Different hats, different thinking? Technocracy, globalization and the Indian cricket team' *Sport in Society* Vol.12 Nos. 4–5 2009 pp.600–12. I wrote the article, using material and suggestions supplied by Sharda.
3 Mike Selvey 'Alf Gover' [Obituary] *The Guardian* 10 October 2001 https://www.theguardian.com/news/2001/oct/10/guardianobituaries.cricket Access 5 May 2017.
4 Selvey 'Alf Gover'.
5 Quoted in David Lemmon *The Crisis of Captaincy: Servant and Master in English Cricket* London: Christopher Helm 1988 p.28.
6 Lemmon *The Crisis* p.40.
7 Rayleigh G. Strutt *Schoolboy Cricket: The Boys' and Masters' Guide* London: Hutchinson 1952 p.52.
8 Strutt *Schoolboy* pp.76–7.
9 Marylebone Cricket Club *The MCC Cricket Coaching Book* London: William Heinemann Ltd 1968 p.1 (first published London: The Naldrett Press 1952).
10 See Mike Marqusee 'The thump of humbug on willow' *The Guardian* 17 July 2006 https://www.theguardian.com/commentisfree/2006/jul/17/disspiritofcricket Access 5 May 2017.
11 Paul Coupar 'England's coaching conundrum: looking back to go forward' *The Guardian* 9 January 2009 https://www.theguardian.com/sport/2009/jan/09/englandcricketteam-peter-moores Access 5 May 2017.
12 Martin Johnson 'Cricket: end of the innings for Mr 120 per cent: Micky Stewart's reign as England team manager comes to a close on Monday' *The Independent* 21 August 1992 http://www.independent.co.uk/sport/cricket-end-of-the-innings-for-mr-120-per-cent-micky-stewarts-reign-as-england-team-manager-comes-to-1541869.html Access 5 May 2017.
13 David Lloyd, with Alan Lee *David Lloyd: The Autobiography* London: Collins Willow 2000 p.169.
14 Viv Richards *Hitting Across the Line* London: BCA/Headline 1991.
15 Ramachandra Guha *India After Gandhi: The History of the World's Largest Democracy* London: HarperCollins 2008 p.737.
16 John Wright, with Sharda Ugra and Paul Thomas *John Wright's Indian Summers* New Delhi: Viking 2006 p.13.
17 Bob Woolmer, with Ivo Tennant *Woolmer on Cricket* London: Virgin Publishing 2000 p.8.
18 See Hilary McD. Beckles *The Development of West Indies Cricket: Volume 2 The Age of Globalization* London: Pluto Press 1998 p.163.
19 See Tim Hector 'One eye on the ball, one eye on the world: cricket, West Indian nationalism and the spirit of C.L.R. James' (compiled and with editorial commentary by Stephen Wagg) in Stephen Wagg (ed.) *Cricket and National Identity in the Postcolonial Age* London: Routledge 2005 pp.159–68.
20 Jo Harman 'Warnie v Buck' http://www.espncricinfo.com/magazine/content/story/912649.html Posted 24 August 2015, Access 6 May 2017.
21 Sambit Bal 'The malaise of bitterness' http://www.espncricinfo.com/magazine/content/story/131785.html Posted 4 November 2003, Access 6 May 2017.
22 See, for example, Andy Bull 'John Buchanan: "Complete fraud" or cricketing mastermind?' *The Guardian* 3 September 2009 https://www.theguardian.com/sport/2009/sep/03/john-buchanan-interview-australia Access 6 May 2017.

23 Suggested by Indian cricket writer Sharda Ugra, email to author 18 February 2007.
24 'S Africa appoint Arthur as coach' http://news.bbc.co.uk/sport1/hi/cricket/other_international/south_africa/4562945.stm Access 15 May 2017.
25 Mike Selvey 'Chappell rides bumps on road paved with passion and pop-star idolatry' http://sport.guardian.co.uk/englandinindia/story/0,,1720518,00.html Posted 1 March 2006, Access 6 May 2017.
26 'Chappell asks players to make their own destiny' http://www.hindu.com/2005/07/14/stories/2005071404312000.htm Posted 14 July 2005, Access 6 May 2017.
27 'Chappell asks' See Edward de Bono *Six Thinking Hats* London: Little, Brown 1985.
28 'Chappell asks'.
29 http://www.deccanherald.com/deccanherald/jul142005/sports1746312005713.asp Access 5 December 2006. No longer available.
30 http://www.answers.com/topic/sourav-ganguly Access 27 February 2007.
31 'Ganguly unfit to lead: Chappell e-mails BCCI' http://in.rediff.com/cricket/2005/sep/23gang.htm Posted 23 September 2005, Access 6 May 2017.
32 'Text of Greg Chappell's email' *Sydney Morning Herald* 26 September 2005 http://www.smh.com.au/news/cricket/text-of-greg-chappells-email/2005/09/26/1127586778800.html Access 6 May 2017.
33 'You can't have it both ways: Frazer' http://m.rediff.com/cricket/2005/oct/04ian.htm Posted 4 October 2005, Access 6 May 2017.
34 *India Today* 10 December 2005 pp.70–1, 76.
35 *India Today* 10 December 2005 p.78.
36 *India Today* 12 December 2005 p.58.
37 'Science in Sehwag art' http://www.indianexpress.com/res/web/pIe/full_story.php?content_id=86108 Posted 18 January 2006, Access 7 May 2017.
38 http://www.indianexpress.com/printerFriendly/5825.html Posted 6 June 2006, Access 5 December 2006.
39 'Kapil clueless on his role as NCA chief' http://www.tribuneindia.com/2006/20061013/sports.htm#2 Posted 12 October 2006, Access 7 May 2017.
40 Ajay S. Shankar 'Politicians bay for his head but Chappell looks to future, won't say no to post-World Cup stint' http://www.indianexpress.com/story/17276.html Posted 25 November 2006, Access 5 December 2006.
41 *Calcutta Times* 5 December 2006.
42 http://cricket.expressindia.com/fulleistory.php?content_id=77982 Access 13 December 2006.
43 Alex Brown 'India's out but Buchanan keeps options open' *Sydney Morning Herald* 4 May 2007 http://www.smh.com.au/news/cricket/indias-out-but-buchanan-keeps-options-open/2007/05/03/1177788317374.html Access 7 May 2017.
44 http://www.merinews.com/catFull.jsp?articleID123885&category=Sports&catID=5... Access 23 February 2007.
45 Simon Hughes *Yakking Around the World* London: Simon and Schuster 2000 p.209.
46 http://www.sportstaronnet.com/stories/20061202010701200.htm Posted 2 December 2006, Access 12 December 2006.
47 Edward W. Said *Orientalism* Harmondsworth: Penguin 1995.
48 Hilary McD. Beckles *The Development of West Indies Cricket*.
49 Hector 'One eye on the ball'.
50 Sharda Ugra 'Play together, live apart: religion, politics and markets in Indian cricket since 1947' in Stephen Wagg (ed.) *Cricket and National Identity* pp.77–93, p.89.

51 Selvey 'Chappell rides bumps'.
52 Ugra 'Play together' p.86.
53 E.P. Thompson 'Time, work-discipline and industrial capitalism' *Past and Present* No.38 1967 p.57. Quoted in Nick Couldry 'Reality TV, or the secret theatre of neoliberalism' https://core.ac.uk/download/pdf/16380907.pdf Access 7 May 2017.
54 Couldry 'Reality TV' p.1.
55 Adrian McGregor *Greg Chappell* London: Collins 1985 p.263.
56 Sunil Khilnani *The Idea of India* London: Penguin 1998 pp.147–8.
57 'Cricket legend Greg Chappell's coaching is now available to all Indians' http://www.1888pressrelease.com/cricket-legend-greg-chappell-s-coaching-is-now-available-to-pr-13ieu6u31.html Posted 24 March 2006, Access 28 February 2007.
58 Samyabrata Ray Goswami 'Pay & Chappell way is yours – Australian company sells cricket training package' http://www.telegraphindia.com/1060331/asp/frontpage/story¬_6038422.asp Posted 31 March 2006, Access 15 May 2017.
59 Goswami 'Pay'.
60 ESPNcricinfo staff 'McGrath takes charge of MRF Pace Foundation' http://www.espncricinfo.com/india/content/current/story/580431.html Posted 2 September 2012, Access 7 May 2017.
61 Ian Chappell 'It's the captain who wins games, not the coach' http://www.espncricinfo.com/magazine/content/story/882341.html Posted 31 May 2015, Access 7 May 2017.
62 'Sri Lanka v Australia: Muttiah Muralitharan hits back at "traitor" jibe' http://www.bbc.co.uk/sport/cricket/36891957 Posted 26 July 2016, Access 15 May 2017.
63 Paul Jones 'Cricket: Leicestershire head coach Andrew McDonald eager to be part of "exciting direction"' *Leicester Mercury* 2 April 2015 http://www.leicestermercury.co.uk/cricket-leicestershire-head-coach-andrew-mcdonald/story-26273144-detail/story.html Access 7 May 2017.
64 http://www.sportingedge.com/sporting-edge-about.html Access 7 May 2017.
65 http://www.paddyupton.com/#ad-image-1 Access 7 May 2017.
66 Andy Bull 'Cricket's great data debate: art v science' *The Guardian* 3 March 2015 https://www.theguardian.com/sport/2015/mar/03/the-spin-cricket-data-analysis-art-science Access 7 May 2017.
67 Michael Vaughan 'Ashes 2013–14: odd selections, timid tactics – England have forgotten their instincts' *The Telegraph* 30 December 2013 http://www.telegraph.co.uk/sport/cricket/international/theashes/10542852/Ashes-2013-14-Odd-selections-timid-tactics-England-have-forgotten-their-instincts.html Access 7 May 2017.

Chapter 16

Beyond the boundaries
The drive to globalise cricket, and its limits

Pakistani banking and real estate businessman Ehsan Mani, who was President of the International Cricket Council between 2003 and 2006, once said 'Cricket cannot call itself a global game when one-fifth of the world's population is not aware of it.'[1] For a sport such as cricket which grew initially within the contours of the British Empire, it might not seem so surprising that one-fifth of the world's population were unfamiliar with it. However, as we have seen in the preceding chapters, the age of British stewardship of cricket seems now to be over; after all, the game's governing body moved their offices to Dubai in 2005. Besides, as Rob Steen suggested in 2010, 'the growth of cricket in recent times should on no account be underestimated. Nor should the ambition of its administrators'. He went on to note the admission of Kenya, Holland, Ireland and Scotland to the senior one-day international circuit and the burgeoning number of ICC affiliates.[2] Nevertheless there have been factors that placed perceptible limits on this ambition. One set of factors relate to the fact that, in the view of many contemporary critics, the ICC now operates less as a benevolent cricket missionary and more as a self-enriching *de facto* oligarchy of three nations: India, Australia and England. The other set is constituted by the obstacles faced by cricket administrators and promoters in pursuit of their avowed aim to make cricket a genuinely world game. The chapter represents an extension and updating of previous work, published originally in 2010.[3]

In the first instance, cricket's governing bodies have faced problems in maintaining the *existing* scope of international cricket competition, never mind extending it. These difficulties, adapting the now-famous terms set out by C.L.R. James lie, it will be suggested, both within and beyond the boundary.[4] There will then be a discussion of which countries have seemed to promise the most fertile cultural soil for the planting and/or full-scale development of cricket and an analysis of two key areas of the current purported evangelism and promotion of the game: the United States and the People's Republic of China.

Cricket and the beginnings of globalisation: from 'imperial' to 'international'

What is now the International Cricket Council was formed in 1909 as the Imperial Cricket Conference. It was based narrowly on the key 'white' dominions of the British Empire, England, Australia and South Africa being its only founding members. With what, in retrospect, must seem a considerable irony, the limits to the globalisation of cricket began to be set even then. The United States, who in 1859, with Canada, had hosted England on the world's first tour by an international cricket team, was excluded. As we saw in Chapter 3 the establishing of the ICC was largely on the initiative of the South African 'Randlord', mining magnate Sir Abe Bailey, and was aimed at cementing imperial and business links with London, where Bailey spent much of his time.[5] Bailey, a friend and political ally of Cecil Rhodes and English imperialist Winston Churchill,[6] had failed to persuade England and Australia to take part in a 'tri-cornered summer of cricket in England involving the hosts, Australia and South Africa'; he has been described as 'basest of racists'.[7]

As we have seen in the earlier chapters, the ICC expanded slowly and within its imperial framework: New Zealand – another 'white' dominion – India and West Indies were all admitted in 1926. Pakistan joined in 1953, following the partition of India in 1947. Still with only seven members, the ICC was re-named the International Cricket Conference in 1965 – recognition of the onset of the formally post-colonial era. Further evidence of this recognition came with the expulsion, however reluctant, of apartheid South Africa in 1971. The ICC, it should be said, came late to an acknowledgement of the anti-racist movement in international sport which had gained strength with the emergence of new, decolonised nations during the 1960s and which had helped provoke South Africa's exclusion from the Olympics of 1964 and 1968. Only a year before South Africa had ceased to be a member of the ICC, a racially exclusive South African team had been invited to tour England, the invitation only being withdrawn at the behest of the British Labour government. As noted in Chapter 3, Home Secretary James Callaghan was concerned about public order and about probable consequences for (mostly likely withdrawals from) the Commonwealth Games, scheduled for later that summer in Edinburgh. Recent evidence suggests, however, that the decision was a close-run thing and that the British government had even considered charging anti-apartheid protestor Peter Hain with seditious conspiracy for threatening to disrupt the cricket tour.[8] (Seditious conspiracy was a serious offence with its roots in highly repressive legislation of the late eighteenth and early nineteenth centuries – several Seditious Meetings Acts were passed during that time.)

This cannot have enhanced cricket's standing among newly independent nations. After 1965, the ICC began, somewhat belatedly, to seek members from both within and outside of what was now the British Commonwealth. Fiji, for example, were admitted in 1965, along with the USA, followed by Bermuda, Denmark and the Netherlands in 1966, Malaysia in 1967, Canada in 1968 and Gibraltar and Hong Kong in 1969. Although steady recruitment has continued, full membership of ICC, which changed its name to the International Cricket Council in 1989, has, as we have seen, not advanced beyond ten.

Only these ten full members of the ICC are permitted to play Test matches. There are, at the time of writing, thirty-nine Associate Members – countries where the ICC deems cricket to be 'firmly established'[9] and which participate in various limited-over competitions – and a further fifty-six nations are currently listed as Affiliate Members – that is, simply countries where the ICC recognises cricket as being played according to the established laws of the game. Some of these latter territories are vast – the People's Republic of China, for instance – and some are not: the Cook Islands, Cyprus, the Falkland Islands, the Isle of Man, the Maldives, St Helena and the Turk and Caicos Islands (the population of which is about 30,000) make up seven of the fifty-six. These 105 countries constitute little more than half the current members of the United Nations – currently 193 – and are spread across five administrative regions: Africa, the Americas, Asia, East Asia and the Pacific and Europe.

Given that for much of the game's recent history Test cricket was its most prestigious and lucrative form, drawing crowds and television revenue when regional, district or county cricket could not, ten full members, out of 193, is not an unduly promising basis for globalisation. Moreover, it is equally manifest that great difficulties now attend the playing of cricket in most of the Test-playing countries. These difficulties lie, as seen in earlier chapters, both within, and beyond, the boundary.

Turning, first of all, to the obstacles to globalisation that lie within cricket culture, these are principally twofold. First, as has been made evident in earlier parts of the book, cricket has begun to lose its appeal, both at the level of participation and as a spectator sport, in several countries. For instance, West Indian cricket is widely accepted to be in long-term crisis: indeed, as observed in Chapter 5, so poor has the West Indies' playing record been since the early 1990s that, in 2007, the influential *Jamaica Gleaner* called on the West Indies Cricket Board to withdraw from Test and major one-day international cricket for two to three years, in order to develop younger Caribbean players to the required standard.[10] Moreover, West Indies Test cricketers have several times in the last twenty years threatened strike action – something unthinkable in what Beckles describes as West Indies 'age of nationalism'.[11] In England fewer and fewer schools play cricket, local clubs regularly cancel fixtures because they can't raise a team and county championship matches are very sparsely attended. Similarly, in New Zealand and Australia regional games attract little interest. Even in India, where cricket is genuinely popular culture, regional games, such as the Ranji Trophy, have scant appeal. There is little enthusiasm to play cricket among the black Zimbabwean majority, cricket having been fostered there by the white settler minority when the country bore the name of the imperialist Cecil Rhodes and was subsequently proselytised by the deeply unpopular and autocratic Robert Mugabe, president since independence. As noted in Chapter 3, Mugabe once said, improbably for a one-time Marxist and opponent of colonial and white settler administrations, that: 'Cricket civilizes people and creates good gentlemen. I want everyone to play cricket in Zimbabwe; I want ours to be a nation of gentlemen.'[12] When, however, fifteen white members of the nation's cricket team went on strike and were dismissed in 2004, the Zimbabwe Cricket Union was obliged to suspend its participation in international cricket, too few credible cricketers being available from among Zimbabwe's black majority.

The English county championship, dating from the late nineteenth century, has survived a number of premature obituaries and there is no doubting the periodic purchase that cricket has on the national imagination – especially during the biennial 'Ashes' tournaments between England and Australia. Indeed, an England victory in one of these series, as in 2005 and again in 2009, will likely bring forth defiant assertions that Test cricket still has an audience – and, therefore, a future – in England.[13] But cricket's roots run conspicuously less deep than fifty years ago, particularly in the public education system. For recruitment, in addition to its historic seedbed of the private schools, first-class cricket relies increasingly on the elite academies, run by the counties or universities with a sport science provision, and on straightforward co-option: white South or southern Africans, it is fair to say, have been a regular feature of the England cricket team since the late 1970s and several recent England players were born and spent the early part of their lives in South Africa including captain Andrew Strauss (100 Tests 2004–12), wicketkeeper Matt Prior (79 Tests 2004–11) and batsmen Kevin Pietersen (104 Tests 2005–14), Jonathan Trott (52 Tests 2009–15) and Keaton Jennings (2 Tests 2016). Jennings is the son of one-time South Africa national coach Ray Jennings.

Second, again as argued in earlier parts of the book, the long-established four- and five- day formats to which first-class cricket has been wedded for so long, may be thought to have a limited future in the postmodern era with its 24-hour cities, multiple leisure options and low boredom thresholds. They last too long for many sports enthusiasts around the world to comprehend and, to widespread international consternation, they can still, after several days' travail, produce no winner. In this regard, the Twenty20 format has met the new leisure imperatives.

Looking beyond the boundary, there seem to be, once again, two strong grounds for pessimism about the future of Test, and perhaps other forms of, cricket. First, poverty greatly afflicts huge swathes of several of the countries that play it – most notably Zimbabwe, where inflation for July 2008 alone was estimated at 47%, Bangladesh and (most) areas of the English-speaking Caribbean. In Bangladesh there is dire poverty by Western standards and Western companies exploit the low-wage Bangladeshi economy: in 2006 skilled garment workers in Bangladesh making products for the Western supermarket chains Primark, Tesco, and Asda were earning a maximum of £16 a month. At the time a living wage in the country was set by economists at £22 per month.[14] A population struggling to subsist is not the most promising market for the sale of Test match tickets. And in the Caribbean, the leading political and cultural commentator Leonard 'Tim' Hector continually argued that the decline of West Indian cricket was linked to the impoverishment of the Caribbean nations visited on them by the privatisation directives of international financial institutions, such as the World Bank and the International Monetary Fund. This 'structural adjustment', to borrow the euphemism favoured by these institutions themselves, had brought forth 'structurally adjusted cricketers'.[15] Moreover, the cricket World Cup of 2007, staged in the Caribbean, while claimed as a commercial success by its organising committee and apparently bringing unprecedentedly high ticket sales[16] is said to have failed in its objective of regenerating interest in cricket on the islands and saddled individual host governments – particularly those of Jamaica and Barbados – with huge debts. One central problem appeared to be the high price of the tickets, which was beyond the pocket of most local people.[17]

All this raises the questions of whether an economic base exists to sustain Test cricket and whether sufficient discretionary income is available in these countries to interest any advertisers who might buy into a televised cricket series.

Moreover, turning now to the second set of problems, several of these countries have severe political difficulties – Sri Lanka over Tamil separatism (currently in abeyance, perhaps, after the military defeat in 2009 of the LTTE or 'Tamil Tigers' who had sought to establish a separate Tamil state in the north and east of the island); Pakistan over its ambiguous stance on Islamism and the Western-defined 'war on terror' and, more specifically, over the attack by gunmen on the Sri Lankan cricket team in the Pakistani city of Lahore in March of 2009, following which the ICC ruled that Pakistan would have to play their matches abroad until further notice; Zimbabwe for much of the twenty-first century on the verge of civil war. In any event, Zimbabwe withdrew from Test cricket between 2004 and 2011. These difficulties readily translate into issues of 'security', deterring players, TV companies and sponsors. All this helped to place many of the Test-playing countries in a weak bargaining position.

Of the thirty-nine Associate Members of the ICC, the majority were recruited after 1989; of its fifty-six Affiliate Members, only two were admitted before 1989 and over two-thirds joined after 2000. On the face of it these recent additions strongly suggest a promotional drive. After all, the ICC is a commercial organisation (its new domicile in Dubai was chosen for the purposes of tax avoidance), and is, supposedly, bent on expanding its markets. But many of these markets lack any obvious promise. There are, as we've seen, a number of constituent countries that cover small geographical areas and have low population figures (Bermuda, the Cayman Islands, Jersey, the Cook Islands, Tonga, the Turks and Caicos Islands . . .) and, equally, there are member countries across the various continents that seem unlikely to develop strong cricket cultures in any foreseeable future – Belgium, Germany, Spain, Greece, Italy, Japan, Brazil, Cameroon, Rwanda, Qatar and Saudi Arabia among them. A recent comic memoir by the writer Angus Bell derives its humour from the improbability of playing cricket in Eastern Europe.[18] And so on.

There are, of course, areas of somewhat greater promise. Some countries have had a sustained, but secluded, place for cricket in their sport cultures. An example here is Denmark, where cricket has been played since the mid-nineteenth century, having been taken there by British railway engineers. As noted, Denmark has been a member of the ICC since 1966. The country has, however, only produced a handful (around half a dozen) professional cricketers – the first of whom was Ole Mortensen, who played in the county championship for Derbyshire between 1983 and 1994. The national team relies heavily on Pakistani Danes, although Denmark is less reliant than, say, Norway (ICC members since 2000), on migrant cricketers. Arguably Denmark's best player has been Amjad Khan, who was born into a Pakistani family in Copenhagen in 1980 and played for Denmark at the age of 17. He signed for Kent, in the English county championship, in 2001 and in 2006 he qualified for England. He made his debut for the England Test team in the West Indies in March of 2009. Khan's case demonstrates the difficulty that smaller nations have in assembling an internationally credible team, given the competitive nature of cricket's global labour market and the flexibility with which nationality is now defined in international sport.

The most progressive European cricket nation, however, is Ireland. Here, as in the West Indies and elsewhere, cricket began as a garrison game, brought by British soldiers, and was first played in the early eighteenth century. It was popular for a while but shunned by many Irish people for being middle class and because it was associated with the British occupation.[19] In 1884 the Gaelic Athletic Association (GAA) had imposed a boycott of British sports; anyone playing or watching such sports would be banned from participating in sports organised by the GAA. This ban was not lifted until 1971. Cricket therefore carried a stigma in Ireland. It is said that the republican politician and founder of Fianna Fáil Eamon de Valera once dropped a cricket bat he was using to demonstrate some cricket strokes when he saw a photographer approaching: 'He knew that a photo like that would mean he wouldn't be invited to Croke Park, the home of Gaelic football'.[20]

The Irish Cricket Union had been founded in 1925 but Ireland did not become a member of the ICC until 1993. Ireland had famously beaten the West Indian touring team in 1969, bowling them out for only 25 at the ground of Sion Mills Cricket Club in County Tyrone, but forty years later their players were still predominantly amateurs and their operation makeshift: South African Adrian Birrell was told when he became Irish national coach in 2007 that the team's kit was stored in the boot of a car.[21] The 'Celtic Tiger' economic boom of the 1990s, however, had brought workers, including some good cricketers, to Ireland[22] and the process of professionalisation was strengthened in 2006 with the appointment of a Chief Executive – Warren Deutrom, who had previously worked for a sports hospitality company.[23] In 2007 they dropped their captain Jason Molins, apparently because he lived in London (where he worked in finance) and had to fly to Ireland for cricket.[24] In 2009 player contracts were introduced and in 2015 twenty-four players were contracted; moreover 'between 2006 and 2013, the total number of cricket players in Ireland almost quadrupled, from 12,202 to 43,838. Ten of the eleven Ireland players that beat the West Indies in its first match at the 2015 Cricket World Cup were born and raised in Ireland'.[25] Commercial revenue had increased but Ireland now needed Test status, largely to stem the flow of defections. As with other forms of Irish labour, a number of the best Irish cricketers had migrated to England. Several of the country's best cricketers – including Ed Joyce (born in Dublin in 1978) Eoin Morgan (born in Dublin in 1986) and Boyd Rankin (born in Derry, Northern Ireland in 1984) – had all played for England. Joyce played for England in the World Cup of 2007, having played for Ireland in the qualifying stages.[26] Morgan became captain of the England ODI team in 2015.

The most dramatically emergent cricket culture, however, is in Afghanistan.

Cricket, plus the shooting: Afghanistan

Perhaps surprisingly for a territory associated historically with British imperialism, Afghanistan only affiliated to the ICC in 2001. Despite fighting three wars there in the nineteenth century, the British, however, never established a full colonial administration in Afghanistan. They saw it instead as a buffer state between the British and Russian empires, in what historians have called 'the Great Game'.[27] Cricket has been played in Afghanistan since the nineteenth century but its recent flourishing there is said to be product of occupation by the USSR (1979–89) and the subsequent civil war between the army and supporters of the left-wing Afghan government and the Islamist Taliban. During this war 2 million Afghans crossed the border into Pakistan and settled among people with whom they already had a common language – Pushto – their separation being a legacy of one of the Anglo-Afghan wars and the drawing of the so-called

Durand Line in 1893. Many learned to play cricket in refugee camps in northern Pakistan.[28] There was also shared television coverage of cricket across Afghanistan and northern Pakistan. National coach Taj Malik Alam told the Global Cricket website:

> After the Russian occupation of Afghanistan, millions of Afghans fled to Pakistan where they saw cricket being played on television. Many youths found trust in this game. In 1998 we announced trials for the national cricket team and hundreds of people came and were keen to play for Afghanistan. The journey started then and now we are knocking on the international door.[29]

The Afghanistan Cricket Federation was formed in 1995 and the country affiliated to the ICC in 2001, the same year as a national team was constituted. 'We aim to become an ICC full member', said Alam, 'have ODI status and have at least five major grounds in Afghanistan. I can say we can beat strong teams in the world.'[30]

Although it competed with the traditional sport of *bushkazi* (conducted on horseback), Alam claimed cricket to be the number one sport in Afghanistan, with 12,000 regular players.[31] It was designated a national sport by the Afghan Ministry for Sport and sponsored by the Roshan Telecoms – a cell phone company owned by an international consortium of investors led by the Aga Khan Fund for Economic Development (AKFED), Monaco Telecom International (MTI) and Swedish–Finnish TeliaSonera. This consortium was Afghanistan's largest private employer. In a lengthy interview posted on the Asian Cricket Council's website in March of 2005 Taj Malik Alam asserted that the Afghanistan cricket team could already 'beat Sri Lanka A and Bangladesh A if given the chance'.[32]

Cricket, it was thought, could be politically important in building a secular modern/Westernised hegemony to counter the Islamised severity of the Taliban and the equally brutal traditional authority of the nation's warlords. Indeed the Taliban, generally speaking hostile to most forms of entertainment, soon recognised the popularity of the game. They readily permitted the playing of cricket and paid for the Afghanistan team's equipment on a tour of Pakistan in 2001.

Ilyas Khan, a journalist who writes regularly on Afghan issues, believes the Taliban agreed to the Pakistani request for a cricket tour to soften its image as a reactionary group. 'Through cricket they are trying to put up a benign face which is more in line with modern times,' he says. 'It's a public-relations stunt to create good will among the people.'[33]

On top of this, the previous year, as revealed by cricket writer Tim Wigmore, the Taliban had 'urged the Afghanistan Cricket Federation to write to the Pakistan Cricket Board requesting support to join the International Cricket Council as an affiliate member. In cricket the Taliban saw a sport that could both promote the regime at home and gain some acceptance abroad'. In time cricket was strongest where the Taliban was strongest.[34] The latter had resolved that cricket resembled the old Afghan game of top danda and that cricket clothing 'accommodated religious and cultural requirements'.[35] Predictably, Afghan women cricketers were less fortunate: despite forming a team in 2010, largely through the efforts of Diana Barakzai, the players were vigorously opposed by mullahs, received threats and disbanded in 2013.[36]

In October 2015, only fourteen years after they had joined the ICC, Afghanistan toured Zimbabwe and beat the home team 3–2 in an ODI series. When they returned home, according to Uthra Ganesan in *The Hindu*, 'it took four hours to complete the 15-minute drive to the Kabul National Cricket Stadium. On Sunday, the entire stretch was once again packed with celebrating Afghans after the feat was repeated, this time at "home" in Sharjah'.[37] In less than two decades Afghanistan had achieved membership of the small, exclusively Asian club of cricket-crazy nations:

> 'The craze began after the 2010 T20 World Cup in the West Indies when the team and the game exploded in the media and on television screens. Then the World Cup last year and now these two series at home and away against Zimbabwe have ensured that, irrespective of age or gender, everyone in Afghanistan follows every performance of the team,' said Tawab Zafarzai, cricket operations manager of Afghanistan Cricket Board.[38]

By now Afghanistan had established cricket leagues in thirty-two of its thirty-four provinces; it had eighty cricket grounds and a thriving professional T20 tournament – the Etisalat Sixes, inaugurated in 2013 and sponsored by a multinational telecommunications corporation based in Abu Dhabi.[39] Early in 2017 Cricinfo reported that 'Afghanistan's progress towards Test status and Full Membership at the ICC took a big step forward after the country's domestic four-day and Twenty20 tournaments were awarded first-class and List A status respectively'.[40]

Afghan cricket has received a lot of help from other nations. The United Arab Emirates and Sri Lanka have both hosted Afghanistan matches and India has given Afghanistan the use of the new Greater Noida stadium outside New Delhi. India and Germany have funded the building of new stadia in Afghanistan – India in Kandahar, the country's second largest city, and Germany in Khost (in the mountainous region near the border with Pakistan).[41]

In 2013 Wigmore asked: 'The national team is making headlines, their domestic cricket is thriving, and money is not an issue. So what's holding them back?' He observed in particular:

The attitude of the Asian Cricket Council. You might think that the Asia Cup would be the perfect opportunity for Afghanistan to get some more experience against Full Members. But the tournament is now an invite-only affair for the four Asian Full Members; Afghanistan are denied even an opportunity to qualify. As Noor [Muhammad, Chief Executive of the Afghanistan board] tersely puts it, 'We are not allowed to play in Asia Cup, which is very disappointing and we have been not even provided with justification'.[42]

It had been suggested that Afghanistan's application for Test status could well fail, however, because of its failure to support the development of women's cricket.[43] That, of course, would have been a perfectly valid reason. However, by this time, a fierce critique of the ICC's role was now gaining currency in cricket circles around the world and this critique was crystallised in a documentary film. The essence of this critique was to question whether the ICC any longer intended to evangelise cricket around the world.

Does cricket make money in order to exist or does it exist to make money? *The Death of a Gentleman*

The documentary film *Death of a Gentleman* was released in 2015.[44] It was made by a team of four men: Sam Collins, Jarrod Kimber, Christopher Hird and Johnny Blank. Collins, a Londoner, and Kimber, an Australian, had both edited cricket publications. Hird, the executive producer, was a leading maker of documentary films, some of which took a critical, leftist stance – *Still the Enemy Within*, for example, which was a retrospective about the miners' strike in the UK in 1984–5, and *The End of the Line*, a critique of over-fishing on the high seas. The title of this new film seemed to have been inspired by the Arthur Miller play *Death of a Salesman*, a parable of disillusionment, first performed on Broadway in 1949. The film was provoked by what many cricket chroniclers have rendered as the 'power grab' of 2014 – a proposal that 62% of ICC revenue would now be channelled to the cricket boards of India, Australia and England. The deal had been sealed by Cricket Australia chairman and company owner Wally Edwards, Somerset chairman and wealthy businessman Giles Clarke of the ECB and ICC chair Narayanaswami Srinivasan, managing director of the India Cements and owner of an franchise in the Indian Premier League (IPL). In 2014, perhaps as a sign of the times, Srinivasan was restrained by the Supreme Court of India from holding the chairmanship of the BCCI while allegations of corrupt practices in relation to the IPL were investigated.

The move/'grab' had garnered little support among cricket correspondents. Scyld Berry in the British right-wing *Daily Telegraph* had seen it as cancelling whatever claim cricket still had to moral superiority: 'In future, the rich cricket countries will get richer. It is the same everywhere else in the world, of course, but this spits in the face of cricket. If it does anything of value, the sport promotes fair play on a level playing field'.[45] In *The Australian* ex-England captain Mike Atherton had also declared the passing of 'a noble ideal', adding:

> As with most things, money is at the heart of this power grab. At the moment, any surplus from the $US1.5 billion ($1.59bn) deal for ICC events (over an eight-year cycle) is shared equally, 75 per cent to the full members and the rest to the associates and affiliates. During the next cycle, India will get the lion's share, with England and Australia receiving the majority of the scraps.[46]

In the film, respected Australian cricket writer Gideon Haigh asked whether cricket makes money in order to exist or if it is now the case that it exists in order to make money.[47]

The implications for the more marginal cricket nations were clear: they could expect much less support. The future of Test cricket too looked less than assured. Berry called the reform 'the worst thing that has ever happened to our sport'.[48]

Small wonder, then, that the film was met with much approbation by cricket writers. For Cricinfo Jonathan Wilson deplored the threat to cricket of 'neo-liberal economics' – a term comparatively new to cricket's customary lexicon. 'The contrast with FIFA is telling', he wrote:

> Blatantly corrupt as it may be, nobody doubts that football's governing body has, over the past 40 years, diverted huge sums from the top of the game to the bottom. There would have been more, of course, had it not been for all the kickbacks and backhanders, but at least some sort of intent was there. Cricket doesn't even have that. India revels in its role as a superpower without ever acknowledging the responsibilities that entails – and England and Australia blinkeredly go along.[49]

'If you care about cricket, you should see it', advised Andy Bull in the British *Guardian*, beneath the headline '*Death of a Gentleman*: call it optimistic, call it idealistic, but it's right'.[50] In the right-wing *Daily Mail*, Lawrence Booth said 'Hats off to DOAG's producers [...] for taking a philosophical conundrum and turning it into a piece of cinema that should trouble all cricket lovers. It may even interest those who do not necessarily love cricket but dislike the corporatisation of modern life'.[51]

The 'power grab' and ensuing critique helped to explain developments – or lack of developments – in cricket's two largest untapped markets: the USA and China. The remainder of this chapter discusses why these two countries have not so far developed a significant cricket culture.

An un-American activity? Cricket in the USA

The game of cricket certainly has a history in the United States, having been taken there, once again by British army officers, in the eighteenth century and adopted by American gentlemen of leisure.[52] It flourished in the period before the American Civil War when American sport was segregated by social class.[53] Indeed, as noted earlier, the first English national team to travel abroad had toured the United States and Canada in September of 1859. Moreover, the first international sport fixture was a cricket match played between the USA and Canada at Bloomingdale Park in New York in 1844. Today, there is still an American cricket culture, but the popularity of the game long since dwindled and it has had a negligible presence in American life since the First World War.

Cricket in eighteenth-century North America, almost inevitably, carried upper-class and British colonial connotations and, while the circumstances of its decline in the US are still argued over[54] the game does seem to have been the victim of these connotations. Deb K. Das has suggested that cricket 'declined in the USA in the 20th century because in the late 1800s it had remained a strictly amateur elite sport at the same time that England, then Australia, were developing a professional system that allowed full-time players to participate'.[55]

And, as Ed Smith has written, while baseball rose in popularity in the American society of the late nineteenth century, cricket 'retreated into pockets of East-Coast anglophilia, arcane strongholds of the old world order on the wrong side of history'.[56] In the time since, the sports that came to stand for America were demotic, marketised and the transparent bearers of an aggressive American nationalism. They were played comparatively little outside of America itself; they took considerably less time than cricket in its three-, four- or five-day form; and, unlike this latter format of cricket, they produced a winner – American sport did not countenance such an outcome as a draw.

Nevertheless, in 2004 the ICC set up Project USA to promote the game of cricket in the United States. Examination of the apparently troubled workings of Project USA, which was scrapped the following year,[57] revealed a divided discourse, which itself suggested a vital political division. The Project's aims were never fully clear. Was it to promote cricket as a mass sport? On the face of it, given the cultural hegemony of 'All American' sports and the huge (if often unacknowledged) enthusiasm for association football among American liberals, women and ethnic minorities, this might have appeared to be a doomed enterprise. Or was it to cater to what were then estimated to be 3 to 4 million cricket lovers in USA? Most members of this latter grouping were drawn from the 10 million or so Indian Americans and Indian migrants or from Caribbean America. Certainly the US cricket scene was (and remains) dominated by Caribbean migrants and most members of the national team had been born in the Caribbean: of the thirteen cricketers listed as representing the United States in one-day internationals in 2005, eight had been born in Caribbean countries and a ninth – Leon Romero – although born in New York in 1974, had previously played for Trinidad and Tobago. Another – Clayton Lambert (b. Berbice, Guyana in 1962) had played for West Indies. Only one of the team – Steve Massiah (b. Guyana in 1979) was under 30.[58]

In the early years of the twenty-first century efforts to speed the growth of cricket in the United States seemed to little avail. A ProCricket League, organised on the Twenty20 format, was begun in 2004 but closed after one season, apparently for lack of funding and an aborted deal for coverage with the Dish satellite TV company. In 2005 the ICC suspended the United States Cricket Association and Project USA, ostensibly because it had failed to organise elections. The suspension was lifted the following year but re-imposed in 2007.[59] A plan, fronted by the ex-West Indian Test player Lance Gibbs, to stage a 2007 World Cup match in Broward County, Florida – one of the USA's few purpose-built cricket grounds – came to nothing. Indeed, there were periodic rumblings about the unavailability of the appropriate soil with which to construct cricket pitches in America. For instance, Martin Williamson of Cricinfo reported in 2007 that California (with New York and Florida one of the three main cricket centres in the USA), would have to import soil in order to prepare cricket pitches for an international tournament and, thus, negotiate the 'strict rules about transportation of soil and grass across state lines'. An expert was quoted as saying that 'soil with the right amount of clay needed to be imported, probably from Georgia, and that meant a mountain of red tape to be overcome before the project could even start'.[60] And an experiment in February of 2008 by the ostentatious entrepreneur Allen Stanford to visit cricket upon the town of Fort Collins, Colorado, brought no conclusive result. Stanford, a US citizen resident in the US Virgin Islands, had set up Stanford 20/20, a cricket competition between Caribbean islands using the Twenty20 format, in 2006 (see Chapter 14). He launched a cricket-publicity campaign in Fort Collins and arranged for Stanford 20/20 to be shown on cable TV there. There was some interest, but one young Fort Collins resident told the local press: 'We're pretty good with the sports we have. We don't even like soccer, and that's the biggest sport in the world.'[61] A year on and Stanford was charged with fraud in the United States, but his interventions in international cricket had raised at least two important questions. First, Stanford had identified cricket specifically as *entertainment* to the American market. He told Andy Bull of *The Observer*:

> This is entertainment, just like going to a movie. The purists lose sight of that: it's entertainment, that's it. If you don't get that then you're living in the Sixties. Dancing, music, 20/20, this is the way we play it, for entertainment. You go to any sporting event in the world right now, it's

being driven by television. And people aren't going to turn on if you do something dry and boring, there's got to be all kinds of stuff happening. If something doesn't give you instant excitement and enthusiasm, you're not going to watch it.[62]

Second, recalling the 'Packer Affair' of 1977 (see Chapter 2), he had raised the issue of governance: Stanford was widely perceived as a maverick, with only a tenuous relationship to the game's international administration. With Stanford eyeing US and Caribbean cricket markets and the official cricket association of the United States intermittently under suspension, the ICC would have to find more reliable 'partners' or risk conceding these markets to an unco-opted and undeniably shifty entrepreneur. As Bull remarked:

> Certainly Stanford has the ambition, money and organisation to have a major impact on the evolution of cricket. While he is seeking to enable cricket in the Caribbean to be financially self-sustaining, at this moment it is very much subject to his whims. If he were to exit the scene suddenly, he would leave a burgeoning organisation behind him, but one with little funding. For now, though, he is massively enthused by the project. Does this make him a threat to the cricket establishment? 'I'll reverse the question: just who is the establishment in cricket at the moment?' It is a pertinent point. Control at the moment seems to rest with whoever has the deepest pockets.[63]

This may help to make sense of some the changes made latterly in US cricket. In February 2007, Gladstone Dainty, then President of the USACA, was subjected to a somewhat challenging interview by Martin Williamson and Will Luke of Cricinfo. In the transcript of the interview Dainty is understandably defensive and the conversation reveals little of why his relations with the ICC had been so poor, but, when pressed over the benefits of a deal he had done with the marketing company Centrex, he replied that 'Youth and Female cricket programs are the priorities of USACA.' Later, when asked to name his achievements, Dainty's reply again stressed grass-roots cricket: under his presidency, the USACA had, he said, 'introduced Under-19 regional and national tournaments; licensed Under-11, Under-13 and Under-15 national tournaments; won the ICC Americas regional Under-19 tournament; qualified for the ICC's 2006 Under-19 World Cup; [and] won the recent ICC Americas Under-15 tournament'.[64]

A programme wherein such a marked priority was given to youth and women's cricket would clearly not be compatible with the sort of promotions that Stanford had envisaged. The promotion of grass-roots sport was expensive and promised no short-term profit to businesspeople. Indeed it might entail the propagation of ideologies incompatible with mainstream American values or the values of a helter-skelter, made-for-TV Twenty20 competition – for example, United States Junior Cricket, based in San Rafael, California has the following ethos on its website:

> Cricketers should be people who do not boast; nor quit; nor make excuses when they fail. They should be cheerful losers, and quiet winners. They should play fairly and as well as they can. They should enjoy the pleasure of risk. They should give their opponents the benefit of the doubt and value the game itself more highly than the result.[65]

Besides which, minds at the USACA and the ICC will have been further concentrated by the Board of Control for Cricket in India's inauguration in 2008 of the IPL – a Twenty20 tournament with huge promotion, attracting satellite TV coverage, substantial sponsorship – from the DLF [Delhi Land and Finance] Group – and some of the world's top players. Moreover, various consortia paid a total of US$723.59 million for the IPL's eight team franchises.[66] The IPL promised to be hugely lucrative – for the BCCI, for the Indian government, for the franchisees, for sponsors and for participant players (see Chapter 14).

In late March of 2009 the USACA announced the appointment of a new Chief Operating Officer – Don Lockerbie, an American who had been CEO and Venue Development Director of the ICC Cricket World Cup 2007 in the West Indies. This World Cup, it may be noted, had made a good deal of money for the organisers, World Cup West Indies 2007 Inc, and for the ICC – although host governments, desperate to boost tourist trade, seem to have borne heavy financial losses. Lockerbie's early statements in office made scant reference to youth, women's or grass-roots cricket in the US. Instead, he was planning a US Twenty20 tournament, using the IPL as a template. Commentators immediately sketched out the political contours of his task. One wrote:

> He [Lockerbie] knows that without official sanction, it may not be possible to create the financial muscle so necessary to sustain any sport in the long term. What the APL needs to decide is if it's going to involve national teams or IPL style franchise. The ICC would not want a rival to the 2010 T20 World Cup scheduled to be held in the Caribbean in April-May so it looks like franchises will be the way to go.[67]

Lockerbie's language was, like Stanford's, determinedly 'top down'; he is looking for corporate funding and ambitious marketing strategies:

> It is too early to say what kind of format it would be, but we're putting out a tender for proposals and see what happens. All we have done is launch a project to look into it. We have not announced a T20 tournament, but we are looking at partners to look at it. We want to attract the best minds in sports marketing.[68]

In 2010 Lockerbie was relieved of his position. According to Williamson this followed 'several months of increasing concern that Lockerbie's bullish promises about changes he was going to make to the game in the USA had come to nothing'.[69] Peter Della Penna wrote a few days later:

> It was refreshing to see an American cricket administrator actively engaging with the media and full of big ideas from outside the box. However, if you're going to talk the talk, you'd better walk the walk too, and there was nothing that Lockerbie loved more than talking about bringing big sponsors and big money to US cricket. He would name-drop from his Rolodex of contacts at will, as if all he had to do was snap his fingers to get his choice of sponsors lining up outside his office door. Lockerbie was like Jimmy Stewart from *It's A Wonderful Life*, gazing into the eyes of USA cricket players, fans and administrators, wooing them by telling them that if they wanted the moon, 'just say the word and I'll throw a lasso around it and pull it down'.[70]

One thing seemed clear from this episode: the big-bucks, all-singing-all-dancing Stanford-IPL model was now accepted as the way forward. Lockerbie's undoing was his failure to bring it about. In 2014 Lockerbie's successor, Australian Darren Beazley, resigned after less than two years in the job after USACA baulked at acceptance of recommendations from an independent governance review by TSE Consulting. Acceptance of these recommendations was a condition of the lifting of the USACA's suspension by the ICC.[71] (The ICC froze USACA funding in 2014.) 'Until we get Americans playing the game and administering the game', Beazley had said at one point, 'you are not going to reach your potential'.[72] The enduring failure to realise this aspiration had meanwhile led to the establishment of a rival American Cricket Federation, whose first head, Jamie Harrison, reiterated the need to develop the game in the United States beyond the existing expatriate and ethnic enclaves. By then there were estimated to be 10 million cricket fans in the US and 32,000 players. Less than 1,000 of the latter, however, were aged 19 or under. Besides, went the rhetorical question, how many of the 10 million fans are fans of US cricket?[73]

In 2017 another tycoon with a grand plan presented himself. Gujarat-born American businessman Jignesh 'Jay' Pandya, real estate developer and chairman of sports development company Global Sports Ventures, announced a $2.4 billion investment in eight new cricket stadia in the US, 'each having a capacity of 26,000 people, in New York, New Jersey, Washington DC, Georgia, Florida, Texas, Illinois and California, would create as many as 17,800 new jobs in the US'.[74] Pandya, like others before him, perceived a sport-mad consumer market and seemed to give less consideration to the indigenous development of this particular sport: 'When you have people of South Asian descent who really understand cricket, it helps. But after that it will probably go mainstream with Americans. I believe that will be very quick, because, as Americans, we just love sports. [And] it doesn't matter what kind of sport'. Gladstone Dainty, still in charge at USACA sold Pandya the association's T20 licensing rights for $70 million.[75]

'We all know or have read about him', sceptical US cricket blogger Tom Melville had written the year before, 'the enthusiastic entrepreneur who, with missionary zeal over the "great potential" of his product, scurries about renting offices, hiring employees, spinning out marketing plans, etc., etc . . . and yet, hasn't made so much as a single sale!' He went on:

> It's long been a settled fact that no sport can reach a sustained and competitive place in a country's sporting scene unless it can establish a following among that country's mainstream populace. [...] With American cricket in a state of persistent cultural invisibility it would be logical to assume the ICC would show some leadership, or at least some direction, in establishing a more productive priority for the game but this has proved to be more wishful than logical. The ICC's guiding principle, throughout the cricket world, has been to only work through the cricket powers that be, which in the United States, has meant those 'stakeholders' who only represent the often feuding factions of the cricket diaspora.[76]

Under the 'Small Balls' Division of the State Sport General Administration: the (slim) prospects for cricket in China

China is the world's biggest command capitalist economy. As Peter Nolan observes, unlike its Eastern European counterparts, communist China has explored 'ways in which market forces could improve the functioning of their economy', without abandoning the rule of the communist party.[77] Since its embrace of capitalism in the mid-1970s, China, with its disciplined, non-unionised workforce subject to central party directive, soon became a magnet for Western capital and commerce. As regards cricket, what may have required a great deal of corporate courtship and the best brains in sports marketing to accomplish elsewhere in the world, was in the early twenty-first century thought more readily achievable by decree of the leadership of the Chinese communist party. As Ashraful Haq, then head of the Asian Cricket Council, said in 2004: 'The government is interested because they feel they can excel in cricket. If the Chinese government backs something, they can make people interested.'[78]

The nature of contemporary China's engagement with the game of cricket is such that the parallel, and usually conflicting, vocabularies of grass-roots participation and heavily capitalised television spectacle were employed with equal vigour – albeit that the game itself, although first played in China in the mid-nineteenth century, had both a negligible history and a minimal contemporary presence there.

China is the world's largest and most populous country with an estimated population in 2015 of 1.37 billion. It is the world's biggest market for mobile phones and, since 2005, for automobiles. In the early twenty-first century China had plans to build 300 new cities by 2012 and, once they were built, China would have 1,000 cities, each with a population of 200,000 or more. Like India, the country had a growing middle class with significant discretionary income and, again like India, it offered plentiful low-cost skilled labour.[79]

A study of sport in China published in 1990 contained an apparently exhaustive list of sports and physical cultural activities – military, medical and recreational – in Chinese history. Not only was there no mention of cricket, but Chinese life had seemingly thrown up no comparable bat-and-ball games at all.[80] This meant that the game in China had been almost entirely confined to expatriates and, even in 2006 – some time after the first government moves to promote the game – the national cricket association estimated that, including foreigners, there were still probably only around 100 cricketers in the country.[81] Like all socialist states, however, China did have a strong government-sponsored sport culture and from the early 1980s it began a quest to become 'a world sports power', entailing, among other things, a place in the top five of the Olympic medal table and the most advanced sports science provision.[82] By the end of that decade China had over 400,000 sports grounds suitable for mass sport activity.[83]

The interest of the Chinese government in developing cricket in China seems to have registered at the Asian Cricket Council (ACC) around 2003. On his visit to China in September of that year ACC representative Rumesh Ratnayake found that, unlike on previous visits, Ministry of Sport officials were anxious to meet him and to discuss a range of objectives, including China's participation in the cricket World Cup and the inclusion of the game in the curriculum of Chinese schools. These objectives would form part of the substance of a five-year plan.[84]

China became an affiliate member of the ICC in 2004 and the plan was fleshed out and published. By the autumn of 2005 there were regular coaching and umpiring courses and cricket was being played in nine Chinese cities – Beijing, Shanghai, Shenyang, Dalian, Guangzhou, Shenzhen, Chongqing, Tianjin and Jinan – and more than 150 schools.[85] 'By 2009', said Cui Weihong, officer in charge of cricket with the Chinese Cricket Association (CCA) in May of 2006, 'we envision there will be 720 teams across the country in a well-organised structure, which will allow promising kids from primary schools to move up through the ranks'; 'Literally no one plays cricket in China' Cricinfo reported, '– but that's likely to change soon'.[86] Hopes were harboured that China might qualify for the World Cup and, perhaps, even gain Test status by the end of the following decade (i.e. 2020).

Chinese officials spoke warmly of cricket and its compatibility with Chinese culture. In 2006 cricket was assigned the name 'shen shi yun dong', which translates as 'the noble game'.[87] It was identified as equally suitable for boys and girls and in 2005 Ratnayake was already attesting to the readiness of Chinese children to learn the game: 'Never in my life have I seen any country's children pick up the game so quickly. They had the basics of the game – hitting and throwing – within just five minutes'[88] Zhang Xioaning of China's Multi-ball Games Administration Centre offered a philosophical rationale for the government's cricket plan:

> What makes cricket special is that it is a game of the physique, it is a game of the heart, and it is a game of the mind. It is a game for the individual within the team. It is truly a noble game that is perfectly suited to the Chinese people. It is being introduced in China at the best time.[89]

And, as Paul Maidment suggested, noting the limitations of the average Chinese physique, in this game 'Skill and strategy count for more than size. Cricket is not a contact sport' – unlike, say, rugby football, at which China had tried its collective hand.[90] Australian barrister Malcolm Speed, Chief Executive Officer of the ICC, visited China in 2006 and was very taken with the enthusiasm and strategic thinking of the Chinese authorities.[91] He said: 'My dream is that in my lifetime I will be able to see India and China playing against each other in Test cricket'.[92]

There was, of course, much more to this development than the exploration of possible sporting benefits to Chinese children. Writing on the Forbes business and financial news website in 2005, Maidment cited the desire of the Chinese government to gain regional prestige in Asia, in many parts of which continent the game already prospered.[93] Cricket administrators in the region, meanwhile:

> Saw dollars. 'The potential benefits and commercial revenues from (China's) presence in the cricket world are enormous,' says Syed Ashraful Huq, chief executive of the Asian Cricket Council, the regional arm of the game's governing body, the International Cricket Council. 'As soon as China breaks though, I foresee the total global revenues for cricket increasing by 30% to 40%'.[94]

With a credible cricket team, the Chinese cricket board could sell television rights for a huge sum, co-opting an array of official sponsors of global and regional cricket eyeing the vast Chinese market. As Maidment pointed out:

> Televised cricket is a $150 million a year advertising market in India alone. An estimated 100 million Chinese watched the basketball competition at the Athens Olympics, so there is a latent market to be tapped.

China would be an attractive market for the ICC's official sponsors, LG Electronics, Pepsico, Hutchison, Hero Honda, India Oil and Cable & Wireless. The ACC already has HSBC, Standard Chartered and Indian Oil sponsoring its regional tournaments. Other potential sponsors include companies like General Motors, which already spends millions of dollars sponsoring golf in China.[95]

This latter reference to golf pointed up something of the nature of the market to which these sponsors would want access – that of a newly enriched middle class which, along with cars and the latest communications technology, might count the mastery of such historically high-status sports as golf and cricket among its inventory of fresh aspirations. Certainly in India, where comparable economic growth had taken place, a growing middle class had formed a market for cricket goods and services: equipment, coaching and how-to-succeed philosophy (see Chapter 15). A similar pattern seemed to be emerging in relation to China, with sections of the global cricket technocracy – notably Cricket Australia – having been engaged to guide Chinese cricket toward elite levels. Ross Turner, Cricket Australia's global development manager, had been working with the Chinese cricket administration since 2005. He told the Indian newspaper *The Age*:

> With its population of 1.3 billion people and its changing economy, China can one day be a cricket power to rival India. It may not be in five years, but it will certainly be within a decade. China has such a strategic approach to everything. They won't be benchmarking against some atoll in the Pacific, they will be saying what is the world standard and trying to better it, seeking prominence and world recognition.[96]

And Ian McCubbin, a lawyer specialising in Chinese–Australian affairs and advisor to the China Central TV network, asserted the now-familiar rhetoric of markets, casting some doubt on the invocation of ennoblement and mass participation in Chinese cricket:

> I don't think the success of cricket in China depends on having hundreds of thousands of people playing it in the park on a Saturday afternoon. I think it depends on promoting it as a television product. Look at India, and the commercialisation of cricket there. There is no reason why that can't happen in China. It's a growing economy, it's a changing economy, but it's also an economy that is becoming an avid consumer of western culture.[97]

In China, as Maidment's business perspective readily suggested, local enthusiasm could be married to 'China's top down approach to sports, which has made it world class in swimming and track in less than 30 years'.[98]

However, less than a decade on from these lip-licking ruminations, there was little sign of the hoped-for rise of Chinese cricket. In 2010 China hosted the Asian Games and played cricket against Malaysia in a purpose-built stadium. They lost heavily and, in 2015, had won only three times in their entire (twenty-two-game) history.[99] There seem to have been several, interlocking reasons for this failure.

The commercial rationale for the development of Chinese cricket remained. Siva Sankar wrote in the *China Daily* in 2016 that cricket and China could still be a 'good match'. Chinese smartphone manufacturer Vivo was now the title sponsor of the Indian Premier League:

> Chinese gadget and appliance makers, and internet giants, already have, or would welcome, opportunities to have a presence in the Indian market that comprises a billion-plus consumers and is second only to, and not very far from, China. Nothing can match cricket's pull insofar as creating instant access to the Indian consumer is concerned. Conceivably, a three-hour India–China T20 match in the near future could create a five-hour prime time viewing bonanza for advertisers, with a potential to reach more than 2 billion consumers in both countries.[100]

There has been little sign, though, that the Chinese government has facilitated the pursuit of these consumers and the undertakings it made to Malcolm Speed in 2006 seem to have been abandoned. There are several factors here. First, as Sahil Dutta observes, the only kind of stage that interests 'media officers, government ministers and private investors' is the world stage. That means medals – as, for example, obtained in the Olympics of 2008 which China spent $1.61 billion in staging[101] and at which China gained ninety-eight medals, forty-eight of them gold. At cricket China promises no immediate or even medium-term prospect of such success. Second, the role of the ACC has been heavily reined in. Founded, as we saw in Chapter 8, in 1983 and seen by many as a Trojan Horse for domination of the ICC by the Indian board, the ACC had its development responsibilities removed as part of the widely condemned 'power grab' reforms of 2014–15. This meant an immediate downgrading of development in the theatre of cricket in which the fabled 2 billion consumers were to be sought. Third, as an apparent consequence, the Chinese Cricket Association remained seriously shorthanded and cricket became side-lined in the Chinese government bureaucracy. In 2015 the CCA was being run by three people, one of whom (ex-Bangladesh player Aminul Islam) travelled this vast country hoping to interest people in cricket. Moreover, the government official responsible for the Small Balls Division of the State Sport General Administration had also to oversee tennis, golf and handball.[102] Fourth, Olympic recognition for cricket, now widely held to offer a way forward for the less established cricket countries, was being blocked. Despite a growing lobby for cricket to be accepted as an

Olympic sport, the ICC was until recently strongly opposed to this. Peter Miller, a close observer of the more marginal cricket nations, wrote in 2015:

> While cricket in the UK does not need the Olympics, that is not the case elsewhere. It makes perfect financial sense for China and a number of other countries. Not because the competition will be the pinnacle of the sport, but because it opens up financial support from governments and sporting bodies. So many funding streams are only available to sports that have those five coloured rings attached. Cricket closing itself off to those because it doesn't suit the privileged elite that are already financially secure is yet another example of the short sighted nature of its administration.[103]

Tim Wigmore, another such observer, pointed out that a survey of ICC members in 2008 had produced a 90% majority in favour of joining the Olympics, having been encouraged by the International Olympic Committee to apply for the Games of 2024:

> China is one of those who could benefit. 'We fully support cricket entering the Olympics,' says Terry Zhang of the Chinese Cricket Association. 'The shortcut for cricket to develop in China is to be in the Olympics.' There has long been fantastical talk of cricket conquering China, but there appears no danger of it doing so anytime soon. 'There is very little awareness in China and very little support from central government,' Zhang admits. China remains 'almost fully dependent on ICC and ACC funding for cricket development'. And the sums on which cricket in China must subsist amount to a pittance: $30,000 a year from the ICC; and around $200,000 a year from the Asian Cricket Council [...] And the tantalising prospect of cricket taking hold in the United States may cease to be a fantasy. Unusually, the US does not provide funding for Olympic sports, but Olympic status would provide a boon for cricket in America. 'Having an Olympic team would greatly enhance not only our ability to fund-raise and to find sponsors, but also the sport's profile among Americans not yet familiar with it,' Jamie Harrison, the chief executive officer of the American Cricket Federation, says.[104]

The architects of the recent 'power grab' were against Olympic membership, seeing it perhaps as a threat to their (newly boosted) interests but in 2017 ICC Chief Executive Dave Richardson said it was possible:

> We need to make a decision by July so we can make an application in time for September, when, as I understand it, the IOC will consider new sports for 2024. I think the majority of the members – and certainly myself – think the time is right and we've come to the conclusion that the overall benefit to the game in terms of globalising and growing it outweigh any negatives, so I'm hoping.[105]

Postscript

In June 2017, as this book was going to press, Ireland and Afghanistan were both awarded Test status by the International Cricket Council. They had been playing as Associate Members of the ICC since 1993 and 2013, respectively. Afghanistan's promotion ran counter to the ICC's previous stipulation that Test-playing countries must foster women's cricket; women's cricket in Afghanistan was by now virtually extinct. It also promised a further boost for the burgeoning cricket scene in the United Arab Emirates (where the ICC was now based), since Afghanistan could not play in their own country for security reasons and were likely to play their 'home' Tests in the UAE.

Notes

1. http://www.asiancricket.org/index.php/members/china Access 8 May 2017.
2. Rob Steen 'Acronym wars: the economics and indianisation of contemporary cricket' in Chris Rumford and Stephen Wagg (eds.) *Cricket and Globalization* Newcastle-upon-Tyne: Cambridge Scholars Publishing 2010 pp.84–102, p.88.
3. See Stephen Wagg 'It's just not shen shi yun dong: exploring the limits to the globalisation of cricket' in Rumford and Wagg (eds.) *Cricket and Globalization* pp.210–30.
4. C.L.R. James *Beyond a Boundary* London: Serpent's Tail 1994 (first published London: Stanley Paul 1963).
5. Jon Gemmell 'An imperialist beast – 100 years of the ICC' Morning Star Online 29 July 2009 http://www.morningstaronline.co.uk/index.php/sport/an_imperialist_beast_100_years_of_the_icc Access 9 August 2009.
6. Bailey's son Derrick captained Gloucestershire in 1952 and 1953: see obituary http://www.telegraph.co.uk/news/obituaries/sport-obituaries/5845170/Sir-Derrick-Bailey-Bt.html Posted 16 July 2009, Access 15 May 2017, which notes Churchill's friendship with his father.
7. Gideon Haigh 'So much done, so little to do' [Profile of Abe Bailey] http://www.espncricinfo.com/magazine/content/story/259254.html Posted 12 September 2006, Access 8 May 2017.
8. http://news.bbc.co.uk/onthisday/hi/dates/stories/may/22/newsid_2504000/2504573.stm Access 8 May 2017.
9. ICC website http://icc-cricket.yahoo.net/the-icc/icc_members/overview.php Access 10 August 2009. No longer available.
10. For an editorial reflecting on this on 1 May 2007, see http://www.jamaica-gleaner.com/gleaner/20070501/cleisure/cleisure2.html Access 13 August 2009. No longer available.
11. Hilary McD. Beckles *The Development of West Indies Cricket Volume One: The Age of Nationalism* London: Pluto Press/ Kingston, Jamaica: University of West Indies Press 1998.
12. See, for example, http://news.bbc.co.uk/sport1/hi/cricket/england/7996501.stm Access 15 May 2017.
13. See, for example, Ed Smith 'Revelations of the Ashes' *The Guardian* 24 August 2009 https://www.theguardian.com/commentisfree/2009/aug/24/ashes-revelations-cricket-cliches Access 8 May 2017.

14 See Aida Edemariam 'What can you buy for 5p in Bangladesh?' *The Guardian* 11 December 2006 https://www.theguardian.com/environment/2006/dec/11/ethicalliving.lifeandhealth Access 8 May 2017.
15 See Leonard Tim 'Will we continue to be annihilated and humiliated?' http://www.candw.ag/~jardinea/fanflame.htm Posted 1 December 2000, Access 16 August 2009; Leonard Tim Hector 'One eye on the ball, one eye on the world' (compiled and with editorial commentary by Stephen Wagg) in Stephen Wagg (ed.) *Cricket and National Identity in the Postcolonial Age* London: Routledge 2005 pp.159–78.
16 Cricinfo Staff 'World Cup profits boost debt-ridden Windies board' http://www.espncricinfo.com/westindies/content/story/301516.html Posted 11 July 2007, Access 8 May 2017.
17 See, for example, Mark Lee 'The $55 million question: Whither West Indies Cricket?' *Abeng News Magazine* http://www.abengnews.com/2009/01/09/the-55-million-question-whither-west-indies-cricket/ Posted 9 January 2009, Access 8 May 2017.
18 Angus Bell *Batting on the Bosphorus: A Skoda-Powered Cricket Tour Through Eastern Europe* Edinburgh: Canongate Books 2008.
19 Tim Wigmore 'Ireland' in Tim Wigmore and Peter Miller (eds.) *Second XI: Cricket in its Outposts* Durrington, West Sussex: Pitch Publishing 2015 pp.36–65, pp.38–40.
20 Jarrod Kimber 'How Ireland got their groove back' http://www.espncricinfo.com/magazine/content/story/670709.html Posted 13 September 2013, Access 9 May 2017.
21 Wigmore 'Ireland' p.48.
22 Tim Wigmore 'After years in shadows, cricket emerges in Ireland' *New York Times* 4 March 2015 https://www.nytimes.com/2015/03/05/sports/cricket/after-years-in-shadows-cricket-emerges-in-ireland.html?_r=0 Access 9 May 2017.
23 'Future of Ireland cricket is in safe hands with Warren Deutrom' http://www.newsletter.co.uk/sport/cricket/future-of-ireland-cricket-is-in-safe-hands-with-warren-deutrom-1-6111232 Posted 11 June 2014, Access 9 May 2017.
24 Wigmore 'Ireland' p.52.
25 Wigmore 'After years'.
26 Alan Bairner and Dominic Malcolm 'Cricket and national identities on the Celtic fringe' in Rumford and Wagg (eds.) *Cricket and Globalization* pp.189–209, p.198.
27 Peter Hopkirk *The Great Game – The Struggle for Empire in Central Asia* New York: Kodansha 1992.
28 See Harry Rice 'A controversial history of cricket in Afghanistan' http://bizarreculture.com/a-controversial-history-of-cricket-in-afghanistan/ Posted 8 March 2017, Access 9 May 2017.
29 An interview with Afghanistan's Taj Malik Alam' http://globalcricket.wordpress.com/2008/02/15/an-interview-with-afghansitans-taj-malik-alam/ Posted 15 February 2008, Access 15 May 2017.
30 'An interview with Afghanistan's Taj Malik Alam'.
31 'An interview with Afghanistan's Taj Malik Alam'.
32 'Cricket warrior' http://www.asiancricket.org/h2_afghan.cfm Posted 2 March 2005, Access 13 August 2008.
33 Nadeem Yaqub 'Bowling over the Taliban' *New Internationalist* July 2001 https://newint.org/columns/currents/2001/07/01/bowlingoverthetaliban/ Access 10 May 2017.

34 Tim Wigmore 'Taliban will cheer the loudest for Afghanistan at Cricket World Cup' https://scroll.in/article/705274/taliban-will-cheer-the-loudest-for-afghanistan-at-cricket-world-cup Posted 9 February 2015, Access 9 May 2017.
35 Tim Wigmore 'Afghanistan' in Wigmore and Miller *Second XI...* pp.15–35, pp.16–17.
36 See Frank Jack Daniel 'Afghan women's cricket crushed by threats, bombs and tradition' http://uk.reuters.com/article/us-afghanistan-women-cricket-idUSKBN0K219R20141224 Posted 24 December 2014, Access 9 May 2017.
37 Uthra Ganesan 'Cricket is now the biggest sport in Afghanistan' http://www.thehindu.com/sport/cricket/%E2%80%98Cricket-is-now-the-biggest-sport-in-Afghanistan%E2%80%99/article13994180.ece Posted 22 September 2016, Access 9 May 2017.
38 Ganesan 'Cricket is now'.
39 Wigmore 'Afghanistan' p.32.
40 Peter Della Penna 'Afghanistan domestic competitions awarded first-class and List A status' http://www.espncricinfo.com/afghanistan/content/story/1080891.html Posted 4 February 2017, Access 9 May 2017.
41 Kate Clark and Sudhanshu Verma 'The great game: the rise of Afghan cricket from exodus and war' https://www.afghanistan-analysts.org/the-great-game-the-rise-of-afghan-cricket-from-exodus-and-war/ Posted 28 March 2017, Access 9 May 2017.
42 Tim Wigmore 'Where do Afghanistan go next?' http://www.espncricinfo.com/magazine/content/story/678293.html Posted 10 October 2013, Access 10 May 2017.
43 Clark and Verma 'The great game'.
44 Issued by Dartmouth Films.
45 Scyld Berry 'England, India and Australia's power grab at the ICC is the worst thing that has ever happened to our sport' *Daily Telegraph* 24 June 2015.
46 Mike Atherton 'Money is at the heart of the big three's ICC power grab' *The Australian* 28 June 2014 http://www.theaustralian.com.au/sport/the-times-sport/money-is-at-the-heart-of-the-big-threes-icc-power-grab/news-story/a82e78bbceee71c0e41855e2c94e1acd?nk=d123696b52bca2a4645c291040edc34f-1494364409 Access 9 May 2017.
47 Quoted in Jonathan Wilson 'Be alarmed, be very alarmed' [Review of *Death of a Gentleman*] http://www.espncricinfo.com/magazine/content/story/903855.html Posted 29 July 2015, Access 9 May 2017.
48 Berry 'England, India'.
49 Wilson 'Be alarmed'.
50 Andy Bull '*Death of a Gentleman*: call it optimistic, call it idealistic, but it's right' *The Guardian* 28 July 2015 https://www.theguardian.com/sport/2015/jul/28/the-spin-death-of-a-gentleman-icc-ecb Access 10 May 2017.
51 Lawrence Booth '*Death of a Gentleman* is a film to trouble all lovers of cricket ... the greed of England, Australia and India is killing the global game' *Daily Mail* 28 July 2015 http://www.dailymail.co.uk/sport/article-3177286/Test-cricket-s-demise-greed-shoddy-governance-Death-Gentleman-film-concern-lovers-sport.html Access 10 May 2017.
52 Deb K. Das 'Cricket in the USA' http://www.cricinfomobile.com/link_to_database/NATIONAL/ICC_MEMBERS/USA/USA_HISTORY.htm Undated. Access 10 May 2017; Mabel Lee *A History of Physical Education and Sport in the USA* New York: John Wiley 1983 pp.14–15.
53 S.W. Pope *Patriotic Games: Sporting Traditions in the American Imagination 1876–1926* New York: Oxford University Press p.5.

54 Dominic Malcolm 'The diffusion of cricket to America: a figurational sociological examination' *Journal of Historical Sociology* Vol.19 No.2 June 2006 pp.151–73.
55 Das 'Cricket in the USA'.
56 Ed Smith 'Patriot game' *The Observer* 3 July 2005 http://www.guardian.co.uk/sport/2005/jul/03/cricket.ussport Access 28 August 2009.
57 Cricinfo staff 'Project USA scrapped' http://www.espncricinfo.com/usa/content/story/146269.html Posted 18 March 2008, Access 15 May 2017.
58 http://en.wikipedia.org/wiki/List_of_American_ODI_cricketers Access 10 May 2017.
59 'USA Cricket hit by ICC suspension' http://news.bbc.co.uk/sport1/hi/cricket/6414625.stm Posted 3 March 2007, Access 10 May 2017.
60 Martin Williamson 'No cricket in the US for the time being!' http://intafrih.blogspot.com/2007/01/no-cricket-in-us-for-time-being.html Posted 23 January 2007, Access 10 May 2017.
61 Cricket blog by Nick Hoult of the *Daily Telegraph* http://blogs.telegraph.co.uk/sport/nickhoult/3952551/Cricket_in_the_USA/ Access 30 August 2009. No longer available.
62 Andy Bull 'We have lift off' *The Observer* 2 March 2008 http://www.guardian.co.uk/sport/2008/mar/02/cricket.news Access 10 May 2017.
63 Bull 'We have lift off'.
64 Martin Williamson and Will Luke 'Dainty: USA cricket will explode into life' http://www.espncricinfo.com/usa/content/story/281354.html Posted 23 February 2007, Access 10 May 2017.
65 http://www.usjuniorcricket.org/ Access 10 May 2017.
66 'Big business and Bollywood grab stakes in IPL' http://www.cricinfo.com/ipl/content/current/story/333193.html Posted 24 January 2008, Access 10 May 2017.
67 Ravi Kant Singh 'Twenty20 cricket league looks to follow IPL example' http://www.mynews.in/fullstory.aspx?storyid=21980 Undated. Access 30 August 2009. No longer available.
68 Peter Simunovich 'USA Cricket Association calling for tenders for possible T20 competition' http://www.dreamcricket.com/articles/dreamcricket-usa-news/usa-cricket-association-calling-for-tenders-for-possible-t20-competition/ Posted 22 July 2009, Access 10 May 2017.
69 Martin Williamson 'Lockerbie ousted as USACA chief executive' http://www.espncricinfo.com/usa/content/story/488156.html Posted 21 November 2010, Access 10 May 2017.
70 Peter Della Penna 'Big ideas, little results' http://www.espncricinfo.com/magazine/content/story/490147.html Posted 4 December 2010, Access 10 May 2017.
71 Peter Della Penna 'USACA chief Darren Beazley resigns' http://www.espncricinfo.com/usa/content/story/731883.html Posted 27 March 2014, Access 10 May 2017; Peter Della Penna 'ICC lays down 39 conditions for USACA reinstatement' http://www.espncricinfo.com/usa/content/story/906669.html Posted 5 August 2015, Access 10 May 2017.
72 Peter Miller 'USA' in Wigmore and Miller *Second XI...* pp.203–23, p.210.
73 Miller 'USA' pp.211–14.
74 'Indian-American businessman Jay Pandya to build 8 cricket stadiums in US' http://www.dnaindia.com/sport/report-indian-american-businessman-jay-pandya-to-build-8-cricket-stadiums-in-us-2307802 Posted 27 February 2017, Access 10 May 2017.

75 James Dator 'Meet the investor spending $2.4 billion to start a cricket league in the USA' http://www.sbnation.com/2017/3/1/14725986/jay-pandya-interview-cricket-usa-2-billion-investment Posted 1 March 2017, Access 10 May 2017.
76 Tom Melville 'Cricket in America and the betrayal of the prime directive' http://www.dreamcricket.com/dreamcricket/news.hspl?nid=17526&ntid=3 Posted 4 August 2016, Access 15 May 2017.
77 Peter Nolan *Transforming China: Globalization, Transition and Development* London: Anthem Press 2005 p.82.
78 Louisa Lim 'China catches cricket bug' BBC Sport website http://news.bbc.co.uk/sport1/hi/cricket/3419585.stm Posted 22 January 2004, Access 10 May 2017.
79 Peter Enderwick *Understanding Emerging Markets: China and India* Abingdon: Routledge 2007 p.193.
80 Howard G. Knuttgen, M.A.Qiwei and W.U. Zhongyan (eds.) *Sport in China* Champaign, Ill.: Human Kinetics 1990 p.5.
81 Mary-Anne Toye 'Howzat! In a quick declaration, China embraces cricket' *Sydney Morning Herald* 4 March 2006 http://www.smh.com.au/news/cricket/howzat-in-a-quick-declaration-china-embraces-cricket/2006/03/03/1141191849511.html Access 10 May 2017.
82 Knuttgen et al. *Sport in China* pp.207–8.
83 Knuttgen et al. *Sport in China* p.25.
84 Report of Mr Rumesh Ratnayake of Asian Cricket Council on visit to China 11th–15th September 2003 http://www.asiancricket.org/v1/rep_china.htm Access 10 May 2017.
85 http://en.wikipedia.org/wiki/China_national_cricket_team Access 10 May 2017.
86 Ranajit Sankar Dam and Wie Jie 'Enter the dragon' http://www.espncricinfo.com/ci/content/story/245632.html Posted May 2006 (no specific day), Access 10 May 2017.
87 Toye 'Howzat!'.
88 'China has arisen into the great world of cricket' http://www.asiancricket.org/h_chinarisen.cfm Access 6 September 2009. No longer available.
89 'China has arisen'.
90 Paul Maidment, 'China's cracking cricket' http://www.forbes.com/2005/09/30/china-india-cricket_cx_pm_1003chinacricket.html Posted 10 March 2005, Access 6 September 2009. No longer available.
91 'Malcolm Speed and Shaharyar Khan: to move cricket forward in China' http://www.asiancricket.org/index.php/component/content/article/68-september-2006/252-malcolm-speed-and-shaharyar-khan-to-move-cricket-forward-in-china Posted 14 September 2006, Access 10 May 2017.
92 Jon Newton 'Cricket's elusive Shangri-La' http://www.espncricinfo.com/magazine/content/story/626559.html Posted 26 March 2013, Access 10 May 2017.
93 Maidment 'China's cracking'.
94 Maidment 'China's cracking'.
95 Maidment 'China's cracking'.
96 Chloe Saltau 'Australia lobbies for China push' *The Age* 9 August 2008 http://www.theage.com.au/news/cricket/australia-lobbies-for-china-push/2008/08/08/1218139086067.html Access 10 May 2017.
97 Saltau 'Australia lobbies'.
98 Maidment 'China's cracking'.
99 Sahil Dutta 'China' in Wigmore and Miller (eds.) *Second XI* pp.179–80.
100 Siva Sankar 'China and cricket will be a good match' *China Daily* 7 September 2016 http://www.chinadaily.com.cn/sports/2016-09/07/content_26722837.htm Access 10 May 2017.

101 Dutta 'China' pp. 179, 184–5.
102 Dutta 'China' p.185.
103 Peter Miller 'China's struggles to develop cricket with ICC reluctant to join Olympics' http://sport360.com/article/international/36803/china-still-struggling-develop-cricket-icc-and-ecb-reluctant-join Posted 16 May 2015, Access 10 May 2017.
104 Tim Wigmore 'A case for Olympic status and wooing China' http://www.espncricinfo.com/magazine/content/story/755727.html Posted 27 June 2014, Access 10 May 2017.
105 Sean Ingle 'Cricket may feature at 2024 Olympic Games, says ICC chief executive' *The Guardian* 30 March 2017 https://www.theguardian.com/sport/2017/mar/30/cricket-could-feature-at-2024-olympic-games-says-icc-president-dave-richardson Access 10 May 2017.

Afterword

In the oft-quoted couplet from his poem *Pride of the Village*, published in 1925, Edmund Blunden wrote 'Cricket to us, like you, was more than play. It was a worship in the summer sun'. These days, those of us who variously play, follow or care about cricket are likely to arrive at somewhat less awestruck judgements of the game, but it is still certainly more than play. Cricket has a politically vexed history – a fact more widely recognised in the last twenty-five years – and this book has been an attempt to show how this has been the case.

Toward the beginning of this book the landed and moneyed gentlemen who ran cricket were seen expressing confidence that the vulgar pedlars of contemporary commerce could be kept at arm's length. It ended with accusations that they, or their successors, had become the monsters that they had thought they could tame. But cricket, despite the idyllic aura with which it has often been surrounded, has always been attended by controversy. Today there are plenty of controversies to choose from. As the journalist Andy Bull observed in his review of the film *Death of a Gentleman*, cricket's devotees constitute 'a loose coalition of the disaffected' and the most recent bone of contention – 'the greed of administrators' – takes its place among a host of others:

> Too little coverage on terrestrial TV. Too few amateur players. Too many amateur administrators. Too many flat pitches. Too much T20. Too much ODI cricket. Too many meaningless Test matches. Too little state school cricket. Too many overworked players. Too many overpaid players. Too many counties. Too many empty stands. Too many exploited fans. Too much self-interest. Too much temptation. Too much money. Too much corruption.[1]

This, more than anything, shows the degree to which cricket's history has been steeped in mythology. As Mike Marqusee pointed out, the widely invoked ethos of 'the spirit of cricket' covered a multitude of sins – racism, class division, imperial pillage . . . – and was often no more than the 'thump of humbug on willow'.[2] Today's hypocrisies and appeals to the 'interests of cricket' are (thin) cover for hyper-commercialism and corporate greed. But, despite it all, cricket seems still to carry special meanings for huge numbers of people across the world. Today many of the custodians of the game are billionaire plutocrats with massive corporate portfolios. Twenty20 is the game of the legions of 'cash rich and time poor' and there is less call for the services of the 'gentlemen in white flannels'. But, as this book has noted more than once, cricket has already survived a number of obituaries. One feels that, so long as makeshift bats, tennis balls and oil drums for wickets can be found, it will survive all depredations.

Notes

1 Andy Bull '*Death of a Gentleman*: call it optimistic, call it idealistic, but it's right' *The Guardian* 28 July 2015 https://www.theguardian.com/sport/2015/jul/28/the-spin-death-of-a-gentleman-icc-ecb Access 10 May 2017.
2 Mike Marqusee 'The thump of humbug on willow' *The Guardian* 17 July 2006 https://www.theguardian.com/commentisfree/2006/jul/17/disspiritofcricket Access 11 May 2017.

Index

A Corner of a Foreign Field (by Ramachandra Guha) 223
A History of Australian Cricket (by Chris Harte and Bernard Whimpress) 223
Abbasi, Kamran 116
Able, Graham 15
ACC (Associated Cement Companies, India) 94
Accelerated Mahaweli Irrigation and Settlement Project 146
Adams, Paul 46
Adidas sports equipment 242
Afghanistan Cricket Federation 291
Afghanistan, cricket in 290–3, 306
African National Congress 38, 44–5, 47, 48, 238
Afrikaner Nationalist Party 37, 42
Agnew, Jonathan/ 'Aggers' 212, 215
Ahmad, Tajuddin 129
Ahson, Haseeb 8
Aird, Ronnie 20
Aitchison College, Lahore 111
Akram, Wasim 118
Akter, Chumki 236
Al Karam studio, Karachi 242
Al Qaeda (terrorist group) 119
Alabaster, Jack 62
Alam, Taj Malik 291
Albees (women's cricket club, Mumbai) 235
Alderson, Andrew 68, 69
Alexander, 'Gerry' 73, 77
Ali Bhutto trophy 144
Ali, Tariq 108, 109, 110
All India Radio (AIR) 95
Alston, Rex 205
Altham, H.S. ('Harry') 5
Amarnath, Lala 94

Ambani, Mukesh 103, 255
American Cricket Federation 299, 305
Amin, Chirayu 259
Anderson, James 175
Anderson, Perry 97
Andrews, David 24
Anglia Ruskin University 14
Anglo American mining company 47
Anglo-Oriental College 111
Anti-Pom rhetoric 167, 168, 170–2, 175
Antonio, Peggy 237–8
Anyone But England (by Mike Marqusee) 3, 214
ANZUS defence treaty 67
Ara, Ismat 236
Archer, Robert 38
Arendse, Norman 49
Arlott, John 4, 9, 12, 22, 39–40, 193, 201, 203–5, 210–14, 216
Armitage, Richard 110
Arthur, Mickey 268, 270
Asda supermarkets 288
Asgiriya Grounds, Kandy 146
Ashmead-Bartlett, Ellis 31
Asian Cricket Council 131–2, 291, 293, 300–2, 305
Asian Games 304
Asif, Mohammad 120
Astill, James 91, 92, 95, 101, 102
Athar, Syed Abbas 126
Atherton, Mike 294
Attlee, Clement 7
Australasian Knock-out Competition 195
Australian Broadcasting Corporation (ABC) 204, 206
Australian Consolidated Press 23
Australian Cricket Academy 27
Australian Cricket Board (ACB) 19–20, 23–4, 26–7, 174

Australian Imperial Force (AIF) 162
Australian Institute of Sport (AIS) 27
Australian International Sports Academy (AISA) 277-8
Australian Services XI 4
Awami League 127-9, 132, 134
Axford, Barrie 214
Azharuddin, Mohammad 120

Bacher, Ali 43, 44
Bacon's City Technical College 15
Baig, Abbas Ali 98, 270
Baig, Anila 120
Bailey, Jack 192, 194-5
Bailey, Sir Abe 38, 285
Bailey, Trevor 76, 79, 163, 211
Bairner, Alan 119
Bakers Mini Cricket 43, 47
Baksh, Vaneisa 241
Baloo, Palwankar 91-2
Bamjee, Aloo 235
Bandookwala, Ayub 279
Bandyopadhyay, Kausik 134, 135
Banerjee, Sudeep 257
Bangbandhu National Stadium, Dhaka 129, 132
Bangladesh Cricket Board (BCB) 129
Bangladesh Premier League 136, 253
Banks, Tony 233
Bantustans 41
Barakzai, Diana 292
Barber, Bob 6
Barmy Army 214
Barnes, Abdullatief ('Tiffy') 42
Barnes, Alan 170
Barnes, Sid 20
Basu, Ajeyo 256
Bates, Suzie 241
Batsford, Sir Brian 193
Baxter, Peter 213
Bayliss, Trevor 268
Beazley, Darren 299
Beckles, Hilary 73, 81, 83, 85-6, 238, 268, 275, 286
Bedford, Duke of 188
Bedi, Bishan Singh 93, 269, 270
Bedser, Alec 51, 93, 166
Bedser, Eric 51
Bee Gees, The 269
Belich, James 60
Benaud, Richie 18-20, 24, 66, 79, 168, 172, 205, 208-9, 217

Benson and Hedges Cup (UK) 10, 193, 194, 195, 251
Benson and Hedges World Cup 65
Bergman-Osterberg, Martina 224
Berry, Scyld 133, 148, 200, 293-4
Beyond a Boundary (by C.L.R. James) 77
Bharatiya Janata Party (BJP) 97, 99, 258, 273
Bhasha Andolon (Language Movement in Bengal) 126
Bhat, Tanmay 102
Bhutto, Zulfikar Ali 109, 114, 115, 121, 126-8, 144
Big Bash League (T20 league, Australia) 252, 253, 280
Bird, Lester 254
Birley, Sir Derek 3, 5, 187, 201, 223
Birmingham City Council 259
Birmingham, Billy 27, 214
Birrell, Adrian 290
Black Homelands Citizenship Act (South Africa) 41
BLACKWASH (1984) 82
Blainey, Geoffrey 26
Blair, Tony 173, 208, 233
Bland, Colin 51
Blank, Johnny 293
Bligh, Ivo 140
Blunden, Edmund 312
Board of Cricket Control in India (BCCI) 92, 99-101, 111, 132, 195, 254-5, 258-9, 271-3, 275, 293, 298
Board of Cricket Control Pakistan (BCCP) 112, 115, 127
Board of Cricket Control Sri Lanka (BCCSL) 146
Bodyline series 22, 24, 94, 141, 159-61, 164, 166, 169, 175, 183
Boers/Afrikaner culture 36-8, 46
Bombay Cricket Association 99
Bono, Edward de 270-1, 276
Boock, Richard 67, 252
Booker Bros McConnell (merchants, plantation owners) 79
Boon, David 174
Booth, Lawrence 294
Border, Allan 172-4, 175
Bose, Mihir 91, 98, 100
Bose, Sugata 97
Botha, P.W. 44
Botham, Ian 12-13, 117, 173, 210-11, 212
Bouillon, Antoine 38

316   Index

Bowen, Rowland 5–6, 10, 15
Boycott, Geoffrey 9, 64, 118, 172, 213
Brabourne Stadium, Bombay 99
Bradman Academy, Adelaide 47
Bradman, Sir Donald 18, 22, 28–30, 66, 75, 114, 149, 159–65, 170–2
Bramley (Surrey village) 224
Brearley, Mike 9, 12–13, 171–2, 265
Britannic Insurance 14
British Empire 3–4, 7, 230, 265
British Empire XI 4; Empire XI v Buccaneers 186
Broad, Chris 174
Broederbond 41
Bromley, John 194
Brown and Company (Sri Lanka) 145
Brown, Freddie 166
Brown, Geoff 109
Bryant and May (matches) 188
Brylcreem 3, 4, 189, 210
Brylcreem Summer (by Eric Midwinter) 3
Buchanan, John 268–70, 273, 278
Bull, Andy 294, 297, 312
Burgher Recreation Club, Colombo 141
Burki, Javed 112
Burnham, Andy 53
Burnham, Forbes 51
Bush, President George W. 110
Bushkazi (tradition Afghan sport) 291
Bustamente, Alexander 76
Butcher, Roland 10
Butler, Tubal ('Buzz') 74
Butt, Salman 120
Byrnes, Rita 43

Cable and Wireless (telecommunications company) 84, 217
Caetano, Marcello 42
Cahn, Sir Julien 64
Cain, Peter J. 185
Callaghan, James 41, 285
Callinicos, Alex 42
Calwell, Arthur 19
Cambridge Marylebone Cricket University 14
Can Pakistan Survive? (by Tariq Ali) 108, 109
Cardiff MCC University 14
Cardus, Neville 199–201

Caribbean Premier League (T20) 253
Caribbean Women's Cricket Federation 235
CARICOM (trade association) 85
Carlton & United Series 101
Carman, Arthur 64
Carnation Revolution (Portugal, 1974) 42
Cary, Clif 22, 162
Cash, Frank 19
Cashman, Richard 24
Castlemaine XXXX lager 25, 174
Centrex (marketing company) 297
Ceylon Broadcasting Corporation 144
Ceylon Cricket Association (CCA) 140
Ceylon Tobacco (company) 144
Chakraborty, Subhash 254
Challenor, George 238
Chance to Shine (cricket promotion scheme) 14, 236–7, 243
Chandler, Martin 65
Chandrasekhar, Bhagwath 93
Channel 4 (coverage of Test cricket in UK) 11, 208–10
Channel Nine (Australia) 24, 206, 210
Chappell, Greg 25, 65–6, 171–2, 267, 269–79 (and *The Chappell Way* cricket programme 277–9)
Chappell, Ian 23, 169–71, 280
Chappell, Trevor 65–6, 277
Charlton Athletic FC 265
Chatterjee, Garga 130
Chauhan, Chetan 273, 274
Chawla, Juhi 256
Chee Quee, Richard 28
Chiesman, Stuart 169
Chifley, Ben 19
China, cricket in 300
Chinese Cricket Association 301–5
Chingoka, Peter 52
Chowdhury, Saber 132–3
Christian nationalism 37
Christian, Dan 26
Churchill, Sir Winston 7, 188, 285
Citizenship Acts (Sri Lanka) 143
Clark Report (1966) 8
Clark, Belinda 241
Clark, Ted 131
Clark, Tom 215
Clarke, Giles 255, 293
Clarke, Michael 175
Cobham, Lord 9

Coca Cola 100, 195
Codrington, George 239
Cohen, Stephen Philip 109, 110
Coke, Christopher 85
Collins, Sam 293
Collins, Tony 166, 167
Colmans Mustard 188, 210
Commonwealth Immigration Act (UK, 1962) 166
Compton, Denis 3–4, 162, 164, 165–6, 189, 192, 205, 210
Congress Party of India 90, 94–7, 102, 276
Conn, David 15
Connor, Clare 242
Constantine, Learie 75, 144
Contractor, Nari 79
Cook, Alastair 175
Cooper, Adam 27
Cornelius, Alvin Robert 112
Cornell, John 24
Cornhill Insurance 11
Cotonou Agreement (between EU and African, Caribbean and Pacific countries) 48
Couldry, Nick 276
Coupar, Paul 265
Cowdrey, Colin 79, 169, 170, 228, 231
Cowdrey, Penny 169
Cox, Vera 226
Craig, Ian 63
Craxton, Anthony 204
Cricinfo (website) 216–17
Cricket Australia 238, 242
Cricket for Women and Girls (by Marjorie Pollard) 225
Cricket Max format 250
Cricket South Africa (CSA) 48, 49, 50
Cricket World Cup 1996 146
Crisp, Bob 51
Crocodile Dundee 24
Croft, Colin 241
Croke Park, Dublin 289
Cronje, Johannes ('Hansie') 46, 120
Crowe, Martin 67, 133, 250–2
Cullinan, Daryll 49
cultural nationalism 28
Currie Cup 38, 51
Currie, Sir Donald 38
Curry, Graham 119
Cyclone Bhola 127

D'Oliveira, Basil 9, 41, 46, 52, 201
Dagnall, Charles 253
Daily Telegraph 202
Dainty, Gladstone 297, 300
Dale College, King William's Town, South Africa 47
Dalmiya, Jagmohan 132–3
Dalrymple, William 92
Darrawella CC (Galle) 140
Dartford College 224
Darwin, Charles 167
Daryanani, Pranay 273
Das, Deb K. 295
Dawood Group, Karachi 115
de Beers mining company 47
de Klerk, F.W. 44
De Mello, Anthony 111–12
De Silva, A.E. 145
Deaker, Murray 'Deaks' 68
Deans, Jason 208
Death of a Salesman (by Arthur Miller) 293
Deccan Chronicle 256
DeFreitas, Phillip 10, 14, 82
Dell, Tony 278
Democratic Labour Party (of Barbados) 74
Dempster, C.S. ('Stewie') 64
Denness, Mike 170
Deodhar Trophy (India) 195
Deodhar, Dinkar Balwant 195
Desai, Ashwin 47, 49
Desai, Morarji 96–7
Deutrom, Warren 290
Dev, Kapil 254, 270, 272–3
Devonshire, Duke of 187
Dexter, Ted 12, 93–4, 144, 167–8, 189–92
Dhaka Metropolis Knockout Tournament 129
Dhoni, M.S. 101
Digicel (company) 84
Dimbulla Athletic and Cricket Club 139–40
Dimmock, Peter 2006
Dish satellite TV 296
Disney Corporation 101, 217
Dissanayake, Gamini 146
DLF (Delhi Land and Finance Group) 298
Dolphins (and other franchises in South African cricket) 48

Donger, T.E. 41
Doordarshan (Indian national TV) 100–1, 132
Douglas, Roger 68
Douglas-Home, Sir Alec 188, 212
Du Preez, Mignon 242
Duke of Norfolk 6
Duleepsinhji 94
Dulwich College 15
Duncan, Sheena 42
Durand Line (between Afghanistan and Pakistan) 291
Durham MCC University 14
Dutch East India Company 37
Dutch Reform Church 46
Dutta, Sahil 304
Dyson, John 268

Eagar, Desmond 168
Earl of Dudley 38
East Asia Forum 134
Eastphalia doctrine 150
Ebrahim, Baboo 48
Eden Gardens, Kolkota 254
Eden, Sir Anthony 5, 188
Edrich, Bill 3–4, 164
Edwards, Charlotte 241, 242
Edwards, T.C.T. 145
Edwards, Wally 293
Engel, Matthew 213
England and Wales Cricket Board (ECB) 11, 13, 14, 208–9, 215, 217, 232–3, 242, 251, 253–5, 260, 293
England Women's Cricket Federation (EWCF) 226
English Schools Cricket Association 5
Equal Opportunities Commission 231
ESPN (media company) 217
Essel Group (Indian business house) 253
Essex CCC 11
Etisalat Sixes 292
Eton College 181
European Common Market 166
European Economic Community (EEC) 61
Evans, Godfrey 162, 192

Fair Play (by Rachel Heyhoe Flint and Netta Rheinberg) 223
Farhart, Patrick 30

Faustin, Veryn 242
Federation of South African Trade Unions 42
Fernando, Tyronne 151
Feroz Shah Kotla Stadium, Delhi 241
Fidler, David 150
FIFA 294
Fingleton, 169
Fingleton, Jack 19
Fingleton, Jack 19, 160–1, 165, 169, 205
Fire in Babylon (film) 81
Firth Cleveland group of companies 230
Fletcher, Duncan 268, 280
Fletcher, Keith 8, 13, 265
Fletcher, Thomas 260
Flintoff, Andrew 118
Flower, Andy 53
Forbes, O.B. 140
Ford, Paul 66, 68
Forward Bloc (left wing group, India) 257
Fosters Oval 11
Fraser, Malcolm 66
Fraser, Peter 61
Frazer, Ian 271–2, 276, 278
Freedom Charter (of African National Congress) 45
Frith, David 82, 117
Frost, David 194
Fry, C.B. 203

Gaddafi Stadium, Lahore 121
Gaddafi, Col. Muammar 121
Gaekwad, Anshuman 270
Gaelic Athletic Association 289
Gaelic football 289
Gallaher Group (multinational tobacco company) 193
Gallaway, Iain 62
Gallipoli (battle in First World War) 30–1
Games of the New Emerging Forces (GANEFO) 40
Gandhi, Indira 51, 94, 96, 99
Gandhi, Mohandas 92
Gandhi, Rajiv 96
Ganguly, Sourav 271
Ganguly, Sumit 150
Gap (clothing stores) 135

Gardner, Ashleigh 238
GATT (General Agreement on Tariffs and Trade) 45
Gatting, Mike 43–4, 117, 265
Gavaskar, Sunil 101, 258
Gayle Chris 84, 85, 241
Gemmell, Jon 39, 40, 53
General Motors 303
Georgie Pie (fast food company, New Zealand) 252
Gibbs, Herschelle 46
Gibbs, Lance 80
Gibson, Owen 214
Gibson, Zak 66
Giddens, Anthony 29
Gilchrist, Adam 29–30
Gilchrist, Roy 77–8
Gill, Sukhinder 26
Gillespie, Jason 26
Gillette razors/ Gillette Cup (UK) 10, 190–4
Gillingham, Rev. Frank 202
Glen Grey Act (1894, Cape Colony) 36–7
Gleneagles Agreement (1977) 9, 41
Global Sports Ventures 299
Goddard, John 75, 76
Goodhart, Philip MP 189
Goonesena, Gamini 143
Gordon, Sir Home 187
Gosden Common (Surrey village) 224
Gouldner, Alvin 180
Gover, Alf 263–4
Government College, Lahore 111
Gower, David 13, 174, 265
Grace, Dr W.G. 188, 210
Grainger, Andrew 24
Grameenphone mobile phone company 135
Grant, George 'Jackie' 75
Grant, Rolph 75
Graveney, Tom 128, 192
Great Trek, The 37, 38
Greater Noida Stadium, New Delhi 292
Green Party (of Australia) 28
Greenwood, Mona 226
Greig, Tony 8, 10, 81, 171, 202, 254
Grey College, Bloemfontein 46
Griffin, Geoff 8
Griffith, Charlie 8, 79

Griffith, Teddy 84
Griffiths, Jim 80
Grimmett, Clarrie 238
Group Areas Act (1950, South Africa) 39
Grout, Wally 22
Guerilla Cricket 215–16
Guha, Isa 216, 237
Guha, Ramachandra 91, 92, 95, 98, 99, 100, 212, 223, 259, 267
Guillen, Simpson ('Sam') 62
Gumede, William 44
Gupta, Amit 256
Guy, John 64
Gyngell, Kathy 239–40

Hadlee, Richard 65
Hadlee, Walter 64–5
Haider, Brigadier R. G. ("Gussy") 113
Haigh, Gideon 19, 20, 22, 171, 258, 294
Hain, Peter 285
Hair, Darrell 149
Hall, Wesley 79
Hambledon (Surrey village) 224
Hammond, Walter ('Wally') 114, 161–4
Haq, Syed Ashraful 300, 302
Harman, Jo 269
Harrild, Theresa 232
Harris, Lord 91, 140, 223
Harrison, Jamie 299, 305
Harrison, Tom 260
Harrow School 181
Harte, Chris 25, 223
Hartley, Mark 25
Harvey, Bagenal/Bagenal Harvey Organisation 189, 194
Hasan, Roqibul 128
Hasina, Sheikh 132
Hassett, Lindsay 19, 163, 164, 169
Hawke, Lord 140
Hawkeye (TV detection device) 207
Hayter, Reg 189
Hayward, Jack 'Union Jack' 230–2
Hayward, Sir Charles 230
Headley, George 75
Healy, Ian 174, 278
Hearst Corporation 217
Hector, Leonard 'Tim' 73, 83, 268, 275, 288
Hendricks, Jackie 77

Henry Holroyd, Lord Sheffield 19
Henry, Omar 42, 46
Herath, Gwen 235
Hero Honda (ICC sponsor) 303
Heron-Maxwell, Mrs Patrick 225–6
Hewlett Packard (multinational information technology company) 277
Heyhoe Flint, Rachel 227, 229–33, 235, 242
Hick, Graeme 10
Hide, Molly 227
Hill, Declan 120
Hill, Jimmy 194
Hillary, Edmund 62
Hindley, Martyn 250
Hindu nationalism/ Hindutva 96–7
Hird, Christopher 293
Hirst, John 31
Hitting Across the Line (by Vivian Richards) 267
Hobbs, Jack 140, 189, 210
Hogan, Hulk 269
Hogan, Paul 24
Hogg, Rodney 172
Holding, Michael 212
Holding, Michael 81
Holt, Richard 224
Holt, Richard 28
Home and Away (TV soap opera) 29
Hopkins, A.G. 185
Hopps, David 152
Horne, Gerald 78
Hot Spot (TV detection device) 207
Howard, Geoffrey 112
Howard, John 18, 26–7, 149
HSBC (sponsor of Asian Cricket Council) 303
Hudson, Robert 203–4
Huggins, Godfrey 36
Huggins, Richard 214
Hughes, Kim 171, 172
Hughes, Merv 25, 174
Hughes, Simon 167, 190, 274
Hunter, Nick 205, 210
Hutchins, Brett 29
Hutchinson (ICC sponsor) 303
Hutton, Len 5, 6, 19, 76, 114, 163, 168–9, 189, 228, 239

ICC Trophy 131, 145
Ikin, Jack 164
Illingworth, Raymond 168–70, 265

Immigration Restriction Act (1901) (in Australia) 20
Imperial Cricket Conference 19, 38, 285
Imperial Tobacco Group 192
Independent Television (ITV) (UK) 205
India Cements 256
India Oil (sponsor of ICC and Asian Cricket Council) 303
Indian Cricket League (ICL) 68, 253–5
Indian Mutiny/ India's First War of Independence 111
Indian National Cricket academy, Bangalore 254
Indian Premier League (IPL) 48, 68, 84–5, 157–8, 250, 253–60, 276, 280, 293, 298–300; franchises 255–6
Industrial Conciliation Amendment Act (1979, South Africa) 42
Ingleby-Mackenzie, Colin 6
Inman, Clive 143
Intel (multinational corporation) 217
International Cricket Council/ Conference (ICC) 47, 52, 54, 68, 101, 130–3, 145, 148, 157, 210, 234–5, 237–8, 241, 243, 253, 284–6, 288–306; Affiliate International Cricket Council/Conference (ICC) Members 286; Associate Members 288–9
International Monetary Fund (IMF) 45, 52, 83, 97, 288
International Olympic Committee (IOC) 305
International Women's Cricket Council (IWCC) 234
Iqbal, Asif 119
Ireland, cricket in 289–90, 306
Irish Cricket Union 290
Isaacs, W.D. 4
Islamia College, Lahore 111
It's a Wonderful Life (film) 299
Ivanhoe (by Sir Walter Scott) 264

Jack Hayward Trophy 230
Jackson Committee Report (1944) 4
Jackson, Michael (Chief Executive, Channel 4, UK) 11
Jackson, Sir Stanley 183, 185, 190
Jagan, Cheddi 76, 78
Jain Academy of Sporting Excellence, Bangalore 278
Jain, R. Chenraj 278

Jalal, Ayesha 97
Jamaican Women's Cricket Association 235
James, C.L.R. 73, 76, 77–8, 284
James, Ken 64
Janatha Vimukthi Peramuna (People's Liberation Front or JVP, Sri Lanka) 147
Jardine, Douglas 141 159, 161, 163, 168–70, 172, 225
Jayasinghe, Stan 143
Jayawickrema, S.S. 'Sargo' 143
Jennings, Keaton 286
Jennings, Ray 286
Jim Crow racism 78
Jinnal, Muhammad Ali 97
John Player League (UK) 10, 192–3
John, George 77
Johnny Miller 96 Not Out (fanzine) 214
Johnson, Bill 22
Johnson, Hophnie Hobah Hines 77
Johnson, Ian 163
Johnson, Ian 20–1, 22
Johnson, Ural Alexis 129
Johnston, Brian/'Johnners' 203–5, 211–14, 216, 228, 232; books in memory of 212
Jones, Simon 118
Joseph, Col. E.H. 140
Joyce, Ed 290

Kabul National Cricket Stadium 292
Kalra, Gaurav 49
Kamilaroi people (of New South Wales) 26
Kanhai, Rohan 79, 267
Kardar, Abdul Hafeez 111, 112–13, 115, 116
Karunatilaka, Shehan 141, 150–1
Kay, John 23
Kennedy, Sally 235
Kenning, David 206
Kent CCC 267
Kentucky Fried Chicken (KFC) 252
Kenyon, Miles 264
Kerr, Pat 236
Khan Ayub 127
Khan, Aftab Gul 128
Khan, Ayub 113, 114, 115
Khan, Ilyas 291
Khan, Imran 112, 116, 118, 119, 152
Khan, Lt. Gen. Azhar 115

Khan, Majid 112, 116
Khan, Mohammad Jahangir 112, 116
Khan, Shah Rukh 256
Khan, Shaiza 235–6
Khan, Sharmeen 235–6
Khan, Yahya 127
Khettarama Stadium/R. Premadasa Stadium, Colombo 146
Khilnani, Sunil 277
Kidambi, Prashant 93, 102
kilikiti (game) 69
Kimber, Jarrold 293
King George VI 204
King, Bennett 270, 275
King, Greg 271
Kishore, Shanshank 236
Kissinger, Dr Henry 129
Klein, Naomi 45
Kolpak ruling (European Court of Justice) 48, 53, 68
Kolpak, Marus 48
Korn, Alison 239
Krishnamohan, Thiviyanthan 152
Kwik cricket 231–2

Labor Party (of Australia) 28
Laden, Osama bin 110, 119
Lahore Gymkhana CC 112
Laker, Jim 163, 167, 192, 205
Lal, Madan 270
Lamb, Allan 10, 118
Lambert, Clayton 296
Land Apportionment Act (1930, Rhodesia) 50
Langer, Justin 29
Lanning, Meg 242
Lara, Brian 83, 85, 254
Larrikin culture 24–6, 29, 62, 160, 164, 168–9, 171–3, 175, 267, 269, 279
Larwood, Harold 161
Lashkar-e-Taiba (terrorist group) 111
Lawry, Bill 23
Leak, Bill 18
Leeds-Bradford MCC University 14
Leicestershire CCC 11, 190
Lemon, Geoff 241, 243
Lewis, Chris 10
LG Electronics (ICC sponsor) 303
Liberal Country League (LCL) 160
Liberation Tigers of Tamil Eelam (LTTE) 147, 288
Lieven, Anatol 108, 110

Lieversz, Darrel 145
Lillee, Dennis 25, 80, 169–72, 175, 251, 279
Lindwall, Ray 161, 162, 164–6
Liptons (tea company) 139
Lister, Joe 144
Littler, Jo 30
Lloyd, Clive 80, 81, 85
Lloyd, David 265–6
Local Government Act (1972) 11
Lockerbie, Don 298–9
London Counties team 4
London Weekend Television 194
Lord Kitchener (calypso player) 7, 79
Lotbiniere, Seymour de 203
Loughborough MCC University 14
Luke, Will 297
Lupton, Major Arthur 264

MacLaurin, Lord 13–14, 208–9, 215, 253
Macmillan, Harold 188; and 'Wind of change' speech 38
Macmillan, William Miller 74
Maddy, Darren 254
Maharajkumar of Vizianagram 94
Mahmood, Fazal 92, 113
Maidment, Paul 302–3
Mailata, Ben 67
Majola, Gerald 49
Major League Baseball (USA) 255
Major, John 208, 233
Majumdar, Boria 256
Malcolm, Devon 10, 82
Malcolm, Dominic 119, 260
Mallett, Ashley 25, 172
Mallya, Vijay 255
Manchester Cricket League 226
Mandela, Nelson 38, 44, 84
Mani, Ehsan 284
Manjrekar, Sanjay 272
Manley, Michael 73, 75, 77, 78
Maori Language Week 66
Maori Wars/New Zealand Wars 60
Marlar, Robin 130–1
Marqusee, Mike 3, 7, 11, 82, 97, 99, 100, 103, 118, 148–9, 152, 185, 188, 204, 214, 258–9, 312
Marsh, Geoff 270
Marsh, Rodney 25
Marshall, Howard 204
Marshall, Malcolm 267

Martin-Jenkins, Christopher 8, 60, 62, 201–4, 211, 214–15
Masakadsa, Hamilton 53
Mascarenhas, Mark 100–2
Mashingaidze, Brigadier Gibson 53
Massiah, Steve 296
May, Peter 163, 166, 167–9
Mbalul, Fikile 49
MCC Coaching Manual 5
MCC Cricket Coaching Book 264
MCC Youth Cricket Association 5
McCauley, Ray 46
McCool, Colin 164
McCubbin, Ian 303
McDonald, Andrew 280
McDonalds (fast food) 252
McDonalds Super Smash (T20 competition, New Zealand) 253
McGilvray, Alan 204
McGlew, Jackie 41
McGrath, Glenn 148, 279
McKechnie, Brian 66
McKibbin, Ross 185
McLaughlin, Mel 241
McLellan, Alastair 79
McQullin, Ian 214
Mdingi (Xhosa village, South Africa) 47
Meckiff, Ian 8
Mehta, Rabindra 118
Melbourne Cricket Ground (MCG) 240
Melford, Michael 202
Melly, Jim 207, 211
Melville, Tom 300
Menzies, Sir Robert 18–19, 21, 23, 24, 26–7
Merritt, Bill 64
Metropolitan Police Operation Swamp (1981) 81
Mezzy Jez (blogger) 216
Miandad, Javed 25
Middlesex CCC 12
Midland Counties Knock-Out Cup 190
Midwinter, Eric 3, 5, 11, 185
Milk Marketing Board 231
Miller, Andrew 215
Miller, Arthur 293
Miller, Keith 18, 23, 79, 162–5, 168–9, 172, 189
Miller, Peter 305
Mitchell, Alison 216
Mitchell, Keith 84
Modi, Lalit 258–9

Mohammad, Hanif 98, 113, 116, 130
Mohammad, Mustaq 114, 116
Mohammad, Wazir 113
Molins, Jason 290
Montreal Olympics (1976) 41
Monty Python's Flying Circus 211
Moody, Tom 270, 275
Moonda, Firdose 49
Moors Sports Club 141
Moravians (religious sect) 163
Morecambe and Wise Christmas Show 213
Morecambe, Eric 213
Morgan, David 209
Morgan, Eoin 290
Morris, Arthur 164
Morrison, Herbert 80
Mortaza, Mashrafe 136
Mosey, Don 211
Movement for Democratic Change (Zimbabwe) 52
MRF Pace Foundation, Chennai 47
Mugabe, Robert 52, 286
Muggeridge, Kitty 194
Muhammad, Noor 293
Mukherjee, Sujit 103
Muktijoddhad (East Pakistan freedom fighters) 136
Muldoon, Robert 61, 65, 66
Muller, Antoinette 240
Multi-ball Games administration Centre, China 302
Mumbai Indians 103
Muralitharan, Muttiah 146, 149–51, 279–80
Murdoch, Rupert 11, 18, 100
Murray, Deryck 118
Musharraf, General Pervez 110
Muslim League 97, 126
Muybridge, Edward 149

Nally, Patrick 193
Nandy, Ashis 90
Napoleonic Wars (1803–15) 36
Nash, Brendan 238
National Basketball Association (NBA, USA) 260
National Football League (NFL, USA) 257, 260
National Union of Mineworkers (South Africa) 42

Native Land Act (1913, South Africa) 37
Native Land Husbandry Act (1951, Rhodesia) 50
Nauright, John 39
Nawab of Pataudi ('Tiger') 93–5, 98
Nawab of Pataudi (Father of 'Tiger') 94
Nayudu, Cottari Kanakaiya ('CK') 92, 140
Ndebele tribe 50
Nehru, Jawaharlal/Nehruism 90, 94–6, 97, 102, 276
Neighbours (TV soap opera) 29
Nenzani, Chris 50
Nestle Australia 170
Nettersole, Noel 'Crab' 75
New Labour (rebranding of British Labour Party) 11
New South Wales Cricket Association 184
New Woman ideal 224
New Zealand Cricket (NZC) 68
New Zealand Cricket Council (NZCC) 63, 64
News Corp Australia 18
News Corporation 100–1
Newsinger, John 7
Nicholas, Mark 85
Nicholson, Rafaelle 223, 242–3
Nissar, Mohammad 93
No Normal Sport in an Abnormal Society (slogan) 43
Nolan, Peter 300
Nondescripts CC (Colombo) 140, 141, 142
Norcross, Daniel 215–16
Norfolk, Duke of 168, 186
Norgay, Tensing 62
Nourse, Dudley 38
NRC (Native Recruiting Corporation) Trophy 37
Ntini, Makhaya 47
Nunes, R.K. 75
Nyoka, Dr Mtutuzeli 49

O'Reilly, Bill 160, 169
Oborne, Peter 108, 111, 112, 116, 121
Official Language Act (Sri Lanka) 143
Olonga, Henry 53
One Nation ideology 6–7
One Unit Programme (in Pakistan) 126
Operation Cyclone 110
Orr-Ewing, Ian 203

Oxford Brookes University 14
Oxford Marylebone Cricket
   University 14
Oxford University CC 14

Pacific Solution policy (Australia) 26
Pacifica Cup 66
Packer 'revolution'/World Series Cricket
   23–5, 80, 83, 115–16, 166, 170–2,
   195, 202, 206–7, 209, 212, 217,
   253–4, 297
Packer, Frank 23–4
Packer, Kerry 23–4, 166, 170
Packer, Robert 23
Packeristanis 116
Pakistan Cricket Board (PCB) 236
Pakistan Eaglets 112
Pakistan People's Party (PPP) 109, 114
Pakistan Women 237
Pakistan: A Hard Country (by Anatol
   Lieven) 108
Pan African Congress 38
Pandya, Jignesh 'Jay' 299
Parker Bowden, Montague 50
Parore, Adam 69
Parsi community in India 91
Passmore, John 39
Patil, Sandeep 270
Patterson, P.J. 85
Pawar, Yogesh 257
PBL Marketing 24–5
Peden, Barbara 226–7
Peden, Betty 226–7
Pentangular Tournament 97
Pentangular Tournament, Bombay
   91, 92
People's National Movement (PNM,
   Trinidad) 73, 74
People's National Party (PNP, Jamaica)
   73, 74
People's Progressive Party (PPP, British
   Guiana)
Pepsi 100, 115, 243
Pepsico (ICC sponsor) 303
Perera, S.S. 139, 143, 144
Personnel Today (website) 13
Physical Training and Recreation Act
   (1937, UK) 229
Piachaud, Dan 143
Pietersen, Kevin 46–7, 280, 286
Pinter, Harold 13
Pir of Pagaro 113

Pirie, Gordon 167
Pitch International 69
Plunket, William 63
Pollard, Kieron 85
Pollard, Marjorie 225, 244
Pollock, Graeme, 48
Pollock, Peter,
Pollot, Lizzie 235
Ponting, Ricky 29, 269
portfolio players 253
Powell, Enoch 201
Prasanna, Erapalli 93
Premadasa, Ranasinghe 151
Preston, Norman 191, 193
Pride of the Village (by Edmund
   Blunden) 312
Priestley. J.B. 200
Primark (stores) 135, 288
Princess Diana 213
Princess Margaret 165
Prior, Matt 286
Proctor, Mike 44, 48, 51
Professional Cricketers Association 254
Profumo Affair (1963) 206
Prohibition of Mixed Marriages Act
   (1949, South Africa) 43
Project USA 295–6
Proteas (South African cricket team) 50
Prudential insurance company 11, 194
Puri, Lakshmi 234

Qayyan Report (on illegal betting in
   Pakistani cricket) 119
Quadrangular Tournament, Bombay 91
Quaid-e-Azam Trophy 113, 127
Quaker Oats 210
Queen Elizabeth II 165, 172–3, 232
Quelch, Tim 6

Radio Pakistan 114
Rahman, Sheikh Mujibur 126, 128,
   129, 132
Rahman, Ziaur 134
Rainbow Nation (South African
   political ideal) 44–50
Rainford Brent, Ebony-Jewel 216, 237
Raising the Standard (business plan for
   English cricket) 14
Raj, Mithali 242
Rajapaksa, Mahinda 150–1
Rajasthan Cricket Association 259
Raleigh bicycles 189

Ramadin, Sonny 80
Rana Plaza building, Dhaka 135
Rana, Shakoor 8, 117
Ranatunga, Arjuna 148
Rand Revolt (1922) 37
Randall, Charles 217
Ranji Trophy 91, 112, 127, 256, 259, 286
Ranjitsinhji 94
Rankin, Boyd 290
Rashtriya Swayamsevak Sangh (RSS) 97
Ratnayake, Rumesh 301–2
Rea, Chris 233
Red Chillies Entertainment 256
Redpath, Ian 170
Reid, Buddy 145
Reid, John 67
Reith, Lord 202–3
Reliance Industries Limited 103, 255
Rembrandt Group (tobacco and industrial conglomerate) 192
Rheinberg, Netta 228–9
Rhodes, Cecil 36–7, 40, 51, 285, 286; Rhodes' Pioneer Column/British South Africa Company 50
Rhodes, Wilfred 200, 204
Rhodesian Front (RF) 51
Rice, Tim 232
Richards, Barry 48
Richards, Dave 172
Richards, Vivian 80, 81, 85, 266
Richardson, Dave 305
Richardson, Vic 22, 160–1, 169, 171
Riekert Commission (South Africa) 42
Robbins, Derrick 42
Roberts, Anderson 'Andy' 212, 267
Roberts, Michael 139, 141–2, 147–50
Roberts, Ron 51
Robertson, Stuart 251
Robertson-Glasgow, R.C. 181–3
Robi Axiate mobile phone network 135
Robinson, Emmott 200
Robinson, Ray 28
Robson, Bobby 266
Rockwood, John 140
Rogernomics 68
Rogers, John 42
Rojek, Chris 210
Romanos, Joseph 251
Romero, Leon 296
Rorke, Gordon 8

Roshan Telecoms 291
Rothmans International Cavaliers 192–4
Rousseau, Pat 84
Rowbotham, Sheila 223
Rowe, David 175
Roy, Arundhati 103
Royal Australian Air Force (RAAF) 162
Royal College (Colombo) 142
Rumford, Chris 118, 253
Ruscoe, Sybil 208
Ryan, Greg 60, 62, 63

Sa Re Ga Ma Pa (reality TV show, India) 254
Sabina Park, Jamaica 240
Said, Edward 93, 275
Samiuddin, Omar 108, 113, 114, 115
Sandham, Andy 263
Sangakkara, Kumar 151–2
Sankar, Siva 304
Saram, F.C. 'Derek' de 141
Savidge, Michelle 79
Schendel, Willem van 133
Schoolboy Cricket (by Rayleigh G. Strutt) 264
Scott, John 188
Seacombe, Mark 236
Seditious Meetings Acts (UK) 285
Selvey, Mike 263
Sen, Satadru 100, 103
Servis Industries, Lahore 115
Sex Discrimination Act (1975, UK) 231
Shaheed Mohtarma Bhutto Women's Cricket Challenge Trophy 240
Shankar, Ajay S. 272
Sharjah, cricket in 101, 117, 119, 132, 292
Sharpeville massacre (1960) 21
Shastri, Ravi 258
Sheffield Shield 19
Sheppard, David 9
Sher-e-Bangla cricket museum, Bangladesh 131
Shiv Sena 99, 102, 257
Shona tribe 50
Simon, Sir John 274
Simpson, Bobby 63, 274
Sinclair, Sir Keith 60
Singh, Charran 79
Singh, Ladhabhai Nakum Amar 93
Singh, Sir Bhupinder 91
Singh, Swaranjit 77

326　Index

Sinhalese Sports Club (Colombo) 141, 142
Sion Mills CC (County Tyrone) 290
Sir Nigel (novel by Sir Arthur Conan Doyle) 264
Sirisena, Maithripala 152
Skirting the Boundary (by Isabelle Duncan) 223
Sky Sports 11, 207–10, 215, 239–40, 250–1
Slazenger cricket bats 189
Small Balls Division of the State Sport General Administration (Chinese government) 300, 304
Smith, A.C. 207, 209
Smith, Chris 10, 208
Smith, Ed 295
Smith, Guy (Bishop of Leicester) 4
Smith, Ian 51
Smith, M.J.K. 12–13
Smith, Robin 10
Smith, William 'Razor' 140
Snape, Jeremy 280
Snickometer (TV detection device) 207
Snow, John 127, 168–9
Sobers, Garfield ('Garry') 51, 79, 80, 85
South African Council of Sport 41
South African Cricket Association (SACA) 42
South African Non-Racial Olympic Committee (SANROC) 40
South African Table Tennis Board 40
South Island Myth, The (New Zealand) 60
Southwark Council 15
Soweto protest, 1976 42
Special Powers Act (Bangladesh) 135
Speed, Malcolm 302, 304
Spinvision (TV detection device) 207
Sport England 14
Sporting Edge (consultancy) 280
Sports Law (1973, Sri Lanka) 145
Springer Handbook of Special Pathology 192
Sri Lanka Freedom Party (SLFP) 142, 152
Srinivasan, Narayanaswami 293
St Thomas College (Colombo) 142, 145
Stalin, Josef 28
Standard Chartered (sponsor of Asian Cricket Council) 303

Stanford, Allen/ Stanford 20/20 254–5, 296–9
Stanley Paul (sport publisher) 199
State Bank of India 94
Statute of Westminster (1931) 61
Steel, A.G. 264
Steen, Rob 48, 255, 284
Steve Waugh Foundation 30 30
Stewart, Graeme 66
Stewart, James 'Jimmy' 299
Stewart, Micky 13, 118, 265–6
Sticky Wicket (fanzine) 214
Still the Enemy Within (documentary film) 293
Strauss, Andrew 286
Streak, Heath 53
structural adjustment 83
Strudwick, Herbert 263
Strutt, Rayleigh G. 264
Subramaniam, Shiva 270
Sumathipala, Thilanga 279
Sunset + Vine (TV company) 173
Sunshine Heights CC (Melbourne) 27
Super 8 cricket 251
Surendran, C.P. 102
Sutcliffe, Herbert 140, 200
Sutherland, James 254
Swann, Graeme 280
Swanton, E.W. ('Jim') 6–7, 12, 51, 191, 201–2, 204–5, 214
Sydney Cricket Ground (SCG) 30

Tagore, Sharmila 94
Takashinga CC (Harare) 52
Taliban 290–2
Tallon, Don 20
Tamil Union Cricket and Athletic Club (Colombo) 141, 142
Tata (Indian corporation) 94
Tata Consultancy Services 270
Tau Devi Lal Stadium, Panchkula 254
Taylor, Clare 241
Taylor, Mark 148
Taylor, Monica 235
Taylor, Ross 66
Taylor, Sarah 244
Taylor, Stafanie 242
Taylor, Will 187
Tedder, Lord 165
Telangana rebellion 95
Television Act (UK, 1954) 188
Ten Pound Poms 61

Tendulkar, Sachin 101–3
Tesco supermarkets 13, 288
Test and County Cricket Board (TCCB) 11, 13, 192, 208, 232
Test Match Sofa 214–16
Test Match Special/ TMS 157, 204, 211–16
Thackeray, Bal 99
That Was the Week That Was (TV satire show) 206
Thatcher, Margaret 52, 117, 208, 233
The Art of Captaincy (by Mike Brearley) 13
The Australian (newspaper) 18
The Barracker at Bay (book) 161
The Conservative Home (website) 239
The Cricketer 201, 215, 232
The Death of a Gentleman (documentary film) 293–4, 312
The End of the Line (documentary film) 293
The Flea (marketing agency, India) 277–8
The Hill (at Sydney Cricket Ground) 163
The White Company (novel by Sir Arthur Conan Doyle) 264
Thomas, Faith 238
Thomas, Grahame 21
Thompson, E.P. 276
Thomson, Jeff 80, 170–2
Threlfall-Sykes, Judy 223
Titan watches 217
Tomlinson, Denis 51
Toohey's lager 25
Transformation Charter (South Africa) 49
Treaty of Waitangi (1940) 61
Tressider, Phil 63
Trott, Jonathan 286
True Colours: My Life (Autobiography of Adam Gilchrist) 30
Trueman, Fred 93, 163, 167, 169 171, 211–12
Tshwete, Steve 46
Tuffey, Daryl 67
Tuke-Hastings, Michael 204
Turnbull, Malcolm 28
Turner, Glenn 26, 64
Turner, Mike 190
Turner, Ross 303
Tutu, Bishop Desmond 46
Twenty20/ T20 format 14, 84, 136, 157, 209, 236, 238, 240–2, 250, 252–5, 258–60, 268, 275, 280, 287, 292, 296–8, 300, 304, 312–13; team names, UK 251–2
Tyronne Fernando Stadium, Moratuwa 146

UCBSA Statement of Intent 47
Ugra, Sharda 27–8, 99, 101, 133, 263, 271, 275–6
UN Development Programme Human Development Index 110
UNICEF 236 Fair Play for Girls (Pakistan) 236
United Breweries, India 255
United Cricket Board of South Africa (ACBSA) 46
United National Party (UNP, Sri Lanka) 142, 146
United Nations Declaration of Human Rights (1948) 40
United Nations Development Programme (UNDP) 44
United States Cricket Association (USACA) 296–8
United States of America, cricket in 295–9
Uni-Vite nutritional products 231
Upton, Paddy 280
Utting, David 26

Vahed, Goolam 47
Vaidyanathan, Siddhartha 254
Valentine, Alf 80
Valera, Eamon de 289
Vanderspar, George 140
Vaslavsky, Anna 257
Vaughan, Michael 69, 280
Vehicle and General insurance company 195
Venkataraghavan, Srinivas 93
Vernon, George 140
Verwoerd, Hendrick 41
Victory Tests 4
Vishal Haryana Party 94
Voce, Bill 77, 164
Vorster, Johannes 41

Wadekar, Ajit 95–6, 270
Wadia, Ness 256
Waitangi Day/New Zealand Day 61
Waitrose supermarkets 14
Wakelam, Teddy 203

Walcott, Clyde 75–6
Walmart (corporation) 135
Walters, Doug 25
Wankhede Stadium, Bombay 99
Wardle, Johnny 166
Warne, Shane 120, 175, 269, 279, 280
Warner, Aucher 74, 75
Warner, Sir Pelham ('Plum') 4, 75, 183, 185–7, 189, 190, 193–4, 205, 213, 215
Warning from the West Indies (by William Miller Macmillan) 74
Warwickshire CCC 259
Washington Redskins (NFL team, USA) 257
Watt, Len 202
Waugh, Austin 30
Waugh, Lilian 30
Waugh, Lynette 30
Waugh, Mark 120
Waugh, Rosalie 30
Waugh, Steve 29–30, 269, 270
WD and HO Wills (tobacco company) 170
Webb, Capt. Matthew 188
Weekes, Everton 75–6
Weerawardhana, Chaminda 150
Weihong, Cui 301
Wessels, Kepler 46
West Indian Federation 78
West Indies Cricket Board (WICB) 83, 85–6, 242
West Indies Players Association (WIPA) 84, 86
West Nally (PR agency) 193
West, Peter 193, 203, 204, 206, 210
Western Province CC 42
Westfield, Mervyn 120
Westminster Strategy (lobbyists) 208
Whatmore, Dav 268, 270
Wheen, Francis 3
Whimpress, Bernard 25, 223
White Australia policy 21, 25
White Ferns (New Zealand Women's cricket team) 241
White Heather Cricket Club 224
Wickramasinghe, Nira 143
Wiener, Martin J. 185
Wigmore, Tim 291, 292
Wijewardena, D.R. 141
Williams, Dr Eric 51, 73

Williams, Jack 213
Williamson, Martin 296, 299
Willis, Bob 13
Wilson, Betty 241
Wilson, Harold 51
Wilson, Jonathan 294
Wiradjuri people (of New South Wales) 26
Wisden 180–4, 191, 193
Wisden Cricket Monthly 8, 10, 82, 117
Wisden India 215
Wolfenden Report (1960, UK) 229
Women's Big Bash (Australia) 238, 240
Women's Cricket Association (WCA) 225–33, 235–6, 244; WCA dress code 226–7
Women's Cricket magazine 225
Woodcock, John 10, 202
Woodward, Kath 243
Woolmer, Bob 118–19, 267–8, 270, 275
Worger, William 43
World Bank 52, 83, 288
World Cup West Indies 2007 Inc 298
World Trade Organisation (WTO) 45
WorldTel (sports marketing) 100–1
Worrell, Frank 75–6, 78, 85
Wright, John 267–70, 275
Wycombe Abbey girls' school 224

Xioaning, Zhang 302

Yardley, Norman 4, 12
Yarrow Stadium, New Plymouth 253
Yeo, Tim 12
Yorkshire Tea 14
Younis, Waqar 118

Zafarzai, Tawab 292
ZANU PF 53
Zee TV 253
Zhang, Terry 305
Zia, Khaleda 134
Zia-ul-Haq, General Muhammad 109, 110, 115
Zimbabwe African National Union (ZANU) 51–2
Zimbabwe African People's Union (ZAPU) 51–2
Zimbabwe Cricket (ZC) 53–4
Zimbabwe Cricket Union 54, 286
Zinta, Preity 256

Printed in Great Britain
by Amazon